GOD AND THE DEVIL

GOD AND **THE DEVIL**

The Life and Work of

INGMAR BERGMAN

PETER COWIE

faber

First published in 2023
by Faber & Faber Ltd
The Bindery, 51 Hatton Garden
London ECIN 8HN

Typeset by Ian Bahrami
Printed and bound in the UK by CPI Group (UK) Ltd, Croydon CRO 4YY

A CIP record for this book
is available from the British Library

ISBN 978–0–571–37090–0

Printed and bound in the UK on FSC® certified paper in line with our continuing
commitment to ethical business practices, sustainability and the environment.
For further information see faber.co.uk/environmental-policy

2 4 6 8 10 9 7 5 3 1

In memory of my father, Donald Cowie,
who first talked to me about Bergman

CONTENTS

INTRODUCTION

He moved forward briskly to shake my hand. Above medium height, with thinning hair, wearing a striped shirt and a charcoal-coloured cardigan, Ingmar Bergman at the age of fifty gave off a restless energy. He was in the midst of rehearsing Büchner's play *Woyzeck* at the Royal Dramatic Theatre in Stockholm. With his aquiline nose and hooded left eye, he allowed himself to look handsome only in rare moments of repose. The landscape of his face seemed always in a state of change, and when he turned his basilisk stare in your direction, you felt scrutinised, instantly accepted or rejected. And a thunderclap of laughter dissolved the tension, as if frivolity were the prelude to a serious conversation.

It was January of 1969, and I was meeting Bergman for the first time. We had corresponded sporadically throughout the previous decade. My first letter from him was dated 6 June 1959: 'I think it is much better that we meet for a personal talk next time you visit Stockholm.' I never went, but when I published my first little pamphlet on Bergman's work, I sent it to him in Sweden. On 9 February 1962, he wrote that he had read it 'with the greatest pleasure'. He had, he continued, 'just finished *The Communicants* [*Winter Light*] and have started to cut the film. In that situation I never talk about my work. I am feeling too frightened.' Another polite letter followed on 4 September: 'I am unfortunately just in the final part of my film *The Silence* and my principle is and has to be not to meet anyone during the shooting. We can perhaps meet later this coming autumn.' By way of apology Bergman would arrange tickets for me at the theatre, and on one occasion even asked Lenn Hjortzberg, his assistant, to take me to dinner. I knew him at one remove, as it were, nourished by the awed, almost reverential tones of those who had spoken to me about the unquestioned 'Master'. Bergman at that time presided like a deity over Swedish cinema, and his opinion on young directors and even industry decisions was decisive.

Two days after our encounter in 1969, however, he invited me to dinner at Teatergrillen, the legendary restaurant adjacent to the Royal Dramatic Theatre, where he had a small table perennially reserved. From this position Bergman could observe not only other guests but also everyone who entered the main door. Occasionally, he would lean forward conspiratorially and make an acid remark about an actor he despised.

A couple of years later we sat down for our first formal conversation, in his austere office on the top floor of the Royal Dramatic Theatre, with its upright chairs, bare walls, small truckle bed, and mineral water and glasses on a table. He talked of *The Touch* – 'It's probably the nearest of my films to reality but nevertheless a dream, full of sadness and desire.' Did he still believe in his dictum that the theatre was his wife and the movies his mistress? 'Forget it,' he laughed. 'Now I'm living in bigamy!'

Two years later we discussed *Cries and Whispers*. 'I intended at first to write something about my mother. She's in all four of the women in the film. My feelings towards her were ambivalent. When I was little I felt she loved my brother more than she did me, and I was jealous.'

The next time I actually met Bergman was in 1980, in Munich. He had taken refuge there after a nasty spat with the Swedish tax authorities, who in 1976 had accused him of declaring insufficient earnings. He was later exonerated, but when I interviewed him for the *New York Times*, he had been shooting *From the Life of the Marionettes*, an anguished, sombre film that reflected his mood. During a Saturday-afternoon chat at the Bavaria Studios, he maintained that 'the cultural climate here in Munich is extremely stimulating and very varied. I miss that in Stockholm, where there is no life-or-death struggle in the cultural field.' After receiving the *Times* piece, he commented that it was 'an indescribable relief to at last be free of this difficult and stressful film [*Marionettes*], which really cost me blood, sweat, and tears'.

Two years later, on 21 March 1982, I sat on the set of *Fanny and Alexander*, as Bergman directed Harriet Andersson in a dream sequence. He had been hailed by the Swedes as a prodigal son and, thanks to funding from Gaumont and other European institutions, he could make what he declared to be his final film in a lavish, epic idiom. But he was – he claimed – retiring: 'I want to stop. I want to stay on Fårö, and read the books I haven't read, find out things I haven't yet found out. I want to write things I haven't written. To listen to music, and talk to my neighbours. To live together with my wife a very calm, very secure, very lazy existence, for the rest of my life.'

The following autumn, we enticed him to London's National Film Theatre. He told me quite candidly that he would not talk about his own work. 'I have just made my last film, and it lasts 3 hours 14

Ingmar on stage with Peter Cowie at the National Film Theatre, London, in September 1982. *Courtesy of the BFI National Archive. Photo by Sten Rosenlund.*

minutes. It was meant to be 2 hours 45 minutes, but as it is my final production I think I can indulge myself just a little!' He agreed to the NFT appearance only if the discussion be devoted to his mentor, Alf Sjöberg, who had just died. I concurred but figured that I could gradually switch the conversation to his own films. Sure enough, after about twenty minutes on stage, we were chatting about the early days of Ingmar's own career, and everyone was delighted. Of course, my ruse was transparent, and Ingmar probably knew as much.

When my first attempt at a critical biography appeared the following year in the United States, Ingmar wrote a warm and thoughtful letter of thanks: 'I have been really impressed by this fine book, in which I encounter understanding, human warmth, and intelligence. I feel a little giddy when obliged to gaze back in time but the friendly tone of your book makes it possible to confront the vanished past.'

In later years, we spoke only on the telephone, around noon on a Sunday if one could get through in those days. When Ingrid, his wife, passed away from cancer in 1995, I wrote him a letter of condolence, but I never heard from Ingmar again.

Why this preamble to what I hope will serve as a more comprehensive critical biography? In the first place, Bergman's workbooks and letters have become available since his death in 2007. Secondly, in the years following my first book on his life and work, Bergman himself wrote various books of a quasi-fictional nature on his parents and on his own childhood. He also published two volumes of memoirs (*The Magic Lantern* in 1987 and *Images* in 1990). And so what, as a young man, I accepted as gospel needed to be questioned and often modified. 'What is Truth?' asked jesting Pilate, and it can be argued that a novel about Bergman's life might be more 'truthful' than the assembly of facts, opinions and quotations that constitutes an orthodox biography.

In 1982, I devoted perhaps an inordinate amount of space to analysing the individual films. In the intervening four decades, however, a plethora of academic studies of Bergman's cinema has appeared. So in this new book I have placed the emphasis on biography rather than redundant exegesis.

A psychological conflict has emerged with ever more force from my research into his letters and workbooks. On the one hand, Bergman was obsessed, in a metaphysical sense, with God. On the other, he had to confront the Devil, manifested in the 'demons' that haunted his sleepless nights from childhood to old age. In essence, his whole life involved a clash between the emotional and the rational.

Looking back across the sixty years since Ingmar Bergman first surged to the forefront of world cinema, one tries to grasp the essential quality that set his work apart from (and often above, and beyond) that of other film directors. At the time, one admired his understanding of the female psyche, his use of close-ups, his direction of actors and his ability to deal with metaphysical issues in cinematic terms. But perhaps his single greatest gift was that of a writer. As his workbooks now reveal, he viewed cinema in literary terms first and foremost. His characters were shaped by their monologues, and their dialogue with lovers and antagonists. He constructed each film with the skill of a great playwright. The scripts did not emerge full-blown from the head of Zeus. Each character took weeks, sometimes months, to evolve; even their names changed more often than not in the course of the writing process.

1

CHILDHOOD SHOWS THE MAN

D. H. Lawrence's precept, 'Never trust the teller, trust the tale', can be applied to innumerable artists, in the sense that their work differs markedly in tone and content from their private lives. For Ingmar Bergman, however, his 'tale' *was* his life, and vice versa. He sought to put on screen or stage each and every experience he traversed, from childhood to old age.

Many an artist gathers inspiration as it lies to hand. So Visconti, reared in ducal luxury, produced *Senso* and *The Leopard* with an authenticity that would have eluded other directors; and Fellini and Truffaut called on their knowledge of the women of the Via Veneto and the prostitutes of the Boulevard de Clichy to give vivacity to their films. Ingmar Bergman found his vision of life in his family household, channelling the rigorous discipline imposed by his parents into the icy, lacerating dialogue that would make his films so compelling.

He liked to calculate his age from the date of his conception, approximately mid-October 1917 and a time of great anxiety in Swedish society. Although the nation had stood neutral since the close of the nineteenth century, the cost of living had doubled during the years of the First World War, and the harvest of 1917 was catastrophic in the wake of exceptionally dry weather. Dairy produce, meat, fuel and other essentials were in short supply. Lenin's revolution to the east would exacerbate these problems, spurring the militant left wing in Swedish politics to cry for a general strike to overcome the entrenched power of the bourgeoisie.

When Ernst Ingmar Bergman was born on Sunday 14 July 1918 at the Academic Hospital in Uppsala, about fifty miles north of

Stockholm, the Spanish flu was raging. This worldwide pandemic caused the death of some 50 million people, for no vaccine against such a virus existed. Ingmar had a caul over his head at birth – a sign of future success and prosperity – and he was a Sunday's child, a token of grace in the eyes of his parents. Because his mother had been recommended to a doctor in Uppsala, Ingmar was reared in the home of his maternal grandmother there.

Controversy surrounds these early days of Ingmar Bergman's life. His father, Erik, was a respected pastor in the Lutheran Church, but marital fidelity proved a virtue hard to attain for the Bergman family. Ingmar's mother, Karin, had a clandestine affair with a younger man, and Erik himself sired three children with his mistress Hedvig Sjöberg, whom he had met in Umeå. By coincidence, Hedvig was pregnant in her ninth month when Karin was about to give birth in July 1918. She signed into the hospital on 13 July, under her maiden name.

Ingmar was born frail and with gummed-up eyes, immediately suffering from fever and diarrhoea. He was christened in emergency by his father and, according to his niece Veronica Ralston, died a few days later. Louise Tillberg, the granddaughter of Hedvig Sjöberg, developed a theory whereby Hedvig's infant son was secretly switched at birth with Karin's child. Karin herself did indeed languish to the point where she could not feed her new son, and a wet nurse took over while Karin was sent home to recover. Some ten days later, Ingmar – or Hedvig's infant – was reunited with Karin.

Veronica Ralston's mother, Ingmar's sister Margareta, inherited the diaries that Karin Bergman had kept in secret throughout her marriage, and Ralston notes that a number of pages have vanished for the days surrounding Ingmar's birth. But that does not confirm what must, until further evidence emerges, remain a romantic theory. Since 2010, DNA testing has been initiated to try to resolve this mystery, but the characteristics of Ingmar's personality are so similar to those of Erik and Karin that the notion that he was a changeling remains not just unproven but also unlikely. Furthermore, Hedvig Sjöberg's son was given up for adoption and was subsequently found to be living in the United States. In *Wild Strawberries*, the professor's son, Evald, mutters rhetorically, 'Is he ever sure I'm his son?', in a possible reference to the suspicion that Ingmar himself might have been a love child.

While Erik Bergman was never without a position as chaplain after 1918, he and Karin suffered from financial inconvenience, if not outright poverty, in their early years of marriage. During Ingmar's first few months, his father was busy from morning to night burying victims of the Spanish flu. Whortleberries became a staple of the family's diet, and the Bergmans found it difficult to scrape together the ingredients for a christening cake for their new son. According to his sister Margareta (known as 'Nitti'), young Ingmar nearly died from poor nutrition.

In the cinemas, however, in the late summer of 1918 Chaplin's *The Pawnshop* enjoyed its first run in Sweden, and at the famous Röda Kvarn theatre (where many of Bergman's films would open), *The Birth of a Nation* was being presented. In the studios, Mauritz Stiller was shooting *The Song of the Blood-Red Flower*, and his friend and colleague Victor Sjöström directed and starred in *The Sons of Ingmar*. The golden age of Swedish silent cinema seemed to be at its zenith.

Bergman's lineage offers insights into the themes and characters in his work as a film director. On his father's side, the Bergman family consisted of pastors and farmers back to the sixteenth century; piety, diligence and an innate conservatism were passed to each new generation. Henrik, Ingmar's great-grandfather, was a pastor and his wife, Augusta Margareta Agrell, was the daughter of the rector of Jacob's School in Stockholm. Ingmar's grandfather, Axel, worked as a chemist on the island of Öland in the Baltic. He died very young, and his wife had to care alone for Erik, Ingmar's father, who also suffered the death of his two-year-old sister, Margareta. Erik Bergman grew up in the town of Gävle, in a household composed of women:

his mother Alma, who was stout and impoverished, teaching the piano to pupils in the community; her sister Emma (a somewhat difficult person who never married and tended to miss trains); and his mother's mother. Forced in the manner of the times to 'say farewell to the dead' by bowing beside the open coffin of deceased relatives, Erik became fond of dressing up as a clergyman and pretending to be at a funeral, an experience that led him towards his life's work.

Ingmar's mother, Karin Bergman, née Åkerblom.
Courtesy of the Ingmar Bergman Foundation.

Karin Åkerblom, Ingmar's mother, was an upper-class girl from the bourgeoisie that had gradually displaced the landed class predominant in Swedish society until the nineteenth century. Her mother's father, Dr Ernst Gottfrid Calwagen, came of pure Walloon stock (from the French-speaking part of Belgium originally) and enjoyed a reputation as a linguist and grammarian. His father in turn had been a rural dean and doctor of theology; the roots of devotion lay deep in Bergman's family. Dr Calwagen's wife, Charlotta Margareta Carsberg, was fascinated by the arts and by music in particular, and their daughter Anna (Karin's mother) travelled, practised several languages and taught French at a school in Uppsala. She married a man twenty years older than herself, Johan Åkerblom, who built the Southern Dalarna Railroad. They made their home in Våroms, and would go for the summer weeks to the island of Smådalarö in the Stockholm archipelago. Both places were dear to the young Ingmar, and he would feature them in his films and screenplays – as was the ten-room apartment that Åkerblom purchased on Trädsgårdsgatan in Uppsala, and that would feature in *Fanny and Alexander*.

Karin Åkerblom loved the piano, and also wanted to train to become a doctor. The Bergmans and the Åkerbloms were related, so while applying himself to theology at the University of Uppsala, Erik called on the family to pay his respects. He promptly fell head over heels in love with his second cousin, Karin. The ardour was not at first entirely reciprocal, but over the years the couple grew to love each other. Karin's mother considered Erik as 'manifestly unsuitable as a husband for her daughter', according to Bergman's novel, *Sunday's Children*.[1] She would not permit Karin to marry him until he had secured a proper job.

The courtship proved turbulent, and Ingmar quoted from his mother's diary: 'I seem to remember we even put an end to our love as well as our engagement. I think a long time went by before we forgave each other. I'm not sure we ever forgave each other, wholly and fully.' Erik was ordained, however, and soon found a post as chaplain of a small mining community, Söderhamn, outside Gävle. The young couple married on 19 September 1913 in Uppsala Cathedral, in the presence of a bevy of relatives and friends. Erik flung himself into his work without reserve, living with Karin in a primitive vicarage, an old wooden house beside a lake.[2] One year later, their first child, Dag, was born, four years prior to Ingmar. The friction between the brothers persisted throughout their lives.

Dag achieved a distinguished career as a diplomat, serving as consul in Hong Kong and as Swedish ambassador in Athens during the Colonels' regime. Dag would torture and despise Ingmar at every opportunity. By his own admission, Dag had to be restrained from beating his younger brother to death.[3] At school, the two boys were always being compared – Dag was hopeless academically, while Ingmar succeeded almost effortlessly at his studies.

With considerable reluctance, the couple moved to Stockholm in 1920, for Erik to take up a curacy at Hedvig Eleonora Church. They rented a small apartment at Villagatan 22 in Östermalm. Hedvig Eleonora, its immense dome grown green with verdigris, was the most perfect church in Stockholm. It still stands foursquare in its own ground on the slope of Östermalm, and its bell tower includes a clock with four faces, which may be seen in both *Prison*, directed by Bergman in 1948, and *Woman without a Face* (which he scripted for Gustaf Molander).

Bergman's parents were in reality decent people, if also prisoners of their class and their beliefs. His mother, just 1.58 metres in height, had a full, soft face and a Cupid's bow mouth. She wore her extremely dark hair in a bun, and had an intense gaze that suggested her Walloon ancestry. Although some were intimidated by her striving after truth, in Ingmar's eyes his mother remained a warm and glowing materfamilias.

In her short book, *Karin by the Sea*, Margareta Bergman evoked the presence of her parents: 'After spending half the night indulging one of her few vices – reading – and having in the second half managed to scrape together a few hours' sleep for herself, [mother] would come stumbling in to breakfast only half awake and in a state of extreme nervous irritability, to find her freshly washed, matitudinally cheerful spouse, already hungry as a hunter, standing by the breakfast table with his gold watch in his hand.'[4]

Erik Bergman was tall, well groomed and good-looking in a Scandinavian way; women always wanted to do things for him,

Portrait of Pastor Erik Bergman at his desk.
Courtesy of the Ingmar Bergman Foundation.

particularly in his later years. He had a special passion for those
screen comedies that so charmed Swedish audiences during the
1930s – frothy, inconsequential capers that diverted the mind from
the impact of the Depression years. Although quite nervous and
prone to insomnia, his comparative weakness vanished the instant
he ascended the steps of his pulpit. His son-in-law, Paul Britten
Austin, reflected that Erik 'should have been a poet. His sermons
were the best thing about him.'[5]

The couple would talk together at the dinner table in a calm, controlled, pleasant manner, but beneath this decorum Ingmar could
sense the enormous tension between them, and an undeclared
aggression. This stemmed in part from a basic conflict of personalities – Karin's wilfulness posing a block to Erik's authoritarianism.
During one phase of the marriage, Karin's repressed passion for
another man – more than ten years younger than herself – made

her even more angry and withdrawn. She described this crisis in her diaries, and Bergman developed it in *Private Confessions*, his novel of 1996. The clandestine affair lasted three years. 'Help me away from myself,' wrote her alter ego Anna, in her diary in *Private Confessions*. 'Free me from this self who wants to think, wants to live, wants to love according to my own will. Obliterate, burn, annihilate this self of mine, for otherwise my lot will be only to destroy other lives and make others unhappy.'[6]

Bergman's parents 'lived completely officially, observed if you like, as a priest and his wife. Like politicians, they had no privacy.'[7] The house was always open to guests, except for Sunday evenings, which were dedicated to the family. Karin Bergman jealously guarded that single interlude of pleasure, when the children and their parents would play games together, or make models, or listen to a novel read aloud by Karin. Margareta was born in 1931, and she proved a more sympathetic sibling for Ingmar than Dag. As late as 1991, he signed handwritten letters to his sister, from 'Your nice old brother'.

Karin's father felt so attached to the railway he had built that he had a villa constructed overlooking the line at Duvnäs so that he could watch the trains go by in his dotage. To this picturesque setting, the infant Ingmar was brought every summer; his friends asserted that his speech betrayed a Dalarna accent throughout his life.

As a child, he adored the blithe summers at 'Våroms' ('our place') near Gagnef; he would sit daydreaming on a bridge near the Åkerblom house for hours on end, gazing into the water below. (Daydreaming, like rising at six o'clock each morning, was a habit he carried with him to the grave.) He also liked to sit with his grandfather, who suffered from muscular dystrophy, a condition that eventually afflicted both Erik Bergman and his elder son, Dag. Sometimes he could accompany his mother to the market in Borlänge: 'In the afternoon we came home with a freight train that made long stops at Lännheden and Repbäcken. Oh, hot summer days with flies and rails – I'll never forget it!'[8]

'Våroms', the Bergman family's summer residence in Dalarna.
Courtesy of the Ingmar Bergman Foundation.

But the environment that left the greatest impact on the young
Ingmar was his grandmother's apartment in Uppsala. The university town has a history second to none in Scandinavia. It is
frequently mentioned in the Icelandic and Norwegian sagas as
being of vital significance in religious and political matters, and
Adam of Bremen described Uppsala as being the centre of blood-
curdling sacrifices at certain periods of the year. A twin-towered
cathedral could be seen from the two-storey house at Trädsgården
12, where Bergman spent his early years, as could the square where
Sweden's mad King Erik XIV had one of his adversaries put to
death. Uppsala implanted a dramatic sense of Nordic history in
Bergman, who would turn to medieval times for his backdrop to
The Seventh Seal and *The Virgin Spring*.

There were fourteen rooms in the apartment, each arranged
exactly as it had been in 1890, when Anna Calwagen had come
there as a bride. Bergman recalled that there were 'lots of big rooms

with ticking clocks, enormous carpets, and massive furniture [...] the combined furniture of two upper-middle-class families, pictures from Italy, palms'.[9] Here his imagination flourished: 'I used to sit under the dining table there, "listening" to the sunshine which came in through the cathedral windows.'[10] On one occasion, he imagined that the statue of the Venus de Milo standing beside one of the windows began suddenly to move: 'It was a kind of secret terror that I recognised again in Cocteau's *Blood of a Poet.'*[11]

About the same time, Bergman discovered the latent magic of the nursery window blind, which when drawn down became a source of strange figures: 'No special little men or animals, or heads or faces, but *something for which no words existed.* In the fleeting darkness they crept out of the curtains and moved toward the green lampshade or to the table where the drinking water stood. They [...] disappeared only if it became really dark or quite light, or when sleep came.'[12]

In 1924 Queen Victoria, the wife of King Gustav V, appointed Erik Bergman as chaplain to the Royal Hospital, Sophiahemmet. She had for many years admired the eloquence and lyrical style of his sermons. At last, the Bergmans were installed in a decent vicarage, a yellow-faced villa in the parkland belonging to the hospital, with a huge rustic kitchen on the ground floor.

In the woods behind Sophiahemmet, Bergman recalled, 'I played very much alone. There was a small chapel in that park, where the dead patients were brought and placed until they were taken for burial.' He made friends with the gardener, whose duty was to take the corpses from the hospital to the mortuary. 'I found it fascinating to go with him; it was my first contact with the human being in death; and the faces looked like those of dolls. It was scary, but also very fascinating.' In the boiler room beneath the hospital, he watched orderlies carrying boxes full of limbs and organs removed during surgery, which were burned in the gigantic, coal-fired furnaces. 'For a child,' said Bergman, 'it was traumatic – and I loved it!'

Erik Bergman and his two young sons, Dag and Ingmar.
Courtesy of the Ingmar Bergman Foundation.

Although the legend developed of his being at odds with his parents from earliest youth – a legend fostered by Bergman himself – the truth is not so harsh. He would accompany his father on bicycle excursions to churches in the Uppland district just north of the capital (evoked in *Sunday's Children*).

On these 'festive journeys' through the Swedish countryside, Bergman's father taught him the names of flowers, trees and birds. 'We spent the day in each other's company,' wrote Bergman in a programme note to accompany the opening of *The Seventh Seal* in 1957, 'without being disturbed by the harassed world around us.'

All three Bergman children were obliged to attend church on Sunday to hear their father preach. Religion was 'something to get hold of, something substantial'. Dag found the sermons so boring that he and Ingmar would play a game, counting how many times their father would use the word 'God', with the winner earning 5 öre. 'Ingmar cheated,' said Dag, 'using all kinds of synonyms for "God".'

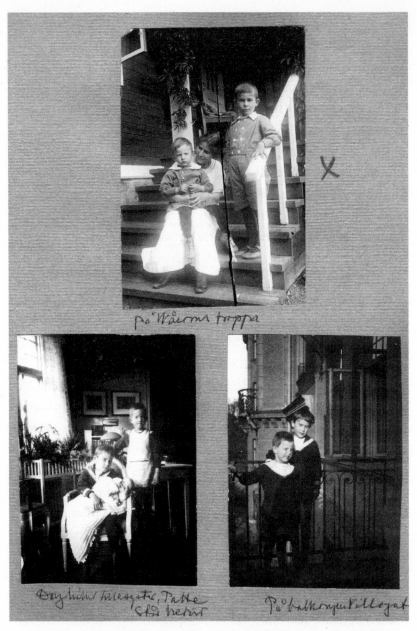

Ingmar and his elder brother Dag, from the Bergman family album.
Courtesy of the Ingmar Bergman Foundation.

Saturday was quiet, for father was composing his sermon. On Sunday morning, a psalm would be read aloud, or brief prayers said, before breakfast. This immersion in religious routine would influence many of Bergman's films, and he once asked, rhetorically, how writers could assess his work if they had not even read Luther's shorter catechism.

The sanctimonious Dag recalled that his younger brother knew how to ingratiate himself with his father by asking him questions about angels and heaven. However, Bergman loathed confession as he would an allergy. He disliked the trappings and dogma that went in train with Swedish Lutheranism, and found his father's fortnightly sermons in the hospital chapel an interminable ordeal. Immediately afterwards, coffee was served for the elderly nursing 'sisters' who lived at home in the Sophiahemmet park. The boys had to be present but escaped as soon as possible because there were matinee performances at the cinemas in Stockholm on Sunday.

Although it was certainly not without its lighter moments, Bergman's childhood was clouded by a terrible fear of punishment and humiliation. Being the elder brother, Dag may have been punished more severely than Ingmar – after a beating from his father, Dag would seek out his mother, who bathed his back and buttocks where the weals flushed red – but Ingmar was made to suffer considerably. When he had wet his bed (and incontinence proved a regular affliction), he was forced to wear a red skirt throughout the day, in front of the family. 'I was always babbling out excuses, asking forgiveness right, left, and centre. I felt unspeakably humiliated.'[13]

The most notorious incident of Ingmar's childhood, when he was locked in a closet, has been embellished and distorted over the years. A picture has emerged of Ingmar's father imprisoning him in a closet on several occasions as a form of vindictive punishment. In fact, it was Ingmar's beloved grandmother, who had come from Uppsala to care for the children, who shut him in a wardrobe in the nursery. Ingmar shouted with shock and anger, and Margareta rushed away searching for the key to the white closet. She was back in a few moments, but in that interval Ingmar had torn the hem of his mother's dress with his teeth. In *Hour of the Wolf*, Johan Borg tells his wife of such a traumatic experience and how he was afraid that a 'little man' lurking in the dark would gnaw his feet.

In an interview for Swedish television in 1981 (which Ingmar himself managed to have suppressed at the time), Dag Bergman claimed that 'Ingmar was a little angel at school, loved by everyone.' He maintained that he, not his younger sibling, was the model for the high-school student played by Alf Kjellin in *Frenzy*. 'Ingmar was without doubt our father's favourite child, and I was Dad's whipping boy.' In *The Magic Lantern*, which appeared a few years later in Sweden, Bergman wrote of Dag: 'He was ruthless, selfish, humorous, always ingratiating with Father despite his hatred, always tied to Mother despite his exhausting conflicts and his attempts to free himself.'[4] Late in his life, Dag showed his brother an 800-page autobiography he had written, and Ingmar arranged for it to be transcribed. However, no trace of the text exists in the Bergman Foundation archives.

The Bergman children inherited a bulky Victorian doll's house. Spurred by his sister Margareta and her friend Lillian, who was virtually adopted by the family, Ingmar – or 'Putte' ('little chap'), as he was called – began to develop an incipient love of theatre. In 1930 he saw Alf Sjöberg's production of the Swedish fairy tale *Big Klas and Little Klas* at the Royal Dramatic Theatre, and this inspired him to build his own puppet playhouse in the nursery. He created a revolving stage, moving scenery and an elaborate lighting system. The stage was formed by turning a large white table upside down, and Ingmar's mother was prevailed on to make a curtain.

One of the first fantasies that Ingmar and Margareta presented was called *When the Ice Troll Melts*. Gramophone records were used to establish a mood, the scenery was carefully sketched, and brother and sister had endless discussions as to which dolls should be assigned to each role.

Ingmar with his sister, Margareta.
Courtesy of the Ingmar Bergman Foundation.

At ten years of age, Ingmar started accompanying his brother to screenings at the Östermalm Grammar School. They were mostly documentaries, nature films and features edited for children's consumption. But the addiction was beginning. If his father remained uninterested in Ingmar's love of films, he fostered it indirectly by showing lantern slides on themes such as the Holy Land in the congregation room of Hedvig Eleonora Church. Ingmar was allowed to sit among the parishioners, watch the show and listen to Pastor Bergman's discourses.

Before long, Ingmar became a confirmed film buff. Theatre held the dominant place among his interests, but the capacity for creating illusionary effects, for gripping an audience by the scruff of the neck, was common to both arts. Film had fascinated him ever since he had been taken to see *Black Beauty*, with its vivid fire sequence, at the age of six. He was so excited by the experience that he stayed in bed with a temperature for three days.

There were matinees every Saturday, the first at one o'clock, the second at three. Admission was 25 öre when Ingmar started attending, but that increased to 35 öre, which was more than Ingmar's allowance. He soon found that his father's small change was kept in his coat pocket in the study, and the necessary coins were filched. His grandmother liked films and used to accompany him to the Castle cinema in Nedre Slottsgatan. 'She was in every way my best friend,' said Bergman.

One of Ingmar's earliest ambitions was to be a projectionist, like the man at the Castle cinema. He regarded him as someone who ascended to heaven every evening. The projectionist sometimes let the boy join him in the booth, but his effusive cuddling in due course discouraged Ingmar.

Then, circa 1928, a munificent aunt sent Dag a movie projector as a Christmas present. On Boxing Day, Ingmar swapped his army of around a hundred lead soldiers for the precious contraption. 'Dag beat me hollow in every war afterwards,' recalled Bergman, 'but I'd got the projector anyway.'[5] It was a rickety apparatus with a chimney and a lamp and a band of film that circulated continuously. Soon Ingmar was assembling his own films from lengths of material that he purchased by the metre from a local photography store. The first subject he bought was called *Frau Holle*, even though the 'Frau' herself did not appear. A girl in national costume was seen asleep in a meadow. She awoke, stretched, pirouetted and then exited right – again, and again, ad infinitum, as long as the projector handle was turned. Three metres of paradise.

Learning to splice film marked a critical stage. Ingmar devised plots to suit the montage of various strips that he joined to one another and wound on a primitive film spool he had built out of Meccano. Pocket money was hoarded whenever possible until an even larger projector could be purchased. From there, it was but a step to the essential acquisition of a box camera. '[I] then made a cinema out of cardboard with a screen, on which I glued up the photos I'd taken. I made a whole series of feature films and ran them through on that screen and made believe it was a cinema.'[16] Although he sold off his collection of films before he went to university, he reconstructed one of them to form the farce watched by the young lovers in *Prison*.

Ingmar visited the cinema whenever he could, sometimes several evenings in succession. Monster movies, such as *The Mummy*, were among his favourites, and the 1931 version of *Frankenstein* proved a memorable experience. In 1935 or 1936 he saw Gustav Machatý's *Ecstasy*, which stunned him. 'And then of course

Ingmar as a young boy. *Courtesy of the Ingmar Bergman Foundation.*

there was that naked woman one saw suddenly, and that was beautiful and disturbing.' He was overwhelmed by Victor Sjöström's *The Phantom Carriage* – 'Certain sequences and images have left an indelible impression,' he told Gösta Werner.[17]

His sense of wonder at the sleight of hand of cinema was enhanced by a visit to the 'film town' at Råsunda, in the suburbs of Stockholm, around 1930. His father had christened the son of the doctor, Vilhelm Bryde, and, in lieu of payment, Erik Bergman suggested that his son be allowed to visit Råsunda, where Bryde worked. 'It was . . . like entering heaven,' recalled Bergman. These were the studios where Victor Sjöström and Mauritz Stiller had made films. The word 'Filmstaden' was printed in large, illuminated letters on an arched sign, just like the huge sign looming above Los Angeles. The rows of terracotta-red buildings seemed like a repository of magic, the factory from which movies emerged full-blown as if by some wondrous alchemy. Bergman always responded to the sights, smells and sounds of the studios: 'For me,' he wrote in the 1950s, '[film-making] is a dreadfully exacting work, a broken back, tired eyes, the smell of make-up, sweat, arc lights, eternal tension, and waiting, a continuous struggle between choice and necessity, vision and reality, ambition and shiftlessness.'

Music, too, was a prime element of Bergman's youth. His father played the piano, and many family friends were adept on violin and cello. There were those who sang, and chamber music gatherings were frequent. An old piano of the Hammerflügel kind stood in his grandmother's home, and Ingmar would sit at it, listening to the casual tunes his fingers could pick out. Later he would go to the opera, where he returned to the gallery week after week, following each production with score in hand. In his room, he played 78 rpm discs at a thunderous volume and would be angry if anyone dared interrupt the storm of melody. His tastes changed as he matured. Bach, Handel, Mozart, Beethoven, Brahms, Wagner, Bartók and Stravinsky joined his pantheon; he fostered a particular affection for the French composer Paul Dukas.

Literature never became quite as vital for him. His passion for Strindberg was significant, and at the age of twelve, he bought the red annotated edition by Landqvist of Strindberg's complete works – in 55 volumes! Around the same time, he had been allowed to sit in the light tower at the Royal Dramatic Theatre and watch Strindberg's *A Dream Play*. He also admired the novels of Agnes von Krusenstjerna, whose view of women influenced his own atti-tudes. He enjoyed 'huge Russian novels' and, as he grew, he turned to Shakespeare, Maupassant, Balzac, Georges Bernanos and the Swede Hjalmar Bergman. But he always found reading a laborious process and liked best to listen to books read aloud (as, for example, the passage from Dickens's *Pickwick Papers* read in *Cries and Whispers*).

2

FIRST FORAYS INTO THEATRE

In his teens, Bergman attended Palmgren's School in Kommendörsgatan, a short scamper in the morning darkness first from Sophiahemmet and then from Storgatan, where his parents lived from 1934, after Erik had been appointed head pastor at Hedvig Eleonora. The structure still stands, five storeys high, although since 1988 it has belonged to the French state and functions as an embassy building. At the time, its echoing stairways were so clearly the inspiration for *Frenzy*, one of Bergman's first screenplays. There was short shrift at Palmgren's for the pupil who might arrive late for morning prayers, and Ingmar's inhibited manner and rather weedy physique made him a favourite target for the mockery of many teachers. At this time, Bergman was thin and puny, with green eyes that would soon turn darker and that, from the earliest years, evinced an intensity remembered by everyone who met him. From infancy onwards he suffered from stomach upsets, which led to a recurrent ulcer in adulthood. He was by nature a maverick when young, and inevitably that collided with the dogma that informed every aspect of life at home.

Two apartments were at the disposal of the Bergman family on the top floor of No. 7 Storgatan in Östermalm. They were linked by a small staircase and a corridor, and Ingmar was given a tiny room behind the kitchen, down the staircase. Hs mother and sister missed the park at Sophiahemmet and placed potted plants in the windows to mask the street view, but Ingmar liked his quarters because he could see far out over central Stockholm and because he felt removed from the household activity. His father did not come back there often, and Ingmar became fast friends with Laila, the aged cook from Småland who had been with the family for nearly half a century by the time Ingmar reached his teens. (Jullan Kindal recreated this character memorably in *Wild Strawberries* and *Smiles of a Summer Night*.)

Bergman was probably more interested in playing his records of *The Threepenny Opera* than in entertaining the female sex. But in Dalarna he did meet one girl in her mid-teens with whom he had a rewarding and liberating relationship. In his autobiography, he describes 'Märta' as having 'powerful shoulders and no hips, her arms and legs long and sunburnt, and covered with golden down. She smelt of the cowshed, as astringent as the marsh." Then, in ninth grade, he met a female contemporary, the sturdy Anna Lindberg, who helped to release him from the emotional strictness of his domestic environment and the lack of any feminine company outside the family circle. The two teenagers would do their homework together and seize every opportunity to make love on the creaking bed in Anna's family apartment at the junction of Nybrogatan and Valhallavägen. It may be that their early-morning excursion by boat during the summer holiday of 1933 on Smådalarö contributed to similar scenes in *Summer Interlude*, although evidence suggests that the model for Marie in that film was Barbro Hiort af Ornäs, to whom in June 1938 Bergman dedicated the first of his workbooks, 'to my Babs', saying that he 'will never forget my days with you on Smådalarö'.[2]

———

In the summer of 1934, Ingmar went to Germany for the first time, on an exchange visit involving some two thousand youngsters. The Swedes would go to Germany for the first part of the summer, and their German counterparts would return home with them to spend the final weeks of sunshine in Swedish homes. Germany and its history already intrigued Ingmar, who was assigned to a pastor's family in the village of Heina, between Weimar and Eisenach. The large household included six sons and three daughters. Hannes, the teenager designated to look after Ingmar, was in the Hitler Youth, and the girls belonged to the German Girls' League. Ingmar attended Hannes's school, and was soon subjected to heavy indoctrination about the might and right of the Nazi cause. The pastor had a tendency to use extracts from *Mein Kampf* for his sermon texts, and Hitler's portrait hung everywhere.

The family made an excursion to Weimar, first to a rally attended by Hitler celebrating the first anniversary of the National Socialist Party coming to power, and then to the opera for a performance of Wagner's *Rienzi*. When Ingmar asked his host at what point during the rally he should say, 'Heil Hitler!', the pastor replied gravely, 'That's considered more than mere courtesy, my dear Ingmar.' For his seventeenth birthday, Ingmar received a photograph of Hitler. Hannes hung it above Ingmar's bed so that 'you will always have the man before your eyes'. In his autobiography, Bergman admitted, 'For many years, I was on Hitler's side, delighted by his successes and saddened by his defeats.'[3]

On another trip, to the house of a neighbouring banker, Ingmar met a girl named Renata, and was smitten. He discovered only later that her family was Jewish. This explained the sudden and ominous silence the following year when, after a correspondence in German, letters no longer came from Renata. On going back to Germany the next summer – the exchange experiment was a success – Ingmar heard that the banker and his family had vanished. In his 1969 TV movie, *The Ritual*, he based some of Ingrid Thulin's dialogue 'almost word for word' on letters he received from Renata.[4]

Ingmar travelled via Berlin on the way home after his initial visit to Germany, and the image of the capital provided him with inspiration for his radio play *The City*, for *The Silence* and for *The Serpent's Egg*.

When Hannes, in turn, came to spend some weeks with the Bergmans, he found himself in a much less regimented milieu than his own. Out at the summer villa on Smådalarö, the Bergman family led a lazy existence free from the demands of city routine. There was tennis, swimming, dancing, even lovemaking. Hannes was thrilled by the presence of Margareta, Ingmar's sister, and the two soon became seriously attached. There were eventually plans for them to marry, but Hannes, a pilot, was shot down on the first day of the German invasion of Poland.

Dag Bergman was one of the founders and organisers of the Swedish National Socialist Party, and Pastor Erik Bergman voted for the party on several occasions. Some of the pastors in his father's parish were 'crypto-Nazis', according to Bergman, and the family's closest friends often talked enthusiastically about 'the new Germany'. But when, after the war, the newsreels of the concentration camps began to be shown in Sweden, Bergman realised the horror with which he had brushed shoulders. 'My feelings were overwhelming,' he told Jörn Donner, 'and I felt great bitterness towards my father and my brother and the schoolteachers and everybody else who'd let me into it. But it was impossible to get rid of the guilt and self-contempt.'[5]

In the 1970s, after almost thirty-five years of reticence, Bergman could admit to having been affected by Nazi propaganda. 'When I came home I was a pro-German fanatic,' he said, although few of his contemporaries recall any pronounced political leanings in him in that period. One of the most meaningful consequences of this episode was that Bergman turned his back on politics in every form. For years he did not vote, did not read political leaders in the papers, and did not listen to speeches.

However, given that Jane Magnusson's major documentary on Bergman, released in 2018 to coincide with the centenary of his birth, asserts so vigorously that he was in denial about Hitler's regime until long after the Führer's death, it's essential to state some facts. He disagreed sharply with his brother Dag and did not belong to the Swedish National Socialist Party. Some of his closest friends and co-workers were of Jewish stock – the actor Erland Josephson, the costume designer Mago (Max Goldstein) and his script assistant and production manager Katinka Faragó. There is no trace of anti-Semitism in Bergman's stage or screen work, and no suggestion that he espoused Nazi ideals such as *Kraft durch Freude* ('Strength through Joy'). Indeed, in 1966 he had the courage to stage Peter Weiss's scarifying play, *The Investigation*, about the Auschwitz trials in Frankfurt. The villain in Bergman's first filmed screenplay, *Frenzy*, is clearly modelled on Heinrich Himmler. In his 1949 feature, *Thirst*, he shows starving Germans pleading for food in the wake of World War II as a train passes through a station on the way home to Sweden. *The Serpent's Egg* (1977) sought to locate the germ cell of Nazi ideology in the Weimar Republic of 1923, with a deranged scientist, Hans Vergérus, explaining that 'It's like a serpent's egg. Through the thin membranes, you can clearly discern the already perfect reptile.'

In 1937 Bergman took what was known in Sweden as the student examination, an equivalent of the English A level (or High School Diploma in the United States) and a prerequisite for anyone intending to go to university. He passed with quite a respectable grade, although he failed Latin. The day before that particular paper, he had been obliged to attend the funeral of one of his father's fellow clergymen, and the incident upset him so much that he made a mess of a subject he had previously enjoyed. He considered himself 'totally, completely devoid of any talent for maths'.[6] He also found geography difficult, whereas history and religion were more engaging. Around this time, he met a young man he called 'Matheus Manders', and shared a cottage with him in a kind of allotment garden. Bergman developed this into a fiction entitled *Matheus Manders, the Fourth Story* or *Om en mördare* in 1942,[7] and the cottage itself would surface in his 1946 feature film, *It Rains on Our Love*.

Before proceeding to Stockholm High School, as the University of Stockholm was known in those times, Bergman did compulsory military service in two stretches, amounting officially to five months each. He was soon sent home, however, thanks to a doctor's amiable assertion that his stomach required more delicate sustenance than the army could offer. 'I don't think I was a very good soldier,' Bergman recalled. His most arduous duty at the military camp in Strangnäs was to manage a machine gun with six other youths. The weapons were obsolescent, and the machine guns, dating from 1914, were as unwieldy as small cannon, mounted on carriages but lacking the horses to drag them along. The officers refused permission for the recruits to wear earplugs during target practice, and Bergman became completely deaf in his right ear. 'But', he wrote in 1994, 'my left ear can still hear a cricket sing,' just as his right eye was 'legally blind' and yet he could 'see like a raven with the left one'.[8]

At university, his chosen subjects were literature and the history of art. Like many another genius, he could not be pinned down to the precise demands of a curriculum. He did not complete the degree course, although he was stimulated by the lectures of Martin Lamm and managed to hand in a paper on Strindberg's play *The Keys of Heaven*.

The years 1938 and 1939 formed a watershed in Bergman's youth. He became friends with Kerstin Högvall, who was a leader of the Storkyrkoflickorna ('Big Church Girls') group at the Mäster-Olofsgården, a club for people of all ages that since 1931 had offered courses and activities, particularly in theatre. 'I *will* be a great director, I *want* to be,' Bergman told her. He had met Sven Hansson, the head of Mäster-Olofsgården, while hunting for books on theatre at Sandberg's Bookshop, where Hansson worked by day. The two men meshed well, and Bergman was asked to teach a course on stage matters at the settlement house. 'When I began at Mäster-Olofsgården,' he told Henrik Sjögren, 'all theatre was for me suggestions, atmosphere, situations. But I came much later to the notion that a stage play has an intellectual aspect. And the idea that I myself could have an intellectual attitude to a production came still later.'[9]

In the spring of 1938, Bergman directed Sutton Vane's *Outward Bound* in Mäster-Olofsgården. He himself played the Reverend Frank Thomson, and another early admirer, Maud Sandvall, appeared as Mrs Cliveden Banks; on 24 May there appeared a factual – if also favourable – notice in the morning newspaper *Svenska Dagbladet*. His next production was a Strindberg play, *Lucky Peter's Journey*. Both contained parts for Barbro Hiort af Ornäs.

Bergman's life might have been governed by his work for stage and screen, but infatuation marked his emotional progress. At least a dozen of the early films that Bergman wrote or directed are marked, almost convulsed, by disputes between the sexes. If at a cultural level the antecedents for this stem from the plays of August Strindberg, on a personal level they owe their vicious, physical turbulence to Bergman's first major erotic relationship. Karin Lannby was two years his senior, and infinitely more mature. Her mother had worked as the Swedish agent for Metro-Goldwyn-Mayer, and in 1925 had travelled with the seventeen-year-old Greta Gustafsson (soon known as Greta Garbo) to Hollywood. The precocious Karin had joined a socialist association in Sweden at the age of fifteen, and soon afterwards became a member of the Swedish Communist Party's youth group. Two years before she encountered Ingmar, Karin Lannby had been a zealous supporter of the Republicans in the Spanish Civil War. She could speak Spanish and French well, and was recruited by Luis Buñuel, no less, to act as a spy on behalf of the Republicans. Seized by Franco's forces while on a mission on the southern side of the Pyrenees, she escaped, suffered a nervous breakdown and eventually found herself in the Langbro Psychiatric Clinic in southern Stockholm.

When Bergman met her in 1939, Karin seemed like the perfect antidote to his brother Dag, whose right-wing views were as extreme as Karin's commitment to the left. In his autobiography, Bergman calls her 'Maria', for she was still alive in 1987, when *The Magic Lantern* appeared. 'She had a thickset body with sloping shoulders, high breasts and big hips and thighs,' he wrote. 'Her face was flat with a long well-shaped nose, broad forehead and expressive dark blue eyes.'[10] Barbro Hiort af Ornäs also noted Lannby's 'fantastic skin' and 'dark-blue eyes'. The chemical attraction between Bergman and Lannby survived all their quarrels, however violent. Bergman drew a corrosive portrait of her in his screenplay *Woman without a Face* (1947), and she doubtless inspired the seductive femme fatale played by Margit Carlqvist in *To Joy* (1950).

Restless, feral and a consummate actress in real life, Karin Lannby pursued her clandestine career in counter-espionage under the code name 'Annette', reporting to the Swedish General Staff on the activities of German and Spanish diplomats after the outbreak of war. Bergman, however, bowed to her sexual power and promoted her as a stage actress in Strindberg's *The Pelican* at the Stockholm Student Theatre in 1940.

Karin seems also to have sparked Bergman's decision to fly the family nest. On 5 September 1939 Bergman had a row with his father, and when the maid went to make up his room the following morning, she found a letter from Ingmar addressed to Erik Bergman, saying he could no longer stay in the house. Three months later Bergman returned to Storgatan on the eve of being called up for military service in Karlskrona. But it was only a matter of months before he quarrelled with his father again.

The break with his parents seemed more severe than it actually proved, and once or twice a week a friend of the family would trek across town to bring him a bottle of red wine and some decent food and retrieve the dirty socks for washing at home. Sven Hansson offered accommodation to Bergman and acted as mediator between him and his family. The rupture diminished to a state of armed neutrality.

Bergman's activity at Mäster-Olofsgården continued for two more years, and his team grew to love him. His demands were onerous, but he never spared himself. Daily rehearsals were essential just before a premiere, and a Sunday-morning rehearsal was scheduled whatever the state of the production. He worked outside Hansson's tiny auditorium as well: Erland Josephson (later to star in such Bergman films as *Scenes from a Marriage, Face to Face* and *Fanny and Alexander*) remembered the young Ingmar coming to the Norra Real High School and directing *The Merchant of Venice* with a cast of pupils, and Josephson playing Antonio. 'It was so absolutely clear what he wanted,' said Josephson later. The climax of this phase of Bergman's career came in April 1940, with his production of *Macbeth*. Maud Sandvall, who played Lady Macbeth, recalled that confusion raged when news broke of the Nazi invasion of Denmark and Norway on 9 April; with the opening only four days away, all the male actors were called up for military service. Sven Hansson quickly contacted officials in high places and succeeded in getting most of the actors released from duty. *Macbeth* opened as planned and, in the shadow of the Occupation, the play assumed an additional symbolic force. Bergman himself played Duncan. Meanwhile, to his credit, Pastor Erik Bergman uttered a powerful sermon against the Nazi threat and made significant efforts to secure the safe passage to Sweden of German refugees.

By 1940, Bergman was producing plays at the Student Theatre in Stockholm as well as at Mäster-Olofsgården. His pace was hectic. He had managed to persuade those in charge of various organisations that he would produce to order for them and, moreover, keep to a tight budget and time schedule. Strindberg's *The Pelican* was Bergman's first production at the Student Theatre. In the autumn season of 1941, he was embroiled in a series of productions at the Medborgarhuset (Civic Centre), among them *A Midsummer Night's Dream* and one of Strindberg's most taxing plays, *The Ghost Sonata*. The 99-seat library at Medborgarhuset was designed as a place where children might be entertained, and Bergman, with Karin at his side, cheerfully staged plays for younger audiences, using professional, adult actors for the leading roles and dubbing his endeavour the

'Sagoteater' (literally, 'Fairy-tale Theatre'). In September, he sought refuge in a garret in his grandparents' summer house in Dalarna, and wrote twelve plays in less than two months.[11]

On 11 June 1941, Bergman and Lannby wrote a joint letter in Spanish to the family of Federico García Lorca about *Blood Wedding*, but in fact Bergman had to wait until 1952 to direct a radio version of Lorca's play. Karin seems to have run the business affairs at the Medborgarhuset, for in October of 1941 a young Gunnar Björnstrand sent her a plea to be paid his pittance for appearing in *The Ghost Sonata*.

Karin Lannby continued her brazen dominance over her partner, effectively ending a two-year relationship between Bergman and the more demure Marianne von Schantz. In fact, Ingmar and Marianne were engaged, informally, two days after the premiere of *Macbeth* in April 1940. She had known Ingmar since her schooldays, and grew up in Skeppargatan, a short distance from the Bergman home on Storgatan.

One day, Sven Hansson's wife surprised Karin alone in Bergman's room at their home in Själagårdsgatan. 'Are you Mr Bergman's sister?' she enquired, and Karin replied, 'No, I'm his wife.'[12] For some months in the autumn of 1941, Bergman shared an apartment with Karin at Tavastgatan 5 in the Söder neighbourhood of Stockholm.[13] By Christmas, their squabbles had degenerated into serious fighting, and Bergman returned to his parents' home. Soon afterwards, he was seduced once more by Karin, but in May of 1942 the relationship foundered in bitterness. Karin's dramatic life continued unabated – after the war she even contacted the Sicilian bandit Salvatore Giuliano (the subject of Francesco Rosi's great 1962 film), and wrote about him in many international newspapers. She settled in Paris, and played the dying mother in Jean-Pierre Melville's *Les enfants terribles*, written by Jean Cocteau. Subsequently, she shared her life with a radical priest named Luis 'Loulou' Bouyer. She outlived Bergman by four months.

The tempestuous liaison with Karin Lannby provided Bergman with a dark well from which he would retrieve accusations, retorts, explosions of anguish and violence for use in future films and plays. It would haunt him as the most erotically charged of all his love affairs.

3

FIRST MARRIAGE, FIRST SCREENPLAYS

It is difficult to establish when Bergman began writing plays, scribbling them in his almost indecipherable longhand. He spent the summer of 1942 in a concentrated burst of energy that yielded several plays; yet only seven seem to have seen the light of day. He once told a French critic that he had written some twenty-three or twenty-four dramas *in toto*. None has become a staple of the Swedish repertoire and, with the exception of pieces written for television and radio, none has been revived since the 1950s. According to his wife at the time, Else Fisher, the first was based on Hans Christian Andersen's story *The Travelling Companion* (a symbol for Death). Entitled *The Death of Punch* (*Kaspers död*), the play describes a man's sardonic attempt to elude the staid decorum of bourgeois marriage. He falls drunk at an inn, is forced to dance on the table (a foretaste of the scene in *The Seventh Seal* where Jof is tormented by the taverners) and borne off to Death. Punch begs to be excluded from Heaven, which appears identical to the crass serendipity of his marriage.

Bergman's Punch figure becomes an embittered Everyman who pops up in almost every script and play written by the Swede during the decade. Jack Kasparsson in *Jack Among the Actors* (1947) addresses the darkness (as will the Knight in *The Seventh Seal*): 'Is there no one there who can help me? Yes, dear God in Heaven, help me, God, you who are somewhere, who must be somewhere, you must help me!' The paradox remains that the clues to Bergman's art (if not to his obsessions) are more clearly defined in his productions of plays by Strindberg, Ibsen, Molière or Tennessee Williams than in his own apprentice works as a playwright. Ironically, since his death, several of Bergman's films – *The Silence, Persona, Cries and Whispers, Scenes from a Marriage* – have been converted into plays and staged at some of the world's leading theatres.

Bergman was anxious to see his own work in performance, and the premiere of *The Death of Punch* at the Student Theatre in September 1942 proved a momentous occasion, not by virtue of the play's brilliance but because of what ensued. Early the next morning, Stina Bergman was reading her newspapers at the headquarters of Svensk Filmindustri, where she was in charge of the script department. This portly woman was the widow of one of Sweden's greatest writers of the century, Hjalmar Bergman, and as soon as she had digested Sten Selander's notice in *Svenska Dagbladet* ('No debut in Swedish has given such unambiguous promise for the future'), she rang the Student Union and asked for Bergman's home number. She was told that Ingmar was still asleep. When he returned the call, he was suspicious and offhand. Stina Bergman invited him to come for a chat that afternoon.

He arrived, according to Stina Bergman, looking 'shabby and discourteous, coarse and unshaven. He seemed to emerge with a scornful laugh from the darkest corner of Hell; a true clown, with a charm so deadly that after a couple of hours' conversation, I had to have three cups of coffee to get back to normal." She suggested on the spot that he should join Svensk Filmindustri as an assistant in the screenwriting division. He was delighted, not only because the job presented a challenge but also because the salary amounted to a princely 500 crowns a month for 'a poor, confused young man' – Bergman's own description of himself. The days were long, with lunches snatched in the canteen. Bergman worked alongside established scriptwriters including Gösta Stevens, Lars-Eric Kjellgren, Gardar Sahlberg and Rune Lindström.

He was given a desk and a tiny office – there were six people there – and he 'washed and polished' scripts. The regimen was tough, and if one of her young men finished editing a screenplay ten minutes before the close of work, Stina Bergman expected him to plunge at once into another script or synopsis. However, the diligent Ingmar found time to originate a screenplay entitled *Episode*, 'a thriller based on the Swedish security police's work during the current war years'. It would ideally have featured Stig Olin or Tord Bernheim in the lead, with parts also for Stig Järrel, Eva Henning and Olof Winnerstrand. It was never made into a film, but some of the dialogue may have crept into Bergman's *This Can't Happen Here* (1950). Allan Ekelund, who became Bergman's line producer on most of his early films, recalls a fledgling effort entitled *Scared to Live*: 'We discussed it quite seriously at the studio; it was based on a novel and it showed considerable talent.'

Gunnar Fischer, Bergman's cameraman from 1948, remembered being in Stina Bergman's office looking over a screenplay. 'A young man came in, didn't say hello or anything, but promptly lay down on the floor with his hands behind his head. Poorly dressed, with rubber boots. He shut his eyes and didn't say a word for about half an hour or so, and then he left without saying goodbye. That was Ingmar.'[2] By his own admission, Bergman dominated any company. He would laugh often and loudly, so much so that in the midst of a general rehearsal at the Nya Teatern, he was asked to tone down his explosions of mirth, as they were disturbing the actors.[3]

The choreographer on *The Death of Punch* was a pert, wide-eyed woman named Else Fisher. Bergman had met her in April 1942 and had asked her to supervise a pantomime programme at the Civic Centre. She called it 'Beppo the Clown', and with it she revealed her gifts for both dancing and choreography. Else had been born in Australia, the daughter of a Norwegian–Swedish marriage. The same age as Ingmar, she was only twenty-one when she took a prize at the International Dance Competition in Brussels; during the 1940s and 1950s she went on to become secretary of the Swedish Dramatists' Association. 'She was kind, clever, and funny,' recalled Bergman in later years.[4] To a certain extent, Bergman portrayed her in *To Joy* and *Summer Interlude*, but her girlish innocence emerges in the person of Bibi Andersson's Mia in *The Seventh Seal*.

In October, Else and Ingmar became engaged. Their relationship was founded on work and romance. Ingmar immersed himself in novels and plays, although he still did not own a typewriter. On 25 March 1943, the couple married with pleasant pomp at Hedvig Eleonora, although, according to his memoirs, Bergman 'ran away a week before the wedding, but came back'.[5]

Else wore the gold crown of the church itself, and Ingmar (who had chosen the hymns and the organ music) was in white tie and tails. There was a reception at No. 7 Storgatan and then a mere two days' honeymoon in Gothenburg. His parents accepted the return, even if temporary, of their prodigal son. The bridal pair lived in a two-room apartment in Abrahamsberg in the western suburbs of Stockholm.

By March of 1943 Bergman had been accepted at Svensk Film-industri as a scriptwriter (his contract ran initially from 16 January for one year). Svensk Filmindustri was the country's largest film

Ingmar with his first wife, Else Fisher.
Courtesy of the Ingmar Bergman Foundation.

company by virtue of its huge chain of cinemas. Sweden was unusual in that its three leading studios produced, distributed and exhibited movies and, although the efforts of Anders Sandrew and Gustav Scheutz created two viable alternatives to Svensk Filmindustri in the late 1930s, there was no doubting the pre-eminence of 'SF', as the enterprise was known. Charles Magnusson had founded SF in 1919, when he absorbed the assets of his chief rival, Skandia, into his own company, Svenska Bio, to which he had already signed Mauritz Stiller and Victor Sjöström. Most of the talented personalities in Swedish cinema had worked at the SF studios in Råsunda, and the administrative headquarters (where Bergman had begun working) were at 36 Kungsgatan, in the very heart of Stockholm. Carl Anders Dymling, a former head of Sveriges Radio, assumed responsibility for SF in 1942 and immediately brought an enlightened mind to bear on the problems of film production. One of his first decisions was to appoint Victor Sjöström as artistic director of the company.

The notion for the screenplay of *Frenzy* or *Torment (Hets)* had germinated since the late 1930s, and Bergman had written the gist by hand in blue ink in an exercise book as early as 1941. It was meticulously structured according to the precepts he had learned at Svensk Filmindustri, with the action on the left half of each page and the dialogue on the right. The protagonist would be Jan-Erik, a high-school student in Stockholm, and the antagonist his sadistic Latin master, nicknamed 'Caligula' by his pupils. In a programme note issued for the premiere of *Frenzy*, Bergman described Caligula as 'a venomous snake' who did not understand the nature of his own evil personality.[6] It would become a full-length treatment when SF asked Bergman to develop an original synopsis of his own.[7]

Sjöström liked Bergman and his work. He was especially impressed by the treatment for *Frenzy* and urged SF to make it into a film. So too did veteran director Gustaf Molander, writing to Dymling that 'this story contain[s] much that [is] objectionable but also a considerable amount of joy and truth'.[8] The studio's 'house directors' refused to direct *Frenzy*, and the screenplay landed on the desk of the distinguished stage and screen maestro Alf Sjöberg, who would win the Palme d'Or at Cannes for *Miss Julie* some years later. 'It was Dymling who told me I should read it because he thought there could be something in it. I read the script and found that it mirrored exactly my own experience as a boy. The atmosphere at my school was very Germanic and full of spiritual pressure. Ingmar Bergman and I had the same teacher – I for eight or nine years!' Their mutual bête noire had been known to boys at both schools as the 'Coachman', driving his class along with cracks of the whip and frequent tongue-lashings.

By 22 March 1943, Bergman had completed a typed 'synopsis' of the film, running to 47 pages, including 418 shots, and concluding with Caligula polishing his pince-nez and gazing out of the school window, as Jan-Erik, hands plunged in trouser pockets, turns away and goes home on graduation day. The first draft was edited by Stina Bergman. Sjöberg developed it from that point on, and asked Bergman to serve as script assistant on set. Shooting commenced on 21 February 1944; at this stage the screenplay concluded with a whimpering Caligula hiding in the cupboard after the murder of the reluctant prostitute Bertha and pleading with Jan-Erik not to leave him alone. The film itself would end with a liberated if chastened Jan-Erik facing the future. The school scenes were shot at the Östra Real School, attended by Sjöberg and by Bergman's brother Dag.

Svensk Filmindustri paid Bergman what seemed like a princely sum of 5,000 crowns (or around forty weeks' wages for a lower-paid worker in Sweden during the 1940s) for the screenplay for *Frenzy*. 'We both felt it as a gift from heaven, a fantastic surprise!' recalled Else Fisher. 'I was expecting our child and lived with my mother in a small house in a small town near Lake Vättern. Ingmar came for one week's visit and brought that fortune with him.'[9] Their daughter Lena was born on 21 December 1943.

———

Ingmar was not entirely the manic bohemian, although he was certainly aware of his own image. He made a point, when attending the cinema, of sitting in the front row with his feet on a bench beside the piano used for accompanying silent films. Letters and articles would be signed with a flourish accompanied by the insignia of a little devil. He took a liking to Else's beret and soon adopted it as a badge of artistic courage. (He remained addicted to berets until Käbi Laretei, his fourth wife, put a stop to the habit.) A beard was of course de rigueur for the times, and Bergman sported a small pointed variety that gave him the guise of a Mephistopheles. More often than not, the beard was grown less at fashion's diktat than to avoid the sheer bother of shaving.

At one point, he was smoking several packs of cigarettes a day and could often be found at his favourite restaurant, Sturehof, in the centre of Stockholm, feet up on the table and friends and admirers in attendance. Ulcer symptoms soon persuaded him to abandon smoking and he was tempted by the bottle only in youth, and abandoned drinking in middle age. A small glass of wine or beer was sufficient, and a *Ramlösa* (the Swedish equivalent of club soda) would be his habitual accompaniment to food or conversation.

Birger Malmsten, who would personify Bergman in films of the 1940s and 1950s, recalls the director in the war years as 'small and skinny, wearing a pair of worn-out suede pants and a brown shirt. He directed the play holding a hammer in his hand, and from time to time he threw it at the young actors.'

———

In April 1944, thanks to a recommendation from the drama critic Herbert Grevenius, Bergman received an offer to become director of the City Theatre in Helsingborg, on the south coast of Sweden. *Frenzy* was still in production, and so Bergman obtained a day's leave from Sjöberg to go down to Helsingborg and sign the contract, thus becoming the youngest head of a major theatre in northern Europe. On his return to the SF studios, he was asked to supervise the last exterior shots on *Frenzy*, as Sjöberg had another commitment. Filmed at dawn, 'they were my first professionally filmed images', he remembered with pride.

Stig Järrel and Alf Kjellin in *Frenzy* (*Torment* in the United States). Copyright © *AB Svensk Filmindustri 1944*. Photo by Louis Huch.

Frenzy captured a large audience in Sweden, as well as a debate in the press. The headmaster of Palmgren's School protested in *Aftonbladet* the day after its premiere on 3 October 1944, claiming that Bergman's father, brother and Ingmar himself had all been satisfied with their education there. Bergman riposted immediately, saying that he abhorred school as a principle, a system and an institution. Sjöberg had based the character of Caligula on Himmler, which he said 'tied in with the anti-Nazi plays I was staging at the Royal Dramatic Theatre, by writers like Pär Lagerkvist'. The teacher reads the pro-Nazi newspaper *Dagsposten* while sipping brandy in

Bertha's flat. At other times his behaviour resembles that of Hitler, with his explosions of rage and his slamming of the cane on desks in the classroom.

For Jan-Erik and his friends, Caligula is the Devil incarnate, but Bergman did not in this first screenplay give vent to his hopes for a Godhead that can combat evil. He does not regard the fiendish teacher as mentally ill; rather he believes that some individuals are inherently evil. The school remains a microcosm of the hell that Bergman's later figures will view as symbolic of the world in general. Bergman's seething rebellion against his family background could easily be heard as a more profound cry of exasperation against the lethargy of Swedish society in the face of World War II. His relationship with his parents can be gauged from the portrayal of Jan-Erik's own mother – considerate and affectionate – and father – more narrow-minded and ineffectual.

During the shoot, he had become friends with the actors Stig Olin and Birger Malmsten, who would serve as his alter ego in his films of the 1940s; one of his closest colleagues through the years ahead, Gunnar Björnstrand, appears as an officious teacher on the prowl for pupils arriving late at school.

Only a few months after his marriage to Else Fisher in 1943, Bergman attended a party at the opera in Stockholm to celebrate the birthday of the conductor Sixten Ehrling; there he met Ellen Lundström, who had the impression of 'a man who talked the whole evening about himself'. Ellen was a dancer and choreographer. In his autobiography, Bergman described her as 'a strikingly beautiful girl who radiated erotic appeal . . . talented, regional and highly emotional'.

Almost as soon as he assumed his post as the head of Helsingborg City Theatre, Bergman assigned Ellen Lundström to choreograph his productions, starting with Brita von Horn's *The Ascheberg Widow at Wittskövle* in September of 1944. This was a role offered at first to Else Fisher, who could not come down to Helsingborg for medical reasons, as both she and the infant Lena were diagnosed as suffering from tuberculosis. Else's disinclination to travel stemmed from the knowledge that Ingmar was no longer faithful to her. She wrote to him on a daily basis, but he did not respond. 'I trusted no one, loved no one, missed no one,' he asserted in *The Magic Lantern*.[10] He was 'obsessed with a sexuality that forced me into constant infidelity' and was 'tormented by desire, fear, anguish, and a guilty conscience'.[11]

Bergman would produce ten plays during a prodigious two seasons in Helsingborg. *Macbeth* opened on 19 November 1944. Herbert Grevenius attended the first night and in his review endorsed Bergman's vision of Shakespeare's tragedy as 'an anti-Nazi drama, a furious settlement of accounts with a murderer and a war criminal. Ruthlessly, consistently, and psychoanalytically, the all-powerful tyrant is taken to pieces.'[12] Another success was *Rabies*, based on a novel by Olle Hedberg, an expert flayer of bourgeois life. The third memorable production proved to be *Requiem*, marking the dramatic debut of a bright young Swedish writer, Björn-Erik Höijer. Bergman summed up his aspirations at Helsingborg in a programme note dated September 1945: 'Our theatre will be, must be, a *young* theatre. It will be a first-rate seedbed for new plants and we cannot tell what they will be like when they grow big. They'll shift and change . . . Our theatre will also be a touchstone for our capacity for self-criticism.'[13] Sally in *A Ship to India* describes her theatre in words that must have represented Bergman's own impression of Helsingborg: 'The same old songs, the out-of-tune piano, the musty costumes. Everything smelling of rats and mould and poverty.' Facilities were indeed modest – twelve spotlights, and just four sets of horizontal lamps – and the capacity was just three hundred. The average age of the company was twenty-three, salaries small, and the theatre's subsidy minuscule – in the region of 50,000 crowns. 'But Ingmar's productions were so good', recalled Erland Josephson, 'that it appeared as though there were a lot of facilities. His use of the stage, the actors, the music, the rhythm, was excellent.'

Bergman habitually harangued his audience in the programme notes even before the curtain went up: 'Take a look at this, my friend, and you'll see what you look like. Just because you happen to live here in Helsingborg, you aren't any better than anyone else. I hope it upsets you. Because we're going to pull the floor from under your feet, plunge you into lethal torture chambers to take a look at the eyeless monsters that lurk there.'

Ellen Lundström had married the photographer Christer Strömholm in 1944, but she and Ingmar had already hurtled into love, and the marriage with Else Fisher was dissolved in 1945. Else may have felt abandoned, but accepted, in her own words, that Ellen 'had much more by way of beauty, strength, and sexual attraction'.[14] She had at least been permitted to leave the sanatorium for two days to attend the first night of *The Ascheberg Widow* in Helsingborg.

Carl Anders Dymling felt from the outset a strong sympathy for Bergman and his writing. When Bergman fell sick in Helsingborg in September of 1944, Dymling wrote to say that Svensk Filmindustri would give him a loan to cover his sanatorium costs. The following spring, Dymling sent Bergman a thoughtful assessment of a screenplay entitled first *Sentimental Journey* and then *Marie*, which would eventually become *Summer Interlude* (1950).

> First of all, undoubtedly you have never written a better love story; it is fine, tender and genuine, and the scenes between the young are authentic and animated.
>
> Less convincing is the framework. Apart from such a minor detail that you never find out from where the diary miraculously materialises, the double perspective doesn't add much, and the fascinating atmosphere surrounding the opera-ballet you have only partially benefited from.
>
> The story is hardly naturally associated with this particular environment but could practically be played out anywhere. This last note is of secondary importance. Much more importantly, as I have

just said, is that the freshness of the first experience of love is not contrasted with a similar experience in the present, a contrast that could be effective, and which one might expect.

Psychologically, it would not be unthinkable, but on the contrary likely, that the girl after fifteen years would win a kind of reconciliation with life and once again experiences love, even if in a completely different form. I am afraid that the story, as cinema, loses a lot by you having focused it so strongly on the memories of youth.

In other words, your synopsis is, I would say, a beautiful short story, in a gentle melancholy mood, but I fear that such a movie would be a little monotonous and flimsy. However, I can easily picture the love story as the core of a film, where present-day Marie is more fully fleshed out. Couldn't one imagine that, at the beginning of the film, she is, using a banal expression, about to enter into a marriage of convenience, but that before marrying she needs to bid farewell to her youth and memories?

It is very possible that I have it all wrong, but you can ponder these points a little.

As usual, Bergman took Dymling's comments to heart, and would revise his screenplay in the coming years, until it materialised as *Summer Interlude* in 1950. He and Ellen rented an apartment on Norra Storgatan in Helsingborg, which included a children's room and a guest room, for when Ingmar's sister Margareta would visit. 'We were happy, Ingmar and I,' wrote Ellen in her reminiscences. 'Ate dinner together at home. Went to concerts and films as time allowed. Made love. And worked, worked in the theatre.'[15]

Ellen's influence on his work was negligible, although when the relationship grew bitter it did provide Bergman with the spur to write the harrowing matrimonial rows in *Thirst*, *Prison* and *To Joy*. Ellen bore him four children. On 5 September 1945 she gave birth to a daughter, Eva, whom Ingmar always accepted as his own child – and in fact adopted, knowing full well that Eva's father was Christer Strömholm. Some days afterwards, Ellen sent Bergman a passionate letter, along with an itemised bill for sundry expenses. She then wrote to him almost continuously, keeping him up to date with Eva's progress. She was a lively soul, writing hastily, often in pencil or ink in a large, generous hand, making little jokes and teasing Bergman. During the month of July 1946 she despatched 14 letters, and no fewer than 21 in the following month. Throughout the summer, while Bergman was travelling or working somewhere other than in Helsingborg, they would write to each other every day, and on the days when they did not write, they would talk on the phone.

Jan was born on 7 September 1946, and the twins Mats and Anna followed in 1948. Jan had a desultory career as an actor and TV director, even appearing as Gunnar Björnstrand's chauffeur in his father's film, *Shame*. Anna married an Englishman and appeared on British TV; in 1979, she directed her first film, *The Stewardess*, in Santo Domingo. In her autobiography, Anna suggests that to some degree her mother was a rival to the young Ingmar Bergman because she was a dancer, choreographer, stage director and actress.[16] Mats made his debut as an actor on Swedish TV in 1969, while Eva became a programme editor at the Royal Dramatic Theatre.

———

The original title of *Crisis* was *My Child Is Mine*, and it stemmed from a play by the Danish writer Leck Fischer. The screenplay is dated May 1945, and was handwritten in ink, but more sloppily than *Frenzy*, as though Bergman had been in haste to complete it – which he did, in fourteen nights. It ran to 444 shots. Dymling had visited Bergman at the theatre in Helsingborg and suggested that he cut his teeth on a film that none of the regular directors in the SF stable was willing to touch. 'I'd have filmed the telephone book if anyone had asked me to at that point,' said Bergman later. Shooting commenced on 4 July, but Bergman recalled in his autobiography that his dream debut swiftly deteriorated into a nightmare. He clashed with his actors; he clashed with Gösta Roosling, the veteran cinematographer; the weather proved unpredictable; and the frustrated Bergman himself succumbed to bouts of drinking. Victor Sjöström, then an adviser to SF, saved the situation by counselling Bergman to be less choleric with his actors and to film each shot in the least complicated way possible.

The wounding of others runs like a bass line through Bergman's work, and dates from this debut. Jack (Stig Olin) is the first of many autobiographical portraits, with the gentler personality of Birger Malmsten taking over the role in subsequent films. Jack holds sway over women both young and of a certain age. His charm and arrogance create havoc in the small-town life of a provincial town (Helsingborg, although unnamed). *Crisis* is a film of light versus shadow, town versus country, the innocent Nelly's biological mother Jenny versus her foster mother Ingeborg.

Jack, the devil's advocate, is brutal and maudlin by turns. As he gazes down at the party guests dancing in the town hotel, he sneers, 'What a bunch of crazy marionettes – and who's pulling the strings? Me!' His suicide in a rain-slicked street by night recalls that of Jean Gabin in Marcel Carné's *Quai des brumes*. Two shots are heard. At a nearby theatre, people can be heard laughing at some entertainment. Jenny shrieks with grief as the ambulance arrives to bear away Jack's corpse. The street empties, and Nelly wanders disconsolate through the night, just as Michèle Morgan did in the Carné film.

Bergman uses an offscreen narrator at the beginning and end of *Crisis*. He would rely on the device at various stages of his career, in films such as *Persona*, *The Passion of Anna*, and in the introduction to several episodes of *Scenes from a Marriage* and *Face to Face*. Other characteristics of Bergman's cinema emerge: the predominance of mirrors for reflecting a person's anxieties and weaknesses; the dream sequence as an evocation of the past; and the close-up, most eloquently showing one character talking away from the camera, while another stares out of the background.

Bergman's self-confidence had been wounded by the experience on *Crisis*. On 15 December 1945 he wrote to Carl Anders Dymling suggesting that Sjöberg should direct his screenplay *Marie*: 'This is the only script I have ever really cared about.' Dymling demurred, but five years later would green-light the project under the title of *Summer Interlude*. Their relationship had grown warmer, with Dymling addressing him as 'Mr Theatre Chief' in 1944, and then 'Dear Ingmar' in the late 1950s. On Bergman's side, even in 1945 he was addressing Dymling as 'Esteemed and Respected Brother' (*Värderade och vördade Broder*).

Crisis opened in February 1946, and flopped, although some reviewers saw promise in Bergman's work. While he continued to write screenplays for Svensk Filmindustri, he would not direct another feature for the studio until *Port of Call* in 1948.

In January 1946, the legendary director Torsten Hammarén invited Bergman to join the Gothenburg City Theatre from the autumn of that year. His stipend would be 8,000 crowns for six months' work, commencing on 1 October 1946.

4

WORKING AT TERRAFILM

The emotional anguish and the financial pressures of Bergman's life at this time might have broken someone less committed to his profession. Instead, he set a tremendous pace, staging plays, writing screenplays, directing films and writing essays and programme notes. He liked to quote Baudelaire: 'It is necessary to *work*, if not from inclination, at least from despair. Everything considered, *work* is less boring than amusing oneself.' Theatre and cinema held equal sway in his career. When a Bergman film proved a fiasco, a Bergman stage production would be acclaimed, and so a creative balance held his world together. At a meeting of the student film society at the University of Uppsala on 13 May 1946, Bergman spoke of his admiration for the French director Marcel Carné and the concept of poetic realism. 'Films must go outside realism, beyond the usual descriptions of reality that surround people,' he claimed.

Another mentor appeared on the Bergman horizon in 1946. Lorens Marmstedt was a maverick producer whose lively little company, Terrafilm, already supported the work of Hasse Ekman and Hampe Faustman, two of the sharpest talents of the period. He was less diffident, less remote than Carl Anders Dymling, and watched the rushes with his directors every evening. He could be brutally candid, too. 'I can't understand your appalling complacency,' he chided Bergman after the failure of *Crisis.*[2]

In the summer of 1946, Bergman found himself shooting *It Rains on Our Love* for Marmstedt. This engaging, if rather trite, love story came from a Norwegian play by Oskar Braaten. Once again, Bergman called on the sober advice of Herbert Grevenius, and even insisted on sharing the director credit with him at the start of the film. Marmstedt encouraged Bergman to use actors with whom he felt at ease – Birger Malmsten in the lead, Gunnar Björnstrand in a minor role, and even Erland Josephson, glimpsed as a clerk in the vicar's office.

Young lovers burdened by an unhappy background appear in more than one Bergman film of the 1940s, and Maggi and David in *It Rains on Our Love* must deal with various crises, some tragic, some frivolous, before deciding to face the future together. Older folk, like the owner of the cottage rented by Maggi and David, are often sly, cynical or scheming in Bergman's early work. The young couple are acquitted in a climactic courtroom sequence added by Bergman and Grevenius, a harbinger of the 'inquisition' sequence in *Wild Strawberries*, when Isak Borg is questioned in front of his acquaintances. All the witnesses at the trial of Maggi and David have appeared earlier in the film. In *Wild Strawberries*, such a coincidence is permitted the status of a dream; here the entire film has a deliberate naivety that makes the finale quite acceptable in its own right.

As in *Crisis*, an offscreen narrator sets the scene, and different stages in the lives of David and Maggi are introduced with charcoal drawings that give the impression of a folk tale. Even the dingy hotel room, with its brass bedstead, where the couple spend their first illicit night together, breathes only a stylised seediness. Bergman owed much at this stage to classic French cinema of the 1930s.

In private, Bergman would frequently succumb to jealousy, and then to rancour. While they were attending a concert, Ellen introduced him to someone called 'Toni'. Bergman was instantly jealous and refused to believe that it was, as she claimed, her father (which was technically true, as Ellen's parents had divorced in her infancy and she never knew her biological father). The romance gathered momentum, however, punctuated by the violent quarrels that disfigured Bergman's early life and which were reflected in films such as *Prison* and *Thirst*. On 30 July 1946 Ellen had told him, 'I don't want to be Mrs Bergman! But you have to adopt the children.' This was somewhat unfair, for Bergman had already signed the birth register as Eva's father.

On 12 August Bergman agreed his first contract with Malmö City Theatre, for the production of his play *Rakel and the Cinema Doorman*, and received the princely sum of 2,000 crowns.

Once moved to Gothenburg, Ingmar and the family lived in Lars-Levi Laestadius's apartment on Eklandagatan, with two large rooms, kitchen, balcony and a loft. 'The autumn of 1946 began well,' Ellen remembered in her unpublished manuscript, *Years with Ingmar*. '[Ingmar] prepared and rehearsed *Caligula*, with the premiere on 29 November, and I did the choreography.'[3] They went to concerts together. But one day Ellen discovered a piece of paper with the words, 'The keys are in the usual place. Welcome.' During the quarrel with Ellen that ensued, Bergman maintained that he felt sorry for 'the woman' in question because she had suffered from syphilis.

During the spring of 1947 Ellen addressed several letters to Bergman at the Hotel Majestic in Cannes, where he was writing under the eagle eye of Lorens Marmstedt, and also care of Terrafilm in the Avenue Montaigne in Paris. By that stage Ingmar was admitting to her in correspondence that he was 'a pathological liar', and pleading for sympathy and understanding. On 16 April 1947 he wrote to Ellen from Cannes after seeing Marmstedt win 3,000 francs, while he had to be satisfied with winning just 20 francs. From Monte Carlo he wrote to her warmly and said he had bought perfume for her. Then he visited the small medieval village of Haut-de-Cagnes. 'We could settle down here when we retire,' he wrote, saying there was a 3-kilometre stretch of sandy beach just for them. *To Joy* reflects much of the anguish and ecstasy of his marriage with Ellen.

Despite the turbulence of the relationship, the young family moved to a two-storey, six-room apartment in Birkagatan in Helsingborg during the early summer of 1947. The relationship was not exactly distinguished for its fidelity. In June of 1947 Ellen went to Paris for a week and slept with four men – a teacher, a sculptor (perhaps the inspiration for the character of Carl-Adam in *A Lesson in Love*), a journalist and an embassy official.[4] Ellen and Ingmar finally married nonetheless in the City Hall of Helsingborg on 22 July 1947, with a meal to follow at the home of their friends Ulla and Lennart Sahlin. Although Ellen was earning her own money, Ingmar insisted on giving her 100 crowns per month for 'pin money'. Early in the marriage they travelled to Copenhagen, and were trapped in a lift after returning from the theatre to the apartment of some friends, where they were staying. This must have been the inspiration for the episode featuring Eva Dahlbeck and Gunnar Björnstrand in *Waiting Women*.

By the end of the year, they had a nanny called Inga-Lill, who proved excellent in caring for the children, especially as Lena had come to stay with them. Bergman wrote repeatedly that he missed the children during his absences, but when he did have the chance to be with them, he showed little interest. Their mother maintained her involvement in theatrical matters, notably at the Atelier Theatre in Gothenburg.

Throughout 1947 Bergman wrote and directed almost without a break. The year would see two of his own films produced (*A Ship Bound for India* and *Music in Darkness*), the screenplay for Gustaf Molander's *Woman without a Face* and three plays staged at Gothenburg City Theatre (*The Day Ends Early* and *Unto My Fear*, both written by Bergman himself, and G. K. Chesterton's *Magic*).

A teacher whom Ellen had known from her schooldays, Miss Larsson, told her with sly complacency that she had seen Ingmar being '*very* intimate' with the author Dagmar Edqvist while he was working with her on the adaptation of her book *Music in Darkness* in the Sigtuna Foundation hotel during the spring of 1947. His financial commitments, with five children to pay for, obliged him to work like a man possessed. He could still be generous and considerate:

for example, when Ellen's mother became a widow, he arranged to send her 500 crowns each month and invited her to live with them. 'Ellen was actually a good and strong friend,' he would maintain in his autobiography. 'We were fighting chained together and were drowning.'[5] Their incessant wrangling would be transmuted by Bergman into some of the most powerful dialogue in *Thirst*, *Prison* and *To Joy*. By the end of 1948, Ingmar and Ellen were exchanging fewer and fewer letters.

Bergman always had respect for his elders, and no stage director influenced him more than Torsten Hammarén. He remembered him as 'a hard, difficult man', but a wonderful teacher.[6] During rehearsals for *Caligula*, Hammarén instilled into his young colleague in Gothenburg the need to be well prepared, to take notes, even when one was planning to improvise scenes. He advised Bergman to keep quiet and let the actors come to him with their comments and suggestions. Hammarén, who stemmed from a wealthy family, had longed to be an army officer. He failed and instead became a benevolent dictator in the theatre.

The actors at the City Theatre in Gothenburg were divided into three distinct groups: old ex-Nazis, Jews and anti-Nazis. One of the most brilliant figures was Anders Ek, who worked with Bergman until, literally, the day he fell mortally ill in 1978, while preparing to appear in *The Dance of Death* in Stockholm. 'He was a tough and critical colleague,' recalled Bergman, 'at once gentle and ruthless.'[7] Ek had embraced existentialist philosophy, which had reached Sweden from the French literary scene, and welcomed the opportunity to appear in Albert Camus's *Caligula* under Bergman's direction. The play met with an ecstatic response from the public and critics alike. Ebbe Lind, one of the most important reviewers of the time, said that 'Gothenburg and Sweden wrote theatre history with *Caligula*, thanks to a new great actor [Ek], a new French dramatic genius [Camus] and a new (for us) important director'.[8] Carl-Johan Ström's set design received acclaim from everyone.

Bergman's second production in Gothenburg was his own play, *The Day Ends Early*, which began with a deranged woman escaping from an asylum and announcing the precise hour of their death to various people she visits. Bitter, elegant even, and up to the minute in sentiment, it painted life as Hell on earth during an otherwise lusty midsummer's night. The final parade of the dead owed something to *Outward Bound*, but while the critics were convinced by Bergman's depiction of a contemporary Sodom and Gomorrah, they doubted his ability to offer any solution to the dilemmas that he posed. Ebbe Lind, objective as ever, made the shrewd observation in the magazine *BLM* that 'Bergman the director is fatal for Bergman the writer, due to his tendency to bring out every effect without regard for the structure of the drama'.

In March of 1947 Bergman staged G. K. Chesterton's *Magic*, which in its setting (an aristocratic household) and theme (art versus philistinism) is a harbinger of Bergman's *The Magician*. Anders Ek again featured in the production, as he had in *Caligula* and *The Day Ends Early*.

Although he was still waiting for the chance to direct one of his own original scripts, Bergman found Svensk Filmindustri willing to accept his screenplay *Woman without a Face*; the company assigned the experienced Gustaf Molander to direct this searing portrait of a young nymphomaniac and her impact on the man who enters her life. Stig Olin plays the world-weary Bogart figure. 'It was the last spring of the war,' he says offscreen. 'I had a novel behind me, quite a success.' Then the film proceeds to describe in flashback a sordid, sadomasochistic love affair that ends with Martin (Alf Kjellin) trying to slash his wrists in a hotel bathroom while a dance band thunders encouragement below.

Rut Köhler (Gunn Wållgren), the cruel and insensitive woman at the heart of this melodramatic script, was undoubtedly based on Karin Lannby. In a mock interview with himself, written at the time, Bergman refers to 'Ruth''s involvement in the Spanish Civil

War, which clearly identifies her as Karin.[9] Bergman had written the first draft of this screenplay in 1946, under the title *The Puzzle Represents Eros*.

As an act of exorcism and vituperation, *Woman without a Face* is fiendishly effective, probably more so under Molander's direction than it would have been under Bergman's aggressive style of the period. Olin's character, Ragnar, is very much the writer's own view of himself – disenchanted, the inevitable cigarette hanging from his lips, a streak of viciousness flickering over his features in moments of stress. The film contains numerous references to Bergman's life – Frida (Anita Björk) is the gentle, clean-cut wife of Martin (Alf Kjellin) and is reminiscent of Else Fisher, while Hedvig Eleonora Church is glimpsed through a window like a guilty reminder of Bergman's 'respectable' upbringing.

During this period, Bergman developed the screen personalities of Stig Olin and Birger Malmsten to present an image of his own youthful fury and uncertainty. His outbursts of frustrated rage and derision are reflected in Olin's character in *Frenzy*, *Crisis*, *Prison* and *To Joy*. The undercurrent of pessimism in Bergman's temperament, allied to an unquenchably romantic vision of life, can be found in Malmsten's character in *It Rains on Our Love*, *A Ship Bound for India*, *Music in Darkness*, *Thirst* and *Summer Interlude*. Stig Olin would become Director of Programmes at Sveriges Radio, and lived to see his daughter, Lena, become a star in her own right, starting with Bergman's *After the Rehearsal*. Birger Malmsten appeared in ten films directed by Bergman, and beneath his boyish good looks he could reveal from time to time an almost diabolical malevolence, as, for example, in *To Joy*.

At about this time, the magazine *Filmnyheter* printed an article by Bergman in which he referred to the motivation behind his screen-writing: 'I want to describe the universal activity of evil, made up of the tiniest and most secret methods of propagating itself, like something independently alive, like a germ or whatever, in a vast chain of cause and effect.[10] The theme haunted Bergman for decades to come, culminating in the declarations of the mad scientist in *The Serpent's Egg*. In *A Ship Bound for India* (*Skepp till Indialand*), this 'evil' resides in the character of Captain Blom (Holger Löwenadler), even if he is ultimately a victim of the malevolence that has possessed him.

Blom remains the most hateful father figure in Bergman's early period. Blindness encroaches on him like the blackness that threatens the dreams of many Bergman personalities. The film consists of a single flashback, as the hunchback Johannes (Birger Malmsten) searches for his beloved Sally (Gertrud Fridh) in the dismal streets of a harbour town and remembers how their affair began. While he has coffee with two women he has not seen for many years, he says that his back is better. 'It wasn't your back that was deformed,' remarks one of his companions, 'but your soul.' In Bergman's work an outwardly visible ailment always offers the clue to an inner psychological defect.

The screenplay for *A Ship Bound for India* had been written in less than two weeks in a small room on the top floor of the Hotel Majestic in Cannes, according to Bergman. For all its glimpses of seafaring life, and the bizarre decor aboard the boat and in the music halls, *A Ship Bound for India* is a chamber work, a string quartet with Blom, his wife, Johannes and Sally as players. Bergman's interest in music manifests itself in his choice of Erland von Koch as composer for the film. The vigorous chords and choral background to the opening of *A Ship Bound for India* are almost worthy of Vaughan Williams. Flaws and virtues abound in this little-seen film. There are too many theatrical exits and entrances, abrupt and awkward transitions. Against that, there is a remarkable crane shot, for example, that follows a drunken Captain Blom out of a cafe, and the powerful scene where Blom destroys his secret hideaway, with its masks and mementoes from his journeys around the world.

A Ship Bound for India offers glimpses of Bergman's own relationship with his parents. Johannes's exchange with his sympathetic mother echoes what probably occurred between Bergman and his own mother, when Johannes criticises his father and she responds, 'We've been married for twenty-five years.' At one point Johannes shouts in fury and frustration at his overbearing father, 'You ruin everything for me!' Yet Blom is a vehicle for evil rather than its embodiment; his malevolence functions as a magnetic field, infecting everyone with whom he comes in contact.

Marmstedt's budget was, as usual, minuscule, and Bergman had to shoot the picture at a dilapidated studio in Djurgården, a park in southern Stockholm. The film opened in September to good reviews, although Bergman himself passed out from drinking too much, too nervously, at the post-premiere party in the Gondolen restaurant in Stockholm. André Bazin, in *L'Écran français*, would congratulate the young Bergman on 'creating a world of blinding cinematic purity'. This was one of the first significant notices Bergman received outside Scandinavia.

Lorens Marmstedt knew how to handle the moods, anger and latent bad temper Bergman had inherited from his father. Both *It Rains on Our Love* and *A Ship Bound for India* lost money for Marmstedt. Now he presented Bergman with a friendly ultimatum: 'Ingmar, you are a flop. Here's a very sentimental story [*Music in Darkness*] that will appeal to the public. You need a box-office success now.' Bergman replied, 'I'll lick your ass if you like; only let me make a picture.'[11] So the autumn months of 1947 were divided between Bergman's production of his new play, *To My Terror*, and the shoot of *Music in Darkness* (*Musik i mörker*, also known as *Night Is My Future*). *To My Terror* struck an autobiographical chord, with Paul, a budding writer, bringing home a fiancée to his grandmother in Uppsala and announcing that he has recognised God's existence, even though he would never accept it just because people told him so.[12] The cast included Gertrud Fridh and Folke Sundquist, both of whom would follow Bergman from Gothenburg to Malmö and act in some of his films.

Bergman's unhappy experience of army service (which left him partially deaf in one ear) is reflected in *Music in Darkness*, which begins with a dramatic scene in which Bengt (Birger Malmsten) is blinded in an accident at a military shooting range. Bergman claimed that Marmstedt 'cut that whole sequence to pieces', and that every day he would come to the studio and demand that scenes be reshot.[13] 'This is too difficult, incomprehensible. You're crazy! She must be beautiful! You must have more light on her hair! You must have some cats in the film! Perhaps you can find a little dog.' Bergman, however, did not resent his producer's attitude. 'He taught me – in a very tough way – much that saved me. I will be grateful to him to my dying day.' Nor was there pique on Marmstedt's side. 'When we had bad disagreements,' he wrote in 1955, 'Ingmar was capable of writing really hateful letters. Often he'd come up himself with the letter, stick it in my hand, and disappear down the stairs. Without a word. But he never harboured a grudge. After a little while, a day at most, all was forgotten.'[14]

Although based on a novel by Dagmar Edqvist, *Music in Darkness* remains unmistakably a Bergman film. There are powerful links with *A Ship Bound for India*. Both Bengt and Captain Blom are weighed down by physical adversity, the one made blind, the other inexorably losing his sight. This disability stimulates an inferiority complex and a latent masochism. But while Blom is doomed, because he is a member of the older generation despised by Bergman, Bengt has youth in his side. Encouraged and adored by Ingrid, a wide-eyed young idealist (played by Mai Zetterling), Bengt finds sustenance in classical music and hones his skill as a pianist.

The film's concern is with the blind man's desire to be treated as an equal, not a pariah. Thus Bengt's greatest humiliation becomes his greatest pleasure, when he is struck a sound blow by Ingrid's jealous and insecure boyfriend (Bengt Eklund). Yet Bergman does not altogether identify with Bengt. There is a flash of his own fractious temperament in the part of the violinist (Gunnar Björnstrand), who vents his loathing of 'the boss' at the restaurant where the two young men play for peanuts. Bergman himself, wearing his trademark beret, is seen in the train that takes Bengt and Ingrid off on their honeymoon.

Despite the commercial success of *Music in Darkness*, doubtless due to its sentimental story, Bergman put aside film plans in order to concentrate on *Macbeth*, which he was about to present at the City Theatre in Gothenburg. He had directed the play earlier, but with the meagre resources of the Helsingborg theatre, and now he could give full rein to his fantasy with the help of his designer, Carl Johan Ström, whose magnificent sets enhanced Bergman's productions in Gothenburg. *Macbeth* opened on 12 March 1948, with Anders Ek in the title role, and Karin Kavli as his scheming wife. The critical reception dwelt on the clash between Bergman's bold visual effects and the intense performances of the actors.

The summer of 1948 can be seen as marking a watershed in Bergman's early career. Although he would make one further feature for Lorens Marmstedt's Terrafilm (*Prison*), he now found himself wooed by Svensk Filmindustri. With *Port of Call*, Bergman returned to the studios in Råsunda, and would remain loyal to Sweden's oldest film company for a majority of his films in the future. Carl Anders Dymling also purchased Bergman's screenplay for *Eva* in February, and assigned it to Gustaf Molander.

With copious flashbacks in the first half to the hero's boyhood, *Eva* harks back to Bergman's childhood and his summer holidays in Dalarna, when he was so fascinated by the trains ascending the gradient near his uncle's station at Dufnäs. In his preface to the screenplay, dated 8 January 1948, Bergman says: 'I have written this as a protest against myself and the new influences I feel within me.' Bo (Birger Malmsten) is still haunted by a tragic event, when as a young boy he had driven an engine in secret with a blind girl, Marthe (Anne Karlsson); the locomotive gathered speed, and Bo lost control. In the accident that followed, Marthe died, and Bo was beaten black and blue by his father. The Bergman protagonist must often relive such shocking circumstances; the process of unburdening oneself of such a memory becomes an act of atonement.

Bo falls in love with another companion from his childhood days, Eva (Eva Stiberg). They spend the summer on a small island whose only other occupant is a widower, Johansson. One morning Bo and Johansson find the body of a German sailor floating by the rocks, reminding them of the war that has so far left Sweden unscathed. The two men put the corpse in the boathouse. Bo keeps the information from Eva, as she's heavily pregnant and subject to bouts of depression. When she finds the body, she has an emotional breakdown, railing about the pointlessness of life and how 'God has abandoned mankind'. She goes into labour and has to be hurriedly rowed in Johansson's boat to a midwife on the mainland. All ends happily, with the birth of their child, Eva content and an emotionally liberated Bo recognising that Death is just one part of life, not its main concern.

Whatever their dramatic failings, these early Bergman scripts and films have a consistency of outlook. People are governed by the trauma of their birth and the terror attached to their dying; they bear a yoke of guilt that may be discarded only by the most painful confrontation with the past and by an abandonment to love. In an interlude of romance there lies redemption, in the psychological rather than the religious sense. For Bergman, however, Bo's new baby may replace the life that he 'took' when Marthe died in the crash, but it must also have been a premonition of the twins to which his wife Ellen would give birth later that same spring.

The return to Svensk Filmindustri also marked an important new relationship at the studio – with Gunnar Fischer, the cinematographer who would endow Bergman's major films of the 1950s with his uncanny flair for lighting and chiaroscuro.

In the spring of 1948, Bergman began commuting between Gothenburg and Stockholm, renting a room in Nylander's boarding house on the corner of Brahegatan and Humlegårdsgatan. It was a popular refuge for actors and others in the theatre. On frequent occasions, he would be late in paying his child maintenance, and 'a furious Child Care official materialised and remonstrated with me about my dissolute life'.[15] As usual, he wove these incidents into the texture of his next screenplay, for *Port of Call* (*Hamnstad*).

On 27 May, Bergman began shooting *Port of Call*, which was set, conveniently, in Gothenburg, where Bergman's theatre activities had ceased for the summer. The dockland atmosphere is established from the outset, as Berit (Nine-Christine Jönsson) tries to drown herself in the harbour. Gösta (Bengt Eklund), the seaman who befriends her, serves as a catalyst for Berit's unhappiness. But he seems solid, pleasant and relaxed, to a degree rare in Bergman's protagonists. Accordingly, when one sees matters through Gösta's eyes, they acquire a surprising emotional strength. At such moments, Bergman uses his camera incisively, to register the joy and anguish, an intimate technique all the more impressive for being juxtaposed with naturalistic shots of the dockland.

The sea offers an illusion of freedom, as it did in *A Ship Bound for India*, and as it would in future Bergman films, including *Summer Interlude*, *Summer with Monika*, *Through a Glass Darkly* and *Shame*. Although *Port of Call* has a similar maritime setting to Carné's *Quai des brumes* (not least in the brooding chords of Erland von Koch's music, reminiscent of Maurice Jaubert's pre-war scores), the prevailing influence is that of Roberto Rossellini, with its harnessing of a documentary style to fictional events. 'At that time I felt it was tremendously relevant,' said Bergman. 'Rossellini's films were a revelation – all that extreme simplicity and poverty, that greyness.'[16]

Gösta is twenty-nine, the same age as Bergman in 1948. He can be obtuse and clumsy. The women around him suffer from a bleak destiny. Berit's friend Gertrud dies after an abortion; her mother is inquisitive and sarcastic, yet yearns for reconciliation with her estranged husband. Bergman's own childhood and early marriages are reflected in the bitterness and frustration of Berit's memories. Already Bergman seems more at home with women than men – for example, the scene in the reformatory, where girls sit idly together during a hot summer, lying close to one another with an easy, lazy sensuality.

The determinism in the final words of *Port of Call* – presaging the mood of *To Joy*, *Summer Interlude* and *Summer with Monika* – is a rejoinder to the squalor and social injustice endured by Berit and her friends.

'We won't give up,' says Gösta.

'And soon it will be summer,' replies Berit, smiling.

5

FROM *PRISON* TO EMOTIONAL LIBERTY

During the summer of 1948, Bergman conceived what would be his final film for the producer Lorens Marmstedt. He called it *True Story*, alluding, he would say later, 'to a very popular genre in weekly magazines at the time that was called "true stories from life"'.[1] Marmstedt disliked the title, and so Bergman decided on *Prison* (*Fängelse*). He completed the screenplay in the summer cottage in Dalarna so familiar to him from childhood vacations, with Ellen and the children in attendance. On 5 May, Ellen had given birth to twins, Mats and Anna. When Mats emerged, his mother thought that her ordeal was over – but 22 minutes later Anna appeared.

In October 1948, the producer David O. Selznick approached Lorens Marmstedt with a view to setting up a screen version of Ibsen's *A Doll's House*. Selznick wanted the film to be scripted by Bergman and directed by Alf Sjöberg, but the project was doomed from the start. 'Sjöberg had too many ideas, and I had too few,' said Bergman, who was nonetheless grateful for the 30,000 crowns fee that came from Hollywood. With the money, he bought himself his first decent 9.5 mm projector and prints of classics such as *The Cabinet of Dr. Caligari*, *The Niebelungen Saga* and several Chaplin movies. This was not the only pointer to Bergman's growing reputation outside Sweden. Both *Music in Darkness* and *Woman without a Face* (based on his screenplay) were screened at the Venice Film Festival in August. At home, Bonnier published three of his plays, under the title *Moralities*.

Rune Waldekranz, the young and enterprising production manager at Sandrew Film, also sought Bergman's services, suggesting to Marmstedt that Bergman might have a contract with both

Terrafilm and Sandrew, with a remake of *Gunnar Hede's Saga* (one of Mauritz Stiller's triumphs in the silent era) in prospect. But nothing transpired.

Everyone acquainted with Bergman in the late 1940s agreed that he relished controversy and delighted in outraging the audience with his inchoate vision. As he himself told an interviewer: 'I don't want to produce a work of art that the public can sit back and suck aesthetically . . . I want to give them a blow in the small of the back, to scorch their indifference, to startle them out of their complacency.'²

Prison went into production in November, at the old Sandrew studio on the outskirts of Stockholm, and Bergman found himself back on Poverty Row. He received no salary from Terrafilm, just the promise of 10 per cent of the profits. He was limited to a budget of around 125,000 crowns, 8,000 metres of film and 18 days in the studio.

A retired schoolteacher tries to persuade one of his former pupils, now a director, to make a film about Hell – Hell on earth. 'I'd open with the Devil making a proclamation,' he says. (Bergman would in fact start a film, *The Devil's Eye*, twelve years later, with just such a proclamation.) In this opening speech, Bergman's writing chimes with that of his artistic contemporaries in Sweden – dread of nuclear holocaust, art for art's sake, suicide as an act of logic rather than cowardice. The teacher even mentions the bombing of Hiroshima.

The film assumes a spiral form, with one character introducing another, and flashbacks abounding. At the heart of the drama stands Birgitta Carolina (Doris Svedlund), a sex worker who has had a brief relationship with the screenwriter Thomas (Birger Malmsten). Birgitta Carolina falls victim to her pimp, played by Stig Olin as the embodiment of evil, a diabolical character worthy of nightmares. The structure of *Prison* may creak and groan from time to time under the pressure that Bergman's symbolism exerts on it. The scenes of pure Grand Guignol belong more to the stage than the screen, and there are gimmicks and situations inspired by the German silent movies

Bergman dozing amid the spider's webs during the shoot of *Prison*.
Copyright © *Terrafilm/Telepicture Marketing Ltd. Photo by Bengt Westfelt.*

that Bergman was collecting at the time. But many sequences reveal Bergman's elation at being able to experiment with the medium and escape the confines of the theatre. The credits, for example, are spoken offscreen (by a voice sounding suspiciously like Bergman's). Göran Strindberg's camera glides and prowls, closing in on faces and creating a sense of space within the frame. Bergman uses simple black-and-white tones to achieve effects that would be impossible in colour.

At the close of *Prison*, the director Martin (Hasse Ekman) tells the old teacher that his film cannot be made because it would end with a question to which there is no response. 'There is one if one believes in God. As one no longer believes, there is no point to it at all.' One can imagine that Bergman's father watched the film with some consternation. Not that Bergman himself identifies with Martin's suave, relaxed and vapid manner. In 1948, Bergman and Hasse Ekman were uneasy colleagues in the Marmstedt stable, and Bergman was quite content to let his rival perpetuate his fastidious image.[3] In *The Magic Lantern*, he maintained that Ekman was 'unswervingly loyal and helpful'.[4] When the film had been edited, Bergman wrote a warm letter to Marmstedt: 'Thank you, kind Lorens. For letting me do *Prison*. I'm both moved and happy when I look back and think how much you supported me and cheered me the whole time [. . .] Thanks, kind Big Brother, and forgive the sentimental expression of these feelings.' Marmstedt, quoting this letter, noted that it revealed the side of Bergman that 'some of us have learned to respect: tact, finesse, real feelings'.

Fifteen years later, Bergman would be roundly castigated by a young Bo Widerberg for ignoring the social realities of his country at the expense of metaphysical concerns. Yet already by the late 1940s Bergman had laid bare some of the injustices and social discrepancies of his native country: the abuse of women needing an abortion (*Port of Call*), the conservatism of the established church (*It Rains on Our Love*), the predicament of sex workers (*Prison*) and the mistreatment of youngsters in remand homes (*Port of Call*). In *Thirst* (*Törst*), filmed in early 1949, he would also touch on lesbianism, a taboo subject in the early post-war years. In yet another reference to abortion, the female lead Rut says, 'I've seen buckets of my own blood. Butchers with sharp knives.'

As soon as *Prison* was in the can, Bergman resumed his shuttling between Stockholm and Gothenburg, where he was preparing Jean Anouilh's *A Wild Bird* and Tennessee Williams's *A Streetcar Named Desire*. On 4 November 1948, Sveriges Radio broadcast his production of Strindberg's *Mother Love*, and the following month his own play, *Draw Blank*, opened in Helsingborg, under the direction of Lars-Levi Laestadius. The notices for *Streetcar* must have pleased Bergman enormously. Ebbe Lind wrote in *Dagens Nyheter*, 'Ingmar Bergman came to Gothenburg City Theatre as a talented eccentric. He leaves it after two years with this masterful proof that shows his mature power as one of the country's most knowledgeable directors.'[5]

Thirst was inspired by a collection of short stories by Birgit Tengroth. Herbert Grevenius, Bergman's trusted fellow screenwriter, wove three different stories together so that, through flashbacks and interlaced plots, they became plausible and suspenseful. Ellen organised the dancers seen briefly in the ballet school.

The first half-hour or so focuses on a married couple, Rut (Eva Henning) and Bertil (Birger Malmsten), travelling home to Sweden from a holiday in Italy. Contempt jousts with affection as they pass through Basel, taking a hotel room for one night. Their train compartment serves as a prison cell in which they can vent their frustration and anger at being trapped in a relationship in which, they eventually conclude, 'Hell together is better than Hell alone.' Rut recalls an affair in the archipelago with Raoul (Bengt Eklund) that prefigures the tone of *Summer Interlude*; Rut, like Marie in the later film, is a ballet dancer. Although Bergman is not credited with work on the screenplay, some of the lines seem drawn from his own life. 'Any healthy man should have two women,' declares Raoul, and his wife might be speaking for Ellen Lundström when she says to Rut with controlled bitterness, 'A woman with three children can't be too concerned about pride.'

Rut is possibly the closest to a Strindberg heroine that Bergman reached. She is jealous even when Bertil lies asleep in the hotel bedroom. He, for his part, dreams that he has struck her with a bottle and on waking is relieved to discover she is still alive. Thus are juxtaposed his true, subconscious desire and his conscious, practical realisation that it is better to have his wife than to be left alone. The wretchedness of the couple's lives is counterpointed by shots of the ruined cities of Germany traversed during the journey. At one station, hungry Germans swarm alongside the train and beg for food. The effect looks clumsy and theatrical, but the meaning is unmistakable. Waiting for his wife in the corridor, Bertil catches sight of his reflection in one of the windows; his features shake, as though he were being jolted in Hell. Rut emerges from the toilet and stares through the window at the alluring night beyond, contemplating suicide. As she does so, Bertil steals up behind her. He stretches out his hand and grasps her shoulder. Rut whirls round and falls into his embrace with a desperation perfectly echoed in the headlong gallop of the train and its long, drawn-out whistle.

The second major thread in *Thirst* concerns the lonely Viola (Birgit Tengroth, who had been acting since 1926 before turning to writing). Grieving the loss of her mother, ailing from encephalitis, Viola is all but seduced by a depraved psychiatrist, played with suave, sardonic assurance by Hasse Ekman. 'Your whole life has been one long mistake,' he tells her. 'Full of foolish liaisons and twisted illusions.' Erland Josephson's doctor in *Cries and Whispers* will accuse Maria in much the same way. Viola almost succumbs to the lesbian advances of Valborg, a former ballet-school friend of Rut, but chooses to attempt suicide instead, jumping into Stockholm harbour just as Rut and Bertil's train arrives in the city.

Thirst may be Bergman's most narcissistic film. The characters are without exception egocentric and afflicted with self-pity. There are mirrors in all the major scenes. Bertil and Rut, Viola and Valborg gaze at their own reflections, fascinated by the confrontation with their wasted features, their ugliness, their fear, their consciences. Bergman's compositions and sense of pace seem more confident than hitherto; the sequences in the train with Bertil and Rut remain among the finest of his early achievements in the cinema.

François Truffaut recognised that Bergman's 'women are not seen through a masculine prism in his films but are observed in a spirit of total complicity. His female characters are infinitely subtle, while his male characters are conventions.'[6] Already in 1949 this principle is established. In the hotel in Basel, for instance, Bertil crouches beneath his duvet while Rut paces in frustration, and the best that Raoul can do after Rut announces her pregnancy is to slap her face and brand her a whore. The men in *Thirst* are sounding boards for the women. They are transparent, pathetic figures who ultimately amuse and disgust their partners.

On 10 April 1949 Ingmar wrote to Ellen that he would not be home for Easter as he had to polish the screenplay for *Marie* (eventually to become *Summer Interlude*), and that he would go down to Basel with Gunnar Fischer to take some shots for the start of *Thirst*. His letters from Cagnes-sur-Mer in May 1949 declared that he was sleeping as much as 16 hours a day, his stomach was better, he was drinking no spirits, only beer, and reading and writing. In fact he returned home drunk every night to his room overlooking fields of carnations in a valley with the Mediterranean beyond. He was, by his own admission, distracted happily by a Russian-American painter. 'She was athletic but well-proportioned, dark as night with bright eyes and a generous mouth, a statuesque Amazon radiating uninhibited sensuality.'[7] In the screenplay for *To Joy* that he completed that summer, Bergman would evoke her feline powers through the character of Nelly, played by Margit Carlqvist.

From early July until the end of August, the shoot of *To Joy* (*Till glädje*) took place in southern Skåne. The film, wrote Bergman later, 'was about Ellen and me, about the conditions imposed by art, about fidelity and infidelity'. Music would 'stream through the film'.[8] The title referred to Beethoven's Ninth Symphony. At this point, a *coup de foudre* occurred that would wreck Bergman's second marriage and lay the ground for his third. The journalist Gun Hagberg came down on location to write about the film, and there was an instant personal rapport between her and Bergman. Gun was a well-educated philologist who could speak six languages, as well as being an athletic, sport-loving young woman who had two sons from her marriage with an engineer named Hugo Grut. She had run barefoot to win the 60-metre race at the Swedish Schools Championships.

In Gun Hagberg, Bergman finally found a woman whom he could respect and admire. In his autobiography, Bergman referred to her 'sincerity, pride, and integrity'. He spends more pages describing his relationship with her than he does his relationship with almost any other woman. Even more significant, she entered several of his films, as it were, under her second name, Marianne. Three of these spring to mind: Eva Dahlbeck as Marianne in *A Lesson in Love*; Ingrid Thulin's character in *Wild Strawberries*; and Liv Ullmann's Marianne in *Scenes from a Marriage*. 'Marianne' in Bergman's work implies a woman of a robust and independent mind. When Albert, the circus-owner in *Sawdust and Tinsel*, makes a half-hearted, almost pathetic attempt to reconcile with his estranged wife, it is evident that Bergman himself must have done the same – all the more so because Harriet Andersson, Albert's lover, was Ingmar's mistress even during his marriage with Gun.

In *Scenes from a Marriage*, Johan tells his wife Marianne that he is going abroad with a new girlfriend, and it seems that this scene reflected the ruthless confession that Bergman made to Ellen Lundström in the late summer of 1949. Ellen decided on the spur of the moment to visit Gun Grut in her home in Johanneberg, and it proved an awkward encounter. Gun agreed that she had children of her own, and when Ellen asked if she was prepared to lose them, she remained silent. Ingmar and Gun arrived in Paris on 1 September and stayed in a small hotel in the rue Saint-Anne, between the Louvre and the Opéra. The view from their window is recreated in *The Silence*. They would, according to Marie Nyreröd's documentary, *The Undefeated Woman*, eat every day at a small restaurant called La Potinière.

'I was escaping from everything,' recalled Bergman. 'It was the first time in my adult life that I did nothing. Absolutely nothing.'[9] That was an exaggeration. He raced round the Paris theatres, and Vilgot Sjöman maintains that Bergman 'lit up like a torch' after coming in contact with the French Molière tradition in a performance of *Le Misanthrope* at the Comédie-Française. He also paid regular visits to the Cinémathèque in the Avenue de Messine and some years later told Amita Malik, perhaps out of gallantry, that he had enjoyed watching a group of dancers from India.[10] He even managed to write a new drama, *Joakim Naked*, but when he offered this and some other plays to Bonnier, the prestigious publishers of his earlier collection, they demurred. In 1980 he told me that Gun 'went to this very famous hairdresser, M. Riffe, and she came back looking terrible, because he had cut off her wonderful hair and made a mess of it, and so [using his name for an article in *Chaplin* magazine in November 1960] was a revenge!'[11]

Knowing that Ingmar and Gun were in Paris, Ellen travelled there on her own initiative. She even saw them in the theatre one evening, a few rows behind her and her friend Monica Schildt. But Ingmar and Gun left at the interval. Ellen returned from France and visited a lawyer, who then wrote to Bergman in Paris. It was the start of proceedings that would occupy 'almost two years'.

Relations between Ingmar and Ellen remained friendly, even warm, and when Ingmar was living on Fårö, Ellen was invited to the island with Jan and had lunch at the kitchen table with Ingmar and his final wife, Ingrid. Ellen was angered by what she read in *The Magic Lantern*, and berated Ingmar in an unpublished manuscript, written in August 1988, directed at her children. 'Why couldn't you have described things as they really were?' Ellen complained. She asserted that their first child, Eva, was 'wanted and planned'. In his autobiography, Bergman claimed that Ellen was suffering from eczema on her feet and hands. But in her own memoirs, entitled *Years with Ingmar*,[12] she asserts that she contracted eczema only during the 1960s, and that had nothing to do with him anyway. She did admit that over the years he had helped her financially when necessary. As late as 2001 and 2002, Ellen was active in staging productions for actors in wheelchairs, at Sibyllans Teater in Stockholm. She died at the age of eighty-eight in March 2007, just three months before Bergman himself passed away. Henning Mankell wrote a sympathetic obituary in *Dagens Nyheter*.

The fine weather in southern Sweden, and perhaps the tinge of Mediterranean sun in the screenplay, rendered *To Joy* the first of those Bergman movies in which the elements play a significant role. 'To me,' Bergman once commented, 'a Swedish summer is full of deep undertones of sensual pleasure, particularly June, the time around midsummer – May and June. But for me July and August, July especially, when the sun shines day after day, are a dreadful torment.'[3]

Although there are close parallels between *To Joy* and Bergman's second marriage – the setting in Helsingborg, the twins born to Martha (Maj-Britt Nilsson) and Stig (Stig Olin), the mentor figure of Torsten Hammarén transfigured into the orchestra conductor Sönderby (Victor Sjöström) – there is no doubt that it remains an idealistic film in comparison with *Thirst*, in which the relationship with Ellen Lundström was hung, drawn and quartered.

Quite aside from the references to Bergman's marriage, *To Joy* offers an intense and probing analysis of the young artist's aspirations. Stig is a violinist, twenty-five years old, the same age as Bergman was when he assisted Sjöberg on *Frenzy*. His striving after harmony and perfection strikes Martha as ugly. She cannot see that Stig wants to order his entire outlook on life. Before his debut as a soloist in the Mendelssohn Violin Concerto, Sönderby tells him, 'Music is a goal, not a means.' But his performance proves a disaster, and Stig unleashes his bitterness and frustration on his wife and on the aged conductor. 'I'm alone, as I always have been,' he exclaims in a temper. No director has torn at his open wounds so insistently as Bergman.

Stig's friend Marcel (Birger Malmsten) plays the cello in the same orchestra, and with his small beard and moustache embodies the diabolical side of Bergman's character. Stig quails beneath the stabbing, sneering comments of Marcel, and promptly succumbs to the smouldering allure of another woman, Nelly (Margit Carlqvist), the wife of an actor and breathing the illicit passion that seduces the Bergman protagonist in so many films. Successive scenes emphasise even further the contrast between a bohemian way of life and an uneventful, perhaps even unintelligent, married existence. Nelly does not resemble Gun Grut, except for the fact that she too will prove a catalytic emblem for Bergman's abandoning his family in Gothenburg.

The tragic death of Martha in a fire at the couple's summer cottage may be a dramatic device, but it spurs Stig to continue playing in the orchestra and to appreciate his young son, who watches him during the climactic performance of Beethoven's Ninth – a symphony described by Sönderby as being 'about joy, a joy so great that it lies beyond pain, beyond despair . . . a joy beyond comprehension'. The film adumbrates what will become the overriding philosophy of Bergman's middle period: that there are brief instances in life of such exquisite beauty that they compensate for all the misery and unhappiness.

———

The new decade began auspiciously, with Bergman announcing to the *Stockholms Tidning* newspaper on 19 January 1950 that he would start work in August at Lorens Marmstedt's Intima Theatre in Odenplan, once he had completed work on *Summer Interlude*, which was scheduled to go before the cameras that spring.

Bergman no longer cultivated quite so outrageous an image. Marmstedt remembered that he 'had a savings book in his pocket and a Ford Prefect he'd bought for 6,200 crowns, cash down. Gone is the beard stubble, gone the rumpled hair, gone the dirty fingernails. But the burning spirit is still there.'[14]

Another intimate of the time said that Bergman was inclined to make great pronouncements, a lot of them drivel and some of them occasionally profound. The composer Erik Nordgren described his first meeting with Bergman to prepare the music for *Thirst*: 'I felt that he had some kind of psychic probe, which he thrust into me, looking everywhere at once. Something frightening. After thirty seconds, he knew everything there was to know about me!'

In February, Bergman was back in Gothenburg, directing a guest production of *Divine Words*, a black comedy by Ramón María del Valle-Inclán that pulsated with sexual power and superstition. Herbert Grevenius wrote of this Bergman swansong in Gothenburg, 'It is customary to call Ingmar Bergman possessed. That has become the cliché. If by it one is trying to describe his artistic passion, then it must be accepted – provided we do not forget that it's a passion for truth and not an aesthetic passion for beauty. But the time has come to take note of the control, the method, a search for form that is, for once in a Swedish director [. . .] more Gallic than Germanic.'[15]

Bergman also collaborated with his friend Herbert Grevenius on the screenplay for *Divorced* (*Frånskild*). This was intended as a vehicle for the distinguished actress Märta Ekström, much admired for her work at the Royal Dramatic Theatre. But she fell sick, and the part went to her contemporary, Inga Tidblad, who was rather more familiar to Swedish filmgoers. There seems little doubt that the melancholy of the piece flows from Bergman. 'My life ends here,' reads an entry in Gertrud Holmgren's diary, as she reflects on her broken marriage. Her son died when very young, her daughter is away studying. Alone in her apartment, on the threshold of middle age, Gertrud considers suicide. Here, as she shuts the window on the sounds of a baby crying in the night, the influence of Bergman is most firmly felt.

During the spring of 1950, while Bergman was preparing *Summer Interlude*, his colleague Lars-Eric Kjellgren was about to direct *While the City Sleeps*. This was scripted from a synopsis Bergman had made of the novel *Hooligans* by P. A. Fogelström.

6

SUMMER LOVE

Throughout his life, Bergman drew with much affection on memories of summer with his family. The Bergmans would spend one part of the holiday period in Dalarna, at the home of grandfather Johan Åkerblom, and the other in the Stockholm archipelago, on the island of Smådalarö and its environs. Scenes from Ingmar's boyhood may be found in several of the films he wrote or directed – *Eva*, *To Joy*, *Summer Interlude*, *Summer with Monika*, *Sunday's Children* . . .

On 15 June 1938, Bergman had dedicated the first of his numerous workbooks to 'my Babs'. The woman in question was Barbro Hiort af Ornäs, a budding actress three years younger than Ingmar. She had worked with him on several occasions in the Mäster-Olofsgården theatre ensemble. It is likely that she inspired the mood and innocence of *Summer Interlude*, if not necessarily the character of Marie. 'This was my first film', Bergman said, 'in which I felt I was functioning independently, with a style of my own, making a film all my own, with a particular appearance of its own, which no one could ape [. . .] For sentimental reasons, too, it was also fun making it. Far back in the past there had been a love story, a romantic experience." The film might also have been inspired by a young girl he had known who had contracted polio; from this tragedy he wrote a short story during the late 1930s entitled 'Marie'. In the film, Bergman replaces the girl's illness with the accidental death of a young man; in this way he is able to develop the character of Marie more thoroughly and rewardingly. She becomes the portal figure in the drama; the men in *Summer Interlude* are subordinate to her psychological importance. Like all Bergman's films, *Summer Interlude* is not attached to the precise moment in history at which it is made. Its mood remains nostalgic, as though Bergman were cherishing that first great love, set against the clouds of war at the close of the 1930s, and seeking to fix in amber the timeless pleasure of a summer in the archipelago.

Marie (Maj-Britt Nilsson) is a ballerina. During a summer vacation on her favourite island outside Stockholm, she becomes infatuated with a youth named Henrik (Birger Malmsten). But their happiness is marred by the jealousy of Marie's Uncle Erland (George Funkquist), who was once keen on her mother and now lives in bitterness with his wife, Elisabeth (Renée Björling). Henrik's aunt and guardian is also a depressing – if somewhat self-mocking – figure, condemned to die from cancer. (Her name is Calwagen, the same as that of Bergman's maternal grandmother.) As autumn creeps in and the time comes to return to the city, Henrik is killed while diving off some rocks. Marie is overwhelmed by grief. More than a dozen years later a journalist, David, tries to comfort her, but it requires much heartache to exorcise the past, and the evil genius of Uncle Erland in particular.

Maj-Britt Nilsson and Birger Malmsten in *Summer Interlude*.
Copyright © AB Svensk Filmindustri 1951.

This most lyrical of Bergman's films required many years of gestation. Bergman's respect for Carl Anders Dymling and the advice he had tendered concerning the first draft led him to revise his script over the ensuing years, until he could at last commence shooting on *Summer Interlude* in April 1950. He was working with the largest crew he had ever commanded – 129 actors and technicians.[2] Ironically, the summer was marred by periods of rain, and Bergman and his crew had to rush out to the island of Smådalarö whenever the sun shone. The interiors were filmed at the studios in Råsunda. 'It was easier to build the ballet stage there,' recalled Bergman's production manager, Allan Ekelund, 'because the studio had all the technical facilities. Besides, the rehearsal rooms at the Royal Ballet were in daily use.' A double acted for Maj-Britt Nilsson in the dance sequences, although the deception is hardly noticeable.

The flashback format suits the film, for Marie is seen to have changed, and to have been chastened by her tragic experience. No other film has caught so well the buoyant sensuality of high summer in Scandinavia. *Summer Interlude* offers a profusion of tranquil images: the stippled waters of an inlet, the wild strawberry patch, the trees in blossom. The serenity of these compositions, enhanced by the photography of Gunnar Fischer and the intelligent music of Erik Nordgren, marks an altogether new phase in Bergman's development as a director. He orchestrates his effects with a confidence that eluded him in the 1940s.

Two of Bergman's most crucial themes persist in *Summer Interlude*, and are developed with more precision than ever before. The first is the idea that mankind is governed by some unseen force beyond its ken, a force with neither scruples nor pity that might strike one down in an instant of happiness. 'I feel like a painted puppet on a string,' says Marie. 'If I cry, the paint runs. Let me mourn my youth in peace.' The milieu in which Marie works – the ballet, with its constant rehearsals and rigid discipline – reminds one again of the notion that humanity flounders through life like a marionette obeying its strings.

In his later films, Bergman locates this manipulative force within society, within education, but whatever its manifestation, it is never far removed from the concept of destiny as such.

The second leitmotif is the lurking presence of Death. When Marie returns to the island to relive the past, she discovers elements of foreboding that she ignored during the summer with Henrik. The sights and sounds that accompanied her romance have vanished. Death and the reminders of Death are all that have survived the intervening years: the pastor she meets on the ferry; the old crone dying of cancer who passes like a black shadow in front of Marie as she walks across the island; the vast drawing room of the family villa, its furniture shrouded for the winter; and her Uncle Erland, presiding like the Evil One himself.

Marie amounts to the first profound female character in Bergman's world. As the son of inhibited parents, he had first met women through his mother and other female relatives such as his aunts, and the feminine world held a mysterious fascination for him. No Bergman actress up to that point had been subjected to such searching scrutiny as Maj-Britt Nilsson in *Summer Interlude*. 'To examine the face of a human being, that's most fascinating for me,' Bergman told Edwin Newman. 'The most fascinating thing of all. All the settings and things like that are not very important.'[3] Liv Ullmann has written, 'When the camera is as close as Ingmar's sometimes gets, it doesn't only show a face but also what kind of life this face has seen.'[4] *Summer Interlude* reached cinemas only a year later – and it attracted excellent reviews. Jean-Luc Godard would return to its merits in 1958, when he wrote in *Cahiers du cinéma* that *Summer Interlude* was 'the most beautiful of films'.

Desperate for funds to support his growing family, and in debt to Svensk Filmindustri, Bergman foolishly agreed to shoot a 'quickie' for the studio, entitled *This Can't Happen Here* (*Sånt hinder inte här*), or *High Tension*. 'Only once has it happened that I've made something I've known from the outset would be rubbish,' he said later, and doubtless he regretted being involved in what was at best a hollow and contrived thriller about the Cold War. Physically exhausted and dispirited, he applied himself to filming the screenplay by the usually reliable Herbert Grevenius. Atkä Natas (Ulf Palme) is an agent trying to sell secrets to the US in exchange for political asylum. When news of his defection leaks out, he is pursued through Stockholm by his associates. There are moments of amusing incongruity – the meeting of secret agents behind the screen of a movie theatre, where a man is humiliated and beaten while a cartoon holds the audience in hysterical laughter. Or the scene in a crowded street where a tyre bursts in the villains' car and passers-by turn a blind eye to the forcible abduction of a young woman. Or the insistent droning of hymns on the radio as a detective recovers from a fight with Natas. The abrasive score by Erik Nordgren maintains the suspense, and Bergman's friend Stig Olin revels in a cameo role as an irate and pompous neighbour. Such incidental pleasures aside, *This Can't Happen Here* is unworthy of Bergman.

Bergman's financial anguish grew worse when in 1951 the film studios shut down in protest against Sweden's crippling entertainment tax. So high was the proportion of box-office revenue paid back to the government that a Swedish film needed to attract an audience of 800,000 if it was to retrieve its costs. If a domestic feature drew 500,000 (which it often did), the producer lost 120,000 crowns, while the state pocketed a tidy 375,000 in taxes. The 'strike' was prolonged because the cinema exhibitors had kept several new films on ice in anticipation of this stoppage, so the public remained unaware of the situation for some time. Finally, in early 1952, the government made certain concessions, agreeing to plough a proportion of the entertainment tax back into the industry.

All this prevented Bergman from making a feature film for eighteen months. 'The child welfare authorities were breathing down my neck,' he commented.[5] His partnership with Lorens Marmstedt came to an end, exacerbated by the coolly received production of *The Threepenny Opera* that Bergman mounted at Marmstedt's Intima Theatre, and by the failure of two subsequent stage productions, *A Shadow* by Hjalmar Bergman and *Medea* by Jean Anouilh. Bergman had to be content with occasional guest productions that yielded some 2,500 crowns a time.

The year 1951 offered more than some crumbs of comfort, however. Gun became pregnant and gave birth to 'lill' Ingmar on 30 April. Ingmar, Gun and the three children (including Christian and Nikolai from the Grut marriage) lived, along with a nanny, in an apartment at Grev Turegatan 69 that Bergman had rented, as his own hideaway in the same street was too small to accommodate everyone. It was a relatively serene period. To the delight of the

Ingmar with his third wife, Gun Grut, née Hagberg.
Courtesy of Marie Nyreröd.

children, Bergman would lay down tracks for his model trains in the apartment. Almost half a century later, Bergman's screenplay for *Faithless* attributes to his alter ego, David, the same traits that exasperated those around him – his possessiveness, his jealousy, his outbreaks of violence, his financial problems and his tendency to forget his children's birthdays.

In *Faithless*, written in 1999, Bergman resurrects this escapade from the perspective of old age, describing his own violent fits of jealousy. The script is replete with acknowledgements of Bergman's remorse and regret for the pain he caused to both Ellen and Gun during this period. The character played by Erland Josephson is even named 'Bergman' in the cast list, and lives in identical circumstances in isolation on Fårö.

On 3 February Ingmar's younger sister Margareta married the British writer Paul Britten Austin, to the delight of Karin and Erik Bergman. On 19 April Bergman directed *Light in the Hovel*, a play about life in northern Sweden by Björn-Erik Höijer – his first major production on the small stage of the Royal Dramatic Theatre. On 9 May Bergman's own play, *The City*, was broadcast on Sveriges Radio, under the direction of the legendary Olof Molander. And in November he produced Tennessee Williams's *The Rose Tattoo* at the municipal theatre in Norrköping.

The City had been written during one of the most miserable periods of his marriage to Ellen Lundström. Some lines from the play capture his mood: 'We were intoxicated with each other's flesh and so deluded our hearts that this was the great truth. But when our bodies grew tired and sated we could not deceive ourselves, and we accused each other for a love that was insufficient.' By now, Bergman thought he could look objectively at his youth. 'All these religious questions, all this talk of guilt and punishment – it's beside the point!' cries Joakim's wife as he raves on. Oliver Mortis (signifying Death, of course) becomes, like all such symbolic figures in Bergman's work, alarming in his ignorance of life's consequences. He knows only that 'from your birth to your death runs a curve, logical, beautiful, absolute'. Some of the dialogue recalls Strindberg's, with the characters rending each other with verbal savagery and then turning their knives on themselves in self-pity.

At this juncture, Bergman received a call from Ragnar M. Lindberg, an executive at Unilever in Stockholm, who asked him to make a series of commercials featuring Sunlight and Gibbs and in particular Bris, the first deodorant soap in Sweden, with a 20 per cent share of the home market. Bergman agreed to tackle the job, providing he could count on the same technical resources as he was accustomed to for a feature film. Thus he insisted on using Gunnar Fischer as cameraman and on shooting the commercials at the SF studios in Råsunda. Unilever accepted these terms and allowed Bergman to prepare his own scripts and storyboards (three different versions for each commercial). Bergman thought that the slogan claiming that Bris killed all bacteria was hokum, but he managed to squeeze it into each of the nine spots.

Most of these Bris commercials are terse and sardonic. Bergman spent no more than two days on each one and used several of the same actors over and over again, notably the genial John Botvid. In 'The Inventor', a man dreams that he is destined to win the Nobel Prize, and his fantasy is an engaging amalgam of animation and pixillation. In 'The Magic Theatre', a gross, sweaty, bulbous figure finds himself engulfed in smoke by a black devil.

Bergman experiments in many of the commercials. He makes use of a television screen as a clever means of expanding and deepening the screen image in 'Film Performance'; in 'Movie Making', a young woman addresses the camera, her face reflected in the lens alongside the man to whom she is talking. The most famous, though not the best, of the nine spots is 'The Princess and the Swineherd' – famous because Bibi Andersson made her screen debut in it at the age of fifteen, bestowing a hundred kisses on the grubby swineherd in gratitude for a bar of soap! As Maaret Koskinen has noted, 'The Bris commercials can justifiably be regarded as a kind of auteur work, not merely commissioned assignments.[6]

In October 1951, Bergman signed a contract with Malmö Municipal Theatre to direct his 'passion play', *Murder in Barjärna*. It would open on 14 February the following year, to a chorus of negative reviews. The play's description of a small community was as horrific and ghoulish as the wildest of film fantasies, and Henrik Sjögren thought it the most shocking of all Bergman's stage productions. This setback, however, proved decisive in convincing Bergman to focus on writing scripts and directing films, rather than creating plays for the theatre.

When the movie strike was settled, a backlog of projects could be processed. Bergman shot two features, one after another, in 1952: *Waiting Women* (*Kvinnors väntan*) and *Summer with Monika* (*Sommaren med Monika*). Gun Grut had conceived the nucleus of *Waiting Women*, with its engaging concept of three wives recounting an adventure from their marriages while they are gathered at a summer house awaiting their husbands' return. Bergman wrote the screenplay, with Gun at his side contributing anecdotes and experiences from her first marriage. He wanted to give her credit on the finished film, but Svensk Filmindustri felt that the public needed convincing that Bergman himself could write a smart, witty film. *Waiting Women* 'was written in a mood of bad temper', he said. 'Sheer terror, grim necessity.' He needed to have a project ready for instant shooting, the moment the studios opened again.

On 30 March 1952, Bergman signed yet another contract with Malmö Municipal Theatre; this, however, was of more substantial import and would prove to be a defining moment in his career as a stage director. The contract stipulated that he would be paid 3,500 crowns per production, plus a per diem of 30 crowns and second-class rail travel between Stockholm and Malmö when required. His fee would increase to 22,000 crowns per annum for the 1953–4 season, and Bergman would be permitted leave to make a maximum of two films per year, providing the dates could be agreed with Lars-Levi Laestadius, the theatre manager.

The divorce between Ingmar Bergman and Ellen Lundström was pronounced final on 9 May. He agreed to pay 200 crowns per month for the children, but nothing to Ellen. Ingmar and Gun promptly married, and *Waiting Women* entered production in June.

The first episode in *Waiting Women* involves an unexpected reunion between two lovers, played by Anita Björk and Jarl Kulle. A direct reworking of Bergman's early play, *Rakel and the Cinema Doorman*, the story deals with infidelity. As in previous Bergman films, sex predominates, followed in turn by the inevitable conversation and outbursts of recrimination. In the second episode, Maj-Britt Nilsson and Birger Malmsten enact a love affair between the ingenuous Märta and an artist, by whom she has a child. A majority of scenes are set in the Paris that Gun and Ingmar remembered with such fondness from their escapade in 1949, and evoke a mood of lyricism reminiscent of *Summer Interlude* (especially when Märta walks along the Seine or through the Bois de Boulogne). These sequences caused Bergman and his crew some difficulty, because they did not realise that one should report to the head of each police precinct – and pay for the right to shoot on location. Märta's radiant joy when she has given birth to her child seemed to express Gun Grut's – and Bergman's – own happiness at having had Ingmar Jnr the previous year.[7]

By far the most significant part of *Waiting Women* remains the final episode, for it furnishes the first evidence of Bergman's gift for the comedy of manners. The premise – a married couple resolve their differences while trapped in an elevator – stemmed from Bergman's personal experience. He had gone on a brief vacation to Copenhagen with Ellen Lundström, where they stayed at the home of some friends who were out of town. But when coming back to the apartment, 'drunk and happy, with everything fully prepared, we put the key in the door – it snapped off! No chance of finding a locksmith. So we spent the night on the stairs.'[8]

Gunnar Björnstrand and Eva Dahlbeck in the
final episode of *Waiting Women*.
Copyright © *AB Svensk Filmindustri 1957. Photo by Louis Huch.*

The sequence posed some tricky problems. Technicians built a cramped model of an elevator interior in the studio at Råsunda. Bergman and Hasse Ekman had embarked on a friendly competition to see who could achieve the longest 'take' (Hitchcock's *Rope* was still in vogue). Bergman insisted on a protracted take inside the elevator, and Gunnar Fischer had to heave the 100 kg camera hither and thither with his assistants. In the end Bergman agreed that certain close-ups would have to be intercut with the main dialogue. Mirrors were used to suggest the inanity of the repartee. The sequence was shot on slow film stock, and a great deal of light was required. It was hot and cramped, and tempers were short.

As Karin and Fredrik, the middle-aged pair returning in evening dress from a centenary dinner, Eva Dahlbeck and Gunnar Björnstrand were the perfect foils. For Björnstrand, his appearance in *Waiting Women* signalled the end of a long estrangement from

Bergman, caused by Bergman's refusal to pay him a decent fee back in the 1940s. From now on, he would become one of the most vital members of Bergman's team. 'He had the ability to remain silent,' Björnstrand said, looking back on Bergman's approach to that film. 'He let the actors develop themselves. We weren't separate, programmed machines – we could work from our own intuition.' Eva Dahlbeck sparkled in the role of Karin, and Bergman knew instinctively how to use her innate talent for delivering the stinging retort. This, combined with her elegance and poise, gave her a formidable image. She is every inch a queen, her comportment a joy to behold. She brooks no rival. Few women can smoke a cigarette so seductively as Eva Dahlbeck; fewer still are so supreme in repartee.

Waiting Women became the first box-office hit of Bergman's career. He was so delighted that he relished waiting in the foyer of Stockholm's most fashionable cinema, Röda Kvarn, and hearing the audience laugh at the Eva Dahlbeck–Gunnar Björnstrand episode.

One of Allan Ekelund's duties at Svensk Filmindustri was to read new books with an eye to their being purchased for filming. He noted Per Anders Fogelström's novel *Summer with Monika*, and forwarded it to Bergman along with another collection of short stories by the same author. 'We wanted the rights,' said Ekelund, 'and then later Ingmar was attracted to it, after first thinking it only a simple little story. It was a convenient break for Ingmar, because I don't think he had a script of his own ready at that point.'

Bergman's recollection differed, unconvincingly, on this issue. 'It was in the first instance a film treatment. Per Anders Fogelström and I met on Kungsgatan, and he told me the plot in ten words. And I said, we have to make a picture out of this; and then we started to write the script. And subsequently he wrote the novel.'

A budget of some 300,000 to 400,000 crowns was established. Carl Anders Dymling had to fight tooth and nail to persuade the board of SF to approve the project. Some members of the board resigned in protest. Even Dymling was shocked by the inclusion of a nude bathing sequence, but Fogelström argued that it was in the original book, and Dymling acquiesced.

Despite Bergman's glowing description of Gun Grut in *The Magic Lantern*, he found that almost as soon as he entered into his third marriage – in June of 1952 – yet another affair would banish their happiness: the very next month, he began pre-production work on *Summer with Monika*, with the neophyte actress Harriet Andersson, and the lightning bolt struck once again.

Early in August of 1952, the entire crew travelled out to Ornö, a large island in the southern sector of the Stockholm archipelago, which Bergman knew from summer holidays in his youth. By modern standards the group was tiny – a mere dozen or so technicians and actors – and they all lived in the parish clerk's house on Ornö.

Harriet Andersson in a publicity shot for *Summer with Monika*.
Copyright © AB Svensk Filmindustri 1953.

'For everyone,' remembered Gunnar Fischer, 'it was our happiest film. Bergman was never secretive and talked eagerly to the crew about what he sought to achieve.'

The shoot lasted over two months. One of the reasons for the protracted schedule was Bergman's infatuation with Harriet, as splendid and uninhibited a relationship as any he ever had. 'I had just seen Harriet in *Defiance*,' he recalled later, 'and no girl it seemed to me could be more "Monika-ish".' Harriet was 'eighteen or nineteen at most, I guess. But she was devastating, and engaged to Per Oscarsson.'[9] Forty years later, he reflected that 'Harriet Andersson is one of cinema's geniuses. You meet only a few of these rare, shimmering individuals on your travels along the twisting road through the movie industry jungle.'[10] As she and Lars Ekborg, who played her lover Harry, were so unknown, Bergman and his project were left in comparative peace.

'Bergman's reputation at that time was very bad,' said Harriet in 2012. 'Everybody was afraid of him, and there were rumours that he kicked his actors and threw things at them.' But after seeing her eight-minute screen test with Ekborg, Bergman's attitude softened, and he even allowed Harriet to buy her own costumes from everyday stores in Stockholm.

When after three weeks the first rushes were viewed, a bad scratch on the negative appeared obvious, so substantial reshooting was necessary. Time and again, Bergman and Harriet returned to the island on some pretext or another – poor sound was a familiar excuse. 'It seemed stupid to put on a bathing costume,' said Harriet. 'You just went into the water and swam, and then dried in the sun. You can have a real sense of freedom in the archipelago. We were in "splendid isolation", you could say, especially because not so many people had boats as they do today.'[11]

In the early scenes, Monika appears to be no more than a common slattern. Fisherman's socks cling to her ankles, and she snivels at the false sentimentality of a cheap Hollywood movie to which Harry, her boyfriend, takes her. But Monika and her gauche, impetuous Harry steal a boat and flee to an island; in the archipelago, removed from the Stockholm crowds, her true potency is revealed and fulfilled. Harriet Andersson as Monika is eroticism incarnate; stills from the film have featured in Truffaut's *The 400 Blows* and elsewhere as symbols of Nordic ecstasy. She wears little make-up, and her allure has a fundamental, carnal quality that thumbs its nose at glamour. The unwashed hair, the mouth perpetually at work on gum, the proud, unboosted bosom: these built a new idiom into film language.

Huddling together in front of a wood fire, Monika tells Harry that she is pregnant. 'We have to make something of our lives,' he responds, the conventional contours of the nuclear family still appealing to them both – as it did, for all his misdemeanours, to Bergman himself. As summer ebbs to its close and the wind grows chill, reality envelops the lovers again. They must return to the city. Monika bears her now unwanted baby girl. The gloomy furnishings of the room where they live with their child drive Monika to frustration. The clumsiness in Harry that at first seemed charming now nauseates her. Monika is an opportunist, not an idealist like Marie in *Summer Interlude*. She has no hesitation, and suffers no remorse, in turning to a new lover. This last passage suggests a return to the bleak, sordid life of early Bergman works. The greater the selfishness, the greater the disillusionment. Rebellious to the end, Monika gives the camera a long stare – a shot copied by both Godard and Truffaut.

Improvisation in the technical departments was obligatory, given the conditions and the minuscule budget of *Summer with Monika*. The dialogue and sound effects had to be dubbed afterwards as Gunnar Fischer had only a silent Mitchell camera on Ornö. Oscar Rosander, Bergman's favourite editor, was unavailable, so the director had to buckle down to the editing himself. Erik Nordgren, who during the 1950s became the regular composer for Bergman's films, says that the music was actually written into the screenplays.

Harriet Andersson and Lars Ekborg in *Summer with Monika.*
Copyright © AB Svensk Filmindustri 1953.

Bergman 'knew exactly at what point he wanted music, and of what sort'. The sequence when the lovers travel out to the archipelago, beneath successive bridges, is reinforced with the sound of church bells and *musique concrète*, and that portion of the score was later broadcast in its own right on Danish radio. 'Ingmar performed it himself,' recalled Nordgren. 'He stood with the two kettle-drum sticks and hammered on the piano strings.'

Harriet Andersson embodies the first great female influence on Bergman's cinema. She starred in *Monika, Sawdust and Tinsel, A Lesson in Love, Dreams* and *Smiles of a Summer Night.* Later she returned to play two memorable roles: Karin in *Through a Glass Darkly* and Agnes in *Cries and Whispers,* as well as a chilling cameo in *Fanny and Alexander.* Bergman relished her wriggling personality, her independence and her quick intelligence. He warmed to her energy and refreshing lack of sophistication. Born, like Greta

Garbo, in the south of Stockholm, she was intent on acting from the start. Lazy in school, Harriet had to find work to pay for her theatre course. She began on the stage by playing Snow White at Oscars Theatre in Stockholm, before appearing in revue ('I was a little tits-and-ass"[12]), then landing a part in Gustaf Molander's *Defiance*.

'Of course when we came back to Stockholm from the islands,' said Harriet later, 'Ingmar wanted to go back to Gun Grut, as the circus-owner does in *Sawdust and Tinsel*, but she refused . . . Still, I can't understand how he left Gun for me. She was a fantastic woman."[13] Bergman installed Harriet in the one-room apartment he had at Grev Turegatan 62, almost opposite the larger flat where he, Gun and the three children lived. If Harriet leaned over her balcony smoking a cigarette, she could sometimes see Gun in her yellow nightgown across the street.

Ingmar and Gun remained fast friends, however, until her untimely death in a car crash while visiting Croatia at the age of just fifty-five. She also helped to create one of Bergman's most intriguing props: the newspaper that Gunnel Lindblom glances at in the cafe in *The Silence*. Bergman would dream of Gun for years afterwards, and as late as 1998 wrote in his workbook, 'I think of Gun with joy, and I see her naked in the light from the little lamp on our sofa-table, or dancing alone in her yellow night-dress."[14] She remains probably the most intelligent and self-assured of all Bergman's wives.

7

TRIUMPH AND DISASTER

Holed up with Harriet in a modest hotel on Mosebacka Square, above the Södra Teatern in the southern quarter of Stockholm, Bergman wrote the screenplay for *Sawdust and Tinsel* (*Gycklarnas afton*).[1] It would be filmed from February to June of the following year. In the interim, Bergman's calendar was as charged as ever: *Summer Interlude* screened at the Venice Festival, without much success; *Waiting Women* opened throughout Sweden; in the same month *The Crown-Bride*, Bergman's first production as resident director at Malmö City Theatre, met with acclaim from the critics.

One of Strindberg's most mystical plays, *The Crown-Bride* is immersed in the folklore of Dalarna. The peasant girl Kersti (Karin Kavli) longs for the purity of a white wedding and drowns her illegitimate baby in order to be accepted as a virgin bride. But although she breaks down at the wedding feast and confesses her crime, fate subsequently leads her to the same death as that of her child – she plunges through the ice of a nearby lake.

Bergman excised the parts of Strindberg's text that dealt too fondly with the provincial and picturesque elements of the drama. Adolf Anderberg wrote in *Skånska Dagbladet*, 'Ingmar Bergman has achieved one of his finest productions. He can be elusive and sometimes difficult to follow. But, confronted with Strindberg's brilliant poetry, he has found his melody and with humility and firmness has brought forth a creation well worth remembering.'[2] Nordisk Tonefilm suggested to Bergman that he make a film from this triumphant production, but the company took so long to clear the rights with the Strindberg estate that the idea languished, and it was only in 1957, when he shot *So Close to Life*, that Bergman fulfilled his obligation to Nordisk.

Malmö is Sweden's third major city, after Stockholm and Gothenburg. A port on the coast of Skåne, it lies less than an hour by train from Denmark. Some of the bustle and excitement of a border town, a port of entry, has accumulated there, and Malmö's newspapers are among the liveliest in the country.

When Ingmar Bergman arrived in the city in August of 1952, the City Theatre (known today as the Malmö Opera) was less than ten years old but already revered. His first two-year contract stipulated that he should act as full-time director and artistic adviser to the management, but neither Bergman nor anyone else could have predicted that he would rule the roost at Malmö for six years, producing seventeen plays and eight films in what might be seen as the richest period of his life.

Each year was programmed with rigour. 'I devote myself to a kind of crop rotation,' Bergman observed. 'I have a piece of land, and sometimes I cultivate rye and sometimes clover.'[3] The theatre season extended from early September to late May, and Bergman directed one or two new productions each year. The actors were engaged for these eight months but for the rest of the year depended on film work. Many had followed him loyally from Gothenburg – Anders Ek, Gertrud Fridh, Karin Kavli, Folke Sundquist, Åke Fridell and others. Bibi Andersson and Ingrid Thulin arrived in the middle years of Bergman's reign at the City Theatre, while Naima Wifstrand joined the troupe in 1954. Gudrun Brost (the clown's wife in *Sawdust and Tinsel*) had played in revue in Stockholm.

The main stage at Malmö consisted of an immense proscenium, which Bergman called 'the big boo'. In the 1950s the maximum seating capacity was 1,695, but false walls could reduce this number to 1,257, 697 or even 553. These walls glided along rails set into the ceiling, and the theatre could be changed in scope within the hour. The huge apron stage, which when fully extended was more than half as wide again as the stage at either Covent Garden or the Paris Opéra Garnier, was capable of rising or sinking in four sections and, when lowered, allowed room for a 70-seat orchestra. Almost all of Bergman's productions took place on the apron stage, while the back stage was often used for projections (in *Urfaust*, for example). Many directors felt it to be a vacuum. How to fill such an area with people and decor? 'I soon discovered that every stage has its magic centre,' said Bergman. 'And the magic centre of that huge stage was six metres in this direction and four metres in that direction – an area of twenty-four square metres.'

Lennart Olsson, Bergman's personal assistant during this period, noted that 'Ingmar always went to the opposite extreme: he took away things, he simplified matters. He presented Molière's *The Misanthrope* with one chair on the big stage, with a painted background and a carpet on the apron stage, and enormous costumes.'

During the early 1950s, television did not dominate the Swedish home. Admission to the theatre sometimes cost less than a cinema ticket and, after a season or two, each new Bergman production came to be regarded as a social event. In 1954 and 1955 no fewer than 90,000 attended his version of the Léhar operetta *The Merry Widow*, referred to by Malmö's denizens quite simply as 'Bergman's Widow'. Not that Bergman embraced his public with affection, and apropos *The Magician*, made in 1958, he described Consul Egerman's family as representing the audience in Malmö.

Malmö City Theatre also stimulated Bergman because there were no limitations on what he could stage. Musicals and operettas were beyond the range of the much smaller Helsingborg Theatre and, in addition, there was at Malmö an 'intimate' theatre in the same building as the main stage. With only 204 seats and a stage 52 feet wide and 30 feet deep, the Intima could be used for modern and off-beat drama, ballet and even opera. Here Bergman staged Molière's *Don Juan*, Kafka's *The Castle* and Hjalmar Bergman's *Sagan*.

Yet another luxury was the main rehearsal room, which was added to the complex in 1955 and had a mirror running along the entire length of one wall. 'It was so wonderful to be at a theatre where there was also an orchestra, a ballet, a chorus, opera singers,' said Bergman. 'My office was behind the small stage, and there was a corridor and at the end of that corridor was the orchestra's rehearsal room. You went to the rehearsal of the symphony orchestra, and the ballet, and it was fantastic.' As usual, Bergman insisted on a private lavatory adjacent to his office, so often did he suffer from bowel irregularities.

Bergman rehearsed very swiftly at Malmö. The actors were all under contract and lived in the city, so there was a daily rhythm to proceedings. 'During rehearsals, the atmosphere was very hearty,' recalled Lennart Olsson. 'They were joking like boys and then all of a sudden very heavily concentrated on what they were doing. Ingmar was so far ahead of everyone in his understanding of the play that you never questioned him. During the first week of rehearsals, he would outline the basic arrangements he required on the stage. Then he left you for two weeks. I had to take over rehearsals for that period. Ingmar felt that if he was there all the time he would grow tired of hearing the lines over and over. So he preferred to come back fresh, with the groundwork already established.'

At first startled and confused, the actors soon began to see the wisdom of Bergman's regimen. They respected the fact that he never changed a classical text. He never used a written script of his own; his notebooks were meagre, almost empty. Unlike many directors, he did not abandon a production once it was afloat. Before each performance he went down to the stage and looked things over, talking to the actors. 'He hated going on stage after a first night,' laughed Olsson, 'although once or twice we managed to push him on!'

Throughout his career, Bergman timed his productions to a point where successive performances all ran to the same length, give or take a minute or so. There was, indeed, only one way in which a Bergman production could be performed by the actors – and yet they never felt restricted. No conflicts occurred between Bergman and his troupe. If he did explode – and he was renowned in Malmö as much for his explosions as for his colossal laugh – it was never for personal reasons but from sheer ambition and the frustration of not being able to attain his goal.

His private life grew subordinate to the demands of work. Thanks to Hartvig Torngren, the then economic director of the theatre, Ingmar and Harriet found accommodation in a three-room apartment on Erikslustsvägen. Åke Fridell, one of Bergman's favourite actors, lived next door. Soon after they had moved in, the bell rang, and it was a very young Bo Widerberg, who asked to meet Ingmar. By nine every morning Bergman and Harriet would be at the theatre, and they did not depart until after ten in the evening. Admittedly, with Bergman's desire for nine hours' sleep a night, there was not much time for social activity. 'I think I went to the town centre just three or four times a year. I just went from the apartment to the theatre, from the theatre back to the apartment. Sometimes I had to travel to Stockholm to cut my films, or do some mixing.' He purchased his first 16 mm sound projector and started collecting films. Friends came happily from the theatre to screenings on a weekday evening.

Forged in the crucible of Bergman's often fiery relationship with Harriet, *Sawdust and Tinsel* has survived the years as his first demonic masterpiece. Charged with betrayal and humiliation, its picaresque story of marital infidelity demonstrated Bergman's growing grasp of his medium. Ostensibly picturesque and provincial, *Sawdust and Tinsel* is distinguished by brilliantly framed and often nightmarish imagery, as well as an eerie, unnerving soundtrack.

The film's gestation had been difficult. Rune Waldekranz, then in charge of production at Sandrew, had heard from Bergman the previous year that Svensk Filmindustri had rejected his synopsis. Anders Sandrew himself passed Bergman's material around various friends and colleagues, and all affirmed that it was the worst script they had ever read. So too did Schamyl Bauman, the popular director, who was in partnership with Anders Sandrew at the time. But Waldekranz prevailed on the company to tackle the project, pointing out the international acclaim for Alf Sjöberg's film of *Miss Julie* two years before and suggesting that the Swedish cinema could acquire a new lease of life on the European market with a prestige production by Ingmar Bergman.

Sawdust and Tinsel became a miracle of improvisation in the face of practical hazards. Waldekranz had promised Bergman that he could have his favourite Sandrew cameraman, Göran Strindberg. But Strindberg was suddenly summoned to Hollywood for a course on the techniques involved in the new process of CinemaScope, and Bergman had to accept the services of a young cinematographer named Sven Nykvist. Bergman was sceptical, and although an autodidact himself, he insisted on subjecting Nykvist to some rigorous tests. Sjöberg was making *Karin Månsdotter*, and Nykvist had been assigned to that production by the studio, so the exteriors on *Sawdust and Tinsel* had to be shot by Hilding Bladh, which added to Bergman's confusion – even if the nightmarish opening sequence on the beach at Arild proved one of the finest in the Bergman canon.

For the music, Bergman approached Karl-Birger Blomdahl, one of Sweden's foremost modern composers. The result was a magnificent and deeply disturbing score, full of stabbing, grating chords and dissonances, even if the optical soundtrack could scarcely cope with music performed by a 40-piece wind orchestra. The costumes, evocative of the turn-of-the-century setting, were designed by Max Goldstein – Mago – who had first met Bergman the day before his wedding to Else Fisher in 1943. They had had a cup of tea together during rehearsals for a production of *Julius Caesar* at Mäster-Olofsgården, and Bergman had said to him, 'One day we'll work together.' Ten years later he called Mago to join the team for *Sawdust and Tinsel* – and it was the start of a long and rewarding collaboration. Bergman studied innumerable sketches and drawings before accepting Mago's designs, which were influenced by the German UFA style, just as Bergman's own visual approach came from the 1920s and the expressionism of Dupont, Lang and Murnau.

The budget was tight as well. Mago remembered the panic that broke out when the one and only pair of bejewelled stockings to be worn by Harriet Andersson during a seduction scene could not be located. Lars-Owe Carlberg, who would become Bergman's regular production manager during the late 1960s, had the devil's own task of nursing and supervising a motley collection of chimpanzees, bears and circus performers. 'Every time I made a film in those days,' Bergman told Marie Nyreröd, 'I was sawing off the branch I was sitting on.'

The unit stayed on location for a month, living in a small hotel in Arild. Then everyone repaired to Stockholm for the interiors. 'By then,' said Bergman, 'we knew each other like sardines in a tin. We'd eaten and quarrelled and got drunk and lived together and had a marvellous time; so the boundary lines between who are the circus artistes and who were the actors and who were film directors or monkeys were by no means clear.'[4]

Åke Grönberg and Harriet Andersson in *Sawdust and Tinsel*.
Copyright © AB Sandrew – AB Svensk Filmindustri 1953.

Like *Thirst* and *To Joy*, *Sawdust and Tinsel* is redolent with the strife and intensity of Bergman's private life. Not until she saw the finished film did Harriet Andersson realise that 'this was our story'.[5] The principal figures in the film are Albert (Åke Grönberg), the circus-owner, and Anne, his mistress (played by Harriet).

During a 24-hour span, each seeks to escape the infernal orbit of altercations and resentment. Albert yearns to return to his 'respectable' wife (as Bergman did to Gun Grut), while Anne succumbs to the wily charms of Frans, a local actor in a small Scanian town where the circus hoists its big top. As Maaret Koskinen has noted, the names Anne and Albert come from Bergman's play *The Fish*, written two years earlier, as does the clown Frost's monologue at the end of the film.[6]

In the course of the evening circus performance, Albert and Frans have a fight in the sawdust ring. Albert is defeated, humiliated, and next morning the troupe moves on, with the circus owner and his mistress again walking beside each other, caught in a vice by their own weakness and vanity. Love is seen by Bergman in this film, as by Strindberg in his plays, as a ghastly, totally unsatisfactory function. Bergman's own guilt at neglecting his offspring emerges in the scene where Albert meets his young son and sees that the boy barely recognises him. Agda, the wife, has achieved independence, as had Gun with her philology studies. Albert comments on how quiet it is in the tobacco shop she runs, and Agda says, 'For me, it's fulfilment.' Albert responds, 'For me, it's emptiness.' Domestic routine and Bergman's way of life were incompatible.

Shortly after the film opens, Albert recalls an incident in which Frost (Anders Ek), his clown, was shamed by his wife Alma (Gudrun Brost). In the original screenplay, the scene takes place in a quarry, where some soldiers are at work beneath a glaring sun. But when Bergman found the perfect location at Simrishamn, he decided to change the setting to the shoreline. Sunlight beats down on the rocks and waves as Alma, dressed in her finery, saunters seductively towards the water and reacts to the soldiers' taunts. As she bathes in the nude, Bergman cuts like a surgeon from face to face, while at the same time restricting the sound to an incessant drumming, punctuated with the reverberation of cannon fire.

This flashback becomes a germ cell for the film. Frost's humiliation, as he drags his naked wife back to the tents across the stony landscape, will be mirrored in Albert's experience in the circus ring after Anne has betrayed him. Grotesque in his gaudy costume and chalky make-up, the clown resembles some baroque martyr as he staggers ever more pitifully over the jagged rocks. Tears of sweat course down his face. At last he collapses like Christ on the way to Calvary, and Alma clings to him in chagrin and remorse.

Huge close-ups of mouths, jeering and shouting, fill the screen, reminiscent of Eisenstein and the Odessa Steps sequence in *Battleship Potemkin*, but it was an association alien to Bergman, who regarded Eisenstein with some disdain in that period and had not seen *Potemkin*. There is a more direct link with E. A. Dupont's silent movie *Variety*, starring Emil Jannings in a similar environment. It was the first film Bergman had bought for his collection: 'It fascinated me so much that I consciously imitated it.'[7] But Dupont did not use light in the way Bergman does in this sequence. 'My nightmares are always saturated in sunshine,' he complained. Harsh sun becomes in his eyes a threat, a terrifying phenomenon of the natural world. Evidence of this 'heliophobia' can be found in later films such as *Wild Strawberries* and *Hour of the Wolf*. The palpable glare of the scene in *Sawdust and Tinsel* was created in the laboratory. A negative was made up from the print, and then a new print from that negative. Yet another negative was struck, until the graininess of the image disappeared entirely, leaving only the stark contrast of black and white.

Anne is attracted to the half-real world of masks and players in the local theatre, as a moth is to a flame. These masks disguise meanings as much as they conceal faces. The moment of truth is the moment when the mask is torn aside and the true face uncovered. Every Bergman film turns on this process. The mask is shown, examined, and then removed. Thus the close-up forms an essential part of Bergman's film grammar.

Frans (Hasse Ekman), the simpering, mannered actor, finds himself aroused by the earthiness and childlike sensuality of Harriet Andersson's bareback rider. The mirror in Frans's dressing room permits the audience to spy on Anne and detect her weakness, her inability to hide her craving for an amulet, dangled before her by the malevolent actor. Like Mephistopheles, Frans persuades his victim to sell herself for a worthless trinket. Bergman was impressed when he read Thomas Mann's *Doctor Faustus*, and this insidious relationship between body and soul has haunted Swedish art since Strindberg. Frans, like all male actors in the Bergman canon, cannot feel true emotion. The artifice of the stage pursues him into private life. He is the epitome of vanity, as Bergman shows so wittily when Frans stabs himself with a stage knife during a rehearsal and proceeds to 'die' before an empty house, to the accompaniment of simulated thunder from the wings. Harriet Andersson recalled in 2021 how Hasse Ekman was so physically weak that during their playful arm-wrestling match in the dressing room, she (who was wiry and fit at the time) put his arm down instantly. Bergman exploded. 'What the hell are you doing! He's supposed to put *your* arm down!'

By comparison, the scenes with Albert are shot in a heavy, almost brutal fashion. The compositions are drained of subtlety, as if to reflect the stupor of Albert's personality. The camera watches him lurch towards it until his puffy face, in gigantic close-up, dominates the screen, excluding all other characters and considerations. Here is a director in total control of his material, able to select with almost diabolical ease the appropriate sound, light or camera angle for any given scene. The mirrors in the theatre and inside Albert's caravan obviate the need for conventional cross-cutting and add a density to the image, a look of abnormality. Reality is confused with its own reflections, as in the opening moments of the film, when the coaches are glimpsed in the polished surface of a river, before the camera swings up to observe the vehicles themselves.

After *Sawdust and Tinsel* had gone to the editing room in June, Bergman and Harriet went on holiday. While she enjoyed the beach, he stayed in the tower room of their small hotel in Arild and began writing a new screenplay, which would become the comedy *A Lesson in Love (En lektion i kärlek)*. He sent the screenplay to Sandrew, but the executives were on vacation. So Bergman forwarded a copy to Carl Anders Dymling at Svensk Filmindustri. Dymling, enthusiastic, summoned Bergman to Stockholm. Two weeks later the budget and schedule had been set. *A Lesson in Love* began filming on 30 July 1953, and concluded two days after the premiere of *Sawdust and Tinsel*.

It proved a short-lived idyll. The reviews for *Sawdust and Tinsel* reduced Bergman to the verge of tears.[8] The film received fair notices from *Dagens Nyheter* and *Svenska Dagbladet*, but the influential critics – those whose opinion counted among the intelligentsia – were violent in their condemnation, especially Bengt Idestam-Almquist, regarded as the doyen of his profession. The fight in the circus ring, although stylised, produced a feeling of revulsion among the Swedes. So too did Bergman's view of life as coarse and sweaty. The film ran quite respectably in Stockholm but failed completely in the provinces. Even in such a large town as Karlstad, it screened over only a single weekend – and then more than a year after its original release, so disliked was the film by exhibitors.

The reception outside Sweden might have comforted Bergman to some extent. After an unofficial screening during the Cannes Festival of 1954, a Latin American distributor from Montevideo was so fascinated by *Sawdust and Tinsel* that he flew to Stockholm and purchased several other Swedish films.

———

The Bergman films made during his Malmö period possessed all the virtues and none of the impediments of a theatrical tradition, while his stage productions drew on the visual devices of the cinema without sacrificing a jot of dramatic or verbal intensity. Each work was suited impeccably to its medium. During the 1950s, Bergman worked seven months out of every twelve in the theatre. With two features behind him in 1953, he still managed to produce both Pirandello's *Six Characters in Search of an Author* and Kafka's *The Castle* on the small stage in Malmö, as well as to prepare a radio version of Strindberg's *The Dutchman*, which was broadcast on 9 October.

Achievements in the theatre are, almost by definition, evanescent. Each performance is unique, and may be altered significantly should a leading actor fall ill, for example. Several of Bergman's stage productions travelled beyond the borders of Scandinavia, but the language barrier created a kind of mist between the foreign audience and what Swedish theatregoers experienced. His films, however, could be released in dozens of countries, and screened in either subtitled or dubbed versions, thanks to a sophisticated system of distribution dating back over a century.

This did not deter Bergman from committing himself to the theatre for more than six decades. Invention and dramatic flair enlivened his stage productions. *The Castle*, for example, took place on a bare stage containing a few sticks of furniture and no set decorations whatsoever. Bergman fought shy of mutilating the original. 'I cannot and will not stage a play contrary to a writer's intentions,' he declared. 'And I never have . . . I've always seen myself as an interpreter, a reflector.'[9] On occasion, one production would open on a Friday, and blocking for the next would commence the following Monday.

On 18 March 1954, Bergman signed a fresh contract with Malmö City Theatre. His salary for the new season was raised to 25,000 crowns, and once again he could take time off to make two feature films, providing that the intendant of the theatre, Lars-Levi

Laestadius, agreed to the dates. This marked the first time that Bergman added the distinctive drawing of a devil to his signature on a formal document – a devil, moreover, with horns and wielding a fearsome trident in the tradition of the Hindu god Shiva and the Poseidon of Greek mythology.

With ten months between completing *A Lesson in Love* and embarking on his next film, *Dreams*, Bergman could concentrate on his stage productions. *The Ghost Sonata*, which opened in March 1954, stretched the cunning and resourcefulness of the stage managers to the full. Bergman narrowed the proscenium opening to 46 feet (from its usual 72), reduced the seating capacity to a mere 1,100 (from the customary 1,700) and raised the stage, extending it out over the auditorium. In his programme notes, he paid tribute to his idol, Olof Molander, whose productions had so impressed him when young. 'This evening's production can perhaps be called a love-child. My Civic Centre experiments [in autumn 1941] are the mother, fructified by Molander's *The Ghost Sonata*. And the child – well, of course, the child takes strongly after both parents, without being a slavish copy of either. Rather the contrary, for he has certainly gone his own way.'[10]

The tone of the drama was muted, as Strindberg had specified, and each character could emerge in clearly defined colours. Benkt-Åke Benktsson, who weighed thirty stone, was a massive Hummel, and Naima Wifstrand (later celebrated for her roles as the old grandmother in both *Wild Strawberries* and *The Magician*) played the Mummy, who finally takes her revenge on the old man and sends Hummel to his death in a dark closet.

In the autumn of 1954 came *The Merry Widow*, in honour of the tenth anniversary of the Malmö City Theatre. Operetta had been ignored by serious producers in Sweden, but now Bergman, sensing the potential of the huge stage and auditorium, established a relationship with the local public that made Lehár's effervescent musical comedy the most popular success in the history of the theatre.

Can-can dancers fanned out over the horseshoe-shaped bridge at the front of the stage, and French perfume was sprayed into the stalls. The performance was as light and heady as champagne, and the audience clamoured to see it. Bergman, said Henrik Sjögren, 'so far from ironing over [*The Merry Widow*'s] fairy-tale world, treated it on the contrary with a kind of tender respect'.[11]

—

Eva Dahlbeck and Gunnar Björnstrand had demonstrated in the concluding episode of *Waiting Women* that they were an adroit comedy team, and their sparring has a more satisfying ring to it than the incessant wrangling of Bergman's younger couples from *Prison*, *Thirst*, *To Joy* and *Summer Interlude*. 'These two actors taught me so much about the technique of comedy and farce, which I was able to use throughout my entire career, including in the theatre,' he reflected later.[12] Their rapport was so good, in the manner of Tracy and Hepburn, that when Bergman suggested cutting a particular scene from the screenplay, they chased him off the set and rehearsed it together. Bergman made some phone calls and cashed some cheques. 'When I got back,' he said, 'they had rehearsed a wildly funny scene.'[13]

Idealism has been supplanted by an empirical wisdom in *A Lesson in Love*, released by Svensk Filmindustri in October of 1954. Intelligence, rather than sexual purity, is at a premium in Bergman's sophisticated comedies. There is a maturity about Dr David Erneman and his wife Marianne (Eva Dahlbeck, based on Gun Grut), if not about their behaviour. Like their youthful predecessors, they appear anxious to flout convention, but are old enough to recognise that they must be bound by the whims of life and that this form of dual survival need be neither as dull nor as stressful as it seems.

David is a gynaecologist who, having been married for sixteen years, yields to the charms of Susanne, a patient in his clinic, and embarks on an affair that disrupts his marriage. Marianne flounces off to Copenhagen to sleep with her former fiancé, Carl-Adam, a rather boorish sculptor. David eventually abandons his relationship with Susanne and recaptures his wife, despite the opposition of Carl-Adam during a brawl in a Danish nightclub. Even within the confines of a light comedy, one is faced with the typical Bergman situation of an individual in whom a crisis brings about a fundamental change of attitude to himself and to life.

Erneman, like Bergman, struggles in the clutches of an early mid-life crisis. 'The conjugal bed is love's demise,' he quips; 'I want your fire to burn away my apathy,' he tells his mistress. But a day in the country with his teenage daughter Nix (Harriet Andersson) shows him that he is out of touch with this girl, his own child. Nix's defiance prompts Erneman to reconsider his philandering way of life, and he sets about retrieving the affections of the liberated Marianne. Deep down, Bergman yearned for the security of a life with Gun Grut, but each time he attempted to return to her he found himself diverted by a fresh affair. 'I'm not taking back the remorseful sinner,' says Marianne, a line that must have been spoken by Gun on more than one occasion.

Erneman's reference to a summer place used by his wife and children 'near Helsingborg' suggests that Bergman knew he was blighting the fledgling lives of his young sons and daughters. To some extent, he caricatured himself in the character of Carl-Adam – 'the world's greatest sculptor', as Marianne calls him sardonically. The bumptious Carl-Adam proclaims that 'women love great artists' and 'only impotent men are faithful'.

Bergman, like Hitchcock, included himself in several of his films. In *A Lesson in Love* he appears in the corridor of a train, reading a newspaper, and then sits in the same compartment as Björnstrand and Dahlbeck. This habit acquired more significance later in Bergman's career, when he would introduce films offscreen (*The Passion of Anna*, *The Fårö Document*, *Scenes from a Marriage*, etc.), as though wanting to underline his own involvement in the material. At the very end of his career, in screenplays including *Sunday's Children* and *Faithless*, he casts himself as a character.

From *Prison* onwards, Bergman often took a prismatic approach to his material, describing life from two or more perspectives. *To Joy*, *Waiting Women* and *Sawdust and Tinsel* all reflected this method, and *Dreams* (*Kvinnodröm*), shot for Sandrew in the summer of 1954, pursued the same structure. Susanne (Eva Dahlbeck) runs a fashion salon, and Doris (Harriet Andersson) is her leading model. Their lives follow opposite paths during the film – Susanne trying to rekindle an affair with a married man named Henrik Lobelius, and Doris fleeing from an unsatisfactory relationship with her conventional boyfriend. The musical form of *Dreams* resembles a double fugue. And again there is the circular, claustrophobic logic of the story line: the film begins and closes in the same setting (the fashion salon), a device that Bergman almost invariably deploys. He does not like his plots to proceed in a straight line. If they did, they would lose the feeling of entrapment that generates the drama.

Once again, however, as in *Sawdust and Tinsel*, the men appear weak and ineffectual. Susanne's lover lacks the courage to leave his wife and children, while Doris's new admirer, a rich and elderly consul (Gunnar Björnstrand), is ailing physically and psychologically. His wife has been in a mental institution for twenty-three years, since the birth of their daughter.

For both Susanne and Doris, their journey to Gothenburg for a photo-shoot (Gothenburg with its memories of Bergman's marriage to Ellen Lundström) becomes an excursion into the nether zone, a brush with Death from which they emerge shaken. Lobelius, on the one hand, and the consul, on the other, are painted in livid, cadaverous terms. In the dingy hotel room where Susanne and Lobelius arrange to meet, the atmosphere of futility and departure dominates the small talk. 'I feel tired and hunted,' sighs Lobelius, telling her he's about to be ruined financially. 'I've no desire, and not enough strength, to start all over again.' Against his better judgement, he makes love to her one last time. When Susanne asks if he will regret the interlude, he answers, 'I shall both have regrets and be happy for it, at the same time' – a remark that might easily be spoken by the consul too. Both men see in these women a chance to return to the tender safety of childhood. Their dreams are interrupted, however, by the bitter intervention of Lobelius's wife and (in the parallel story) by the consul's daughter. Doris, who reacts naively to gifts showered on her by the consul, has something of both Else Fisher and Ellen Lundström in her personality; Susanne possesses much of the determination and professional independence of Gun Grut.

Bergman's characters in this middle period are forever attempting to break out of their set pattern of existence. They always fail. In the finale of *Dreams*, Doris flings herself into the arms of her patient and boring fiancé, while Susanne resumes her role as the chic, elegantly coiffured proprietress of her salon. Both women had laid aside their masks for a brief moment, but the security of their daily lives proves more compelling than the temptations of an arid, furtive affair.

Bergman seems to be chiding his characters for essaying emotional risks. He also reveals his innate conservatism. Time and again throughout his turbulent life he would return to the emotional status quo. While shooting *Dreams*, Harriet Andersson became pregnant, and had an abortion in the third month. Ingmar visited her in the hospital with a bouquet of flowers, and when she returned home he cooked a fish meal, which Harriet said he never normally did. 'I think he was relieved not to have another child,' she said in 2021.

Katinka Faragó served as script assistant on *Dreams*, the first of her many films with Bergman. The studio had warned her: "If he spits at you, spit back. If he stares at you, stare back." He had a very bad reputation at the time. We finally met in a very narrow corridor – it was a very primitive studio, with nothing fancy about it. And he stared at me, and I stared back as I'd been told to do. It seemed like a year, but in fact it was probably no more than half a minute. Then he finally laughed and said, "Don't worry, it'll be all right.""[4]

Dreams may be viewed as both the last film of Bergman's youth and the first of his middle age. In the years ahead, he would learn to express his reactionary pessimism in more stimulating and inspiring terms.

8

THE GOLDEN YEARS BEGIN

During the early months of 1955, Bergman produced three plays at the Malmö City Theatre. *Don Juan* opened on 4 January on the small Intima stage. Some critics felt that Bergman's desire for shock effects might have diminished his intellectual conception of Molière's play. But on the whole the response was enthusiastic. The appearance of the awesome Statue, who consigns Don Juan to hell, beside the Ghost of Donna Elvira (her face a skull behind a veil) proved one of those *echt*-Bergman touches and a scene he would create for the cinema in *The Devil's Eye* five years later. Another coup was the first entrance of Don Juan, described by the critic Henrik Sjögren as 'yawning after the night's pleasures, with his bare thigh protruding from the elegant pleating of his nightshirt, itching himself from the fleabites, and on his head a cap with two bright red horns, those attributes of the buck and the Devil, adorned with crests and bells'.[1]

A month later, on the big stage, Bergman directed John Patrick's study of the clash between East and West, *The Teahouse of the August Moon*, set during the American occupation of Okinawa after World War II. This comedy was not entirely to Bergman's taste, nor perhaps within his grasp. He abandoned the idea of verisimilitude in casting or setting, opting instead for coarse-cut caricature and satire.

By this time, Bergman had acquired a steadiness of purpose and pattern of life that enabled him to rein in his innermost fears and insecurities. Carl Anders Dymling would look back on his extraordinary will power. 'He is a high-strung personality, passionately alive, enormously sensitive, very short-tempered, sometimes quite ruthless in the pursuit of his own goals, suspicious, stubborn, capricious, and unpredictable."² Bergman, despite the truth of this unflattering picture, aroused an intense loyalty, affection even, among those who worked and lived alongside him in Malmö. Friendship was always important for him.

His routine extended to Stockholm, where he stayed in the small apartment on Grev Turegatan when shooting interiors or editing a new movie. He gathered with friends at the Sturehof brasserie on Stureplan, famous for its fish dishes. Harriet Andersson, Gunnar Björnstrand, Ulla Jacobsson, Eva Dahlbeck, Mago and others would sit around the regular table discussing the film of the day and the issues of the moment. Tillie Björnstrand, Gunnar's wife, recalled 'Bergman's violent sense of humour, which concealed a deep streak of angst and melancholy'.³

These dinners constituted Bergman's main meal of the day. Bibi Andersson described his invariable lunch as consisting of 'some kind of whipped sour milk, very fat, and strawberry jam, very sweet – a strange kind of baby food he eats with cornflakes'.⁴ On occasion, he would indulge in a Droste chocolate. He spent so much of his waking time in Malmö at the theatre that few hours remained for reading or relaxation. But he could not have survived without a diet of old movies. 'I had a longing for contact,' he said apropos of his screening sessions with the crew and the actors. 'I couldn't stay away from my friends. We gave each other experiences, we taught each other things, we lived together. We were all in a permanent state of curiosity.' As Mago remarked, 'With Bergman, you can have a personal contact from morning to night – other directors were always surrounded by assistants.' Gunnel Lindblom recalled that in Malmö, 'once a week we had no performance, because on Tuesdays the symphony orchestra gave concerts on the main stage. That was when a movie-crazed gang of actors gathered at Ingmar's apartment in Erikslust, where he had a film projector.'⁵

Bergman's state of depression in 1955 grew so serious that he contemplated suicide during a brief trip to Switzerland (an incident evoked in *Through a Glass Darkly* some years later), and found himself in Karolinska Hospital, vomiting and suffering from suspected cancer of the stomach.[6] His doctor, Sture Helander, became a lifelong friend. Once recovered, Bergman took a room at his favourite refuge, the quaint Hotel Siljansborg in Dalarna, and set to work on the screenplay of *Smiles of a Summer Night*. The success of Lehár's *The Merry Widow* and Molière's *Don Juan* might have cast a spell over his writing, for never before had he established such an effervescent mood in a screenplay. He set aside his work on an adaptation of Birgit Tengroth's story *Jungfruburen* (*Virgin*) for either stage or screen.

Although *Dreams* had been made for Sandrews, Bergman persuaded Svensk Filmindustri to accept his new comedy, reminding Dymling that *A Lesson in Love* had performed well for the studio. He claimed that the budget was between 350,000 and 400,000 crowns (around $75,000 at the time), although others have put the figure as high as 750,000 crowns ($150,000). *Smiles* certainly cost more than any of the 37 Swedish features made in 1955. It was also the most expensive film Bergman had ever shot. The unit and actors were on call for 55 days, until, Bergman recalled, 'We were all on the verge of a nervous breakdown.'[7] Exterior photography began on 21 July, in Jordeberga Castle, three miles south of Malmö. The delightful little theatre in which Desirée Armfeldt (Eva Dahlbeck) performs was inspired by the small rococo stage in the town of Ystad. Harriet Andersson recalls that the mood was wonderful, with Gunnar Björnstrand and Åke Fridell making everyone laugh day and night. Katinka Faragó, the script assistant, remembers that the three weeks of scheduled location work were achieved in just ten days; she was so stressed that the assistant director wrote in his diary, 'We are all very tired. Katinka cries as soon as anyone asks her to shut up.'

The summer of 1955 in Sweden grew almost unbearably hot. The gas lamps in the studio 'theatre' expired for want of oxygen, and tempers ran high. On some occasions, Bergman would announce that his stomach was giving him hell, and Lennart Olsson was asked to take over and deal with the large crew and cast, most of whom were made up and ready to perform. Bergman told Olsson of his fear that, if the film proved a flop, Svensk Filmindustri might sever relations with him altogether. To complicate matters further, his leading lady, Ulla Jacobsson, was pregnant when filming began. The secret was restricted to a very few members of the cast, and Mago had to design costumes that would conceal any changes in the actress's figure.

Gunnar Fischer took full advantage of the late-evening and dawn summer light to conjure a miracle in monochrome photography, with white for once prevailing over black. For lighting and set-up run-throughs, he had to ask the crew to help him; there were no stand-ins. Bergman himself checked the framing of each shot and used to build up his scenery 'through the camera' (in those days an ancient Debrie, wrapped in pillows and blankets to smother its whirring complaints).

The sumptuous costumes and the period sets (created by Bergman's loyal designer, P. A. Lundgren) contributed to the evocation of a vanished world of wealth and fastidiousness. When Stephen Sondheim's stage version of the film, *A Little Night Music*, opened on Broadway, there was a similar emphasis on costume design and extravagant settings.

Smiles of a Summer Night, set at the close of the nineteenth century, shuffles its variegated characters around the theme of fidelity. The film's upper-middle-class milieux prefigure the world of *Fanny and Alexander* – a world for which Bergman remained nostalgic throughout his life: one of refined luxury upstairs, and attendant vulgarity below stairs. *Smiles* demonstrates Bergman's consummate talent for writing dialogue – apothegms worthy of Oscar Wilde, waspish comments ('If they're actors, they must sleep in the stables,' says the aged Mrs Armfeldt) and the worldly wisdom dispensed by Desirée ('For the past three years I've been twenty-nine, and that's

Gunnar Björnstrand and Eva Dahlbeck in *Smiles of a Summer Night.*
Copyright © AB Svensk Filmindustri 1955. Photo by Louis Huch.

no age for a woman of my age') and Fredrik ('The years have given
your body the perfection which perfection itself lacks . . .').

Fredrik Egerman (Gunnar Björnstrand), a prosperous lawyer,
has a new young wife, Anne (Ulla Jacobsson). During a visit to the
theatre, he goes backstage to arrange a rendezvous with his former
mistress, Desirée Armfeldt (Eva Dahlbeck). Desirée's lover of the
moment is Count Malcolm (Jarl Kulle), who is affronted by the
presence of Egerman. Desirée engineers an elaborate house party at
her mother's country manor in order to bring about a confrontation
between Malcolm and Egerman, to whom she is drawn somewhat
more profoundly than she will admit.

At the party, stretching over a long midsummer's night, lust
and love manifest themselves in the form of an elegant quad-
rille. Egerman's son by an earlier marriage, Henrik, finds himself
attracted to the innocent Anne; Petra (Harriet Andersson), Anne's
maid, strikes up a lusty relationship with Frid (Åke Fridell), old Mrs

Armfeldt's groom; and the lawyer himself is seduced by the Count's wife, Charlotte (Margit Carlqvist), with the result that he must fight a duel by Russian roulette with his rival. But the gun contains a blank cartridge filled with soot, and Egerman, although humiliated, survives to regain the affections of Desirée.

Egerman comes close to being a tragic figure. He suffers the fate of all those Bergman men who cannot yield to instinct. He finds himself too circumscribed by pedantic dignity to indulge his fancies. Yet this suave, courtly individual remains the most sympathetic person in the film because he recognises that the male must revise his values if he is to endure. He makes one smile with him when he scores in repartee with the bristling Count in Desirée's dressing room. He makes one nod in agreement when he teases young Henrik for his hypocrisy.

Desirée is the perfect partner for him because she possesses both a sense of social comportment and an ability to express her appetites in language that Egerman can accept without being appalled. Her self-pity is organised along strictly practical lines. Aware of her fading youth, Desirée refuses to settle for promises of paradise. 'No, Fredrik Egerman, I want my reward in *this* world,' she demands, biting his finger savagely. Desirée is a woman acclaimed in her own right as a stage diva, and she exercises a steely control over her private life, asserting both her independence of men as well as her right to motherhood.

Such hedonism also runs in the veins of Fredrik's meek and virgin wife, Anne. When the opportunity arises, however, she snatches at it eagerly, without the sardonic calculation that Desirée brings to such matters. She runs off with Henrik, while Egerman watches aghast in the background. And so Egerman is left to arrive most painfully at his eventual salvation – a relationship with Desirée.

Frid, the groom at the manor, behaves like an uninhibited satyr whose lust for Petra, the maid, emerges in two beautifully patterned sequences: the first in the park, where Frid pursues his giggling prey between the trees to the accompaniment of equine whinnying, and the second in the hay, where the couple frolic lasciviously and Frid exclaims in exultant tones, 'There isn't a better life than this!'

The sweet-and-sour mood of *Smiles of a Summer Night* is embodied in the character of Charlotte, a calculating seductress who despises her husband, Count Malcolm, and suddenly cries to Anne in an unguarded moment: 'I hate him! I hate him! Men are beastly! They are stupid and vain and have hair all over their bodies. Love is a disgusting business.' This outburst is flung into the camera with such controlled viciousness that one recoils, mainly irritated that one's preconceptions about these elegant characters should be so roughly destroyed. Margit Carlqvist's gazing directly into the camera is as disturbing as the moment in *Summer with Monika* when Harriet Andersson does the same.

Eva Dahlbeck gives her finest performance in *Smiles of a Summer Night*. Bergman dubbed her 'a battleship of femininity', and she would elude any advances he might have made to her, although he held her in such respect that an erotic dimension to their relationship would never have developed. Dahlbeck turned to writing fiction, and lived abroad for decades. Happy in her marriage to an air force officer from 1944 to 2007, she outlived Bergman by less than a year.

On Boxing Day 1955, Bergman attended the premiere of *Smiles of a Summer Night* in a state of trepidation. '[I] sat there thinking this is the worst fiasco I've ever known. Not a soul seemed to laugh, nobody was enjoying it, they all sat grim and silent.'[8] Had the film failed at the box office, Bergman's screen career might have petered out. With his child-support obligations, he grasped at any project that would bring him a fee. His indifferent screenplay for Alf Sjöberg's *Last Pair Out* (*Sista paret ut*) featured roles for both Harriet and Bibi and reflected the concerns of Bergman's earlier period – students versus adults, intellectuals versus the bourgeoisie.[9]

The critics were divided over *Smiles of a Summer Night*. Olof Lagerkrantz attacked it sharply in *Dagens Nyheter*, saying, with a bitchiness worthy of old Mrs Armfeldt, that its jokes were suitable for the stable yard. Hanserik Hjertén, later to become critic at the same influential newspaper, also poured scorn on *Smiles* in a film magazine of the period. Word of mouth, however, was good, and once the film had won a major award at Cannes the following spring, foreign sales began to accelerate.

Like *Smiles of a Summer Night*, Bergman's private life in 1955 was a kaleidoscope of liaisons. He had parted from Gun Grut, his third wife, but kept in touch with her while she pursued her career and brought up their son, Lill-Ingmar. By the autumn, the relationship with Harriet Andersson had come to an end. They had not slept in the same bed for many months, and Bergman had been involved with Bibi Andersson since late the previous year. In February 1956 Harriet would travel to Stockholm to be with her new lover, the actor Gunnar Hellström.

Bibi Andersson (no kin to Harriet) had first met Bergman as a teenager, when she appeared in the commercials for Bris soap. She had a promising career at the Royal Dramatic Theatre in Stockholm and was attached to Svensk Filmindustri's pool of actors and actresses. Bergman knew her sister, Gerd, quite well and invited her out to KB restaurant in Stockholm with Bibi and the actor Björn Bjelvenstam; and when Bjelvenstam, during a drive up to Stockholm in Bergman's ancient Volvo, suggested a midsummer night's party with Gerd and Bibi, the seeds of romance were sown. Bergman promised Bibi that she could have the part of Anne in *Smiles*, should Ulla Jacobsson's pregnancy rule her out of the film. When this failed to happen, Bergman felt embarrassed and offered Bibi a small role instead. So she can be glimpsed fluttering about on stage in the tiny theatre where Desirée Armfeldt reigns supreme.

Bibi meant a great deal to Bergman during these years. 'Now Bibi arrives, and everything seems better,' he wrote in his workbook.[10] Her youth and guileless ardour inspired some of his greatest creations – Mia in *The Seventh Seal*, the two Saras in *Wild Strawberries*, Hjördis in *So Close to Life* and, on the stage, Sagan in Hjalmar Bergman's play. She was fiercely loyal to him and could stimulate him even in his moments of severe depression. Her presence coincided with – or perhaps prompted – Bergman's most idealistic period. On 16 July 1955, Bergman noted, 'Bibi is right. I've done enough comedy now. There must be something else, more serious.'[11] And she was indeed right. Bergman's next film, *The Seventh Seal*, would propel him to the forefront of world cinema. On the eve of Bibi's flight to Cannes for the presentation of *The Seventh Seal* in May 1957, Bergman confided in his workbook that the relationship with her was 'a manifest and absolute communion between us'.[12] They lived in Erikslust, which Bibi termed 'a sad district of Malmö', in a three-room apartment that 'was neat from the start; Ingmar's style being spartan but in good taste'.[13]

Although they never married, Bergman and Bibi continued to work with each other through the years, their mutual successes reflecting a growing maturity on either side: *Persona*, *The Passion of Anna*, *The Touch*, and then *Twelfth Night* at the Royal Dramatic Theatre. 'In all the years I knew him,' she reflected, 'I was strengthened in the belief that utter certainty is also utter strength. Ingmar had both.'[14] In 1979 Bibi wrote an impassioned defence of Bergman's cinema in *Dagens Nyheter*, responding to those critics who had condemned it for dealing only with the upper classes. 'But Bergman's films have been concerned with *feelings*,' she insisted, 'and we *need* to be concerned with feelings.'

In March 1955, Bergman's play about medieval Sweden, *Wood Painting* (*Trämålning*), ran for just eighteen performances at Malmö City Theatre. But the reviews for what had been designed as an exercise for Bergman's students at the theatre proved so enthusiastic that on 16 September the production transferred to the Royal Dramatic Theatre in Stockholm, again as an exercise for the drama students. The one-act play had undergone a sea change, however. Bengt Ekerot was the director. Ekerot, a member of the literary group known as the '40-talisterna', had become an accomplished stage producer, and the man who would play Death in *The Seventh Seal*. Bibi Andersson now featured as the blacksmith's wife. Six weeks later, Bergman himself directed Vilhelm Moberg's *Leah and Rachel* on the small stage at Malmö, even as he was already developing his next film – *The Seventh Seal* (*Det sjunde inseglet*).

Wood Painting contains several elements of *The Seventh Seal*: the fear of the plague, the burning of the witch, the Dance of Death. But the concept of the 'holy couple', Jof and Mia, is missing, as is the motif of the chess game between Death and the Knight, Antonius Block. Bergman instead laid perhaps too heavy an emphasis on the tomfoolery between the smith and his wife. Only one character may be found fully formed, namely Jöns, the Squire, whose dialogue in both play and film is almost identical, line for line. Bergman's original handwritten text ends with Karin, the Knight's wife, telling everyone that they must hold hands and follow the 'Lord' to the dark lands. In the radio version of the play, broadcast back in the autumn of 1954, the 'silent girl' was played by Nine-Christine Jönsson (familiar from *Port of Call*). Eva Dahlbeck was the witch, who also had a more vocal role than in *The Seventh Seal*.

To trace the origins of what became Bergman's most celebrated film, one must go back to his childhood. Henrik Sjögren regarded the central theme of Bergman's plays as being 'Everyman between God and the Devil',[15] and this Manichaean vision of the world was fostered by his parents. Ever since the Reformation, Sweden had been a Protestant society in which the pastors had occupied a central place. In his scathing book on the country, *The New Totalitarians*, Roland Huntford commented that it remained 'one of the rare countries in which men are often anti-religious, but rarely anti-clerical'.[16]

Even during the later stages of the nineteenth century, when a revolution in thought was sweeping through most European nations, Scandinavia clung to its religious ideals, adumbrated in the world of Kierkegaard and in plays such as Ibsen's *Brand*. The image of the deity was exclusively of God the Father. Jesus as a creature of flesh and blood is absent. Instead, he is confined to a secondary role, an anguished figure on the Cross, set above the altar in innumerable small, bare, well-lit churches. The asceticism of Luther prevailed, and in private life Pastor Erik Bergman acted as a high priest. The odour of sanctity permeated the household. Candles were lit before breakfast on Sundays.

Of course, Bergman reacted against this upbringing. But just as certain antidotes contain a degree of the poison they are meant to counteract, so the artist needs to draw on the experiences that he seeks to expunge. Orthodox religion ran in Bergman's blood. He often signed his scripts with the initials S:D:G: ('*Soli Deo Gloria*' – 'To God Alone the Glory'), as did J. S. Bach at the end of every composition. He was fond of quoting Eugene O'Neill's dictum that all dramatic art is worthless unless it deals with man's relationship to God.

In 1955, when Bergman was already thirty-seven years of age, the images of the frescoes he had seen in his youth still seared his mind. Albertus Pictor had been the finest of all Swedish medieval church painters. In his murals, and in those by other, anonymous artists, the theme of Death is paramount. Bergman announces at the beginning of *Wood Painting* that the story is taken direct from one such fresco, in the vestibule of a church in southern Småland. The ravages of the plague are charted over a twelve-foot span, from the entrance, where 'the sun is playing over a green landscape', to 'the dark corner where the final incidents occur in the greyish, rain-laden dawn'. In his later autobiographical novel, *Sunday's Children*, Bergman described similar murals in affectionate detail.

Another key source of the film was Carl Orff's *Carmina Burana*, a medley of medieval songs written by minstrels, often during the plague years. Bergman had bought Ferenc Fricsay's recording of the music and played it at high volume each morning before leaving for rehearsals at the theatre.

The Seventh Seal was difficult for Bergman to sell. While making *Dreams*, he had spoken to Rune Waldekranz at Sandrew about the notion of a screen version of *Wood Painting*, but there was no opportunity at that juncture to persuade Anders Sandrew to finance such a nebulous and potentially expensive project. Even Svensk Filmindustri remained dubious, in view of the extravagance of *Smiles of a Summer Night* (Bergman having insisted on re-upholstering all the furniture to create the 'whiteish' look of the film).

He pressed ahead with his screenplay, however, and on 8 April completed one of the longest dialogues between Death and the Knight. By 11 April he noted in his workbook that he had written what would be regarded as one of the finest sequences in the film – the Knight reflecting on life over strawberries and cream on the hillside. Then, in May 1956, *Smiles of a Summer Night* won the Jury Prize at Cannes (for its 'poetic humour'). Bergman did not realise that the film was entered in the festival. He had been reading *Svenska Dagbladet* in the toilet when a headline caught his eye – 'Swedish Success in Cannes'. Stunned and excited, he borrowed money from Bibi for the flight to Nice and joined Carl Anders Dymling and the Swedish delegation in Cannes. He presented Dymling with the screenplay for *The Seventh Seal* and declared, 'Now or never, Carl Anders!'[17] Dymling read the script once more, and agreed to support the project, providing it required no more than thirty-six days to shoot (in fact, Bergman would complete the film with a day to spare).

Bergman tinkered with the script, rewriting it five times, at first in the Hotel Siljansborg in Dalarna, and then 'hidden in a small room in the gatekeeper's cabin in Råsunda'.[18] The major development was the replacement of Jöns in the main role by the Knight. Originally, the Knight's character was silent. 'The Saracens had cut out his tongue,' commented Bergman, with a nice sense of historical verisimilitude, although the true reason was that, while one of the director's pupils at Malmö was sufficiently handsome to take the part, he could not deliver dialogue.[19]

Already over Easter Bergman had told Allan Ekelund, his production manager, how intractable the script was proving to be. Although Bergman was no scholarly researcher, he found himself responding to all manner of rich influences, as well as *Carmina Burana* – Picasso's picture of the two acrobats, the two jesters and the child; Strindberg's *Saga of the Folkungs* and *To Damascus*; the concluding portion of *Outward Bound* (Death's omniscience, coupled with an occasional engaging disclaimer), which recalls the 'Examiner', the Reverend Frank Thomson, whom Bergman himself had played on stage back in 1938.

He visited Härkeberga Church, north of Stockholm, to look at the paintings and murals. He was accompanied by Ekelund and by P. A. Lundgren, his art director, who needed only a nudge from Bergman to devise some brilliant designs. Lundgren seized on the most arresting of the tiny figures depicted in the church frescoes and enlarged them to grotesque proportions so they could adorn the side of a caravan or a surrogate stage backdrop.

By 5 June, the screenplay was ready – and dedicated to Bibi Andersson. Preparations for shooting in July began at breakneck pace. Ove Svensson, a student at Uppsala University, was an assistant on the film, providing Bergman with his favourite wafer biscuits, as well as selecting extras from among hundreds of eager applicants.

The budget was set at between 700,000 and 800,000 crowns (the equivalent of $150,000 at the time), and only three scenes were shot on location. The opening sequence by the seashore and a few other hillside scenes were shot at Hovs Hallar, on the southwest coast. Lennart Olsson had spent two weeks searching for the right spot. Hovs Hallar, with its sense of a mountain coming literally down into the sea, struck Bergman as exactly right. He also liked filming in the province of Skåne because the light was so much softer than in the northern parts of the country; colours, landscape, atmosphere, all were smooth and gentle. Gunnar Fischer and his crew manhandled the 40 kg Mitchell camera down to the shoreline. The crew stayed in a hotel in Torekov, a short distance along the coast.

As so often in Swedish cinema, improvisation offered the key to success. Some actors could not work in harmony with Bergman, or each other, and had to be replaced during filming.[20] Costumes were borrowed from Malmö City Theatre. (The description of a circus setting up shop in *Sawdust and Tinsel* is not so far from the truth where Bergman's productions were concerned.) Everyone fetched and carried. Else Fisher, Bergman's first wife, was called on to choreograph the dance performed by Jof and Mia in the village. Anders Ek, Bergman's close friend and colleague from far back in the 1940s, played the monk who harangues the flagellants. The poor folk in the tavern sequence consisted of extras found by Bergman and Olsson in Stockholm's seniors' residences. The scene with the flagellants was shot from 8 a.m. to 7 p.m. in a single day. 'It was such a fantastic time,' said Bergman later, with only a touch of hyperbole. 'We never slept. We only rehearsed and shot.'[21]

The most famous scene, the Dance of Death, was achieved *par hasard*. Early one morning at Hovs Hallar the unit was preparing quite another shot, when suddenly the skies grew rather dramatic. The light changed. Bergman announced on the spur of the moment that he would shoot the Dance of Death. But some of the actors had joined a party the previous evening. Åke Fridell (who played the blacksmith) had suffered a minor 'accident' and could not walk properly when he arrived on location. Bergman asked Ove Svensson to take his place. A costume was found, the scene was shot by Gunnar Fischer, and the student Svensson's silhouette joined the immortals of film history. There was but a single take.

Most of the principal sequences (such as the burning of the witch and the uproar in the tavern) were shot in or around the studios at Råsunda. The bonfire lit for the immolation got out of hand. Bergman claimed that the residents of surrounding suburbs were cleaning oil off their windows for days afterwards.

Bergman preferred the organised precision of studio interiors. 'Ingmar always came into a freshly built set and *sniffed* for the atmosphere,' recalled Lennart Olsson. 'Not checking for minute details, but for the smell and the mood.' His savage sense of humour never deserted him. Ove Svensson, for example, was made up with a putrid skull to play the dead monk addressed by Jöns on the coast near the start of the film. Bergman delighted in despatching him to the commissary at Råsunda and seeing how the other diners lost their appetite.

Bergman created an abundance of personalities in *The Seventh Seal*, not until *Fanny and Alexander* in 1982 would he revel in such a diversity of characters. Each reflects an aspect of his own approach, and response, to life and work. Jof and Mia embody an idealism that hovered always just beyond Bergman's grasp. The Knight, Antonius Block, expresses his yearning for belief beyond mere dogma. The Squire gives vent to the tetchy, waspish side of Bergman. The actor Skat and Lisa, the blacksmith's errant wife, seize the moment with hedonistic abandon, like Frid and Petra in *Smiles of a Summer Night*. In the chaos of existence, they are all elements of the artist's psyche engaged in a kind of centrifugal dance away from their source. However much at odds two Bergman personalities may be, one can rest assured that beneath the bitter arguments there lie fragments of the same soul. Thus, inherent in the matrix of Bergman's greatest work is the conflict between life and death, belief and doubt, light and darkness, sadism and suffering, vengeance and magnanimity, hope and despair, and above all God and the demons that oppose Him. Antagonists, protagonists, innocents or cynics, all enhance the dialectic that runs through so much of his work.

Like many of Bergman's films, *The Seventh Seal* unfolds within a 24-hour cycle, from dawn to dawn, as though the very turning of the earth were exacting a kind of magnetic force on the characters. The predicament of the Knight and his Squire on their return from the Crusades, and those they encounter in a plague-infested Sweden, touched a chord among a new generation coming of age in the shadow of nuclear armageddon, just as the film's abiding relevance has recently been accentuated by a worldwide pandemic.

The significance of the Knight's character emerges as soon as he realises he has been tricked by Death in the confessional scene. Nowhere is Block closer to Bergman than when he leans back against the stone wall of the church and flexes his hand with courage unquenched. 'This my hand,' he says ardently. 'I can move it, feel the blood pulsing through it. The sun is still high in the sky and I, Antonius Block, am playing chess with Death.' The action becomes a stirring symbol of the will to live, the source of human love and ideals. Like the Knight, Bergman has reacted with a wry smile to misfortune and deception; like him, too, he is animated by a boundless curiosity.

Bergman's view of the medieval Church is filled with revulsion and loathing. Death is a surrogate priest in the confessional; the monk harangues the flagellants with the cynicism of a modern demagogue and a total disrespect for humanity (Anders Ek looking uncannily like the portraits of the turbulent Florentine friar Savonarola); yet another cleric, Raval, robs a dead man and is about to rape a serving girl when the Squire discovers him. This same Raval – 'Doctor Mirabilis, Coelestis et Diabilis', as Jöns calls him sarcastically – had urged the Knight to embark on his Crusade so that he and his accomplices could indulge their thieving instincts at home. Raval embodies active, malicious evidence of the unethical advantage the ministers of the Church took of most men's naivety during the Middle Ages.

Set against the viciousness of Raval, the masochistic wailing of the flagellants as they pass through the village and the burning of a waif of a girl somehow condemned as a witch are the pathos and serenity of the hillside gathering, when the Knight and the Squire join Jof and Mia at dusk. Bergman transmutes the wine and the wafers of Holy Communion into the fresh milk and strawberries passed from hand to hand with a kind of unadulterated reverence.

As the Knight watches the death agony of the young girl burned at the stake, he asks her, 'I too want to meet the Devil. I want to ask him about God. He, if anyone, must know.' But the girl cannot respond, and the Squire comments drily, 'Look at her eyes, my Lord. Her poor brain has just made a discovery – emptiness.' Although Block shakes his head vehemently at the Squire's assertion, it's obvious that he has become emotionally aware of what earlier he had suspected intellectually – that human beings must rely on their own resources to counter Death. Block is not quite a zealot, not quite an Ahab, not even an atheist obsessed with God, like the hero of Flannery O'Connor's *Wise Blood*. He longs to believe, to effect a reconciliation between the world's pain and beauty.

Bergman's concept of Death is intriguing. He endows him with the sardonic stare of the intellectual, who is both afraid and bereft of emotion. Death glides into the frame from one side or the other, always unexpected. Only a few – Jof, the Knight, the serving girl – can discern him for what he is. Even the actor Skat, when he hears him sawing away at the tree trunk below, treats him like a cheeky woodsman. Bergman has pounced on the fact that in those medieval church paintings Death has a fondness for chess, for the game is emblematic of the logic and lack of imagination he abhors. Bergman may sympathise with the Squire, but he identifies with the Knight when he sweeps the pieces off the chessboard and thus covers the flight of Jof, Mia and baby Mikael – the 'Holy Family'. Perhaps he even feels a twinge of sympathy with Death himself when, after defeating the Knight, he confesses his ignorance. Like the humans he overwhelms, Death cannot see beyond the encroaching darkness.

The film opened in Stockholm on 16 February 1957. The reviews were uniformly excellent (with the exception of Hanserik Hjertén's dismissal in *Arbetaren*). But Bergman felt alone. 'Nobody, not even the actors, phoned me after the premiere,' he told Käbi Laretei (his fourth wife) some years afterwards. Pastor Erik Bergman,

Nils Poppe and Bibi Andersson in *The Seventh Seal*.
Copyright © AB Svensk Filmindustri 1957. Photo by Louis Huch.

now retired from his duties at Hedvig Eleonora Church, wrote an
appreciative note to his son, saying that he thought the film very
good. Even those international critics who disliked *The Seventh Seal*
admitted its power, as did Dilys Powell in the London *Sunday Times*,
declaring that 'it has the impact of one of those spiked iron balls
chained to a club, so popular in films about goodwill in the Middle
Ages'. One of the most respected American critics in Europe, Gene
Moskowitz, wrote in *Variety* after the film's screening in Cannes that
the 'characters abound with vitality and Bergman wraps this into
an absorbing film . . . Superior technical narrative, impressive lens-
ing and thespians makes this a definite U.S. art house possibility.'[22]
Late in life, during a conversation with his son Daniel on a bench
beside his house on Fårö, Bergman evoked the scene where Death
appears before the Knight at the start of *The Seventh Seal*, and asked
the rhetorical question: Will the audience just laugh and say that

it's Bengt Ekerot with his white make-up and black cape – or will people somehow accept the scene and its magic?[23]

Coming on the heels of *Smiles of a Summer Night* in France and Britain, *The Seventh Seal* established Bergman in the top flight of contemporary directors. It remains a work of immense force – Bergman's *Faust*, his *Hamlet*, his *Odyssey*. Critics and audiences alike were stunned not just by the ambitious theme but also by the assurance of the performances and the brilliance of Gunnar Fischer's black-and-white cinematography. Swedish craftsmanship was second to none in the film world at that point. And in Max von Sydow, who at the age of twenty-seven brought to the role of the Knight a distinction and a gravitas worthy of Alec Guinness, Bergman had found a major new star.

In the wake of his triumphs at Cannes with *Smiles of a Summer Night* and *The Seventh Seal*, Bergman could look forward at last to a future free of rejections by producers and critics. But this new-found confidence concealed the seeds of an attitude that would grow ever more autocratic. In his creative work, Bergman needed colleagues he could dominate and colleagues he could protect. He relied on an assistant more than perhaps he would admit. From 1954 until the end of the Malmö period the 'sorcerer's apprentice' was Lennart Olsson. It was a factotum's role, for Bergman squeezed every ounce of potential from the day, and the stage or film set had to be prepared exactly to his prior instructions by the time he made his appearance.

Towards the end of 1955, Bergman had engaged a dancer from Malmö City Theatre named Lenn Hjortzberg, who would become his secretary for more than a decade, fending off fans, ex-wives and sundry petitioners of every type. The fastidious Hjortzberg devoted himself to Bergman's business and administrative chores, even to rounding up the livestock to fill the farmyard in *The Virgin Spring*.

By now, Bergman's discipline rendered him seemingly unemotional, objective, prone to dissect those with whom he came in contact. 'You cannot refuse Ingmar' was a refrain one heard from those associated with him through the years. Indeed, when Bergman laughed, the world was expected to laugh with him. He admitted that he was aggressive by nature, 'and I often find it hard to repress my aggressiveness'.[24] The big feuds with a younger generation of filmmakers, including Bo Widerberg, lay ahead. Only in old age would he admit that during his finest hours he missed the advice and criticism of a mentor such as Lorens Marmstedt.[25]

9

BEHIND THE MASK

Bergman's loyalty to the theatre never wavered. In the eyes of the international public, *The Seventh Seal* would tower over his other work achieved in 1956, but during that year he produced three plays at Malmö City Theatre, and in early 1957, while writing the screenplay for *Wild Strawberries*, he flung himself into rehearsals for Ibsen's monumental play *Peer Gynt*.

Max von Sydow appeared in all three of these productions, as well as in Molière's *The Misanthrope*, which Bergman directed in late 1957. Tall, slender, with an oblong, expressive face, von Sydow dominated any stage, his majestic voice sounding much older than his years. In 1954, at the age of fifteen, he had attended a performance of *A Midsummer Night's Dream* on the big stage of the freshly opened Malmö City Theatre. This 'fantastic experience' spurred him and some friends to form an amateur dramatic society. Some years later he entered the Acting Academy of the Royal Dramatic Theatre in Stockholm. Gunnar Björnstrand watched him in rehearsals and thought that this twenty-year-old looked at least forty. Having worked with Alf Sjöberg, and appearing in stage productions in Norrköping and Helsingborg, von Sydow received an invitation from Bergman to join his troupe in Malmö. After just two roles at the City Theatre, he joined the cast of *The Seventh Seal*. Already in 1957 Bergman told the French critic Jean Béranger, 'You'll see that posterity will consider [Max von Sydow] one of the greatest actors of our time.'[1]

As soon as the film entered post-production, Bergman returned to the theatre with gusto. On 19 October 1956, he directed Max as Brick in Tennessee Williams's *Cat on a Hot Tin Roof*, which had been published the previous year. With its claustrophobic atmosphere of family guilt, the dominance of a dying paterfamilias and much sexual innuendo, Williams's drama was an ideal vehicle for Bergman, whose own plays had never attained such a pitch of intensity, even when dealing with similar themes. Henrik Sjögren noted how Max contrasted Brick's nervous tension and disgust with life with a tireless passion for truth.[2]

For the final production of the year, Bergman created an almost poignant portrayal of Strindberg's *Erik XIV*, with Toivo Pawlo as the medieval Swedish king stretched between cruelty and remorse, laughter and tears, loneliness and the flattery of a huge court. Bibi Andersson played Karin Månsdotter, the peasant girl taken by the king as his mistress and left alone at the age of twenty-six.

For most of those who lived and worked in Malmö during the 1950s, *Peer Gynt*, which opened on 8 March 1957, was Bergman's finest production. In terms of sheer length, it dwarfed the others. The performance ran for some four hours, with one decent interval after the third act and a shorter one between the fourth and fifth. Ibsen's gigantic play contains some forty scenes and sprang almost entirely from his fantasy. (Peer Gynt was a real person who lived in Norway in the late eighteenth or early nineteenth century, but few hard facts are known about his life.) Michael Meyer called the drama the direct ancestor of Strindberg's *A Dream Play*, a 'struggle between the divine purpose and our undermining passions and egocentricities, between man's deeper self and his animal, or troll, self'.[3]

One observer was struck by Bergman's habit of working at a high level of tension in rehearsal and then suddenly breaking the mood by telling a funny story, quite irrelevant to the play. He was careful not to take his actors to the absolute peak too early; instead, he brought them to within a few degrees of perfection. Arne Ericsson, a journalist in Malmö during this period, remembered Bergman's precision inside the theatre. 'He loved silence so much that he had a board erected, with the words *shut up!* written on it in ninety-seven different languages!' He always followed his intuition; he might arrive for a crowd sequence on stage and announce that the previous day he had been utterly certain of how to handle the scene but that during the night he had dreamed of it in a different form – 'And now I'm going to improvise.' This was in vivid contrast to his approach to the cinema, where he detested improvisation.

The settings for *Peer Gynt* appeared quite conventional (e.g. the Norwegian house) in the early stages of Bergman's production, but in the fourth and fifth acts the style grew more and more impressionistic. The scene in the Cairo madhouse proved unforgettable, with each of the twenty or so inmates a distorted personality in his or her own right. But during the final act the stage was almost bare, with Max von Sydow and Åke Fridell (as the Mountain King) face to face, and then Peer alone with his beloved Solveig (Gunnel Lindblom). 'It all becomes simple and grand,' wrote Nils Beyer in *Morgon-Tidningen*. 'Just two human beings on an empty stage. And in the background, silent and twisted, the figure of the Buttonmaker, holding his ladle, with his box on his back.'[4]

There were some awkward moments. Naima Wifstrand, playing Mother Aase, was in her late sixties and so fragile that for Max von Sydow to hoist her up on to the roof of the house proved a hazardous operation. During rehearsals she cracked a rib but managed to soldier on. Like everybody else, she adored Bergman, and featured regularly in his screen productions.

Bergman's authority at Malmö City Theatre was strengthened after the triumph of *Smiles of a Summer Night*. Lars-Levi Laestadius was head of the theatre but was smart enough to give Bergman free rein. 'Ingmar would arrive in the winter, do his plays, leave, come back the next winter,' said his assistant director, Lennart Olsson. 'He himself chose the plays, and would talk his way round Laestadius who was a clever individual and never tried to argue. After all, it was a privilege for him to have Ingmar in the house. But there was a problem for the other directors, because if there were three or four

Bergman productions during one season, you had to have between five and eight other productions, and they were, in some way, sandwiched in between Ingmar's.'

Throughout this busy season, Bergman had been nurturing the idea that would evolve into *Wild Strawberries* (*Smultronstället*). First, he had to direct a television version of Hjalmar Bergman's *Mr Sleeman Is Coming*, his initial contact with the young medium. On 25 March he had scoffed to himself, 'My next film will be called "He Lies on His Back in the Sun and Recovers".' In his second volume of autobiography, Bergman asserted that he wrote the script for *Wild Strawberries* while under observation and treatment in Karolinska Hospital in Stockholm – although in his workbook for April 1957 he refers to being in Sophiahemmet. He seemed happy enough to avoid the trek to Cannes for the screening of *The Seventh Seal* in May, and Bibi Andersson represented him and the film.

The character of Isak Borg had been conceived the previous year, when Bergman had driven from Dalarna down to Stockholm and paused in Uppsala at dawn. The town was quiet and rather deserted, and the silence had a suggestive quality. Bergman looked up the house in Nedre Slottsgatan where his grandmother had lived, turned the door handle, and thought to himself that when he opened the door he would enter the world of his childhood once again.[5] 'If I'm upset about something or feel sad or lonely, I think back to my childhood, to the summer house by the sea or the nursery with its toys,' he confided to his workbook in May of 1957.[6]

Carl Anders Dymling persuaded the aged and ailing Victor Sjöström to take the part of Isak Borg, which had been written, according to Bergman, with the legendary actor in mind. Bergman readily admitted that 'Isak Borg equals me. I.B. equals Ice and Borg (the Swedish word for fortress). Simple and facile [...] a figure who, on the outside, looked like my father but *was me, through and through*.'[7] Borg, a distinguished professor emeritus who lives alone with his housekeeper, can come to terms with his egocentricity only by travelling back in time to his earliest youth, finding there the seeds of his failure as husband, lover and father.

So much of the film echoes Bergman's life at the time. His relationship with Bibi Andersson, 'a life filled with kindness and creativity, was beginning to crumble'.[8] He was not on speaking terms with his father, and his mother made frequent but futile attempts to achieve reconciliation. The chilling character of Isak's mother was originally Isak's father, a doctor.[9] But on 16 May Bergman decided to cast Naima Wifstrand as the ninety-eight-year-old mother and created a meticulous family tree for the Borgs. The feuding couple, Alman and Berit, picked up on the road by Borg, stemmed from the waspish author and critic Stig Ahlgren and his actual wife, Birgit Tengroth (the author of *Thirst*). The nightmarish inquisition in the middle of the film was inspired by Bergman's own 'calamitous final examination in school'.[10]

Isak is unusual among Bergman characters in that he does not set out of his own accord on a quest for self-knowledge. At every juncture, he must confront the evidence of his own shortcomings. He reacts with bewilderment rather than complacency. His personality and his past are reflected in the life around him. Evald, his son (Gunnar Björnstrand), Alman and Isak's mother all appear as thinly disguised images of himself. The photographs on his desk at home and in his mother's collection are of the dead. (Bergman always uses photographs to suggest mortality, as opposed to drawings, which are much more vibrant. The photographs the waiter shows to Johan in *The Silence* are similarly deathlike.)

In his opening soliloquy, Isak admits he's an old pedant and toys for a moment over a chess move after hearing his housekeeper's announcement that dinner is served. There seems nothing mean or vicious about his behaviour. But Bergman's purpose in *Wild Strawberries* is to reach behind the façade that keeps the skeletons concealed in a respectable life. As Miss Julie says in Strindberg's play, 'Oh, you may run and run, but your memories are in the baggage-car, and with them remorse and repentance.'[11] Isak's personality contains much of Pastor Erik Bergman but, basically, he was Bergman himself – by his own admission 'a complete failure at thirty-eight'.[12] As a father, as a husband, certainly; but, with *Smiles of a Summer Night* and *The Seventh Seal* already acclaimed, hardly a failure in his career. Just like Isak Borg, in fact.

As late as 22 February 1957, Bergman was referring to his next project as 'the Uppsala film',[13] and three days later was already jotting down the first elements of the plot of *The Magician*. 'God give me strength to make this film [*Wild Strawberries*] without fear, without distractions, and without despondency,' he wrote in his workbook on 2 May. Filming began in early July and would continue uninterrupted until 27 August, when Bergman had to begin preparing Molière's *The Misanthrope*, his first production of the new season at Malmö City Theatre.

The scenes with Victor Sjöström posed the most formidable challenge. The greatest personality of Swedish silent cinema was seventy-eight years old and sometimes querulous. A lonely man, a widower, his health was poor, and during the filming he often forgot his lines. Gunnar Fischer said that several scenes had to be shot indoors for Sjöström's sake: 'We had to make some very bad back-projections in the car because we never knew if Victor would come back alive the next day.' Still, as long as Sjöström was home by 5.15 p.m. each day 'and had his whisky punctually, all went well'.[14]

An enchanting kinship developed between Sjöström and the young Bibi Andersson. She revived in him the flair of a ladies' man, and he treated her seriously and with great charm. Bergman, who frequently used his 16 mm camera to keep a record of his film productions, has a shot of Bibi and Victor flirting quite harmlessly, oblivious to the activity of the crew around them. In the diary he maintained during the shoot, Bergman noted of Sjöström, 'I never stop prying, shamelessly studying this powerful face. Sometimes it's like a dumb cry of pain, sometimes it's distorted by mistrustful cruelty and senile querulousness, sometimes it dissolves into self-pity and astoundingly sentimental effusions.' In the final close-ups of Isak Borg, said Bergman, 'his face shone with secretive light as if reflected from another reality. His features became suddenly mild, almost effete. His look was open, smiling, tender. [...] Then complete stillness – peace and clarity of soul. Never before or since have I experienced a face so noble and liberated.'[15] Bergman had inherited some of Sjöström's distinctive characteristics – a meticulous efficiency and attention to detail, and an irritability in the face of things not going well.

The opening nightmare, replete with symbols of death and disaster, seems a tribute to Sjöström's own great silent film, *The Phantom Carriage*. Sound effects, as in the opening flashback of *Sawdust and Tinsel*, are harsh and abrupt. The silence at one point is so profound that Isak becomes aware of his own massive heartbeat. When the hearse-like carriage crashes into a lamp-post and disgorges its casket, the axle squeals insistently, like a newborn baby, suggesting the proximity of birth and death.

The set for this sequence was built on the lot at Råsunda, but the shot of the carriage rounding the street corner was taken by Gunnar Fischer in Stockholm's deserted Old Town at almost 2 a.m. one summer morning. A couple emerging late from a restaurant were startled by the spectacle of a coach without a driver hurtling down the narrow cobbled lane. The dummy that Borg mistakes for a pedestrian was constructed from a balloon and a silk stocking. All the walls and floors had to be painted a pure white to achieve the glare required by Bergman.

In *Wild Strawberries*, Bergman strove to reconcile age and youth – Isak Borg on the one hand and, on the other, his daughter-in-law, Marianne (Ingrid Thulin), the feisty, pipe-smoking hitchhiker Sara (Bibi Andersson) and Isak's boyhood crush, also named Sara. Yet the everyday sequences involving the young people remain far less persuasive than the dreams experienced by Borg. Bergman's vision of the young Sara is just too ardent, too cheerful, too quaint. Her dialogue with her hitchhiking pals Viktor and Anders has a naive ring to it in comparison with the tautness of the exchanges between other characters in the film. Throughout his career, Bergman was much more at ease in the past than in the present. Personalities such as the contemporary Sara here, or the homosexual played by Gösta Ekman in *Face to Face*, are contrived to the point of embarrassment.

Victor Sjöström as Isak Borg revisiting his youth in *Wild Strawberries*.
Copyright © AB Svensk Filmindustri 1957. Photo by Louis Huch.

In *Wild Strawberries*, the true parallels with Bergman's own life emerge with alarming conviction within his dreams. The Sara of Isak's youth marries his brother Sigfrid, a sneering, patronising individual much akin to Bergman's elder brother Dag. 'You know so much, and you don't know anything,' says Sara, as she holds a mirror up to his trembling features. Bergman's men and women abhor the mirror; it reflects the truth that they are unwilling to accept. As Denis Marion has observed, facial expressions and bodily behaviour are more suggestive of inner feelings than the words pronounced by Bergman's characters.[16]

The dream in which Isak must confront his wife's infidelity on 1 May 1917 is a reference to Karin Bergman's affair with a young man named Tomas at the same time (and described in Bergman's later screenplay, *Private Confessions*). The flashbacks to the Borg family's summer villa mark an affectionate reconstruction of Bergman's own summers on Smådalarö in the years before World War II. In fact, the house used by the unit was outside the resort of Saltsjöbaden, but the spotless tablecloth, the sparkling appointments, the bickering among the relatives and the aunt's dominance all evoke the world in which Bergman grew up.

En route for Lund, where Isak will receive his honorary doctorate, the car is involved in a collision with a Volkswagen. Alman and Berit – husband and wife – tender their apologies for careless driving. Their hideous relationship obviously resembles Isak's own marriage, and in large measure that of Bergman's parents. The sparring between these two pathetic creatures matches some of Strindberg's clashes, where married life is depicted as 'a war to the knife'. When, at last, Marianne stops the car and insists that they leave, Alman and Berit stand together in the empty road, shackled like so many Bergman couples by their own vulnerability and mutual loathing. As Mummy says in Strindberg's *The Ghost Sonata*: 'Crime and guilt and secrets bind us together, don't you know? Our ties have snapped so that we've slipped apart innumerable times, but we are always drawn together again.'

Wild Strawberries concludes on a note of serenity and acceptance. Isak, having been honoured by the university in Lund, falls asleep, under the illusion that Marianne and his son have agreed to resume their marriage. He lets his mind glide back yet again to childhood in the archipelago. Sara leads him to a slope overlooking the inlet, and his father and mother wave to him kindly from across the water. Bergman has said, 'We go away from our parents and then back to our parents. Suddenly one understands them, recognises them as human beings, and in that moment one has grown up.' Bergman showed his own sympathetic awareness of that past by casting Else Fisher as the mother, glimpsed in long shot in that final sequence, and their daughter, Lena, as one of the fractious twins in the Borg household.

Wild Strawberries won the Golden Bear at the Berlin Film Festival in 1958, and was acknowledged around the world as the seal on Bergman's career to that point. Some months after the opening of the film, Bergman was in Dalarna and met a childhood friend, who told him that while he was watching *Wild Strawberries* he 'began to think of Aunt Berta, who was sitting all alone in Borlänge. I couldn't get her out of my thoughts and when my wife and I came home, I said let's invite Aunt Berta over at Easter.'[7] That, said Bergman, was the best review he had ever had.

As Bergman's films became more assured, so the affinities with Strindberg grew clearer. *The Seventh Seal* shares common ground with *The Saga of the Folkungs*. The plague rages in both dramas; flagellants scourge themselves and one another; the Kyrie eleison sounds like a last trump. Bergman presents historical characters, as did Strindberg, as more than mere figures of heroic myth and legend. *Wild Strawberries* exhibits the same tightly woven texture of dream and reality as Strindberg's *To Damascus* and contains two characters – Alman and his wife – who are the spiritual heirs of the Captain and Alice in *The Dance of Death*. Forever bickering, they aggravate each other and everyone within range. 'But we're welded together and can't get free!' cries Alice. The couple chained together in misery, locked in a combat that only death can resolve, is a theme that runs vividly through the work of both Strindberg and Bergman. Marriage is, at best, 'a pact between friendly warriors' (*Creditors*) and, as a result, the partners gradually began to resemble each other. In *Creditors*, the notion of the wife's second husband amounts to a blend of the first husband *and* her. In Bergman's *Hour of the Wolf*, Liv Ullmann as Alma suggests that 'a woman who lives for a long time together with a man at last comes to be like that man'. Martin

Lamm, whose lectures Bergman attended, noted the tautness of Strindberg's *The Father* in terms that apply also to Bergman's later films: 'A compact and simple structure, a small cast of characters, an action limited almost entirely to the moment of catastrophe, intensified pathos, and the universal sense of the tragic.'[18]

———

Distribution of Bergman's films outside Scandinavia proved sporadic and, at first, not altogether successful. An enterprising distributor from Uruguay had discovered Bergman's early films and had released some titles in 1953. *Summer with Monika* opened in West Germany and Austria soon after its domestic release, and by 1954 *Cahiers du cinéma* in France was singing the praises of Bergman and Harriet Andersson. But distribution in the United States, the largest and most important global market, did not gather momentum until the late 1950s. Cy Harvey, a partner in the fledgling art-house distributor Janus Films, was visiting Paris in 1956, when he discovered that *Summer with Monika* was 'playing in an exploitation theater, dubbed in French, in Montmartre, with all the young ladies of the night padding in front of the theater!'[19] William Becker, later co-president of Janus, noted that the early Bergman titles were shown mainly by exploitation exhibitors. 'There was one fellow up in Connecticut who shot a bunch of footage of naked girls on a lake, and he cut more or less the same footage into three or four different Bergman films [including *Sawdust and Tinsel*, which he dubbed 'The Naked Night']. He thought they did not contain enough nudity. When Janus got these movies, they all had to be gone through carefully, and the interpolations removed.'[20]

Smiles of a Summer Night opened in the US through Rank Film Distributors in late 1957, but the Bergman bandwagon gathered momentum only when Janus began releasing titles such as *The Seventh Seal* and *Wild Strawberries* in prestige art houses across the nation. 'An uncommon and fascinating film,' wrote Bosley Crowther of *The Seventh Seal* in the *New York Times*. Archer Winsten in the *New York Post* found it 'wholly extraordinary, being at once mystical, realistic and poetic. It stands in the company of the great foreign films.'

———

Despite Bergman's assertion that his life with Bibi Andersson was approaching its end, the actress continued to bloom in virtually all his films and stage productions of the period: *Wild Strawberries, So Close to Life, The Magician* and *The Devil's Eye,* and *The Misanthrope, Sagan* and *Faust* at Malmö City Theatre. According to Bibi in her autobiography, the relationship ended only in the spring of 1959, when Bergman met his fourth wife, Käbi Laretei. And in the late autumn of 1957, Bergman first made the acquaintance of Ingrid von Rosen, who some fourteen years later would become his fifth – and final – wife.

10

THEATRE AS WIFE, FILM AS MISTRESS

Even in the midst of such a hectic working schedule during 1956–8, Bergman attended diligently to his workbooks and his private diary. It may be true that keeping a diary is a form of vanity, narcissism even, but for Bergman his workbook served as a private conversation between him and his doubts and his ideas. There would be gaps in the narrative, of course, and during and after the shoot of *Wild Strawberries* he did not write in his workbook. In November 1957, he developed the idea for a screenplay entitled *Gillis's Revelation* (*Gillis uppenbarelse*), about a young priest coming to Stockholm from the provinces, but it never bore fruit.

During November and December 1957, Bergman applied himself to directing *So Close to Life* (*Nära livet*), from a screenplay by Ulla Isaksson. Bergman had been friends with Isaksson for some time and had been intrigued by her novel about witchcraft trials. They resolved to collaborate in some way, and when Bergman wanted to settle an old commitment to Nordisk Tonefilm, he proposed *So Close to Life*, which stemmed from a short story by Isaksson entitled 'The Aunt of Death'.

So Close to Life is the first of those Bergman films in which dialogue and characterisation take precedence over scenery and locations. *The Ritual, From the Life of the Marionettes* and *After the Rehearsal*, three later works, belong to the same category. For all its refined craftsmanship and consummate acting, *So Close to Life* lies in the margin of Bergman's work. In form, it resembles a play. One main set: the maternity ward in a Stockholm hospital. An opening crisis: Cecilia arriving after a miscarriage. A dramatic conflict with links to an unseen outside world: Hjordis's relationship to her lover. And the climax: Stina's unexpected loss of her baby during labour.

In her preface to the screenplay, Isaksson writes, 'There is a secret with life, with life and death, a secret as to why some are called to live, while others are called to die. We may assail heaven and science with questions – all the answers are only partial. But life goes on, crowning the living with torment and with happiness.' Bergman felt drawn to this apparent lack of discrimination between survival and extinction. When Stina (Eva Dahlbeck), the healthiest and most radiant of the three women, wakes up after losing her baby, she listens to the doctor who stands before her both in judgement and ignorance, a dispassionate figure with affinities to Death in *The Seventh Seal*. 'On the threshold, life failed him,' he says, without a trace of sentimentality. Only nature knows why Stina, possessed of everything in life, suffers such a tragedy. The film demonstrates that, at this juncture, Bergman was as ashamed by childbirth as he was by death. He had already fathered six children, and three more awaited him in the years ahead.

The men involved in *So Close to Life* are shown as insensitive, crass and patronising. Each reflects something of Bergman's own behaviour as a father. Cecilia's husband, Professor Ellius (Erland Josephson), tells her with an aloof and ingratiating smile: 'Ellius expects his wife to do her duty.' Hjördis pleads anxiously with her unseen boyfriend to acknowledge his responsibilities. Only Harry (Max von Sydow) appears tender and solicitous; but behind the smiles and the flowers he brings to Cecilia lurks a naivety reminiscent of the marriages in *To Joy* and *Waiting Women*. The ward sister is the personification of goodness and understanding, and helps to reconcile Hjördis with her mother. She is played by Barbro Hiort af Ornäs, one of Bergman's earliest girlfriends, for whom he retained a warm affection.[1]

Hjördis was a role created by Bergman for Bibi Andersson. She does not figure in Isaksson's original story. With her rebellious spirit in the wake of a stern upbringing, her fragility and femininity at odds with her shield of resolution and indiscretion, Hjördis embodies many of the traits of both Bibi and Bergman. She seeks an abortion because her lover refuses to marry her; she even loathes the fact that her pregnancy deprives her cigarette of its taste. Yet beneath this disgust for the business of reproduction Hjördis continues to be allured by the image of an untroubled domestic life. She offers unstinting help to her fellow patients. She talks with Cecilia (Ingrid Thulin), and in one of the film's few concessions to lyricism, she brushes Stina's hair and applies her make-up.

Although the hospital may, by definition, be a place of succour, to Bergman it represents a hostile zone. Throughout the film, he lays stress on inanimate objects, such as surgeon's gloves and electric clocks. The only music comes from a radio in the sister's room. The corridors are deserted and inhospitable, a token of barren emptiness. *So Close to Life* looks like the sort of film that Bergman would have made for television a decade later. It relies on few of the traditional advantages of the big screen. No special effects, no exotic characterisations, no 'masks', no flashbacks. For the purposes of documentary realism, Bergman shot much of the film in Karolinska Hospital in Stockholm, where he himself had languished earlier in the year. Upstairs, his sister Margareta was having a daughter, Rose; when Bergman heard about his new niece, he sent up a huge bouquet of roses.

So Close to Life opened in Stockholm in March 1958 and met with excellent reviews. Carl Björkman in *Dagens Nyheter* even hailed it as Bergman's 'best film and indeed one of the best films ever produced in Sweden'. At the Cannes Festival two months later, the reception was equally warm, and news of the special acting award given to the four principal actresses cheered Bergman while he lay in bed in Sophiahemmet and wrote the screenplay of *The Magician*.

Bergman and two members of his cast – Max von Sydow and Bibi Andersson – had to shuttle between Stockholm and Skåne for the final rehearsals and opening of *The Misanthrope* at Malmö City Theatre. The premiere of Molière's play took place on 6 December, and dazzled reviewers and audiences alike. Nils Beyer in *Morgon-Tidningen* hailed it as 'the finest Molière presentation that has appeared on a Swedish stage in our lifetime'.[2] Henrik Sjögren, in *Kvällsposten*, congratulated Bergman for 'the finest, richest, and most sensitive production that the Malmö City Theatre has ever shown'.[3]

The violent rebellion of Alceste (Max von Sydow) against the confines of seventeenth-century society was embellished by

Max von Sydow and Gertrud Fridh in Bergman's production of Molière's *The Misanthrope* at Malmö City Theatre in 1957. *Courtesy of Malmö Opera. Photo by Alice Stridh.*

Bergman's use of splendid and elaborate costumes. It was not difficult to perceive a connection between Bergman's production of *The Misanthrope* and the 'angry young men' of the British stage at that point in the decade. Nils Beyer extolled Gertrud Fridh as Célimène, who, 'switching with stunning self-control from ploy to ploy, showed what a brilliant comedienne she could be – now soft, evasive, feline; now captivatingly abusive; now murderously swift in riposte'.

Sooner or later every director lets slip a comment that will brand their career. In 1950, Bergman declared that 'the theatre is like a loyal wife; film is the great adventure, the costly and demanding mistress – you worship both, each in its own way'.[4] Twenty years later, he cheerfully recanted. 'Forget it – now I'm living in bigamy,' he told me in 1971.

Max von Sydow felt that subtle links existed between Bergman's films and stage productions during the 1950s. In *The Misanthrope*

– and not just in von Sydow's performance – may be discerned the seeds of *The Magician*, where Vogler, like Alceste, is mocked, exposed, and then – in a flourish of dramatic licence – vindicated. In the next play Bergman produced, *The Saga* (*Sagan*), lie harbingers of *The Virgin Spring*, particularly in the notion of the spring and the supernatural properties contained within it. Hjalmar Bergman, who wrote *The Saga*, was inspired by a spring in which a young woman had drowned herself over a century earlier because her lover had abandoned her. The play was written in 1919–20 but received its first performance only in 1942; it embodies all Hjalmar Bergman's talent for condensing action and deploying a poetic, even ardent imagination. Bibi Andersson played The Saga in Ingmar Bergman's production in Malmö (and again when he revived it in Stockholm).

Bergman relied on his ensemble of players to make up the cast of each new film. There was a practical consideration, too: the actors were paid for only part of the year by Malmö City Theatre, so it was important for them to work in the summer months. Some of these actors would pursue an international career – notably Max von Sydow, Ingrid Thulin and Bibi Andersson.

An annual ritual had been established. Bergman would write his screenplay in the spring, send copies of it to his principal performers and technicians, and often travel up to Dalarna. Several of those involved in the production would gather alongside Bergman at the Hotel Siljansborg, near Rättvik. There the details of the script came under discussion, as well as Bergman's objectives. Max von Sydow recalled how he was approached by Bergman to play the part of Vogler in *The Magician*: 'I'm thinking about a film about a magician who no longer believes in his powers. Would you be interested in that role?' Once Max had accepted, he was sent the complete screenplay.

On 28 February 1958, Bergman confided to his workbook that he would embark on the story of a 'hypnotist', and called it, at first, *The*

Charlatans, and then *The Face* (*Ansiktet*). Although this title would be retained by distributors in Europe, Janus Films in the United States persuaded Bergman and SF to change it to *The Magician*. This might give a clue to another source of inspiration: G. K. Chesterton's play *Magic*, about a conjuror forced to entertain some philistine guests at a duke's house, and which Bergman had staged back in 1947 in Gothenburg.[5] Dr Sture Helander once again recommended a stay in the clinic for his friend, and Bergman enjoyed his enforced isolation, 'all the more so because I don't feel ill in the least'.[6] He would sit on a chair in the silence of his room, with its white walls and a view of woodland beyond the window – an image he would use in *From the Life of the Marionettes* more than twenty years later. He could work on the new screenplay, while reflecting on the unexpected success of *So Close to Life* after its premiere in March. 'I think it's a decent piece of work, but bloody good it isn't. In fact, I find it rather boring.'[7]

Max von Sydow and Gunnar Björnstrand in *The Magician*.
Copyright © AB Svensk Filmindustri 1958. Photo by Rolf Holmqvist.

The Magician offered Bergman the chance to retaliate against some of the audiences at Malmö City Theatre – and the doctor, the consul, his overweening wife and the police chief who mock and seek to discredit the hypnotist, Albert Emanuel Vogler, all stand for the cynical critics and spectators so abhorrent to Bergman. The character of Dr Vergérus (Gunnar Björnstrand) was born, wrote Bergman, 'out of an irresistible desire to take a small revenge on Harry Schein'.[8] The film critic of the influential magazine *BLM* at the time, Schein would go on to found the Swedish Film Institute and remained a friend and ally of Bergman until his death in 2006. He was married to Ingrid Thulin at the time, which made the parallels even more intriguing.

A film audience cannot truly be measured, except in statistics concerning age and social standing; the individual filmgoers come into the dark screening room and remain well behaved throughout, rarely applauding or booing at the end of the projection. Theatre audiences, however, become an integral part of the atmosphere of each stage performance. Bergman could not help but be aware of their sneers and sniggers as he prowled around backstage. Most of his productions in Malmö met with ecstatic enthusiasm, but as Bergman often said, you remember the bad reviews more than the good. It is not surprising, then, that underlying the Gothic intrigue of *The Magician* was Bergman's persistent fear of humiliation.

Vogler, the 'magician', is caught in the grip of a paradox. He makes his living from cajoling and diverting his public and yet stands at the mercy of its ridicule and disdain. Arriving one night at the gates of the capital in 1846, he is held under house arrest and interrogated with his troupe by the local authorities. Vogler, like Egerman in *Smiles of a Summer Night*, wears a beard as a mask of protection. Like any mask, it attracts a suspicious gaze instead of evading it. (Bergman made a habit of letting his beard grow until shooting on a film was completed.) Vogler remains silent before his inquisitors, just like Mrs Vogler, the actress in *Persona*. Bergman's Austrian aunt Caroline bore the family name Vogler.

From the first instance they clap eyes on each other, Vogler and Vergérus are locked in battle. They accept that they are opponents and that each possesses part of the other – and furthermore Vergérus is jealous of Vogler's wife, Manda. Reduced to its simplest state, their duel is that of religion versus rationalism. Bergman is not unsympathetic towards Vergérus, an analytical realist as dubious of scientific facts as Vogler remains aware of the flimsiness of the illusions he creates. Vergérus will be tortured by Vogler in an attic room with a series of ghoulish deceptions and legerdemain. 'Miracles don't happen,' he tells Manda. 'It's always the apparatus and the *spiel* that have to do the work. The clergy have the same sad experience. God is silent and the people chatter.'

Bergman delights in deluding his own audience even as he unmasks Albert Emanuel Vogler in the film. He does so by resorting to unashamedly theatrical effects. During the attic sequence, in which Vergérus dips his pen into an inkwell containing a human eyeball and is shocked by the appearance of a dismembered hand, the camera movements and editing rhythm are wholly subjective, compelling the spectator to identify with Vergérus. The arrogant doctor in *The Magician* is forced to his knees, like Albert in the circus ring in *Sawdust and Tinsel*. Again, the theme of God and the Devil may be discerned: one part of Vogler is compassionate towards Spegel, the dying actor he meets in the forest; the other revels in a sadistic abasement of Vergérus in the attic. Or again, for the consul's wife Bergman is a saviour, while for Antonsson, the coachman, 'a face like Vogler's makes you furious, you want to bash it in'.

Without his disguise, Vogler is helpless. 'I liked his face better than yours,' smiles Vergérus. 'I've never seen you before!' cries the consul's wife, Ottilia, who had sought to seduce Vogler in her boudoir only the previous night. But the humiliation is peremptorily dispelled by the arrival of a royal proclamation summoning Vogler to appear before the king on 14 July (Bergman's birthday!).

As late as early June, the ending of the film had still perplexed Bergman, and the solution was inspired by an unexpected grant he received from the King's Fund, which impressed his parents enormously. The cobbled street up which Vogler in his coach vanishes in jubilation was found by Bergman in the Skansen open-air museum in Stockholm, with its replicas of the past constructed for the inquisitive eyes of tourists.

The shoot for *The Magician* ran from 30 June to 27 August, 'when the summer vacation was over and it was time to return to the theatre'.[9] Bergman's voracious, insatiable need for an audience sustained his growth and development as both artist and entertainer. When Gunnar Björnstrand arrived at the studio one morning suffering from migraine, he and Bergman agreed to proceed with a close-up, to register the extra tension and pain in Vergérus's features.[10] Such are the exigencies of art – and truth becomes illusion as clearly as vice versa.

———

The stage and costume designer Kerstin Hedeby earned fewer accolades than Bergman's other colleagues at Malmö, chiefly because she did not work on his films as much as other members of the City Theatre (although she acted a small but devilish part in *Dreams*). Her sets and costumes contributed enormously to the impact of Bergman's stage productions, and in *Urfaust*, which opened on 17 October 1958, she surpassed herself. The garments were reminiscent of fourteenth-century German paintings, while the basic set consisted of Gothic arches adorned by a Madonna on one side and a gargoyle on the other. Hedeby was married to Toivo Pawlo, who played Mephistopheles in this production.

Goethe's first, youthful draft of *Faust*, usually referred to as the '*Urfaust*', was divided into twenty scenes by Bergman and presented Faust as a philosopher–lover – 'a cross between Romeo and Hamlet', wrote the anonymous correspondent of the London *Times*.

The opening of the play was enthralling even by Bergman's standards. The house lights dimmed until the theatre, with curtain up over the huge apron stage, lay in pitch darkness. Then a single spotlight from high in the auditorium picked out the face of Max von Sydow's Faust, as he entered from stage right. The effect was that of a head floating in space, a cinematic device and a harbinger of the brilliant lighting that distinguished the entire production. Minor characters loomed as silhouettes against the backdrop; livid greens and reds prevailed among the costumes (with Mephistopheles in a scarlet cloak); props were sacrificed in favour of pantomime in certain scenes. Lennart Olsson pointed out that Bergman had a tendency to find the right sound, especially at the beginning of his productions, so as to get a grip on the audience. He nearly always started with the auditorium in darkness, then curtain up, stage dark, next the sound starting somewhere, a very specific sound, and finally the light very slowly coming up on the stage.

Gunnel Lindblom, 'austere and honest and magnificent' (Bergman's words), played Margareta, condemned to die in prison after her illegitimate child was born – and died.[11] Her erotic presence is wedded to a fine sense of tragedy as she gazes with horror into the face of Mephistopheles, who bends over her saying, 'Judgement has been pronounced,' and she perceives in his features those of her beloved Faust. Another outstanding performance was that of Gudrun Brost playing Martha, the inamorata of Mephistopheles.

In theme, there were affinities between *Urfaust* and *The Devil's Eye* (Bergman's 1960 film, in which Don Juan makes a pact with the Devil). In visual texture, however, the stage production displayed close ties with *The Magician*, with Max von Sydow's facial make-up almost identical and the lighting hard and expressionistic.

The final three months of 1958 were among the busiest in Bergman's career. *Urfaust* premiered on 17 October; his revival of Olle Hedberg's play *Rabies* aired on television on 7 November; his last production at Malmö City Theatre – *The People of Värmland*

– opened on 19 December; and a week later *The Magician* was unveiled at Röda Kvarn cinema in Stockholm.

In November, Bergman and Victor Sjöström were awarded Gold Plaques by the Swedish Film Academy. 'Now I've received all the prizes that exist,' sighed Bergman. 'All that remains is for someone to stuff me and place me in a showcase in a film museum.'[12]

The People of Värmland is a folk comedy by F. A. Dahlgren, 'a sort of village *Romeo and Juliet*, padded out with songs and popular anecdotes'.[13] As well as Max von Sydow and Bibi Andersson in prominent roles, the presence of Åke Askner, a popular star of operetta, gave the Malmö audience something to cheer. But, as Henrik Sjögren wrote, 'The laughter died away and stuck in the audience's throat when, in the end, Askner revealed how tragically and desperately empty is the liar's life-role. It was one of those magical moments one sometimes gets at the theatre.'[14] By slightly exaggerating the bucolic nature of the entertainment, Bergman set it in a perspective that enabled his satirical, but also affectionate, treatment to be appreciated.

11

NEW DIRECTIONS

The year 1959 marked a milestone in Bergman's work as well as in his private life. He and Bibi Andersson would part ways. He would divorce Gun Grut and marry his fourth wife, Käbi Laretei, who was to exert an enduring influence on his work. He would leave behind the glorious period at Malmö City Theatre and would not create any new stage productions for two years. During 1959 he would also change his cinematographer – from Gunnar Fischer, who had been at his side since the 1940s, to Sven Nykvist, who would become his soulmate behind the camera until his final screen production in 2001. He would shoot two features, *The Virgin Spring* and *The Devil's Eye*. Finally, his seventh child, a girl christened Maria, was born in secret to Ingrid von Rosen, married at the time to Count Jan-Carl von Rosen (who assumed the daughter to be his own).

By early 1959 Bergman's love affair with Bibi Andersson was over. It had been a singularly rewarding involvement. Bergman retained with Bibi, as he did with all the women in his life, a profound symbiosis. 'I must be able to exchange souls with my partner,' he said. 'The ones I've been together with for the other thing – well, I can count them on the fingers of one hand. And deep down I am faithful – though no one will believe it. My being is actually fidelity: all those whom I have grown fond of in some way, I am faithful to afterward." Bergman's influence, allied to Andersson's own determination and intelligence, succeeded in establishing Bibi as an international actress without, in any degree, subverting that first, fine, careless rapture of her youth. Throughout that great scene on the hillside in *The Seventh Seal*, when the Knight speaks to her of his unhappiness and spiritual confusion, Bibi's lines are stitched unaffectedly alongside the embroidery of the Knight's eloquence. Yet she is the catalyst, the force that gives the Knight courage to pursue his destiny. So it was with her and Bergman for more than three entrancing years.

Throughout March, Bergman suffered from knee problems and recurrent insomnia. He retreated to the Hotel Siljansborg in Rättvik and worked with Ulla Isaksson on the screenplay for his next film, *The Virgin Spring*. He declined an offer to become head of Stockholm City Theatre. He spent happy moments with his editor, Ulla Ryghe, and the new love of his life, Käbi Laretei, who practised her piano downstairs. He had met this elegant, accomplished woman at a rehearsal for Beethoven's Fourth Piano Concerto in the theatre auditorium in Malmö, during the summer of 1957. She was already renowned throughout Scandinavia, Europe and the United States as a pianist of high calibre. Her performance of Hindemith's *Ludus Tonalis* at Carnegie Hall, shortly before the composer's death, marked a high point in her career. She had style and wit and verve. Käbi's husband was Gunnar Staern, a conductor, and there was a four-year-old daughter named Linda. She and Bergman corresponded in secret, and by 10 January 1958 Käbi was calling him 'beloved Ingmar' and began her letters with the words 'Ingmar, *my* Ingmar'.[2]

Many a film festival invited Bergman to attend a premiere or a retrospective, and so often did he refuse that by the end of his life his reputation was almost that of a hermit, living apart from the world on his cherished island of Fårö. In fact, Bergman did travel quite extensively during his life. He belonged to a generation for whom the Far East, Africa and Latin America were exotic locations beyond the range of most tourists. He visited all the major countries of Western Europe, some more than once, as well as the United States.

When he agreed to accompany the Malmö City Theatre team to Paris and London with *Urfaust* in May of 1959, he had romantic reasons for doing so. But Bergman's visit to Paris, where *A Saga* was presented by the organisers of the Théâtre des Nations, left a sour taste, because the press had claimed – falsely – that he had dined with Jeanne Moreau after the performance. His dismal mood might have been due to his having to return to Sweden for a minor operation, before taking the plane for London with his facial scars not yet completely healed.[3] In London, Käbi performed at the Royal Festival Hall on the same evening as *Urfaust* opened in Peter Daubeny's World Theatre Season. The Swedish press pursued the couple relentlessly, their curiosity whetted by the fact that Käbi was still married. Bergman was more excited by the reception for the play. 'I was in the audience and the experience of their reaction was overwhelming. It was a miracle suddenly to understand these human beings who did not speak a word of our language and to feel the enormous, secret power of the theatre.'[4] On his return to Stockholm, Bergman wrote to Peter Daubeny, 'The days in London seem like a dream to me. Part of it was a nightmare and part of it was very, very pleasant.' He thanked Daubeny for arranging a 'quiet and fascinating evening together with David Lean and your charming wife [Molly]'.

Back in Sweden, Bergman again found refuge in Dalarna, and scouted locations for *The Virgin Spring*. Exchanging letters with Carl Anders Dymling, he first dismissed the idea that Hasse Ekman should direct *The Devil's Eye*. Bergman had agreed to make this comedy for SF as a form of insurance should *The Virgin Spring*, a potentially downbeat project from a box-office point of view, lose money. He also castigated the sound engineers sent to work with him by Aga-Baltic, who for years had been the main partner of Svensk Filmindustri where sound was concerned. Dymling responded by urging Bergman to shoot *The Devil's Eye* in the autumn, so that Hasse Ekman could use the studios to film his own project, *Falskspelet*, before the end of the year. Bergman was in a frustrated mood. The shoot of *The Virgin Spring* had been delayed by Gunnel Lindblom's suffering from appendicitis, and he had discovered that some of the prints of his films circulating in London were in poor condition and badly subtitled. SF's British agent, Cecil Cattermoul, whom Bergman had dismissed as 'an alcoholic old hippo', stoutly denied these claims.

———

The themes of God and the Devil, good and evil, Christianity and paganism, run like a watermark through *The Virgin Spring* (*Jungfrukällan*). Ulla Isaksson generated her screenplay from a medieval ballad, which originated in the Romance languages and assumed the status of a legend in the Nordic lands, about a young virgin, Karin, who is waylaid and killed by three brigands while riding to early Mass. In some versions of the legend, three girls are ravished, but in the province of Östergötland there exists a recorded incident involving the daughter of a farmer near Linköping who was kidnapped, raped and murdered by a group of vagabonds. The spring said to have welled up beneath the corpse of the dead girl still exists in the churchyard of Kärna parish and is thought to possess healing powers.

Bergman had been fascinated by the ballad, known as 'The Daughter of Töre of Vänge', since his university days. He first thought of transposing it to the ballet, then to the theatre. But finally he recognised that it had 'a filmic dimension'.[5]

Ulla Isaksson responded to the purity and rigour of the song, which falls into clearly defined segments and marches relentlessly along its appointed course. The dramatic and visual elements are foremost, creating the basis not only for a religious miracle play but also for a film in which Christian and pagan teachings are in conflict – just as in *The Seventh Seal* the atheism of the Squire is opposed to the yearning belief of the Knight.

Bergman encouraged Isaksson to preserve the archaic and primitive spirit of the original legend. Sweden had been converted to

Christianity long before the ballad emerged, but the Black Mass, a deliberate travesty of Christian ritual, began to percolate through Europe in the twelfth century, and weird sacrifices were performed behind closed doors on the farms of Dalarna and other Swedish provinces. During the 1950s, Bergman was drawn compulsively to this metaphysical and religious debate: 'I needed a severe and schematic conception of the world to get away from the formless, the vague and the obscure, in which I was stuck. So I turned to the dogmatic Christianity of the Middle Ages with its clear dividing lines between Good and Evil. Later I felt tied by it, I felt as though I were imprisoned.'[6]

It was a happy shoot, in part because of Bergman's burgeoning love for Käbi. His regular cinematographer, Gunnar Fischer, had been engaged by the Walt Disney company to shoot a feature in the far north of Sweden during the bitterly cold winter of 1958–9 and so could not join Bergman on preparatory work for *The Virgin Spring*. In his place Bergman took on Sven Nykvist, who had worked with him on *Sawdust and Tinsel*. Their understanding was immediate, and with the exception of Bergman's next project, *The Devil's Eye*, Nykvist would become a major element in the Bergman team.

Birgitta Pettersson found herself cast as Karin at the age of just twenty. She had been one of six pupils at the City Theatre's acting school in Malmö, and Bergman was on the jury as well as a teacher. He gave her a small part in *The Magician*. 'He was very kind to us students,' she recalled. 'Although he was not an old man at the time, he struck us as very wise, and he was always on our side in the big theatre.' Her ordeal on screen was made more palatable in reality because both actors who played the rapists – Axel Duberg and Tor Isedal – were friends of hers. She thanked Bergman for giving her the part, and on 26 October he replied with words of encouragement for her developing career: 'I *know* that you will become a very good actress, but, in the long run, you must work with all the calm and clarity and intelligence that you have in your heart.'

Gunnel Lindblom and Birgitta Pettersson in *The Virgin Spring*.
Copyright © *AB Svensk Filmindustri 1961. Photo by Rolf Holmqvist.*

He also wrote very enthusiastically about her performance in Arne
Sucksdorff's *The Boy in the Tree*. 'However, don't forget patience and
self-development. Both terribly boring but necessary and indispens-
able in the long run.'

Many exteriors were filmed at Styggförsen in Dalarna, not far
from Rättvik. The summer weather proved mediocre, and Bergman
recounted his feelings one rain-swept morning when he and the
crew were preparing an elaborate tracking shot through the forest. Just twenty-two people were present. The facilities were rather
primitive, and complex technical rehearsals were necessary.

Suddenly a break appeared in the clouds, the sun shone, and
Bergman elected to shoot. Then a colleague cried out and pointed
upwards. Two majestic cranes soared above the pine trees. 'We
dropped what we were doing and raced up to the crest of a small hill

above the stream in order to get a better view of the birds in flight.' Eventually, the cranes disappeared over the western horizon, and Bergman and his crew returned to work, invigorated by the sight. 'I felt a sudden happiness and relief,' he wrote in his diary. 'I felt secure and at home.'[7]

According to the script, the buds on the trees should have been just sprouting, but the leaves were too far advanced, and Bergman had to keep moving further north to new locations. In one scene Max von Sydow, as Töre, uproots a solitary birch tree as the first stage in his solemn cleansing and preparation for the slaughter of the three robbers. But although Sweden is literally covered with birch trees, no stretch of ground containing merely a *single* sapling or tree could be found. So Bergman took his actors and crew to a different area altogether, where, in an open field, they planted a tree. The sun was going down, and Nykvist waited for the evening light; when he viewed the rushes two days later he realised that everything was in silhouette – too much light had penetrated the film because the focus-puller had forgotten to close the camera. A fortnight later the scene had to be shot again.

Bergman did not attempt to pursue the American and Italian style of historical filmmaking, whereby every detail is minutely reconstructed. He relied on a few evocative touches to achieve a startling mood of verisimilitude. Karin, for instance, uses the surface of a cask of water as a mirror. Skins are strung for stretching on the walls, and Töre carries his cutlery in a pouch at his belt. Bergman also found a place for 'Jacob', the raven who had behaved so impeccably as a symbol of foreboding in *The Magician*, and who appeared in other films produced by the studio.

Gunnel Lindblom, who played Ingeri, the 'evil' foster sister of Karin who is misled by her credulous acceptance of pagan belief, had to lose eight kilos before the shoot began, even though she was pregnant at the time. Bergman insisted that she should look gaunt. Ingeri is perhaps the most intriguing character in *The Virgin Spring*.

Her worship of Odin, and her susceptibility to the sinister old man she meets at the mill race, suggests that she has an awareness of the diabolical. She finally confesses to her foster father, Töre, that 'I willed [the tragedy] to happen. They fell on her like devils.'

If Karin represents the unsullied beauty that, by its very nature, tempts the rapists, Töre embodies the Christian ideal of the Middle Ages. He is seen at first with his wife, Märeta (Birgitta Valberg), performing daily prayers beneath a wooden crucifix. His conduct, however, springs full-blooded from the Old Testament, and he has no compunction in putting the goatherds to death in brutal fashion. Töre gazes at his bloodied hands, and his fury drains from him. He leads his family and retainers in a precipitous journey through the forest to recover Karin's body. Now, he appears stunned, entranced. When Märeta declares that she loved her daughter too much, 'more than God Himself', her husband replies that she is not alone in her guilt. He had urged Ingeri to go with Karin; he acknowledges that he had been too proud of Karin, and had elevated her to an almost biblical symbol of goodness and virginity.

While his wife weeps over Karin's corpse, Töre is virtually struck to his knees by some abstract force. He stares skyward in supplication, uttering the words of baffled incomprehension common to such disparate Bergman characters as the Knight in *The Seventh Seal* and the pastor in *Cries and Whispers*: 'I don't understand you, God . . . yet I ask for forgiveness, for I know of no other way to live.' Immediately, after Töre vows to build a church of limestone and granite to atone for his sin, the spring wells up from beneath Karin's head. As a final act of absolution, Ingeri bathes her face in the fresh stream, thereby exorcising the evil that her summons to a pagan god had provoked.

For perhaps the final time in his career, Bergman emphasises the symbols of good and evil: the toad that Ingeri secretes in the bread for Karin's lunch; the shrivelled, sacrificial items cherished by the old man at the ford; the owl's squawking cry as the guilty herdsmen enter the farm by night; Töre's throne-like chair with its engraved images of saints; the self-flagellation of Töre in the sauna; his straddling the birch tree after he has uprooted it, his breath emerging in a groan of relief and fulfilment. Some years later, Bergman dismissed *The Virgin Spring* as an aberration. 'It's touristic, a lousy imitation of Kurosawa.'[8] He believed that by permeating the tale with the notion of therapy and redemption through sacrifice, he blurred and corrupted the original ballad and its stark outline.

Bergman's affection for Kurosawa and the Japanese cinema may be felt in the rhythm of the film, in the juxtaposition of bouts of action and allusive silence, and in the tracking shots that accompany Karin and Ingeri (and later Töre and his family) as they hasten through the forest. The moral ambivalence of the film recalls *Rashomon*. Bergman might have wanted his work to breathe a psychological complexity. But while in *Wild Strawberries*, *Persona* or *Hour of the Wolf* he succeeds in peering deep into the personalities of his major characters, in *The Virgin Spring* the simple fabric of the legend prevents him from dealing with the dramatis personae in anything other than emblematic terms. The most durable sequences enact the narrative tension of the original ballad – the ride through the forest, the rape and murder of Karin, and Töre's vengeance 'with unsheathed knife'.

—

On 28 June, with *The Virgin Spring* in the can and *The Devil's Eye* in pre-production, Bergman attended the confirmation of his daughter Lena, in the presence of his parents and of Else Fisher, Lena's mother.

With his divorce from Gun amicably settled, Bergman could marry Käbi Laretei (also now divorced) only two months after shooting *The Virgin Spring*. The ceremony took place in Boda Church in Dalarna on 1 September. A few close friends were invited, among them Ulla Isaksson, Sture Helander and Britt Arp, who ran the Hotel Siljansborg. The couple moved into a handsome villa on Ymervägen in the fashionable district of Djursholm. Just six days after the wedding, Bergman heard that *The Magician* had won the Special Jury Prize at the Venice Film Festival.

Although he had been engaged by the Royal Dramatic Theatre in Stockholm, Bergman had temporarily lost his passion for the stage. His stomach was troubling him, and he was furious with himself for having agreed to make a comedy for Svensk Filmindustri so soon after the arduous production of *The Virgin Spring*. 'I detest the idea', he admitted later, 'that some of my films, especially the bad ones, are going to survive.'[9] His irritability showed in an exchange with the boss of Janus Films, Cy Harvey. Bergman wrote on 22 October urging him not to release *Dreams*, *Waiting Women* or *A Lesson in Love*: 'I find it very wrong and dangerous to present these films, which are of a remarkably lower quality than the ones now shown.' Harvey replied in defence of these titles, saying they had been well received critically in Paris and London: 'You certainly do not create films simply in order to make money, and we do not distribute your films solely for the profits involved.' Bergman wrote back contritely on 20 November: 'I was very happy for your letter and your [comments] made me a little more peaceful.' However, he disliked the dubbed version of *The Magician* that Janus had prepared: 'Dubbing is a grotesque and demoniacal process, which has no justification other than economic.' In fact, this dubbed version was released only outside the major urban areas in the US, and the film screened with subtitles in all the major cities and in seventy-five theatres in the New York area alone. Harvey reminded Bergman that *The Seventh Seal* had flopped when premiered in the US in early 1958: 'Yet now it is playing some theatres for the third time and doing better than the second and the first.' American critics including Andrew Sarris, Eugene Archer, Stanley Kauffmann and Hollis Alpert were all singing Bergman's praises throughout 1959. In France, the cradle of cinephilia, entire books had already appeared extolling the auteur virtues of the greatest Nordic director since Dreyer and Sjöström. In London, a 1959 retrospective of Swedish film, entitled 'The Passionate Cinema', included several Bergman titles at that point unknown in the UK.

The Devil's Eye (*Djävulens öga*) proved an unhappy experience in every respect. Apart from Bergman's nausea, there was not the burning desire between Jarl Kulle (as an arrogant, swaggering Don Juan) and Bibi Andersson (as Britt-Marie, the pastor's daughter) so necessary for the relationship to appear satisfactory. More serious, from a long-term point of view, was Bergman's friction with Gunnar Fischer. On the second day, when the unit sat in the screening room viewing the rushes, he pounced on Fischer for some error of lighting.

Next day, Bergman apologised – as he usually did – but he wounded Fischer by telling him that after working with Sven Nykvist on *The Virgin Spring*, he felt spoilt. The relationship had reached its end. Fischer had photographed a dozen of Bergman's films, and his powerful use of monochrome technique had contributed enormously to their reputation around the world. There was no violent quarrel, and in 1970 Bergman asked Fischer to shoot the credits sequence for *The Touch* – and paid him handsomely.

The Devil's Eye was based on a somewhat dusty Danish radio play, *Don Juan Returns*, written by Oluf Bang. Bergman found it in the archives of Svensk Filmindustri. At first glance, it is difficult to see what attracted him to the subject. In all likelihood, it was his desire to place on film some of his enjoyable staging of Molière's *Don Juan* at Malmö City Theatre in 1955. The fundamental conceit – Don Juan being despatched from Hell by the Devil, whose painful eye may be cured only if a woman's chastity is breached – is engaging. The dialogue, too, bubbles with irony and epigrams. During the opening scenes in Hell – a marbled hall where the Devil (the comedian Stig Järrel) struts about in dark business attire – some of Bergman's finest writing crackles with wit. The only blasphemous words refer to God and the Church, while Satan's noble and respected advisers are

Count de Rochefoucauld and the Marquis de Maccopazza, whose 'perversions in their time sent voluptuous shudders right up into the archangel's pinions'.

Up on earth, Bergman revels in his attack on petty bourgeois pretence. Don Juan takes aim at Britt-Marie (Bibi Andersson), the innocent daughter of a country pastor (Nils Poppe). Asked by his wife if he could ever forgive her infidelities, he replies solemnly, 'I must love you whatever happens.' He is not the only prisoner of staid convention in Bergman's world, and like Fredrik Egerman in *Smiles of a Summer Night* and Isak Borg in *Wild Strawberries*, he must undergo the painful experience of watching his wife embrace a lover.

Bergman's love affair with the young Bibi Andersson seems to echo in the tantalising relationship between Britt-Marie and Don Juan. Thus, Bergman scrutinises his own affections. His alter ego (with a receding hairline, like Bergman's at the time) is mortified at the end because his passion lacks feeling and simplicity. He can never ape the simple nuptial bliss of Britt-Marie and Jonas, her fiancé on earth.

Don Juan's final descent into Hell recalls Bergman's stage production of 1955, with the immense bearded statue thundering at the door and the Great Lover sinking into a mass of flames while the monumental effigy gazes on. The scene has been described by every major writer dealing with the legend of Don Juan, from Tirso de Molina to Lord Byron. In such moments Bergman can, with a snap of his fingers, blend the elements of the theatre with those of the cinema and create a frisson that stays in the mind longer than all the courtly dialogue.

Other parts of the film betray Bergman's lethargy. The storm around the pastor's house, for example, and the flames in Hell appear crude even by the standards of amateur filmmaking. Certain scenes are too attenuated and lack vibrancy. The entire film sports a misanthropic tone, even if redeemed with a final, deadly thrust to the heart of the bourgeois ideal: Britt-Marie tells Jonas on their wedding night that she has never been kissed by another man, thus denying her contact with Don Juan. The lie is sufficiently horrendous to cure Satan's stye! Far from being grateful, the Devil condemns Don Juan to dream of love and earth's unattainable paradise.

12

THE DISCOVERY OF FÅRÖ

The new decade began well for Bergman. Simon and Schuster, aided and abetted by Cy Harvey at Janus Films, proposed publishing four of his screenplays. Bergman had declined such offers, even in Sweden, up to that juncture. But Harvey, in a letter dated 5 January 1960, said, 'Let me assure you on two points: you will have complete artistic control of the book. Secondly, we will obtain the best terms for you that are possible.' Bergman agreed, and the book soon went into a second printing. By May, Bergman was asking when 'the money from Simon and Schuster will arrive? My wife wants a new lipstick and my secretary needs a fountain pen.'

On 8 February, Stanley Kubrick sent a letter to Bergman during the shoot of *Spartacus*: 'Your vision of life has moved me deeply, much more deeply than I have ever been moved by any films. I believe you are the greatest filmmaker at work today. Beyond that, allow me to say, you are unsurpassed by anyone in the creation of mood and atmosphere, the subtlety of performances, the avoidance of the obvious, the truthfulness and completeness of characterisation.' This must have cheered Bergman considerably when it reached him just a day or two after the Swedish premiere of *The Virgin Spring*. The Swedish critics assumed distinct positions vis-à-vis the film. For Carl Björkman in *Dagens Nyheter*, this was not just Bergman's best film to date, but one of the finest examples of Swedish art and poetry. Jurgen Schildt wrote in *Aftonbladet* that the film was 'a bit loose in its grip, and a bit jerky in composition'. Soon afterwards the much respected Olof Lagerkrantz (who would become editor of *Dagens Nyheter* that same year) launched a biting attack on the film, declaring that Bergman had manipulated his medium in order to achieve sensational effect. The graphic detail of the rape sequence shocked many Swedish viewers, although the censor did not cut the film for domestic release.

On 14 March, *Time* magazine featured Bergman on its front cover, seen against a backdrop of a Nordic forest, with a slinky blonde leaning against a tree. The profile resounded with characteristic hyperbole and alliteration: 'The Bergman boom fits into the cultural context of the times. His is a voice crying in the midst of prosperity that man cannot live by prosperity alone.' This marked the Swede's consecration as a major cultural figure of the period, and throughout 1960 the Janus offices were besieged with requests for prints of Bergman's films. On 22 April, Bryant Halliday, who ran the company with Cy Harvey, wrote to Bergman that *Wild Strawberries* was in its 32nd week in Los Angeles and a fortnight later reported that *Summer Interlude* had been re-released 'in its original version, exactly as you made it. The success is tremendous, and it is doing better than almost every foreign film now playing in New York.'

Although working full tilt on the screenplay for his next film (twenty pages at a single stretch on certain days), Bergman kept busy by dictating letters to Lenn Hjortzberg. He was becoming more excited by the business side of filmmaking, and on 15 July had the temerity to ask Cy Harvey, 'in strict confidence, how much Janus Films Inc. has paid to AB Svensk Filmindustri for the period 1/1 to 1/4 1960'. Harvey, of course, demurred, but the question seemed relevant to Bergman because Janus had persuaded SF to let the company take over distribution of his films in Canada as well as the United States. Janus also acted as agent in selling *The Magician* to parts of South America and the Far East. Bergman trusted Harvey implicitly. This might explain his rejection of Paramount's offer that spring to make a film on any subject he wished.[1]

Walter Wanger at Twentieth Century Fox wanted Bergman to direct a version of Albert Camus's *La Chute* in Sweden, in English. But on 14 July, his birthday, Bergman wrote back that his agency,

William Morris, had told him that Wanger 'had other and more important things to do'. They advised him he would have to take Cary Grant for the main role, and when he objected to that they suggested Laurence Olivier. Bergman had made up his mind to refuse any such offer: 'I lost my interest for William Morris Agency as well as for *La Chute* and American pictures on the whole.' Bergman then cancelled his contract with WMA. He told Wanger, 'If I am going to make a picture in a foreign language, I want to make it here in Sweden with my own crew and together with actors I have chosen myself (English or American ones doesn't matter, but they must be real actors).'

On 3 May 1960 he informed Carl Anders Dymling that he wanted to shoot *The Wallpaper* (soon to become *Through a Glass Darkly*) in colour. Ten days later, writing from the Cannes Festival, Dymling questioned the title of *The Wallpaper*, and suggested *Secret Games* instead. He had sent a cable to Bergman a day or two earlier, in English: 'Brilliantly written and deeply touching stop Letter follows but comments few and unimportant stop Well done Ingmar.' Once again Bergman's mentor had encouraged him when he needed it, for the script for *Through a Glass Darkly* differed dramatically from all his previous work.

Käbi's influence on Bergman's habits soon became apparent. She persuaded him to forsake the beret he usually wore when on location. He refused, however, to relinquish his leather jacket. 'It contained my past,' he grumbled. Käbi succeeded in claiming the jacket, but Bergman clung to his old car. 'I'm not letting the Volvo go; I'll hold on to that to my dying day.'² Bergman would give her bunches of yellow roses. On Sunday mornings he would bring her breakfast in bed, and they would chat and listen to music. They shared the same birthday, although Käbi was four years his junior. Bergman's relationship with Käbi constituted a significant phase of his life. On the one hand, it marked a return to the bourgeois world in which he had been reared. On the other, it awoke in him the need

Ingmar with his fourth wife, Käbi Laretei, in 1959.
Photo © Lennart Nilsson/TT.

for an altogether fresh approach to the cinema, an approach at once austere and distilled.

Three of Bergman's first four wives were involved in music: Else Fisher as a choreographer, Ellen Lundström as a dancer and choreographer, and now Käbi Laretei as a concert pianist. This only confirms the cardinal place that music occupied in his life and work. From the earliest films (*Music in Darkness, To Joy, Summer Interlude*) to the later works (*The Magic Flute, Autumn Sonata* and *Saraband*), music influenced either the content or the form of his cinema. He had presented Käbi with a harpsichord, on condition that she select and record some Scarlatti sonatas for *The Devil's Eye*. The film begins and ends with the familiar sonata in E major, and when Don Juan and Pablo emerge on earth, they are accompanied by another burst of Scarlatti.

Although some friends claimed that Bergman was a rebel who came home to the arms of the bourgeoisie when he married Käbi Laretei, the director never regarded himself as a fugitive from his well-upholstered environment. On the contrary, his films of the early 1960s are more 'revolutionary' in texture than any of those he made during his bohemian days in post-war Stockholm. During this period, his emphasis switches from one's place in the universe to the condition and validity of the artist in society, to a closer examination of human weakness and the mysterious labyrinth of the imagination. The concept of faith no longer obsessed him. His work henceforth would be devoid of the romance that always accompanies a tacit belief in a god.

As a foretaste of the new style he would adopt, Bergman directed a television version of Strindberg's chamber play *Stormy Weather*, which aired on 22 January 1960 and placed a strong emphasis on close-ups. He also received new impulses from another source – Käbi herself. Her love and knowledge of music impressed Bergman. He relished concerts, and collected records himself, but through Käbi he met many of the world's greatest musicians, striking up a stimulating acquaintance with Igor Stravinsky. 'I'd like to make films the way Bartók makes music,' he told his wife after she had played the Hungarian's Third Piano Concerto for him.

Their evenings were calm. Bergman urged Käbi to read aloud to him – Russian literature, including the Chekhov short stories, and musical biography were among the favourites. 'He would lie back on the sofa with his eyes closed,' recalled Käbi. 'If I accused him of falling asleep, he would recite back an entire passage parrot fashion!' She gave him a set of the Beethoven Quartets, together with the scores, and years later Bergman called from Fårö to say that he was still enjoying them.

The villa in Djursholm dated from 1907. Bergman described it as 'a wooden structure surrounded by an overgrown and impenetrable garden as big as Gustaf Adolf's Square. The kitchen is as huge as the one in *Miss Julie*, and the living room is the same size as a full apartment . . . In all my life I've never seen a house so reminiscent of a colossal circus wagon.'[3] Etchings by Hogarth adorned the walls.[4]

Bergman was struck by Käbi's attitude towards the press. She remained unconcerned by newspaper articles and reviews. Bergman would wake up early the day after one of her concerts and bring the papers into their bedroom in excitement, while Käbi preferred to sleep until the afternoon. He, on the other hand, devoured the Swedish notices after a premiere of one of his films; the foreign ones meant more to him. In the same vein, he would seek an immediate reaction from Käbi to any new screenplay, as soon as Lenn Hjortzberg had finished typing it up from Bergman's hand-written sheets.

In April of 1960, Bergman, almost by chance, alighted on the island of Fårö, the location that would, for the rest of his life, be associated with him and his films. He wanted to shoot *Through a Glass Darkly* (*Såsom i en spegel*) in the Orkney islands north of Scotland, but the studio winced at the financial and logistical challenge. Bergman then combed the Swedish coast for a possible location, and failed. When someone suggested Fårö, he agreed to reconnoitre the island, but still believed that the Orkneys would be the best solution. As the taxi took him and Sven Nykvist along the primitive roads and the raw, pebbled shoreline, Bergman felt that he had found 'my landscape, my real home'.[5] Fårö is divided by a slender strip of water from Gotland, a much larger island frequented by Swedes in summer. At that time, Fårö could not be visited by foreigners, and served as a restricted area for Swedish military exercises. Bergman found precisely the sites he had dreamed of; even the wrecked ship in the film was a Danish trawler that had run aground off the coast of Fårö during a blizzard in 1950.

By 12 May, the screenplay for the film had been completed during yet another sojourn at the Hotel Siljansborg in Dalarna. It was dedicated 'To Käbi, my wife'.

Fårö was not always tranquil. In the evening, the sheep made a din, and while Bergman was filming the 'play within a play' sequence at dusk, the army regiment in Fårösund blew the Last Post, much to the director's chagrin. But the crew and actors formed a cheerful group, eating together at night and then often watching films such as Jacques Tati's *Mr Hulot's Holiday*. ('It's the fiftieth time I've seen it!' Bergman exclaimed amid laughter.) For all the concentration on the task at hand, Bergman thought of his children, and especially Lena, the eldest. On 2 August he wrote that he was not sure that it would be possible to bring her to Gotland as accommodation on the island was limited, but he sent money for her rail fare and sundry

Gunnar Björnstrand and Lars Passgård amid the steles on the shores of Fårö in *Through a Glass Darkly*.
Copyright © *AB Svensk Filmindustri 1961. Photo by Rolf Holmqvist.*

other expenses. He was sorry that she was not doing well in German at school, although, he said, at sixteen one forgets quickly, as he himself had experienced.

Through a Glass Darkly was the first of seven films shot by Bergman on Fårö. Harriet Andersson remembered the shoot: 'We stayed at a youth hostel. Two in each room. The beds were tiny, like shoe boxes. The food was always good. Freshly caught fish, flounder, which were fried in butter, piping hot. It was delicious.'

Through a Glass Darkly opens with a quotation – containing the film's title – from St Paul's letter to the Corinthians: 'For now we see through a glass darkly; but then face to face: now I know in part; but then shall I know even as I am known.' The four characters emerge from the sea. They might be aliens. But soon the air is filled with the ritual chaff of family holidays, recalling Bergman's comment that as a youth he had rebelled against the 'atmosphere of hearty wholesomeness' in his home.[6] Each of the four is introverted. The daughter Karin (Harriet Andersson) suffers from schizophrenia and has just been discharged from a clinic. The father David (Gunnar Björnstrand) is a novelist who, since the death of his first wife, has pursued his career at the expense of the family. The seventeen-year-old son, Minus (Lars Passgård), has the typical teenager's self-conscious attitude to sex and resents the teasing of his older sister.[7] And Karin's husband Martin (Max von Sydow) conceals this longing for freedom beneath a Swedish stoicism and a somewhat patronising attitude towards those less capable than himself of coping with the anguish of life.

Bergman's exposition of the issues at stake is admirable in its terseness and simplicity during the early part of the film. David might have brought presents for his family, but they are unsuitable or mere duplicates of what they already own. And now he announces that he will be leaving them again, to conduct a cultural delegation to Yugoslavia. He is finishing another novel, and while, on the surface, he seems able to place his work ahead of his domestic ties, at root he feels shattered with remorse. Minus and Karin have conceived a small play with which to welcome their father's return. As he sits in the dusk, watching like Claudius in *Hamlet*, David recognises that Minus's portrayal of a magniloquent artist is modelled on himself. 'I am the ruler of my own kingdom, small and poor though it may be . . .' he intones. The artist loses his love because he dare not take the plunge into eternity to join the dead princess (played by Karin). The sacrifice might be easy, pronounces Minus; what is life to a *real* artist? But love seems not worth the sacrifice of a masterpiece. David, too, cannot forsake his notions of art for the warmth of family affection. 'I let David explore my aborted suicide in Switzerland during the time before *Smiles of a Summer Night*,' wrote Bergman later.[8] In Strindberg's *The Dance of Death*, Curt describes the Captain in words that might be applied to David in *Through a Glass Darkly*: 'He is actually the most conceited person I have ever met. "I am; therefore, God must be".'

Each of the four characters in *Through a Glass Darkly* reflects an aspect of Bergman's personality. David, the selfish writer who neglects his children. Karin, the schizophrenic daughter, obsessed with her health and susceptible to visions of God. Minus, the gangling teenage son whose frustration and inexperience in the shadow of his big sister mirror Bergman's distress at the hands of his elder brother, Dag. Martin, the obtuse husband who sleeps like a lamb and proves so inadequate in caring for his wife.

Here, at the dawn of a new decade, Bergman abandons his dogmatic concept of God as part of the Lutheran ethic in which he was steeped as a youth. Karin yearns for a godhead she can worship, a godhead greater than the emotions and ideals discernible in the everyday world. Her warped quest for the beneficence of a Christian God is emphasised in the crisis of the film. During a convulsive, orgasmic fit in the upstairs room of the cottage, she begs Martin to kneel beside her and pray – 'Even though you don't believe.' The reverberation of the helicopter arriving to bring Karin to hospital causes the door in the wall of the room to swing open. But the 'God' that emerges, so eagerly awaited, is according to Karin no more than a spider, a creature that seeks to penetrate her body. 'I had always dreaded spiders,' said Harriet Andersson, 'and could imagine it trying to consume my personality, consume me like a worm, and crawl over my body, face, and hands.'

As Bergman remarked some years later, *Through a Glass Darkly* is marked by 'the idea of the Christian God as something destructive and fantastically dangerous, something filled with risk for the human being and bringing out in him dark destructive forces instead of the opposite'.[9] In April, while writing the screenplay, Bergman had noted in his workbook, 'Love is life and loss of love is death, as I know from my own bitter experience.'[10]

The film concludes with a kind of litany in David's room. When he was down in the wrecked ship with Karin – and, in effect, being raped by her – Minus tells his father, 'Reality burst, and I tumbled out.' David responds to his son's plea for some proof of God's existence. He recites the lineaments of a new philosophy in Bergman's world: God is love, love in all its forms. 'I don't know if love proves God's existence, or if God Himself *is* love,' says David. But 'suddenly the emptiness turns into wealth, and hopelessness into life. It's like a reprieve from the death penalty.'

The environment dictates the mood of *Through a Glass Darkly*. The slender division between night and day affords no rest; only Martin, the most obtuse of the four, can sleep at all. During the early 1960s, Bergman's insomnia 'became chronic'. He referred to the 'hours of the wolf' between 3 a.m. and 5 a.m. 'That's when the demons come: mortification, loathing, fear, and rage.'[11]

The presence of the quiescent sea, the barren rock-strewn shore near the cottage, establishes a sensitivity of sound and image against which the slightest human foible or deviation shows up like a tremor on a seismograph. The forlorn, threatening wail of a foghorn accentuates the sense of space and desolation. The severe chords of

Bach's Cello Suite No. 2 in D minor bring a fresh tone to Bergman's cinema, and were yet another vindication of the influence of Käbi Laretei at that juncture.

The editing of the film occupied more than two months. Ulla Ryghe, who had learned the rudiments of film editing at Europa Film but who was still, by her own admission, inexperienced, worked late almost every night to correct her mistakes. Bergman arrived at the editing room at around 9 a.m. He could never be accused of being prodigal with his shooting. He would present Ryghe with about 26,000 feet of finished film, which had to be reduced to around 8,000 feet. He made his choice between different takes as soon as he saw the daily rushes. 'I have never worked', she said, 'with any other director who has given me so little material that has been at the same time so rich. One of the very important things Bergman taught me was, first of all, to edit a movie as it has been planned and shot. If you do that, then you have a structure, you have discovered the backbone of the film.'

The Devil's Eye opened to dismal reviews on 17 October, and five days later Bergman vented his spleen on Cy Harvey of Janus Films: 'If [*The Virgin Spring*] is going to be shown in America, it must be shown with a very clear marking of what has been cut from the original print.' He resented Carl Anders Dymling's acquiescing in Janus's proposed minuscule trimming of the rape sequence in order to satisfy the US censor boards. Three days later he added, 'I am not going to start a fight with Dr Dymling and I am not causing a scandal in America. But, dear Cy, if you are an honest man, please tell the press that you [will] show them a cut version of my picture.' Bergman knew by that stage that Dymling was suffering from cancer. So he was relieved to hear, in a letter from Cy Harvey dated 18 November, that Gunnel Lindblom and her husband, Dr Sture Helander, had seen *The Virgin Spring* on its opening night at the Beekman Theatre in Manhattan, 'and both said that the cut was so small that they hardly noticed it, and remember – what they saw was the New York version. In the rest of the United States the cut is even less.'

For his return to the theatre after a hiatus of almost three years, Bergman produced Chekhov's *The Seagull* at the Royal Dramatic Theatre. He had rarely gathered together such a distinguished cast: Eva Dahlbeck as Irina, Ulf Palme as Boris, alongside Christina Schollin, Aino Taube, Kristina Adolphson and Uno Henning. When it opened on 6 January 1961, few critics were in a position to see the links between this production and *Through a Glass Darkly*. The staging of the 'play within a play' in Act One was handled in a similar manner to its counterpart at the beginning of the film. The delicacy of nuance, so natural to Chekhov, proved harder for Bergman to attain. Ebbe Lind in *Dagens Nyheter* recognised that Bergman's strength lay in the strongly coloured scene, the bizarre, the unexpected clutch at the throat. Ivar Harrie in the tabloid *Expressen* charged Bergman with exaggerating and even caricaturing the personalities of the play. Chekhov and Bergman are joined, however, by their acknowledgement of the impossibility of love and the egotism of art.

Three months later, Bergman brought off a more striking coup – a staging of Stravinsky's *The Rake's Progress* at the Royal Opera in Stockholm. Set Svanholm, the great tenor and now director at the Royal Opera, had contacted Bergman and asked if he would direct something for him. They discussed *Otello* and *Don Giovanni*, but settled on *The Rake's Progress*, which Bergman had seen in Hamburg in the very early 1950s. The journey of Tom Rakewell and his bride-to-be Anne Trulove through the nether regions and eventually to the madhouse was one that took Bergman's fancy.

His staging was inspired, allowing the singers room in which to turn and manoeuvre without diminishing the acoustical impact of the music or the arias, and contrasting moments of silence with loud and tumultuous scenes. The costumes by Kerstin Hedeby were not the only reminders of earlier Bergman productions such as *Urfaust* and *Peer Gynt*. Curt Berg, reviewing the opera in *Dagens Nyheter*, expressed delight that Bergman 'has in his direction worked with almost the same chamber music method as Stravinsky. The entire production is *orchestrated* in accordance with the score.' (During rehearsals, a fire broke out at the opera house, but Bergman was comforted by the news that *The Virgin Spring* had won an Academy Award as Best Foreign Language Picture in Hollywood.)

Fourteen months would elapse before Bergman returned to the theatre. The cinema possessed him in the interval.

On 12 September, Dymling wrote to say that the ad agency Leo Burnett wanted Bergman to make some commercials for their client, Marlboro. On 1 October, Stina Bergman wired him that an American company was considering making a film from *The Saga*, providing he would shoot it in Sweden, from his own screenplay. 'My heart is pounding as I await your response,' concluded the telegram. Bergman confirmed that he would refuse the offer 'because I find it very difficult to think of *The Saga* as a film'. Nonetheless, the final weeks of 1960 brought the first real whiff of reaction against the Bergman bandwagon at home and abroad. The magazine *Chaplin* published a special 'anti-Bergman' issue, in which the most amusing article was nothing less than a sarcastic piece written by the director himself under the pseudonym of 'Ernest Riffe'.[12] His contemptuous dismissal of Bergman includes some damning accusations: 'In film after film he provides examples of his profound misanthropy and lack of contact with his surroundings. [...] He tells us nothing about ourselves and the life we live, or about God. He does not even tell us anything about his own insignificance or greatness. He is merely a frightening testimony to the terrible decline of our cinematic art.'[13]

Meanwhile, Bergman adopted a defensive tone towards Janus Films, who were reporting phenomenal attendance figures for *The Virgin Spring*, despite an initial panning by Bosley Crowther in the *New York Times*. After all the wrangling with the New York state censors, a mere twenty seconds had to be cut from prints screened at cinemas. Bergman, however, felt that his distributors had been guilty of 'complaisant prevarications' in their handling of the matter. He referred to himself in correspondence as 'an old Swedish prima donna director, who has only one passion: his work'.

13

A NEW LANGUAGE

In early 1961, a crisis developed at Svensk Filmindustri. Carl Anders Dymling, for twenty years the head of the group, fell mortally ill with cancer. There was confusion. No successor lay obviously to hand. Bergman joined some senior members of the company in a kind of interregnum. The studios, with 135 staff on the payroll, had to be used. So Bergman and Erland Josephson, using the pseudonym Buntel Ericsson, cobbled together a comedy entitled *The Pleasure Garden*, revolving around the elegant indiscretions of a schoolmaster – played by Gunnar Björnstrand – in a small Swedish town at the turn of the century. Bergman took an active interest in the processing of the Eastmancolor film, for Svensk Filmindustri had not made many productions in colour up to that point. Alf Kjellin served as director, and the film contained several amusing incidents, while the costume and production design were distinguished. In all other respects, *The Pleasure Garden* remains a footnote in Bergman's film career.

So, almost in spite of himself, Bergman became involved in matters of state at Svensk Filmindustri. Soon he had recommended the actor, producer and director Kenne Fant as Dymling's successor, and established a cordial relationship with him. Bergman would, however, become a portal figure at SF and an 'artistic adviser' in effect, just like Victor Sjöström during the 1940s. His room at the studios in Råsunda stood on the ground floor of the main building, its window facing the famous entrance gate. A visitor described it as 'furnished with impeccable Swedish good taste. A soft grey rug on the floor, a small divan covered with a moss green and grey blanket, a comfortable cane chair and, alas, three telephones. But on the walls, photos of only two people: Chaplin [. . .] and Victor Sjöström.'

Käbi Laretei recalled that, before their marriage, Bergman had never taken a holiday in the orthodox sense of the term. So they rented a house at the seaside, in a small place called Torö. Bergman loved the stunted, barren shoreline and the denuded landscape, an early harbinger of his devotion to Fårö. He had been struck by the idea for *Winter Light* (*Nattvardsgästerna*) during the Easter break. He had listened to Stravinsky's *Symphony of Psalms* on the radio and conceived a film somehow concerned with 'a solitary church on the plains of Uppland'.[2]

At forty-three Bergman still could not shake off the Lutheran dogma that had clung to him like a shroud since childhood. He would scratch and tear at it from time to time, and in the spring of 1961 resolved to make one final attempt to rid himself of doubt and angst. The germ cell of *Winter Light* can also be traced to May of 1961, when by chance Bergman had witnessed a funeral in Rättvik Church with about twenty mourners.[3] On 14 June, he first enunciated the idea for the film: 'A parson shuts himself up in his church. And says to God: I'm going to wait here until you reveal yourself.' Two days earlier, he had attended the burial of his mentor, Carl Anders Dymling: 'A boring, official ceremony without any religious or spiritual atmosphere [. . .] People were utterly silent as the earth was tossed over the casket.'[4] During the weeks that followed, Bergman wrote most of the script for *Winter Light* on Torö. Once a week he drove into the city for meetings at Svensk Filmindustri, working through the pile of letters or keeping an eye on production plans.

Another impulse for the film dated back to the previous autumn, when, after Bergman and Käbi had married, they returned to the church in Boda to see the pastor. There they learned that a small girl's father had committed suicide, in spite of the pastor's efforts to support him. The death of Jonas Persson in *Winter Light* derives from this incident. There might also have been a recollection in Bergman's mind from his play *The Day Ends Early*, in which

Pastor Broms finds that his faith is too weak to dispel his fear of death. The obsession with eczema, described by Märta in the film, sprang from Bergman's second marriage. Ellen Lundström had, he claimed, suffered from allergic eczema. Ellen denied this in her unpublished memoirs, saying that she contracted the disease only much later.[5]

While still writing the script, Bergman drove around the country churches in Uppland, north of Stockholm, accompanied by his father. He wanted to absorb the atmosphere of the small buildings, with their simple, unadorned architecture and spartan interiors. He inspected the organs, which always appealed to him, in particular the small eighteenth-century models. Bergman had studied the organ in his youth, and continued to play it well into his senior years.

On 24 October, Bergman told Cy Harvey of Janus Films that 'the opening night of *Through a Glass Darkly* was a terrible trial and afterwards I became ill, but now we are about to start shooting *The Communicants* [*Nattvardsgästerna*] and work with great pleasure'. By that stage, P. A. Lundgren had reconstructed the interior of Torsång Church in the studios at Råsunda. 'It was a church in winter,' said Sven Nykvist, 'and there was no sun at all. There was no light coming in except from the cloudy sky, so we couldn't have any shadows at all. And we tried to make it look exactly like that.'[6] Double-X film had just become available in Sweden, and it enabled Nykvist to achieve a luminosity and density of image.

Much of the shooting for *Winter Light* was done on location in Dalarna, in the village of Finnbacka and in nearby Skattungby, with its church used for the final scenes. Bergman found the schedule demanding, and altogether principal photography required 56 days. Gunnar Björnstrand, playing the leading role of Pastor Tomas Ericsson, had to transfer almost without pause from his part in *The Pleasure Garden* to the rigours of shooting *Winter Light*, and his health cracked. Many thought he might die. Sture Helander, Bergman's physician, prescribed some pills, and they made Gunnar

Gunnar Björnstrand as the troubled pastor in *Winter Light*.
Copyright © AB Svensk Filmindustri 1963. Photo by Rolf Holmqvist.

feel even worse, and unusually tired into the bargain. Ironically, this state of health was ideal for the part.

The tension between Bergman and Björnstrand caused problems in the early days of the schedule. Bergman found himself waking at two in the morning with 'snakes in [his] stomach'.[7] But lighter moments occurred. Late one afternoon, worn out after shooting, Gunnar and Ingrid Thulin, playing Märta, traipsed off to a roadside cafe. They played a record on the jukebox and danced – Björnstrand still in his pastor's robe – provoking curious stares from the other customers. Bergman, meanwhile, satisfied his hunger with boiled ham and a fried egg, with a box of Droste chocolates and a packet of biscuits on the side.[8]

In the early stages of the script, Märta was the pastor's wife, not his mistress. She acts as a foil to Tomas's doubt and inertia. Their relationship is crumbling just as the pastor's religious convictions are under siege. Tomas's spiritual despair is corroborated by the problems of Jonas the fisherman and his wife; Jonas believes that the

Chinese have been brought up to hate people – soon they will possess nuclear weapons, and the world will be destroyed. 'God seems so remote,' the pastor tells them. 'I feel so helpless.'

Winter Light deals with what C. S. Lewis called 'the Problem of Pain'. Both Tomas and Märta suffer from heavy colds. Märta tears off her bandage to reveal hands stricken by eczema. The sexton, Algot Frövik, is a hunchback but bears his disability with courage and equanimity. Bergman, who in his workbook had described Frövik as an angel, noted, 'It's a terrible moment when Tomas realises that this man in his naivety has understood Christ far more deeply than he has.'[9] Thus, physical ailments become, as always in Bergman's cinema, the symbols of an inner, psychological malady.

When Jonas Persson commits suicide (offscreen) and Tomas views his corpse by the river bank, Bergman's camera makes plain the pastor's discomfiture through a series of long shots. The dull, fateful roar of the rapids and the spectacle of the frozen roads counterpoint Tomas's congealed attitude and unassuageable despair. It is indeed, as Märta comments, 'a Sunday in the Vale of Tears'. The tragedy triggers in Tomas a bitter determination to rid himself of his mistress. Alone with her in a school classroom, he launches into the most terrifying harangue in the film. He rejects Märta's offer of love. 'The real reason is that I don't want you,' he informs her with uncompromising bluntness. 'When my wife died, I died. She was everything you can never be.' The air grows full of pain and resentment; Tomas's speech rises like black bile, devoid of Christian understanding. Tomas begins to perceive the Church as a profession rather than a vocation. In these moments, Bergman seems to be freeing himself of the religious burden that his father's heritage had imposed upon him. When Tomas admits that he failed to see the terrible reality of the Spanish Civil War while attending a seamen's mission in Lisbon, it may be that Bergman was reflecting on his own purblind attitude to Nazi Germany in World War II.

Winter Light might be the most austere film in the Bergman canon, but it runs a mere 80 minutes and the editing is so rigorous that complex ideas and emotions are conveyed with remarkable fluency. In a single scene lasting more than six minutes, Ingrid Thulin as Märta, facing the camera in close-up, reads a letter she has sent to Tomas.[10] She cannot understand his indifference to Christ, but declares her love for him in spite of everything. *Winter Light* owes more to the Bible than any other Bergman film. The pastor's name, Tomas, refers to the apostle who doubted that the resurrected Jesus had appeared to the other ten apostles. Jonas in the Hebrew Bible fled from God and was swallowed by an immense whale. Märta was the sister of Lazarus, whom Jesus raised from the dead. 'Guess what has occurred to me!' exclaimed Bergman during the shoot. 'Märta Lundberg's eczema – it's placed on the stigmata spots. The hands and forehead, the hair-line.'[11] Some lines are taken directly from the scriptures: 'God, why hast Thou forsaken me?' asks Tomas, alone in the vestry, with its barred, cell-like window recalling the window of David's room in *Through a Glass Darkly* or the confessional in *The Seventh Seal*. The sexton utters the same phrase and talks at length about the Garden of Gethsemane.

In the closing scene, Pastor Tomas Ericsson indites the opening words he knows by heart: 'Holy, Holy, Holy, is the Lord God Almighty. The earth is full of his glory.' At last a line of communication somehow exists. Communication. Communion. The original Swedish title of the film means 'The Communicants'. Severe though *Winter Light* may be, the film is remarkable for Bergman's ability to discuss Christian issues at a time when the religious debate was in decline. Käbi's reaction was fair. 'Yes, Ingmar, it's a masterpiece; but it's a dreary masterpiece.'[12] Herbert Grevenius sent Bergman a postcard on 9 February 1963, hailing his 'incredibly bold movie'.

The Swedish critics were respectful, if reluctant to praise the film for anything other than its uncompromising quality. Jurgen Schildt in *Aftonbladet* complained that *Winter Light* 'moves at a snail's pace and barely gets there in the end. It discusses a problem, but from prepared viewpoints. It is simple, but the simplicity is seldom fascinating and almost never evocative.' Bergman, however, felt secretly relieved: 'With *Winter Light* I've closed the religious debate, and accounted for the result,' he wrote in his workbook. 'The film is a gravestone marking the end of a painful conflict that has plagued me throughout my conscious life."[13]

Even more than in *Through a Glass Darkly*, the camera in *Winter Light* replaces the mirror at whose reflections earlier Bergman characters had gazed in search of the absolute. From now on, Bergman addresses his audience more directly. There is no escape, either for the characters or the spectator. Music, for example, would have sounded vulgar in *Winter Light*. Yet the very structure of the film owes much to music. The tick of the vestry clock, like a penitential lash, the boom of the rapids, the noise of tyres on a snow-covered road make up the rhythm of the soundtrack. 'Film', Bergman would write in his introduction to the screenplay of *Persona*, 'is a language, the sentences of which are literally spoken by one soul to another and which escapes the control of the intellect in an almost sensual fashion.'

———

Filming on *Winter Light* finished on 12 December 1961. Next, Bergman found himself attracted to a burlesque film entitled *The Folktale*. It would feature traditional folk elements and star Naima Wifstrand as 'the princess who has grown old waiting for all the dull suitors' and Ingrid Thulin as a forest sprite, as well as the usual suspects Gunnar Björnstrand, Max von Sydow, Allan Edwall and Martin Ljung.[14] The idea never came to fruition, and two days after Christmas, Bergman jotted down his initial ideas for *The Silence* (*Tystnaden*). By 23 January, the first outline of the plot had emerged – two women, one of whom has a ten-year-old son, travelling in a foreign country. The title mutated from *Timoka* (the name of a city), to *God's Silence*, and finally *The Silence*.[15] Bergman also reflected that the screenplay grew out of Bartók's Concerto for Orchestra: 'the dull, continuous note, and then the sudden explosion'.[16]

Never averse to stealing from his past, Bergman plundered his radio play *The City* (first broadcast in 1951) for the setting – the visit to a city where the language is impenetrable, with long streets and silent houses. To this Bergman added his memories of a visit to Hamburg in 1946, where tanks still patrolled the streets by night, and of the gloomy hotel room in Paris where he had stayed with Gun Grut. He envisioned the room in *The Silence* 'as an island of reality in this stream of impressions'.[17] He even asked Gun to help with creating an alien language, as seen in newspapers or spoken over loudspeakers on the train.

While Käbi departed for a concert engagement in Stuttgart, Bergman threw himself into writing *The Silence*, mostly in his favourite retreat in Rättvik. 'Christmas wasn't particularly easy for either of us,' he wrote in his workbook. 'But despite everything, we're fighting for our marriage.' Soon after her return from Germany, Käbi became pregnant, and Bergman spent March and April at home in Djursholm completing his screenplay. 'O God, help me to hold fast. Not to be afraid. To do [the screenplay] right,' he scribbled in his workbook on 17 March. During the same month, press reports circulated to the effect that Bergman intended to turn his back on filmmaking for an entire year, devoting his energies to a study of the life and work of Johann Sebastian Bach. 'Once in a lifetime,' he was quoted as saying, 'one must try to realise one's dream and break away from the drudgery of everyday work.'[18] Käbi would join him in this research.

His sovereign position in Swedish culture came under attack in January 1962 from the young Bo Widerberg, who wrote a series of polemical articles in the newspaper *Expressen*, entitled 'Vision in Swedish Cinema'. The two had first met in 1953, when Bergman was head of the Malmö City Theatre and making *Sawdust and*

Tinsel. Bergman suggested to Svensk Filmindustri that they develop Widerberg's project *The Emperor of Capri.* Instead, they worked together on another idea, *Kissing (Kyssas),* but Carl Anders Dymling turned down the script, and this caused the bad blood between Widerberg and his would-be mentor.

In his later articles in *Expressen,* Widerberg castigated Bergman for prattling on about God in 'one of the world's least religious countries'. He condemned Bergman for his 'vertical', metaphysical vision of human problems, dealing merely with man's relation to God. Instead, declared Widerberg, 'more than ever we need a horizontal film, a lateral art'. Bergman replied in an open letter to Widerberg: 'Swedish film is today a burned-out land. If you can build something serious with us, that will last many years, then you are very welcome.'[19]

Throughout his adult life, Bergman had an uncanny gift for being alert to practical issues even in the midst of writing or filming. For example, on 3 April 1962, he told Cy Harvey that he had just signed a contract with Svensk Filmindustri for the next six years. Janus, riding high on the success of *Through a Glass Darkly* at the Academy Awards, continued to send prints of films to Bergman for his private collection; the arrival of De Sica's *Umberto D.* that spring made him especially happy.

He considered shooting *The Silence* partly in the French town of Grenoble, which he recalled as 'grimy and awful and lacking in culture: no culture at all, no theatre, only striptease'.[20] At first Bergman wanted his son, Lill-Ingmar, to play the boy in the film, before he settled on Jörgen Lindström.[21] He also wanted the part of the waiter with whom Anna (Gunnel Lindblom) has a one-night stand to be played by Thommy Berggren. But although the young stage actor accepted, he fell ill with acute appendicitis in London and had to be hospitalised.[22] The role was assigned to Bergman's friend of the 1940s, Birger Malmsten. The original idea called for Anna and the waiter to enter a church and make love in one of the crypts; perhaps feeling that to be too provocative, Bergman decided that they should copulate in a hotel room.

Another unspecified role may have been offered to Greta Garbo, who had visited Bergman at the studios on 4 January. 'Her voice is so nice and gentle,' he told Vilgot Sjöman. 'It has a quiet huskiness that makes it interesting. And her eyes! And a quiet sense of humour.'[23] But no part for a woman of her age materialised in the film.

While Ingrid Thulin as Ester in *The Silence* to a recognisable extent reprises her role in *Winter Light* – long-suffering, frustrated for want of love – Jörgen Lindström as her nephew is the first child character of any significance in Bergman's work. He was exactly the same age as Lill-Ingmar, and so Johan in *The Silence* received the attention from his director that Lill-Ingmar had in real life lacked. Bergman would occasionally spend a Sunday with Gun and Lill-Ingmar, and his half-brothers, and play with their model train set. He did the same with Jörgen Lindström when there was a break in filming. In *The Silence* Johan is the innocent observer, the one character not yet stunted and embittered by life. During the course of the film he escapes from his fatal subservience to his mother. He watches, and in sympathy with him the camera becomes a voyeur, peering and prowling, pausing before gliding this way and that.

On 15 June 1962, the technicians contracted for *The Silence* met Bergman in Rättvik. In the bridge salon of the Hotel Siljansborg, they discussed the problems the film might pose. 'There must not be any of the old, hackneyed dream effects, such as visions in soft focus or dissolves. The film itself must have the character of a dream,' Bergman told Sven Nykvist.[24] They decided to use Eastman Double-X negative, which could be developed to a higher gamma than usual. 'During the shoot,' recalled Katinka Faragó, 'Bergman slept very badly, because Käbi's pregnancy caused her to suffer from restless legs, and she had to walk around a lot at night.'[25]

Ester becomes the quintessence of bitterness and self-disgust. Anna, the body to Ester's spirit, radiates a lazy eroticism, whether drawing a pair of bangles off her arm and laying them with a subtle clink on a bedside table, or flicking open a lipstick as though freeing a penis from its pouch. Once arrived at their mysterious hotel, Anna seeks gratification in the town. At first she is repelled by the spectacle of a couple making love in an adjacent seat at a cabaret (a scene that fired the indignation of censors around the world), a scene made even more grotesque by being intercut with a display by a troupe of dwarfs on stage, cavorting like dogs to the command of their full-grown trainer.

Gunnel Lindblom in *The Silence*.
Copyright © *AB Svensk Filmindustri 1963. Photo by Rolf Holmqvist.*

While Anna is copulating with the waiter from a nearby bar, Ester remains in the hotel room, smoking, drinking some harsh spirit brought to her by the old retainer and listening to the radio. Then she masturbates. Onanism in Bergman suggests that a person's whole psyche has grown inward, feeding on itself instead of drawing nourishment from the outer world. From the window she sees an emaciated horse dragging a load of junk through the narrow street. The image counterpoints her own misery and meagreness of soul.

The barman behaves as a 'servant' to Anna in the same way as the elderly waiter in the hotel ministers to Ester's needs. Each bows reverently to his charge, the hotel waiter presenting Ester with a drink, and the barman bending lasciviously to breathe over Anna's calf and knee. The act of giving is achieved without speech, for the language of the strange country sounds impenetrable to the sister. (Bergman made it up himself, basing it in part on Estonian phrases and words. 'Timoka', for example, the name of the city, refers to 'the hangman' in Estonian; Bergman saw it on the wrapper of a book of poetry on Käbi's shelves.) Communication thus becomes spiritual – Ester drinks the glass of spirit with the reverence of a worshipper accepting the chalice – and carnal, flesh on flesh, slaking the body's desire. Bergman wanted to make a film virtually without conversation. Dialogue seemed less significant than the mood of a film, than the feelings between the sentences. *Winter Light* can be regarded as a literary film; *The Silence* cannot.

Music, too, forms a link between civilisations. When Bach's *Goldberg Variations* is played on the radio, Ester and the waiter both know the name of the composer. J. S. Bach is the only comprehensible term in the newspaper Anna scans in the cafe. (Bach wrote the *Goldberg Variations* for the young Johann Theophilus Goldberg to play at night to his protector, Count Keyserlingk, to alleviate the pain and insomnia caused by a serious illness.) Bergman was also, as noted above, inspired by Bartók. The sudden wave of tubercular agony that grips Ester recalls the unpredictable spasm of notes at the climax of the Concerto for Orchestra. As she clings to the bedstead and opens her mouth in a rictus of pain, sirens boom out over the city. The sound is harsh and dissonant, as imperious as the knocking on the door at the close of *Through a Glass Darkly*.

The Silence should not be considered in cultural isolation. Bergman, true, was involved in his *voyage au bout de la nuit*, but his film was modulated to the same pitch as other works by major directors in the early 1960s. Antonioni, for example, detected in the lethargy of the contemporary world a tendency towards spiritual dissatisfaction. Resnais, in *Last Year in Marienbad*, had chosen as his theatre a chateau with corridors as interminable as those in the hotel in Timoka. Robbe-Grillet and Beckett were two prominent authors who shared Bergman's impression that mankind was at the most aimless stage of his development (or retardation). The prosperity of the post-war period had led to a boredom and cantankerousness among the bourgeoisie. Material gains had been acquired at the expense of moral equilibrium. Society's goals were obscure; the individual felt at the mercy of an overwhelming laxity. Purblind and disconcerted, the ego rejected the outer world and writhed in on itself, unable to communicate with those around it. *The Silence*, made in a distant Nordic land, recorded with the accuracy of a sonar the echoes of this universal malaise.

Although from a strictly thematic point of view *Through a Glass Darkly*, *Winter Light* and *The Silence* might not constitute a trilogy, they are umbilically linked in terms of the severity and concision of their screen language.

During the shoot of *The Silence*, Bergman noted in his workbook that although he yearned to return to the stage, 'this is the best part of my life and I believe absolutely decisive for my continuing [to work]'.[26] Ever conscious of the importance of the American market, he told Cy Harvey he was open to suggestions for an alternative English title for *The Communicants*. He proffered two titles of his own: *The Unbelieving* and *The Incredulous*. Harvey responded by suggesting *Light in Winter*, and on 23 October Bergman writes, 'In my opinion it sounds better to call the film *Winter Light*.'

On 7 September 1962, Bergman's fourth son, Daniel, was born, and Bergman spent time at home filming him with a 16 mm camera – footage that he would later edit into a short contribution to the portmanteau production *Stimulantia* (1967). Despite this, Daniel would, decades later, agree with the German filmmaker Margarethe von Trotta, who said that Bergman 'was much closer to his own childhood than he was to his own children'.[27] On 16 December Ingmar's mother, Karin, reported in her diary that she and Erik Bergman had been to the villa in Djursholm for the christening of Daniel Sebastian: 'The music room was so beautifully arranged with a tall, candlelit Christmas tree, and the christening table right next to it.'[28]

14

ADMINISTRATOR, INNOVATOR

During the year 1963, Bergman's financial worries began at last to recede. His salary for a film at Svensk Filmindustri was not huge, and had remained the same for almost ten years – around 25,000 crowns for the script and a further 25,000 for directing (for which he could have purchased four new Volvo Amazon cars!¹) – but from the sale of his *Four Screenplays* in the United States, he earned over $10,000 on the first edition, and Simon and Schuster urged him to let them publish six more scripts. Janus Films continued to enjoy excellent results with the films in distribution; Bergman liked Cy Harvey and respected his business acumen. Harvey confessed that he was a trifle alarmed by the static nature of Bergman's camera in the productions of the early 1960s but remained constant to the leading light of his catalogue. He even obtained permission from the owner of the rights to D. W. Griffith's *The Birth of a Nation* to strike a print for Bergman's personal use.

On 14 January, the Royal Dramatic Theatre in Stockholm announced that Bergman would become managing director for the next three years, taking over the responsibility from Karl Ragnar Gierow. This was, and remains, the most influential and glamorous stage post in Scandinavia. Founded in 1788 by Gustav III, 'Dramaten', as it is known in Sweden, has been situated since 1907 in a massive, ornate building overlooking Nybroplan. At its rear lies a small auditorium, Lilla Scenen, where chamber plays and other productions involving small casts and modest settings have been performed since 1947. Eugene O'Neill was among the foreign playwrights championed by Dramaten, and as a result the theatre was entrusted with the world premiere of *Long Day's Journey into Night* in 1956, after O'Neill's death.

As he lay in bed with Käbi one evening, Bergman asked if she felt he should accept the offer. She was silent for a minute, and then replied, 'I know that you are going to accept. And I believe that it may be the beginning of the end of our marriage.'[2] Certainly, the administration of Dramaten was demanding. In 1945, when the building contained just one stage, there were 45 players attached to it; in 1964, with three stages involved, there were still a mere 56 under contract. 'It's a nasty post, loaded with responsibilities,' said Bergman in late January 1963. 'And amusing at the same time; to tackle and solve problems and complications is my ideal way of life – if I can only stay fit.'[3] His own office, high up in the building, appeared characteristically spartan. Outside the door, white plastic letters arranged on a black signboard spelled 'BERGMAN'. Within, a bed for resting, a couple of chairs, a pot plant and some bottles of mineral water and glasses on a tray.

Bergman's term of residence commenced formally on 1 July. As usual, he wrung the last drop from the months prior to assuming the post. The year began inauspiciously, with *Winter Light* dividing the critics. While on a brief holiday in Switzerland, Bergman received a telegram from Kenne Fant, head of SF, on the day after the premiere: 'Two for, two against, one in between.'

During the spring he staged Strindberg's *The Ghost Sonata* on Swedish television, and rumours circulated that he would make a ballet film in four episodes with Birgit Cullberg, the country's leading choreographer. On 2 May yet another of his productions for television was broadcast: *A Dream Play*, featuring Ingrid Thulin as Indra's Daughter and Uno Henning as the Officer, against ultra-ascetic decor. Two days later, Bergman travelled up to Dalarna with his technical team to prepare for his next film, *All These Women* (*För att inte tala om alla dessa kvinnor*), in the tranquil comfort of Hotel Siljansborg.

The screenplay credit on *All These Women* is attributed to Erland Josephson and Ingmar Bergman. The two friends collaborated with a fair amount of ease and good humour. Erland proved a dab hand at writing dialogue, while Bergman's imagination brought forth a flow of stories and incidents that could be woven into a script. In 1961 their comedy *The Pleasure Garden* had escaped with a good-natured reception, and now, in the aftermath of the spiritual trilogy, Bergman felt it would be an excellent idea to relax and take a swipe at the critics. He was fond of quoting Buñuel's retort to the question, for whom do you make your films? 'I make them', said Buñuel, 'for my friends and my enemies.'

At first titled *The Moral Lecture* or *A Hole in the Middle*,[4] *All These Women* stemmed, like so much during those years, from Bergman's relationship with Käbi Laretei. She had told him of various Don Juan types in the musical field and, in particular, of one of her teachers, who was married to a celebrated German violinist. He would tour the world in that lady's company, staying at castles and manor houses. 'He was a fat, boss-eyed man who had something remarkably demonic about him, and she had to play traffic cop to all his women.'[5] Erland Josephson contributed several of the plot developments. Once a week he would meet Ingmar and Käbi at their villa in Djursholm for work on the screenplay. 'My idea,' said Josephson, 'and also his idea, was that the important thing in the film should be the women, and the part of the critic was not at all significant. In the event, Jarl Kulle was so dynamic, and Ingmar found him so funny, that it became a film *about* women.'

Set around 1920, *All These Women* proved insufferably ponderous in some parts and eggshell-delicate in others. Cornelius (Jarl Kulle), the fastidious music critic who visits the summer residence of a great cellist named Felix, is Public Enemy Number One in Bergman's eyes. With his monocle and dandified clothes, he is a direct descendant of the line that includes Alman in *Wild Strawberries* and Vergérus in *The Magician*, yet rendered on this occasion in satirical terms. (He even makes a note of the maestro's hat size.)

Cornelius is bent on writing the biography of the late-lamented virtuoso and intends to annotate and analyse every word, gesture and relationship in Felix's life. As he stands beside the open bier, he asks pompously, 'What is genius?' Jillker (Allan Edwall), the dead man's business manager, reminds Cornelius drily that Goethe defined genius as the ability to make a critic change his mind. Cornelius stumbles about like Groucho Marx in a fruitless effort to penetrate the defences of awe and ridicule surrounding Felix, who is inscrutable save to his mistresses. He swims in the manorial pool, supported by a dummy ring in the shape of a swan. Later he pursues Jillker through the fountains, dressed in Neronic garb with laurelled brow; Bergman runs the scene in fast motion, ridiculing the pomp of artistic recognition.

The bulk of *All These Women* consists of a flashback describing Cornelius's hapless attempts to gain admittance to Felix's inner circle. Surrounded by a bevy of women, who act as a human smoke-screen for the maestro, he grows more and more frustrated and compromised. Bergman and Josephson add a wicked barb of their own, showing that Cornelius is concerned not so much about his proposed biography as about a composition that he has sent earlier for Felix's consideration. In a final, ironic twist, Cornelius finds himself assuming the role of the dead man and, with the smiling encouragement of the harem, he himself becomes enshrined while a down-at-heel young cellist arrives to take *his* place.

There can be no compromise between artist and analyst; Cornelius is denied a glimpse of Felix's face, as is the audience. Thus Bergman underlines the artist's claim to privacy.

In spite of his tension and weariness in the wake of *The Silence*, and on the verge of his new job at the Royal Dramatic Theatre, Bergman approached *All These Women* with painstaking devotion. This was to be his first film in colour, and the entire crew underwent checks for symptoms of colour blindness. Svensk Filmindustri paid for a 'colour-film school' for several weeks, with lectures by experts on painting and so on. Sven Nykvist exposed 18,000 feet of Eastmancolor stock before shooting even began, experimenting with tones and effects.

Harriet Andersson recalled that Bergman himself seemed under the weather, but that 'we girls had a wonderful fun time', especially in the Norrviken Gardens, outside Båstad in southern Sweden, where much of the film was shot on location. Three of the female stars of the film had been romantically involved with Bergman (Barbro Hiort af Ornäs, Harriet Andersson and Bibi Andersson) and others had appeared in some of his greatest screen and stage productions – Eva Dahlbeck, Gertrud Fridh and Karin Kavli.

'I think the picture was very stiff,' conceded Sven Nykvist, 'because we didn't do anything at all with the lighting – we overlit everything so it would be technically perfect. It was, but it had no atmosphere at all.' Such criticism could scarcely be applied to the film's most diverting sequence, when Felix is glimpsed on the balustrade amid a spectacular display of fireworks.

———

At the time few could have sensed it, but Bergman's international reputation had reached its crest. During the year 1963, the cream began to curdle, and the habitual synchronicity between theatre and film failed to improve the situation. Various factors contributed to this change in Bergman's attitude – as well as the attitudes of others in Sweden towards him. *All These Women*, shot in the summer, seemed a disaster foretold, and Bergman knew it. The Swedish Film Institute, founded that year by his friend Harry Schein and functioning from 1 July, sought to stimulate fresh talent in domestic filmmaking, thus obliging Bergman to share the spotlight with Bo Widerberg, Vilgot Sjöman, Mai Zetterling, Jörn Donner, Jan Halldoff, Jonas Cornell and Jan Troell.

Bergman reacted to the arrival of a younger generation of filmmakers with ostensible satisfaction, but underneath he was bitter about Bo Widerberg's withering critique of his own work. He even told aspiring young directors such as Roy Andersson, 'If you get involved with Bo Widerberg, you'll be fucked in the film world here.[6] He showed an unexpected asperity when writing about the proposed film school due to open in 1964 under the leadership of producer and historian Rune Waldekranz. He deplored the likely emphasis on film theory as opposed to practical work. He called for the establishment of a first-class film museum. Film should be experienced, he wrote, and students should have access to technology enabling them to study sequences from great films. More than that, he proposed that the most talented film students should be given a modest sum to embark on the project that most inspired them.[7] (He was far ahead of his time, for the Biennale College Cinema programme at the Venice Festival takes exactly that form.)

The opening of *The Silence* in Sweden on 23 September provoked a violent reaction. Some newspapers ran a permanent column for some weeks, printing arguments for and against the picture. Over 600,000 people saw the film during its first seven weeks of release, at a mere twenty-seven cinemas. At first, the Swedish censorship bureau intended to make cuts in the cabaret sequence. But a campaign in the liberal press led to an amendment to the rules, whereby a film should not be cut if its artistic quality was beyond reproach. This new statute came into effect just three days before *The Silence* was due to receive its certificate – in July 1963.

The Silence looks tame by comparison with even the soft porn of the 1970s. Audiences and authorities of the time, however, felt disturbed by the authenticity of its carnal mood. In France, the censorship board refused at first to issue a certificate for *The Silence*. The minister responsible, Alain Peyrefitte, requested certain cuts in the cabaret sequence and in the lovers' rendezvous in the hotel room. In the German Federal Republic, debate over the film reached parliament; millions flocked to the cinemas, making a temporary fortune for the distributor, Atlas Film. *Soviet Screen* ran a sharp attack on Bergman for the latent fascism and hatred of mankind displayed by *The Silence*. The film attracted large audiences in Britain and the

United States, even though most people were drawn to it for the wrong reasons. Bergman quoted a venerable member of the Swedish Academy apropos of *Lady Chatterley's Lover*, who had declared, 'This book is going to have a lot of unwanted readers.'[8] Bergman added, 'And this film is going to have a lot of unwanted viewers!' At an earlier stage, when screening the film for Kenne Fant, head of Svensk Filmindustri, he had predicted that no more than 100,000 spectators throughout the world would pay to see it.

The anonymous letters were sickening. One contained soiled lavatory paper. Käbi supported her husband loyally but was a little puzzled that Bergman could make such a despondent film while they were so happy in their marriage. Ingmar's reply was that, alongside her, he now felt strong enough to tackle such themes.

When *The Silence* was released in the United States the following February, it screened in Manhattan at the Rialto (known for its striptease movies) and the Trans-Lux East. Bosley Crowther, in the *New York Times*, praised the acting but complained that Bergman had not given the audience sufficient material to find the underlying meaning or emotional satisfaction in the film. In *Esquire*, Dwight Macdonald criticised the lack of motivation, which made the sisters' actions seem arbitrary and increasingly boring. He regretted Bergman's vision of himself as a philosopher in recent films, when his talent was for the concrete rather than the abstract. Even John Simon, later to become one of Bergman's greatest advocates, wrote in the *New Republic* of his disappointment with *The Silence*. The acting and the photography were excellent, but Simon noted the absence of forward thrust, a want of 'human content'.

The responsibilities at Dramaten weighed on Bergman. He wanted more time for his own productions, as well as his films, while also trying to effect radical changes at the theatre. Some actors and directors were angered and confused by this new policy, but they could not deny that Bergman was fighting like a tiger with the authorities for more recognition of Dramaten's role. When he joined the institution in 1963, its subsidy was in the order of 4 million crowns per annum, and when he left three years later the figure had climbed to some 10 million. One of his revolutionary steps was to mount a series of classical plays for children; Dramaten had always ignored the needs of young people who might be attracted to the theatre.

'I started in the morning at eight o'clock,' recalled Bergman of his stewardship of Dramaten, 'and was there until eleven at night; then I went home and slept. I was at it ten months a year, and there was no place left for demons and dreams.'[9] The first prickly decision confronting him concerned the legendary stage director Olof Molander. Then in his seventies, Molander had held sway over Dramaten in the late 1930s, but, to cite Bergman's own words, had 'become a tormented man who tormented others'.[10] Procrastination was not in Bergman's nature, in either public or private life, and at a meeting in his office he informed Molander that he would not be mounting any productions in the forthcoming season. The elegant, immaculately dressed Molander left the office abruptly, refusing to shake Bergman's hand.

Bergman and his executive assistant Margot Wirström had to fend off numerous invitations for the theatre to tour with some of its productions – as well as declining offers from foreign playwrights eager to see their work performed in Sweden. Georg Solti wrote to Bergman asking if he would produce Schoenberg's *Moses und Aron* at the Royal Opera House, which Solti would conduct. Bergman declined, citing his new responsibilities and saying, 'Of course I must devote all my time and efforts to this theatre alone for the next few years.'

He even refused his friend Peter Daubeny of the Royal Shakespeare Company in London, pleading 'a complicated reorganisation which is very delicate'. Actors besieged him, hoping to join the prestigious Dramaten troupe. On 19 December, for example, he wrote warmly to Gerd Hagman, explaining that he had inherited 'an awful mass of women' from his predecessor Karl Ragnar Gierow, and had no room for more that year. Inga Landgré sent him two letters after his appointment at Dramaten had been announced, hoping for work and pointing out that he had 'treated all his mistresses so well', and what a pity it was that the two of them had never been in love. Bergman sent a waspish retort: 'You had your chance when we met on *Crisis*. Right now I can't do anything for you. Merry Christmas, in any event!'

His iron discipline, however, enabled him to continue with his own stage productions. Edward Albee's lacerating play *Who's Afraid of Virginia Woolf?* opened on 4 October. The critic Derek Prouse was struck by Bergman's rejection of the seedy realism that had marked other productions of the play. 'One enters the theatre to find the stage uncurtained, a bare, grey back wall surrounded by black tabs, four pieces of grey furniture, a drinks table and one book. The mood is heightened by changing intensities of light from unrealistic sources.'[11] With Karin Kavli as Martha, Georg Rydeberg as George and Bibi Andersson and Thommy Berggren as the young couple who witness – and participate in – George and Martha's sterile war of words and nerves, *Who's Afraid of Virginia Woolf?* impressed the Swedish critics. It was the continent's first production of the play, and Bergman demonstrated that he had lost none of his power to grip an audience, that he knew how to veer from sordid naturalism to frenzied absurdity.

At the end of 1963, Bergman was invited to meet King Gustaf Adolf VI at a court reception. He did not want to attend, but Käbi persuaded him to do so. The other guests made crass remarks, at second hand, about *The Silence*. Then the King led Bergman away into an adjoining room for a chat. Afterwards, Bergman told his wife that the King had in fact been rather nice.

15

PERSONA AND LIV ULLMANN

At the age of forty-five, Bergman seemed to have resolved the religious issues that had plagued him since early youth. But now, in the darkest moments of the night, he was pursued not by God but rather by the Devil – in the form of demons. These demons did not assail him in the guise of Lucifer or Mephistopheles. They were, he said, for the most part pale-faced and well-dressed. The demons he encountered frequently included Disaster, Fear (for example, of birds or large crowds), Work, Failure, Sloth, Grudges, Rage, Pedantry and so on. The only two he did not suffer from, he told Marie Nyeröd towards the end of his life, were Nothingness and Boredom. For the Greeks, a demon meant a supernatural power, and Homer used the term in conjunction with *theos*, a god. In the Middle Ages, the Seven Deadly Sins were demons in their own right. Mahatma Gandhi once said, 'The only devils in this world are those running around in our own hearts.' Bergman would have agreed.

Thus haunted, Bergman embarked on a script he entitled *The Cannibals*. It would be his longest piece of writing to that point, and he intended the film to run for four hours and be released in two parts. In his workbook, he referred to it as 'almost a ghost story', and that one of the 'demons' wears a mask like a bird. On 22 July he jotted down the idea of photographing it in black and white with the 'scope format.' Locations were scouted on the Shetland Islands and on Hallands Väderö, a small island off the southwest coast of Sweden with somewhat exotic vegetation. Although *The Cannibals* never came to fruition, the screenplay was resuscitated as *Hour of the Wolf* in 1966.

Meanwhile, he mounted a stage production of Harry Martinson's new play, *Three Knives from Wei*. Throughout the winter months he had laboured on this reconstruction of life during the Tang dynasty of China, with its massive cast and its essential conflict between decorum and reality. He staged it, wrote Henrik Sjögren, as a poetic tale, 'a necklace of lyrical scenes. Kerstin Hedeby's sets and costumes gave the drama a shimmering, pastel quality like that of a silk painting, against which only the rig-out of the two concubines, with their strong, saturated colours, stood out.' The reviewers were united in their praise for Hedeby's designs but less than happy with Bergman's (and Martinson's) grasp of the subtle discords that were implied beneath the ritualistic performances.

All These Women opened a few days later and was roundly condemned by the critics. 'A convincing and well-deserved fiasco,' noted Bergman in his autobiography more than twenty years later. As usual, however, the reviewers sidestepped the condemnation of themselves and attacked Bergman for the clumsiness and flatness of the comedy. Mauritz Edström in *Dagens Nyheter* said, tartly and concisely, that the film was just not funny enough. Swedish audiences also felt disappointed. Just as they had assumed Bergman would follow *The Virgin Spring* with a masterpiece and had found only *The Devil's Eye*, so now they felt cheated by Bergman's tomfoolery in the wake of *The Silence*.

Some pride was salvaged in September, when the Swedish Film Institute, inaugurating a series of annual awards, gave Bergman a 'Gold Bug' for *The Silence*, the equivalent of an Oscar for Best Direction. He was also now the 'Inspector' of the Institute's Film School. Herbert von Karajan invited him to mount a guest production at the Salzburg Festival, but nothing transpired. And in August he had begun rehearsals for Ibsen's *Hedda Gabler*, destined to become one of his most brilliant stage productions. Mago designed the scenery as well as the costumes and persuaded Bergman that the overall colour should be red. Seven screens were erected to define the acting areas, and each screen was covered with scarlet material, giving the entire stage a womb-like impression. Bergman would return to the notion of enveloping crimson textures in *Cries and Whispers*.

Mago based his main set on a typical Norwegian interior of the 1890s, with large bookshelves. 'Hedda's first costume was a dressing gown made of dull silk in champagne tints,' he said. 'Its severe lines were relieved by a touch of lace at the wrists. Another dress was peacock green.' Gertrud Fridh, playing Hedda, had naturally copper-coloured hair, which stood out in striking contrast to the deep red screens. Bergman himself took care of the lighting. 'The morning scenes were brilliant and hot,' according to Mago, 'the evening ones dim and cool. The set contained no windows or any other obvious sources of light.'[2]

The stimulus behind *Hedda Gabler*, claimed Bergman, was a woman Ibsen encountered, but the voices in the play belong to Ibsen alone. 'That's what I felt a terrible need to release.' But in successive revivals of his production (with, in the English and German stagings, Maggie Smith and Christine Buchegger replacing Gertrud Fridh as Hedda) the feeling was one of entrapment rather than release. Even in her most private moments of anguish and indecision, Hedda remained in full view of the audience; she was hardly ever offstage, and in scenes not involving her she was shielded from the other players by the red screens. As she placed the gun to her head at the climax of the play, she stooped to a foetal crouch, suggesting Bergman's familiar vision of death and birth as inextricably mixed.

Although this production never reached Norway, it was invited to a festival in West Berlin, and four years later Bergman would accompany it to London, with Gertrud Fridh reprising the title role, in the context of Peter Daubeny's World Theatre Season. Ronald Bryden in the *Observer* hailed Fridh's 'magnificent performance', and J. W. Lambert in the *Sunday Times* averred that Bergman's direction 'restored the balance of the drama'.

His talents were still solicited on all sides. Invitations arrived from the Lincoln Center in New York, and from theatres in London and Oslo. Bergman refused almost without exception, citing the shooting of a new film as his excuse. Between October 1963 and the end of January 1964, Nicolas Nabokov of the Berliner Festwoche urged Bergman to stage Stravinsky's *The Soldier's Tale*. (The composer apparently wanted Bergman to direct the play.)

Sometimes Bergman himself pursued playwrights – Lars Forssell, for example, who had sent him a new play in April 1964. He invited Bernard Frechtman (translator of Jean Genet's *The Balcony*) to Stockholm, paid for his flight from Paris, and took him to dinner in February 1965. He maintained contact with his old mentor Stina Bergman, asking her if Dramaten could stage some of Hjalmar Bergman's plays in 1965, when Max von Sydow would be available to the theatre. 'My dearest Ingmar,' she replied, apologising that *Swedenhielms* had already been contracted to Stockholm City Theatre. In December 1964 he wrote to one of his closest early friends, Stig Olin, saying that should he lose his job at Sveriges Radio, 'I would naturally be ready to hire you and your whole family immediately at Dramaten.'

Käbi and Ingmar spent Christmas 1964 in Zurich, a few days of peace and relaxation from the pressures of the theatre. In January, however, a lung infection took hold of him. It was thought to be an ordinary cold, but a high temperature persisted and by March, when he became very sick, the doctors were talking of pneumonia (as well as an unpleasant ailment of the ear, Ménière's disease). Bergman began to suffer from a reaction to antibiotics.[3] Käbi remembered that 'the warm-hearted sisters at the clinic were like substitute mothers'.[4] Early in the year his mother called to say that Erik Bergman would be entering hospital for an operation on a malignant tumour in his gullet. He had smoked some sixty cigarettes a day throughout his adult life.[5]

In April, all plans to film *The Cannibals* were shelved. Anders Ek, Bibi Andersson and the young Norwegian actress Liv Ullmann had been contracted by Svensk Filmindustri. More cancellations were forced on Bergman. His assistant at Dramaten, Margot Wirström, wrote to the British critic Ossia Trilling on 1 April that 'Mr Bergman is seriously ill for some time and in hospital.' That did not deter him from sending a telegram eight days later to Åke Grönberg, urging him to join the theatre's ensemble from January 1966: 'We really need you!' The actor's reply was clearly positive because Bergman sent him a note from his hospital bed saying he already felt better after reading his telegram.

He also had to relinquish his commitment to stage *The Magic Flute* in Hamburg, and his illness prevented him from travelling to Utrecht on 24 June to accept the Erasmus Prize from Prince Bernhard of the Netherlands, an award he shared with Charles Chaplin. Kenne Fant went in his stead, and read a speech devised by Bergman for maximum impact on the audience. It became one of his most widely quoted declarations.

Speaking of his childhood, he remarked, 'I made myself understood in a language that bypassed words, which I lacked; music, which I have never mastered; and painting, which left me unmoved.' Why, he asked, does one continue to practise art?

> The reason is curiosity: a boundless, never satisfied, constantly renewed, unbearable curiosity that urges me on, that never lets me rest, that has entirely replaced the past hunger for fellowship. I feel like a prisoner who has tumbled out into the booming, shrieking, snorting world after a long period of confinement. I am seized by an irrepressible curiosity. I take note, observe, keep watch; everything is unreal, fantastic, frightening, or foolish. I catch a flying speck of dust, perhaps it is a film. What importance does it have? None whatsoever, but I personally find it interesting and it becomes a film.

The artist, he said, lives exactly like every other creature that exists only for its own sake. 'This makes a rather numerous brotherhood living together egotistically on the hot, dirty earth under a cold and empty sky.'

What few people knew at the time, however, was that Bergman continued to write with passion while restricted to the clinic. 'I want to make a fresh start,' he noted in his workbook on 12 April. The new film would revolve around two women: a nurse, Sister Alma, who 'is searching for her true self' through the patient assigned to her, Elisabet Vogler. Throughout the month of April 1965, the screenplay gathered momentum. 'Mrs Vogler has a strict expression but also a childish softness,' he wrote in his workbook. He conceived the idea of Elisabet watching an atrocity on television – either the hanging of the Israeli spy, Eli Cohen, in Damascus in 1965, or the scene of the Vietnamese Buddhist monk setting fire to himself in Saigon in 1963. On 19 May, he reflected, 'I think it will end with Alma writing a letter to Elisabet in which she is thankful for all she has learnt through her.'[6] The screenplay was completed on Örnö and bears the date 17 June 1965.

The members of Bergman's crew dispersed for the summer holidays, disappointed that *The Cannibals* had been at best postponed. Three weeks later, though, Mago, who was in Copenhagen for a meeting with Marlene Dietrich, received a call from Bergman's production manager, Lars-Owe Carlberg, asking him to return to Stockholm immediately to design a film entitled *Persona*. At first Bergman had wanted to call it *Cinematography*, but Kenne Fant, loyal though he was to Bergman's whims, 'had a fit' and felt that Svensk Filmindustri could not proceed without a better title than that. Bergman considered *Sonata for Two Women*, *A Piece of Cinema* and even *Opus 27* before finally selecting *Persona*, the ancient Latin word for 'mask'.

He appeared at a press conference, looking bronzed and surprisingly fit. He explained that during his spell in hospital he had started writing to ward off boredom, just to maintain a working routine. And from this activity *Persona*, 'a sonata for two instruments', had been born. 'In hospital one has a strong sense of corpses floating up through the bedstead. Besides which I had a view of the morgue, people marching in and out with little coffins, in and out.'[7]

Bergman's viral infection had been so pernicious that it had affected his balance. For four months, he claimed, he sat staring at a spot on the wall. 'If I moved my head, the whole world seemed to turn upside down.' (Such an image probably inspired those final clinic scenes in both *The Serpent's Egg* and *From the Life of the Marionettes*.) So he began to contemplate a film involving just two characters, one talking, the other silent. Perhaps Bergman had returned to Strindberg and his play *The Stronger*, in which 'Mrs X reads Miss Y's thoughts, but at the same time she feels Miss Y is inducing her to express everything she is thinking'.[8] Suddenly, he began to imagine two intermingled faces, 'and that was the beginning, the place where it started'.[9] In another interview, Bergman gave Stig Björkman a slightly different account: 'One day I suddenly saw in front of me two women sitting next to each other and comparing hands. I thought to myself that one of them is mute and the other speaks.'[10]

Persona has only four speaking parts, and two of these are minor. So for Bibi Andersson, playing Sister Alma, and Liv Ullmann, as Elisabet Vogler, the film presented an arduous challenge. They had been friends since 1962, when Bibi had been appearing in *Pan* (a Nordic co-production), and Liv – then only twenty-four – had acted alongside her. When Bibi returned to Stockholm, she told Bergman that she had met a girl of the type that he liked and that he might be able to use her on stage or screen. So, when Liv came subsequently to Sweden with her theatre group, Bergman met her and found her engaging. The apocryphal story is that Bergman encountered both women by chance on a street corner and was struck by the resemblance between them. The actual idea for *Persona* is far more likely to have sprung from a Polaroid photo of Bibi and Liv together, although Bergman's explanation about the image of two women caressing hands seems more cogent still. Some months after that first meeting, Bergman contacted Ullmann and said that he had a part for her in the screenplay he was writing.

The romance between Ingmar Bergman and Liv Ullmann became as notorious in Scandinavia as Ingrid Bergman's relationship with Roberto Rossellini. Liv, born in Tokyo of Norwegian parents and partly educated in England, would possibly have achieved some fame as an actress without Bergman's influence. 'One of the things I am most grateful to Ingmar for teaching me', she said, 'is that if you keep yourself open to whatever comes out, something will happen. I was very young [on *Persona*] and I couldn't have verbalised my feelings about the actress.'[11]

During the first week of shooting in the studios at Råsunda, Liv recalled that Bergman was rather worried, but once the unit moved to Fårö on location, his mood became more positive. He felt at home, far more so on the island than he did in the bourgeois environment of his wedded life with Käbi in Stockholm. Liv stayed with Bibi and the make-up artist in a small house near the sea. An affection grew steadily between Liv and her director. They would walk together on the way home after the day's shooting, while Bibi Andersson, ever tactful, ran ahead with Sven Nykvist to give the couple some privacy.

The circumstances could not have been more difficult. Liv had a husband in Oslo. Ingmar was married to Käbi Laretei. Their son, Daniel, was not yet three years of age. No stranger to infidelity, however, Bergman could be quite ruthless where emotional disengagement was concerned. Käbi maintained to the end of her life that Daniel had been 'a love child', but an incident during his infancy revealed the need for both his parents to enjoy their own space, their own careers. When Daniel's nanny, Silja Pennanen, wanted to leave, Bergman suggested that, at his expense, she and Daniel should move into a house or flat somewhere in Djursholm, so they could see the Bergmans easily. She was so shocked that an infant could be virtually discarded without a qualm that she resigned immediately.[12]

At first, Bergman refused to contemplate yet another messy divorce. Many of his love letters to Liv were written, in longhand, from the villa at Ymervägen 22 in Djursholm – every day or every other day. Liv returned to her home in Oslo when filming had finished, but Bergman pursued her, and contacted her friends in the city. With their help, he persuaded Liv to return to Fårö with him. He had decided to move permanently to the island. 'We walked on the beach,' wrote Liv in her autobiography, 'which was nothing but rocks, and took pictures of each other.'[13] In another interview: 'To me, he was God. I was only twenty-five [sic], too young, and he was forty-six. When he spoke, I blushed.'[14] Bergman was unstinting in his recognition of her gifts as an actress: 'Liv, like the best of all creative artists, has marvellous integrity and enormous faith in her own intuition.' And Liv Ullmann would appear in all his major films over the next twelve years.

'The pressures of both our careers built up a kind of tension that made the break-up of our marriage inevitable,' said Käbi Laretei. The press pursued her without mercy while she was in New York for a concert, pressing her to comment on the rumours linking Liv and Ingmar.

Persona has provoked innumerable interpretations, scholarly, psychological and aesthetic. It deserves its abiding place among the most inventive and audacious films of the twentieth century. At every stage, from the kaleidoscopic prologue to the merging of Alma's and Elisabet's faces on screen, Bergman seemed bent on testing and stretching the limits of cinematography. As early as 1964, Bergman told an interviewer that he saw 'more and more clearly that film as an art form is approaching a discovery of its essential self. It should communicate psychic states, not merely project images of external actions.'[15]

Everything one says about *Persona* can be contradicted; the opposite will also be true. Once again, facets of Bergman's own personality emerge from the behaviour of the two women: his propensity for observing human beings, his tenderness towards those he loved, his almost vampiric habit of sucking ideas from those with whom he was intimate, his neglect of his children and his use of dreams as a source of inspiration.

From the outset, Bergman insisted on reminding everyone that *Persona* had been created literally on celluloid; the early stills for the film showed the sprocket holes on the left-hand side, until finally Bergman relented and allowed Svensk Filmindustri to issue them as regular 10 × 8 photographs. The opening shot embodies the very essence of cinema. It's as iconic as Adam and Eve in the Garden of Eden, the start of everything in cinema. Without these carbons bursting into life there would be no projection. And the high-pitched keening, a discordant, intensifying drone, of Lars Johan Werle's music gives it an other-worldly timbre. A sexual undertone runs through the sequence, commencing with the idea of fertilisation by light, giving life to an otherwise dead void. Film as a medium of communication comes under scrutiny in *Persona*. The film leader passes through the projector with its descending numbers flipping up every twenty-four frames, to the accompaniment of harsh whining noises. Then, a series of images that evoke Bergman's state of mind in the clinic where he wrote the script, as well as the motifs of humiliation and death that permeate the film: a hand being nailed to a cross, a lamb being slaughtered, deserted parkland, steps, a pile of sand-like material – all fading away and being succeeded by pictures from a morgue. A dead woman lying in profile, a boy beneath a sheet. And, on the soundtrack, the inexorable drip of water.

The boy stirs and comes awake. He wipes his hand over the screen. But he does so because he is mystified by the image of a woman's face on that screen. As the audience watches the boy, the audience becomes the fused image of two women's features. Much later in *Persona*, Elisabet pops up into frame and takes a snapshot of the camera – the audience – while out on the seashore. Bergman thus dissolves the habitual acceptance of a celluloid barrier between the spectators and the characters in a film.

Bergman with Sven Nykvist, Bibi Andersson and Liv Ullmann
during the shoot of *Persona*.
Copyright © AB Svensk Filmindustri 1966. Photo by Lars Johnsson.

The audience clings anxiously to the lineaments of traditional narrative furnished by Bergman – the nurse accompanying her patient
out to a holiday cottage on the advice of her doctor – but the key to
the film is the concept of life and personality as a mirror: the notion
that the image staring back at one from a mirror is a double, the other
half of one's psyche. Both Alma and Elisabet are divided in two; each
is the other's missing half. Carl Jung identified the *persona* (the outer
mask presented to the world) as intellectual, and the *alma* (the inner
soul) as quite certainly sentimental. Long before Bergman, Jung realised that liberation becomes an urgent necessity when the individual
is caught between the conflicting demands of *persona* and *alma*. The
fact that Bibi Andersson's character bears the name Alma is a gesture
of acknowledgement by Bergman towards Jung's research in this area.
For Jung, the *alma* remains that person in dark cloak with shadowed
face who crouches in the cellar of the subconscious.

Reflection. Duplication. The mirror serves as the central emotional motif in the film. In a symphony, a theme is frequently recapitulated. Rarely in a film. In *Persona*, when Alma lectures Elisabet about her pregnancy and hatred for her child, Bergman's camera watches the actress's face as she talks. But almost immediately afterwards she repeats the speech word for word. This time the camera observes Alma's face. At the very end of the film, Alma is back in nurse's uniform, cleaning up and closing the cottage for the winter. As she adjusts her hair in a mirror, she suddenly sees the image of Elisabet caressing her in the same manner, a reminder of the other woman's presence within her and of the three-dimensional property of the 'mirror'.

There are no readily identifiable border posts between fantasy and reality. Alma enters her patient's room in the hospital almost, it seems, by the same door through which she had arrived to answer the doctor's summons. On the island, Elisabet denies visiting Alma's room by night and stroking her hair, when Bergman has shown the audience such a sequence without giving any clue as to its falsity. Later in the film, Alma appears to sleepwalk when answering the call of the sinister Mr Vogler.

'The reality we experience today', declared Bergman on television in 1968, 'is in fact as absurd, as horrible and as obtrusive as our dreams. We are as defenceless before it as we are in our dreams.' The 'horrible' reality that Bergman mentions leaks into even such a hermetic film as *Persona*: the newsreel shots of a Buddhist monk immolating himself, or the photo of Jews being rounded up in the Warsaw Ghetto. The more appalled Alma and Elisabet are by reality, the more they take refuge in a dream state. But, as the actor tells Elisabet sternly, 'Your hiding place isn't tight enough. Life trickles in from outside. And you are forced to react. No one asks whether it's true or false, whether you're genuine or just a sham. Such things are important only in the theatre.' Bergman addresses himself here; the doctor refers to Elisabet's 'constant hunger to be exposed', a line evocative of Bergman's Malmö period, when his innermost feelings seemed to colour his stage direction.

Fear and its accomplice, guilt, lie at the heart of Bergman's work. Humiliation is both the cause of, and the response to, such fear. Every remark in *Persona* aims to wound, every question to provoke, every answer to lacerate. As with the sisters in *The Virgin Spring* and *The Silence*, the humiliation suffered by the one is suffered vicariously by the other. Dualities govern much of Bergman's cinema. From *Persona* onwards, Liv Ullmann and Max von Sydow would embody the Janus-like concept in *Hour of the Wolf*, *Shame* and *The Passion of Anna*.

The moment of most wilful humiliation occurs midway through *Persona*, when Alma plans her revenge on Elisabet for having written such spiteful comments to the doctor in her letter. She has broken a glass on the terrace outside the cottage and deliberately leaves one jagged fragment on the path in the expectation that Elisabet will emerge and cut her foot. So eloquent is the expression on Alma's face that one knows, long before Elisabet winces in pain, that Alma by sheer force of will has drawn her towards the shard. Almost immediately, the film burns in the projector, a caesura that suggests that not even the celluloid can withstand the ferocious assault of Alma's retaliation, allied to the audience's complicity with her. Ulla Ryghe, Bergman's editor, recalled that projectionists stopped their machines the first time they ran *Persona*, assuming that the actual film was melting. Large red labels were pasted on the appropriate reel cans, informing users that the film was neither on fire nor breaking up.

Persona also comprises a struggle between the artist and his public. Elisabet, the artist, exerts a voodoo-like hold over her companion – the philistine or spectator. Alma's speech degenerates into incoherence, like a word processor gone berserk. Her exasperation represents the familiar attack mounted by Bergman's antagonists against the artist, for not divulging his secrets. How amusing that Bergman should give Elisabet Vogler the same family name as he did his other 'mute' protagonist – Albert Emanuel Vogler in *The*

Magician. He is all too aware of the leech-like role played by the artist, devouring his audience in order to glean his material – as Somerset Maugham used to acquire the gist of his Far East stories by listening to the experiences of people he met.

Before starting to edit *Persona*, Bergman had to take over the direction of *Tiny Alice*, Albee's play about what Hjalmar Söderberg had called 'the desire of the flesh and the incurable loneliness of the soul', because Bengt Ekerot had fallen sick during rehearsals. The moment the opening had taken place at Dramaten's Lilla Scenen, Bergman drove up to the Hotel Siljansborg in Rättvik, with Ulla Ryghe and his assistant Lenn Hjortzberg in attendance and the temperature outside declining to -26°C. In the evenings the talk turned to *Auschwitz*, the Peter Weiss play due to be unveiled at the Royal Dramatic Theatre on 13 February 1966. As always, Bergman would use the verso of each page of the play's text on which to make notes and scribble rough designs for blocking and positioning. Only occasionally would he tamper with a playwright's dialogue, but if so, the lines were struck through without hesitation.

Ulla Ryghe found Bergman to be open to suggestions, even if he put up a struggle before accepting ideas. 'When we thought *Persona* was in good shape,' she said,

> we screened it for the first time – Ingmar, Sven Nykvist and I. When the lights came up in the cinema I knew that at one point something was wrong. Bergman asked what I thought, and I told him my feeling. He got very irritated about my being so vague. After some shouting, we started to go through the movie, sequence by sequence, and I was able finally to explain what I had felt: the scene where the two women's faces merge was coming too early in the film. It didn't have enough build-up at that juncture. Bergman must have felt similarly, for we took it out, moved it around, tried it in one or two different places and then finally found the right spot for it.

One of the most evocative and difficult sequences in *Persona* is Alma's recollection of an orgy on the beach. Some people to whom Bergman mentioned this scene thought he should not include it. Bibi Andersson believed it should be, however, providing she could omit certain male sex words that she judged Alma would not use. And by 11 a.m. on the first morning of trying the scene, it was in the can. Liv Ullmann had to remain silent throughout Bibi's monologue. 'I told Liv how she must gather all her feeling into her lips,' said Bergman. 'She had to concentrate on placing her sensibility here – it's possible, you know, to place one's feeling into one's little finger, or one's big toe, or into one buttock, or your lips.'[16]

16

AT WORK ON THE ISLAND

Ingmar walking alone on the shore on Fårö in 1970.
Courtesy of Leif Engberg.

Bergman's life and career were undergoing another sea change. The pressures of administration at Dramaten were colossal, and in early 1966 Bergman resigned. He yearned to concentrate on his own creative work instead of responding to endless letters and telegrams from within and beyond Sweden. At least his production of Peter Weiss's *The Investigation*, an oratorio for the victims – and perpetrators – of the Nazi death camps, met with glowing notices. He had also hoped to stage Vilhelm Moberg's new play, *Your Hour on Earth*, but, after lengthy correspondence, this was abandoned. Until the final weeks of his tenure as managing director, Bergman and his secretary were busy postponing engagements and apologising to those affected by the situation. Laurence Olivier had asked Bergman if he would consider a production of Strindberg's *The Dance of Death* for the National Theatre in London, to open in September 1966. On 11 February, Bergman replied, 'Your proposal made me feel very happy and honoured, but unfortunately I already have made other arrangements. With admiration and warmest personal regards.'

Less than a month after the premiere of *The Investigation*, Bergman lost his mother. On 8 March 1966 he talked to her just days prior to her death and confessed that Liv was pregnant. The next day, Karin wrote in her diary, 'This evening I received a wonderful big azalea from Ingmar. Lenn [Hjortzberg] brought it up to me. And then Ingmar himself called to thank me for yesterday.' Liv Ullmann arrived from Norway hours after Karin Bergman had suffered her third heart attack. The doctors wanted to call Bergman, according to Liv, but his mother had said, 'He's so busy. Leave him alone.' She was dead by the time her son reached her room at the hospital. Erik Bergman, after more than half a century of marriage, was shattered by his wife's passing. Ingmar was the only member of the family able to care for him. Margareta, the daughter, was in England and Ingmar's elder brother Dag was on diplomatic service abroad. On 30 May 1965, his mother had written to Ingmar urging him to care for Dag and Margareta after her death.[1]

Karin Bergman died at the age of seventy-four. 'My feelings toward her are ambivalent,' Ingmar told me. 'When I was young I felt that she loved my brother more than me, and I was jealous.' He discovered a diary among her possessions. The entries had been maintained scrupulously since 1916. 'She wrote in a microscopically small script, with many abbreviations,' noted Bergman. 'But suddenly we discovered an unknown woman – intelligent, impatient, furious, rebellious – who had lived under this disciplined, perfect housewife.'[2] Custody of the diaries passed to Margareta, and thence to her daughter Veronica.

The funeral took place at Hedvig Eleonora Church. In a packed congregation, Bergman sat next to his niece Veronica. The organist at Hedvig Eleonora had nursed an infatuation for Karin, and just before the funeral he suffered a heart attack and died.

Bergman paid a tribute to his mother's death in the opening scene of *The Touch* (1970), showing Bibi Andersson's character arriving at a clinic after her mother had passed away. As a personality, Karin emerges most clearly in triptych form, in *Cries and Whispers* (1971). She and Ingmar had different artistic tastes, but a sympathy had persisted between them to the last. 'We were both extremely headstrong with a fiery temperament,' he told a schoolteacher on Fårö. 'We had an innate ability to fall out. But we became really good friends the last years, and it wasn't because she was my mother, but she was my friend, who was fun to meet and have a chat with.'[3]

Now that his father felt lonely and depressed, Bergman behaved towards him with relative kindness and affection. In his workbook, however, he had written on 20 May 1965, 'My parents never spoke to me about *gentleness* and *love* and *humility*.' Erik moved to smaller quarters in the Grev Turegatan but was eventually compelled to enter hospital. Bergman visited him every day when he could, and Erik, according to friends and relatives, much appreciated this consideration. He died in 1970.

Daniel, not yet four years of age, saw little of his father during this turbulent spell. Bergman was, at best, an absentee parent. But, almost aware of this failing, he had shot a home movie about his son on 16 mm. Now he sifted through several thousand feet of film and tried to assemble 'a testament, something he could have when he grew up'.[4] The result became a short documentary, ready for inclusion in Svensk Filmindustri's portmanteau production, *Stimulantia*, which featured short contributions from nine directors. 'Daniel's face is the finest, most stimulating thing I know,' says Bergman offscreen. He shows the child gathering mushrooms, reacting to his mother, Käbi, as she plays children's songs on her piano in the family villa in Djursholm. In a final, frozen shot, Bergman seizes Daniel's innocence, as he flings up a hand to ward off the gaze of the camera while he lies in a hammock with his grandma.

The intense privacy of this little film gives it the tone of a monody for Bergman's life with Käbi Laretei. It had been a rich period in the director's middle age, and to Käbi he owed his fascination with ever more ascetic, ever more disciplined and ever more 'musical' cinema. Like Arnold Schoenberg when he had composed *Verklärte Nacht* in 1899, Bergman must have felt that, with *Persona*, he had tested the frontiers of his medium. He continued to do so during the next six years.

Käbi had already acquired an aura and a reputation as a concert pianist when she married Bergman. Liv Ullmann was at a much younger and more vulnerable stage of her life, and her new partner watched over her with love – 'You are my Stradivarius,' he said – but also possessiveness. Now settled on Fårö, he felt free of the constraints that a bourgeois existence in Stockholm had imposed on him. 'His hunger for togetherness was insatiable,' recalled Liv. 'I know that Ingmar had found his island, and I tried to love it in the way he did.'[5]

Bergman had believed in the screenplay for *The Cannibals*, even if the project foundered, because he had sent Lasse Bergström, his editor at Norstedts, a copy for him to read but not publish. Now, in early 1966, he developed the script for *Hour of the Wolf*, retaining elements from *The Cannibals*. Indeed, the main characters and narrative ingredients in *Hour of the Wolf* had already been listed by Bergman in his workbook on 22 July 1964. Like all good chefs, he retained anything that could be used in a future recipe. Writing now in a quiet, isolated room, he found it difficult to sleep. 'The demons would come to me and wake me up, and they would stand there and talk to me.'[6] The first draft of his screenplay began with Alma's offscreen monologue, in which she announces she is expecting a baby in about a month. (In fact, Liv gave birth to their daughter,

Linn, on the same day that Bergman filmed Tamino's entrance into the palace court in *Hour of the Wolf*.)[7]

In July 1967, Bergman purchased a stretch of land on Fårö at Djaupadal, between the woodland and the beach at Braidaur. Kjell Abramson, a colleague from Bergman's days at Dramaten, drew up the building plans for a one-storey building. Bergman's study would face the sea, and a part of the house would be devoted to a library for Bergman's books – and, much later, his video collection. His sanctuary could not have been more remote. Fårö itself was at that juncture off-limits to foreigners. To reach Fårö one first had to travel to Gotland, and then take the ferry over the sound. A further fifteen- to twenty-minute ride over rough roads would then bring Bergman's home into view.

The island looks as though it had emerged from the primeval sea of its own volition. Liv Ullmann described the landscape as covered with 'gnarled spruce trees of strange green colours, most of them stunted and bent along the ground. Only the strongest managed to lift themselves upward [...] The ground was grey and brown – wide fields covered by dry moss.'[8] Max von Sydow was struck by the 'limestone rock full of fossils, with a lovely grey tone. And there are areas which are absolutely barren, almost like a rock desert. The forests have very low fir trees and juniper bushes, green against the grey.'[9] Ingmar and Liv's daughter Linn Ullmann, who knew her first years on Fårö, would refer to the tall steles along the shore: 'The four-hundred-million-year-old stacks force their way up and out of the sea, reaching for the sky.'[10] In winter the temperature can sink as low as −22°C when lambing commences in March, and survival for the local fauna is a matter of chance and fitness.

Income tax is much higher on Fårö than it is in the Stockholm area, but that did not deter Bergman from becoming a permanent resident there in 1967. Once installed on the island, he could be as lazy as he wished. He could observe the waves advancing and retreating on the barren shore, and listen to the subdued hiss of the wind in the pine trees. He could write in peace. He could become acquainted with virtually all the inhabitants of the island (only some 700 at the time). 'Human understanding and human interaction are authentic there, not artificial as in the big cities,' he commented.[11] By the end of the decade, he had established a pattern of life on Fårö. A man attended to the garden and helped on the property in other ways; two elderly ladies took care of the housework. Soon afterwards, a studio was built in the seventeenth-century village of Dämba, in the southwest corner of Fårö, five minutes by car from Bergman's house.

Bergman drove in his favourite Peugeot, catching the 4.45 p.m. ferry to Fårösund to buy the newspapers. Each morning, soon after 8 a.m., he would take a walk along the seashore. He liked to point out to visitors that Fårö had been a crossroads for traders and merchants in the eleventh and twelfth centuries. 'Russia is only 130 kilometres away,' he would remark.[12]

Hour of the Wolf began production in late May of 1966, and shooting continued into September. Most of the exteriors were filmed not on Fårö but at Hovs Hallar in southern Sweden, the location also used for the opening of *The Seventh Seal. Hour of the Wolf* forms part of an unofficial trilogy featuring Max von Sydow as Bergman's alter ego – the artist as fugitive, retreating into his tiny world and gradually bending his thoughts in on himself, until dream and reality merge in terrifying collusion. In *Hour of the Wolf,* he is a painter, Johan Borg. In *Shame,* a violinist. In *The Passion of Anna,* he has no pretensions to artistic achievement: 'This time his name was Andreas Winkelmann,' intones Bergman's voice offscreen at the close of the film.

Bergman explained the title thus: 'According to the ancient Romans, the Hour of the Wolf means the time between night and dawn, just before the light comes; people believed it to be the time when demons had a heightened power and vitality, the hour when most people died and most children were born, and when nightmares came to one.'[13]

If the shadow of God in some form hovers over Bergman's major works of the 1950s and early 1960s, then the Devil (in the form of demons) holds sway in the 'island trilogy'. Erland Josephson plays the Mephistophelean figure of Baron von Merkens in *Hour of the Wolf*. He claims, with an ingratiating smile, that he and his wife are among Borg's 'warmest admirers' and invites the painter to dinner. At the Baron's castle, Borg is paraded like a zoological specimen before the assembled guests. Sven Nykvist's wide-angle lens gives the face of each of the Baron's acolytes an enveloping, predatory look. The dinner begins with one complete counter-clockwise movement around the table; during the meal, the camera whirls about, pausing haphazardly on each person's shoulder like a bird in flight.

Bergman had a great fondness for *Dracula*, especially the screen version starring Bela Lugosi. *Hour of the Wolf* has been widely compared with Mozart's *The Magic Flute* (and, by extension, the work of E. T. A. Hoffmann), but in technique and visual power it remains a tribute to Bram Stoker's creation. Bird references proliferate throughout the film. The first sign of Johan's illness, for example, comes as he greets his wife Alma outside the cottage after climbing the slope from the seashore; washed sheets hang on a line beside the couple, and the wind causes them to make a noise like the beating of great wings. After dinner at the castle, Lindhorst (Georg Rydeberg) fixes his gaze on Johan, and his face is lit in such a way as to suggest the beak-like nose and cold, ornithic eyes. Much later, Lindhorst appears again, despatching Johan into the castle vault to search for his beloved mistress, Veronica Vogler (Ingrid Thulin); surrounded by hundreds of small birds, Lindhorst stretches his arms wide like a huge bat in flight. Finally, in the swamp where Johan disappears, Lindhorst's features are transmogrified into those of a vampire bat. The whirring, shrieking music of Lars Johan Werle heightens this association with birds and, of course, with the 'bird catcher' Papageno in *The Magic Flute*. 'I am terribly afraid of birds,' admitted Bergman.

Gertrud Fridh and Max von Sydow in *Hour of the Wolf.*
Copyright © AB Svensk Filmindustri 1968. Photo by Roland Lundin.

'I become frightened, extremely frightened, when a bird gets into the room if I am sitting there."[4]

To some degree, *Hour of the Wolf* is a remake of *The Magician.* Once again, Bergman deceives the audience with his sleight of hand, just as he confuses the characters within the film. Alma (Liv Ullmann) is alone outside the cottage when an old lady (Naima Wifstrand, in her final role for Bergman) suddenly materialises on the hillside. Because the sequence is edited so subjectively, one never for an instant suspects Alma's vision. Instead, one shares her apprehension. One *believes.* Later in the castle the same ancient woman drops her eyeball into wine glass and peels off her facial mask with a crackling sound so tangible that for a moment one thinks that flesh is being torn apart.

In this film Bergman alights on a cinematic vocabulary commensurate with the dreams and hallucinations he seeks to describe. Sometimes he uses a harsh, gleaming light to suffuse the imagery, as in Johan's meeting on the shore with Veronica Vogler, or the fantasy beside the inlet when Johan is attacked by a young boy. On other occasions, Bergman resorts to heavy penumbras of shadow, inside the castle and its windowless rooms. By contrast, there is the unmistakable 'realism' of Alma's and Johan's return to their cottage after the dinner party: sunspots are reflected on the lens of Sven Nykvist's slightly shuddering, hand-held camera. In the penultimate sequence, in the swamp, Bergman deploys the optical printer in the laboratory in such a way as to undermine the constituents of the image; faces are glimpsed in huge, grainy close-up, and the background is coarse and obscure.

In the end, Johan Borg appears to be consumed by his tormentors. The 'demons' possess a loathsome strength. Heerbrand, the archivist, calmly enters through a door that has just been double-locked. Von Merkens, like Death in *The Seventh Seal*, informs Johan: 'Nothing you do will escape me.' In a flashback from the painter's diary, a small, apparently innocuous boy flings himself on Johan while he is fishing and seems endowed with almost superhuman force. When, in desperation, Johan dashes his head against a rock, the boy dies with cawing, bird-like cries. Even when Johan has lowered his corpse into the water, the boy's head rises to the surface, like violence emerging in the human personality.

Bergman has the courage in *Hour of the Wolf* to confront some of his innermost feelings and proclivities. Is the boy the son of Johan by an earlier marriage? Or an illegitimate child? Certainly, shame permeates this most bizarre of sequences. It may be that Bergman felt prone to homosexual instincts from time to time. When the boy peers into Johan's boots beside the water, Johan whips up his fishing rod in a frenzy of movement, as though trying to conceal some erotic response. Even the mortal struggle between the two has the rhythm of a violent orgasm. The boy incarnates a part of himself that Johan dare not acknowledge, and one detects in his attitude, as he lowers the body into the pool, the faintest nuance of regret.

For a long period, Bergman relied on the services of Lenn Hjortzberg, a dancer who gave up his career to assist Bergman, to shield him from unnecessary meetings and type all his letters. Daniel Bergman has described him as 'a short, lean, and thin-haired man with a quick but gracious voice'.[15] Hjortzberg once told me that he knew 'every detail of Ingmar's testament', although that was before he became so drunk on the set of *Shame* that Bergman finally let him go. The character of Tim in *From the Life of the Marionettes* was based on Lenn. There is no evidence that Bergman ever had a gay lover, but certainly he feared his own instincts in that area. In *Hour of the Wolf*, after being humiliated in public, in the arms of his naked mistress, a harassed Borg is seen in a close-up that is supplanted by a repeat shot of the boy's head immersed in the water, linking the ambivalence of Johan's painted and made-up face with his own dread of homosexuality. 'Sometimes I think that I'm a lesbian man obsessed with other women,' he reflected in his workbook a few years later. 'Sometimes I think that my impressions and feelings are extremely feminine and not really masculine.'[16]

Memories of his childhood still weighed on Bergman. In the cottage, Johan tells Alma about an incident based directly on Bergman's own memory of being locked in his nursery closet. He believed that in that cupboard dwelt a little man who 'could gnaw the toes off guilty children'. Release was followed by a ritual caning. 'Then father said, how many strokes do you deserve? And I said, as many as possible.' Thus, for Johan, if not for Bergman himself, humiliation serves also as expiation.

———

The women played by Liv Ullmann in the island trilogy mirrored to some extent a real-life situation. Alma in *Hour of the Wolf* and Eva in *Shame* find themselves tethered to their partner not just by love but by fear. For the media, Liv and Ingmar appeared to be enjoying an idyllic, almost Walden-like existence on Fårö. They had the company of 'Pet', a female dachshund whom Liv had brought with her from Norway. A daughter, Linn, was born to the couple during the shoot of *Hour of the Wolf*. 'I let it happen,' said Liv of the pregnancy. 'I wasn't afraid. I felt it was very right.' Bergman's divorce had not yet been pronounced final, and the Lutheran Church refused to baptise the baby. 'We did not marry', remarked Liv later, 'because we were both married when we met and it was never needed. [. . .] There was no lawyer, no priest in our relationship; it was our friendship, and our love.'[17] Many years later, she would concede that Bergman's possessiveness assumed claustrophobic proportions. He built a high stone wall around the property on Fårö, to keep prying visitors at bay. He requested Liv to stay at home throughout the week, save on Wednesdays, when she could join the rest of the crew for an outing. She had to be back by a certain time, and Bergman would wait for her, leaning against one of the sheep fences.

Bergman would make brief visits to Stockholm, to have a mole moved from his cheek or to fly to Holland to collect at last the Erasmus Prize of 100,000 Dutch florins. In late autumn and winter, Fårö's harsh winds and bleak landscape made it inhospitable to all but the most doughty of visitors. Bergman continued to oversee the construction of his new home on the island, however, and welcomed his hermit-like routine.

On 18 October, *Persona* at last opened in Sweden, to enthusiastic notices. Mauritz Edström, reviewing for *Dagens Nyheter*, described it as 'a confession of fear: fear of your fellow man, fear of failure, fear of being seen through, fear of disappointment, fear of your neighbour's strength and insight – and the wish to see the security of others shattered by a naked dread of death'.[18] Attendances, however, were mediocre: only 110,725 Swedes saw the film, compared with the 1,459,031 who had bought tickets for *The Silence* three years earlier. The pattern persisted abroad, where *Persona* became the focus of long articles in the serious film magazines but brought only modest returns at the box office. This was discouraging for United Artists, the American studio that had purchased a majority of the world rights to *Persona* and Bergman's next film for $1 million. The money went to Svensk Filmindustri, and indeed Bergman's income for the fiscal year 1967 was reported as being 853,180 crowns (about $170,000 at the time) before tax – more than others in the Swedish film sector, but not excessive by international standards and considering the director's enormous workload and level of creativity.

Erland Josephson, who had succeeded Bergman as head of the Royal Dramatic Theatre, asked him to guest direct Molière's *The School for Wives*. The production met with hostile reviews, and Bergman would not return to Dramaten until 1969. Instead, he followed Liv Ullmann to Oslo, where he spent six weeks preparing for the April opening of Pirandello's *Six Characters in Search of an Author* at the National Theatre of Norway. Liv played the daughter, Kurt Wigert her father. Sven Barthel wrote in the Stockholm daily *Dagens Nyheter* that Bergman had presented 'a vision of man's vulnerability and impotence, his nakedness'. A local critic commented that the applause was as resounding as if Norway had defeated Sweden in a football match at the Ullevål Stadium.

While in Oslo, Bergman began writing a screenplay about a scientist who conducts experiments. 'He shuts up two people in his laboratory, exposes them to various psychic pressures, and observes them.'[19] Both Jan and Jacobi in *Shame* originate in this script, but so does the Vergérus of *The Serpent's Egg*. In February, Bergman had changed the name of Max von Sydow's character from Abel to Jan: 'A tall, confused person, unpractical, a little decayed, who has sometimes shat on himself and his fellow beings.'[20] During the spring, Bergman's ideas for *Shame* (entitled in draft *The War*, and later *Dreams of Shame*) became more concrete. Lenn Hjortzberg was despatched to Fårö to prepare the buildings and buy furniture for its production, which would begin in September. Bergman himself, restless, wrote yet another script in July, a kind of play almost completely dependent on dialogue. He placed it to one side, and the following year developed it into *The Ritual*.

Family issues preoccupied Bergman during this period. Anna, the wife of his brother Dag, had been confined to a mental clinic in Athens in the spring of 1965, and had reacted sharply against her confinement. The doctors told Dag that she would need a long course of treatment. Bergman arranged for Anna to enter Sophiahemmet in Stockholm. Anna was forty-seven and the mother of two boys. Divorce proceedings were currently in progress.

In the spring of 1966, stationed in Athens, Dag wrote frequently to Ingmar in the wake of their mother's death. He then asked his brother to lend him 2,000 crowns, because the cost of Anna's healthcare demanded it. He offered to repay the money at the rate of 200 crowns per month. On 28 May, Ingmar pointed out that their father's recent stay at Sophiahemmet had cost more than 10,000 crowns. He said his margins were small, but that once again he would step into the breach. Relations continued to be fraught. Seven years earlier, Dag had written, 'It is sometimes difficult to be your brother because people expect you to be profound and have a good way with women – something I never had.' Dag's bitter, sardonic nature poisoned the well of their relationship.

Using a crew of forty-five – extremely large by Swedish standards – Bergman spent the final four months of 1967 on *Shame*. The team spirit so conspicuous in Scandinavian filmmaking now prevailed. The script called for the trees to be utterly bare, devastated by fire and bombs. But in the autumn of 1967 the trees were still flourishing, and Max von Sydow and others had to climb up ladders and pick off the remaining leaves, one by one. Max remembered the crew gathering with Bergman 'at a quiet lunch of ham and eggs, or at the tea table with the cookie package and the chocolate box'.[21] Bergman's script supervisor, Katinka Faragó, remembers that 'on Fårö we had no water, we had to pump it up by hand, and the loo was in the woods. I had a big house, because of my children, and often the crew would gather for cocktails at my place, and we had to use our imagination to come up with food to have with the wine, because there was just one shop on Fårö, and not a fancy one by any means.' The noise of jets screaming over the refugees was generated by two J34 Hawker Hunters, which could fly at up to 1,000 km per hour and had been hired from a military base near Gothenburg.[22] In the screenplay, a submarine surfaces to rescue those fleeing the war; Bergman shot the sequence, but in the finished film everyone perishes.

Behind the scenes, though, the clouds were gathering around Ingmar and Liv. In private letters to Liv, he even referred to 'the demons' that harassed him. On the ground, he regarded Liv's family and friends as a threat to their relationship. 'His jealousy was violent – a psychological rather than physical force,' she recalled.[23] During the shoot of *Shame*, tensions reached a peak. For the final sequence, Liv was left in a rowing boat in freezing temperatures. 'He was so cruel to me,' she said. Katinka Faragó, meanwhile, was going to the post office to arrange for alimony and support cheques to be sent to Bergman's ex-wives and children, recalling how Pastor Erik Bergman had despatched funds from Hedvig Eleonora Church to Hedvig Sjöberg to help with the raising of the illegitimate children he had sired.

In the late 1960s, with the Vietnam War still raging, *Shame* seemed to offer Bergman the opportunity to respond to Bo Widerberg's caustic comments about his cinema being irrelevant to contemporary society. In fact, the film concerned not so much war as Bergman's own complexes – the moral turpitude personified by Max von Sydow's Jan Rosenberg, his self-pity, his indecisiveness, his consuming commitment to music (read 'film and theatre'). All this at the expense of his love for the tolerant Eva, who yearns to have babies, while he prefers to play and practise the violin.

Shame had been written more than a year before the Soviet Union invaded Czechoslovakia and before the conflict in Vietnam had assumed catastrophic proportions. 'If those two things had already happened,' said Bergman, 'the film would have worn a different aspect.'[24] Although he cited the tragedy of civilians caught up in the struggle in southeast Asia as his inspiration, he recognised that the film originated 'in a panicky question. How would I have behaved in the Nazi period if Sweden had been occupied and if I'd held some position of responsibility or been connected with home institutions?'[25] For this reason, the character of the craven 'mayor' Jacobi (Gunnar Björnstrand) reflects as much of Bergman's inner turmoil as does Jan Rosenberg, and evokes, however obliquely, the director's reactions to Hitler and the concentration camps. Bergman did not live to witness Sweden's abandonment of its traditional neutrality in May 2022, when the country applied to join NATO during the Ukraine War.

Jan cannot call on the convenient aid of either fascist or communist convictions. He and his partner Eva (Liv Ullmann) are musicians who have withdrawn to a remote Baltic island, where they eke out their livelihood by growing and selling fruit. The island is invaded. A guerrilla movement arises, involving many civilians, and Jan's old friend Jacobi proves to be a quisling. He arrests Jan and Eva but soon releases them. When he comes to their cottage, he sneers at 'the sacred freedom of art, the sacred spinelessness of art', and ascribes his behaviour to 'towering guilt and a great pain'. He tells Eva how he went to see his ailing mother, only to be told by the doctor that she had just died (exactly what happened to Bergman himself). In the turmoil, Jan finds himself assigned to execute the perfidious Jacobi. But nothing can save either him or Eva.

To Bergman, who found it difficult to stray beyond very personal dilemmas, to discuss social issues other than in terms of his own familiar characters, the confusion in *Shame* is exemplified in the relationship between Jan and Eva. As in *Hour of the Wolf*, the woman appears more practical than her partner. She sounds as punctilious as Alma about her housekeeping budget. When they awake in the cottage, Eva puts coffee on the stove and washes fearlessly in cold water. Jan can only swallow a tablet, feel an aching tooth and pick absentmindedly at his toes. Strange portents disturb their breakfast. Jan notes that the church bells are tolling on a Friday, and the phone rings incessantly, even when Eva lifts the receiver. 'It's best to know nothing,' says Jan. 'I'm sick of your escapism,' responds Eva. All this may have mirrored the everyday life of Liv and Ingmar on Fårö.

Art, for Bergman, must be a profession or it amounts to nothing. Significantly, therefore, neither Johan Borg in *Hour of the Wolf* nor Jan Rosenberg in *Shame* is seen to be practising his art. Johan essays a quick sketch of his wife and dabs painfully at a canvas on the beach before confronting Veronica Vogler. But Jan does little more than caress his violin – and then only in order to mention that Pampini, a contemporary of Beethoven who had made the instrument in 1814, had fought with the Russian armies against Napoleon, the implication being that he, the musician of today, fails to accept his obligations in a similar crisis.

At home one evening before their world crumbles, Jan and Eva eat fish and drink white wine and talk tenderly to each other. They make resolutions about their music that will never be honoured. At such moments Bergman may be seen to cherish the togetherness that sex and marriage can bring. Harriet Bosse wrote to Strindberg, in the wake of their break-up, 'I am very fond of you – whatever may happen – I love you, perhaps because, through such deep and boundless sorrow, you have infused my life with meaning.'[26] Liv Ullmann said of Bergman, 'His hunger for togetherness was insatiable.'[27]

The concluding sequences of *Shame* rank among the most pessimistic moments in Bergman's cinema. Marooned at sea with other refugees, Jan and Eva have been tested and found wanting. Rations are handed round like a Last Supper. (Religious connotations run through even the most naturalistic of Bergman's films. Jan, for instance, denies thrice that he knows where Jacobi has hidden his cash, even though it is he who has stolen it.) As the boat dwindles to a speck in the indifferent ocean, Eva mentions a dream, not hers, but 'someone else's that I'm part of. And what happens when that person wakes up and is ashamed?'

Bergman felt frustrated with the final edit of *Shame*. 'The first half, which is about the events of the war, is bad,' he wrote in *Images*. 'The second half, which is about the effects of war, is good. [. . .] Once the outer violence stops and the inner violence begins, *Shame* becomes a good film.'[28] Perhaps the ultimate courage of the film is that Bergman thrusts his characters out of the warm, secure, womb-like refuge that constitutes the bourgeois family into an environment as hostile and uncaring as a lunar landscape. As he wrote in the screenplay, 'They're alone, and the world is coming to an end.'

Back in 1951, Bergman had established his own production company, Cinematograph AB. Bergman had named it in affectionate tribute to Louis Lumière's early motion-picture machine. For years the company lay almost dormant, until it featured on the credits of films from *Shame* onwards. In 1968, quarters were found at Floragatan 4 (the street where Bergman's parents had lived in the early 1920s), adjacent to the offices of Sandrew Film & Theatre company. At the top of the winding stair stood the ship's figurehead that featured in both *Persona* and *The Passion of Anna*, and that became an emblem for Cinematograph. Bergman cherished the copy that his set designer P. A. Lundgren made of the wooden sculpture in 1973; he had come upon it while visiting the Bunge Museum in Fårösund.

During the ensuing eight years, he made Floragatan 4 his headquarters in Stockholm, and it became a more vital centre as Cinematograph branched out into production in the early 1970s. 'Bergman' was inscribed on a brass plate beneath the company plaque, and within the premises a screening room was constructed, with sumptuous armchairs in yellow velvet.

In early February, Bergman and Liv Ullmann journeyed to Rome for a few weeks' break, with 'each day filled with very special and fantastic experiences'. He had a dream one night of a woman and burning horses, an image he would use in *The Passion of Anna*, then just starting to germinate in his mind. In fact, his workbook for January 1968 includes mention of 'Annandreas', the working title for *The Passion of Anna*. He and Liv found time for lunch with Dino De Laurentiis, a meeting with Alberto Moravia and visits to the Vatican and the Colosseum. Away from the stress and pressures of the film set, their relationship recovered its joy and passion.

In Rome, Bergman had his first memorable encounter with Fellini. Within an instant they were brothers, recalled Ullmann. 'They embraced, laughed together as if they had lived the same life. They wandered through the streets in the night, arms around each other, Fellini wearing a dramatic black cape, Ingmar in his little cap and an old winter coat.'[29] The admiration was mutual. When *Amarcord* opened a few years later, Bergman saw it several times. In an interview in 1966, Fellini had waxed enthusiastic about Bergman's 'seductive quality of mesmerising your attention. Even if you're not in full agreement with what he says, you enjoy the way he says it, his way of seeing the world with such intensity.' He expressed amusement at Bergman's gait: 'With his hands on his back, he walked with long steps like an inspector *à la* Kierkegaard or Beckett . . .'[30]

In 1962, Fellini had written to Bergman saying that the Italian producer Tonino Cervi 'has talked to me of an idea of producing a film in three episodes to be directed by you, by Kurosawa and by me'. On 10 October that year, Bergman responded, emphasising his admiration for Fellini and that 'to make a picture together with you should be a great honour to me'. On 18 March 1965, Fellini again wrote to Bergman, confirming that 'now this project seems to have more chances of materialising, and Cervi is working on it with great enthusiasm'.

By the time Bergman and Liv Ullmann arrived in Rome in early 1968, the project had somehow lost the involvement of Akira Kurosawa. Fellini and Bergman would create a joint film, entitled *Love Duet*, to be shot in Stockholm and Rome. Martin Poll would be the producer, and filming was scheduled tentatively for the autumn of 1969, after Bergman had completed *The Passion of Anna*. Fellini declared, 'It will be a poker game in which we hide aces up our sleeves. The only person we may hide things from is the producer.'

On 19 February, *Hour of the Wolf* opened in Stockholm. Many critics noted that the screenplay had been written prior to the making of *Persona*, and that Bergman's style, heavily symbolic, did not mark a leap forward. The novelist Per Olov Enquist, writing in *Chaplin*, made an interesting comment. Bergman, he said, resembled a deadly black mamba in the bourgeois drawing room, 'lying in a corner, coiled up and remorseful, sobbing over his hostility and his neuroses, and how his tail had been trampled on as a child'.[31]

Shrugging off the tepid response to *Hour of the Wolf*, Bergman rehearsed *The Ritual* (*Riten*) for a month in the spring with his four actors, Gunnar Björnstrand, Ingrid Thulin, Anders Ek and Erik Hell, and then filmed it in a mere nine days in May and June in the studios at Råsunda. Essentially a TV movie, *The Ritual* was made with Bergman's habitual stringency: 'I'd set the footage to a maximum of 15,000 metres [almost 50,000 feet]. We used up 13,500 or something of that order, so I had to know exactly what we were going to include.'[32] He and Mago ransacked the studio storerooms for all the tables and chairs they could find to save costs in production design.

With the small screen in mind, Bergman relied on large close-ups for most of the 74 minutes of the film, occasionally whip-panning from person to person during a sharp exchange of words, but more often cutting from face to face. The backgrounds – office walls, hotel rooms, a confessional, a bar, a dressing room – are grey and neutral.

The Ritual consists of nine scenes, during which three cabaret entertainers are examined by a civil judge. At first they are interviewed together, and the judge then seeks to impose his will on them as individuals. Meanwhile, the entertainers round on one another, railing at their humiliating profession and their own emotional inadequacies. Eventually, they cause the judge's death by heart failure as they perform their 'ritual'. Although in several Bergman films there are faint harbingers of events or developments in his personal life, the parallels between the content of *The Ritual* and the tax investigation to which Bergman would be submitted in 1976 is uncanny.

The four characters in *The Ritual* appear intimately related to one another, in their quest for freedom and their disillusion with their life and profession. Their names echo those of other Bergman characters – Albert Emanuel Fisher (Anders Ek) or Hans Winkelmann (Gunnar Björnstrand). Hans's marriage is on the rocks, and he articulates the flaws familiar in so many Bergman relationships: 'Our words don't fit. There's an absolute lack of understanding.' In the fourth scene, 'A Confessional', the judge, like some fugitive from a Graham Greene novel, blurts out his fear of imminent death – to Bergman himself, no less, who plays the priest. The confessional is a central plank in several of Bergman's films, whether or not they be tinged with religious overtones. The act of avowal becomes one of expiation, of liberation. Alma recollects the orgy on the beach in *Persona*. Ester pours out her heart to the old waiter at the end of *The Silence*. Jacobi bares his soul to Jan and Eva in *Shame*.

The Ritual amounts to a personal catechism for Bergman. His characters pronounce lines that he himself has delivered in interviews. Sebastian, forced on the defensive by the judge's questions, asserts his independence: 'I'm my own god. I supply my own angels and demons.' Winkelmann admits that he has one great horror – being left alone. Later he says he has learned almost everything about humiliation. 'Something about me seems to invite it. The really great artists can't be hurt. I'm not one of them.' Like Bergman, Sebastian must support various children, but 'my lawyer knows more about it than I do'. Again, like Bergman, Abrahamson and the others are obsessed with their physical metabolism. Thea tells the judge she has suffered from eczema for two years. Sebastian complains of eye-ache and diarrhoea. The scrofulous Abrahamson cannot prevent himself from perspiring freely. 'I'm sorry if the smell upsets you,' he apologises to Sebastian. Even a passing reference to cancer carries a cold menace, an implacability that matches Fisher's own attitude to life. Bodily sickness becomes, for the umpteenth time, a sign of spiritual malaise.

The Ritual hints at money being concealed by the entertainers in Switzerland, and, ironically, Bergman was persuaded by his advisers in late 1967 to set up a company in Switzerland called Persona AG. He even named an offscreen character 'Bauer' in *The Ritual* – it was Sven Harald Bauer who handled Bergman's legal and financial affairs. This would cause him enormous heartache in 1976.

'At ten past nine this morning, I wrote the first page of this new screenplay [*The Passion of Anna*],' noted Bergman in his workbook on 5 July 1968. He spent the summer weeks completing the script, so that production could begin in September. He had accepted an invitation to attend the Sorrento Film Festival in Italy, where *Shame* would have its world premiere. At the last minute he pleaded an ear infection, leaving Liv Ullmann to appear in his stead. The fact that many of Sweden's most prominent film critics gathered in Sorrento – the festival was devoted entirely to Swedish cinema that year – may have deterred Bergman from journeying south.

Shame met with an unexpected amalgam of scorn and admiration when it opened in Stockholm on the same day as it premiered in Sorrento. Bergman's film undermined the complacency of the ordinary Swede; it enraged the politically committed observer, however, by its refusal to take sides. It clung, in short, to the traditional Swedish neutrality at a time when opinion was running strongly against the United States and its participation in the Vietnam War. A week after the premiere, Sara Lidman condemned Bergman in the evening paper *Aftonbladet* for granting 'the contemporary Western intelligentsia total freedom from responsibility for Vietnam by turning this war into a metaphysical issue'.[33] In *Dagens Nyheter*, Torsten Bergmark described Bergman's position as coinciding with the sort of intolerable aloofness that the artist attempts to maintain. 'It results in the deepest human degradation,' he wrote, 'and the kind of conduct that is less morally defensible than even that of the quislings.'[34]

Bergman's attitude was defiant, if hazy. 'I do not know of any party that is for frightened and terrified people who are experiencing the period of dusk and the fact that it has begun and the plane is definitely inclined downwards. I cannot really engage myself in any political activity.'[35] He often reacted against the idea of coercion against the artist and would tell the story of Shostakovich being asked to rewrite a symphony on the grounds that it was insufficiently socialistic in thought.

Pauline Kael, writing in *The New Yorker* magazine, spent most of her notice on dismembering Bergman's career, while at the same time describing *Shame* as a masterpiece, 'a flawless work and a masterly vision. Treating the most dreaded of subjects, the film makes one feel elated. The subject is our responses to death, but a work of art is a true sign of life.' *Shame* earned a nomination for an Academy Award but did not win. The film received a pitiful distribution in the US and the UK.

———

On 30 June 1968, Bergman decided to change the title of his next film from *Annaandreas* to *A Passion*. Just as *Winter Light* was listed as production number L136 in the Svensk Filmindustri files, now *The Passion of Anna* is L182. When United Artists later informed him that for copyright reasons it could not be released under that name in the United States, Bergman suggested 'The Passion of Anna'.

Not since *Winter Light* had Bergman felt so ill at ease when making a film. Max von Sydow was under pressure also, for he was appearing at the Royal Dramatic Theatre for two performances each weekend during the 45-day production schedule and had to commute by boat during the late autumn season. Sven Nykvist and Bergman frustrated each other; Bergman felt a recurrence of his old stomach ulcer, and Nykvist suffered from giddy spells. In the final stages, even the editing proved difficult, and over 11,000 feet were left on the cutting-room floor.

The most serious issue may have been the deteriorating relationship between Liv and Ingmar. Bergman described her character in *The Passion of Anna* as 'sensitive, terribly intense, sickly, and timorous', while he himself identified strongly with Andreas.[36] He had not even attended the christening of baby Linn. The circumstances conspired against them. Liv had been cast as Kristina in Jan Troell's massive production of *The Emigrants* and *The New Land*, which would entail location work in the United States.

'My philosophy [...] is that there exists an evil that cannot be explained,' wrote Bergman, 'a virulent, terrifying evil – and humans are the only animals to possess it. An evil that is irrational and not bound by law. Cosmic. Causeless. Nothing frightens people more than incomprehensible, unexplainable evil.'[37]

This sense of malevolence runs like a filament through *The Passion of Anna*. Andreas Winkelmann (Max von Sydow) has parted from his wife and withdrawn from the world to live in solitude on an island in the Baltic. But without warning he finds himself confronted by two kinds of violence: physical, in the shape of an unidentified maniac who slaughters sheep, and psychic, in the presence of Anna Fromm (Liv Ullmann), a crippled widow whose husband is also named Andreas.

The suspense of *The Passion of Anna* originates in this sinister 'duplication', the feeling that Andreas is being sucked inexorably along the same path to disaster as his namesake was – deluded, exasperated and finally driven insane by the passionate idealism of Anna.

The mood engendered by Bergman is sinister and bizarre. The identity of the mysterious psychopath who slaughters the sheep, tortures a dog in the woods and humiliates Andreas's ailing neighbour, Johan of Skir (Erik Hell), is never disclosed. But the violence growls in the background, like the bass line in a piece of music, and permeates Andreas himself until, in a horrifying outburst, he swings an axe at Anna's head and beats her furiously. Bemused and ashamed, Andreas drifts into a light sleep, only to be roused by the noise of fire engines. The island's assailant has poured petrol over an unfortunate horse, set it alight, locked the door of the stables and vanished. Nobody is apprehended. *The Passion of Anna* might be described as a detective story without a solution.

The other engrossing theme of the film is more familiar to Bergman devotees: the probing beneath the mask that each person offers to the world. Anna speaks ardently of the honesty and harmony of her marriage, only to provoke a replica of the terminal clash with her husband. Elis (Erland Josephson), an opulent architect and photographer who lives close to Andreas on the island, appears painfully aware of the infidelity of his wife Eva (Bibi Andersson), despite the sarcastic indifference he affects. Andreas himself, whether he is regarded as a Christ-like figure or a criminal on the run, smarts under the well-meaning contempt of his neighbours.

Andreas is caught between the forces of light and darkness. When he visits Elis's studio, he flinches under the bright lights used by the photographer. Bergman introduces lamps and shade to suggest a penumbra close to the dream state. And, in one of the film's most alarming sequences, when Anna, by now living with Andreas, tightens her embrace around his neck so tightly that in her eyes one glimpses an urge to strangle her partner, the light in her room has been extinguished.

Sleep and the subconscious state beckon Andreas. Eva is found dozing in her car at the roadside. 'Sometimes I can't sleep at night,' she tells Andreas. 'So I fall asleep during the day.' Again and again, Bergman shows people half asleep, discovered in the grey region between waking and dreaming. While one Andreas lives in actuality, the other dwells in a dream zone. When Andreas falls asleep, he enters the world of his namesake. In the original screenplay, Andreas informs Anna that he is afraid of 'the sleep, which is always dreams that hunt me here or there, or merely the darkness that rustles with ghosts and memories'. Dreams are the repository of guilt for Andreas. He succumbs slowly to the contagion of guilt, the legacy of the 'dead' Andreas, who perished in a car crash while Anna was driving. The ultimate logic of the film is that Andreas should find himself seated beside Anna in a similar situation.

One of Bergman's experiments has dated badly. He asks each of the four main actors to talk about their character, wearing everyday clothes and talking conversationally into the camera. This Brechtian *Verfremdungseffekt* looks and sounds self-conscious, and redolent of the 1960s. Sven Nykvist's camerawork, however, could not be better suited to the material. It forces the spectator to enter the drama – to hasten and lurch through the snow beside a deranged Andreas, to duck and veer away as Andreas attacks Anna outside his cottage, and to pore over the words evoking violence in the letter Andreas has found in Anna's handbag. This was Bergman's first dramatic film to be shot in colour, and chromatic effects and a jagged editing technique heighten the audience's apprehension of violence. Blue has been drained from the negative. Grey, brown, green and, above all, red predominate, so that the revolving amber light on a police vehicle, the splash of Anna's scarlet scarf in the snow and the hectic orange of the stable inferno carry an authentic charge of frenzy.

In the final shot, Andreas collapses in a landscape that slowly dissolves before the audience's eyes. The ground becomes a pattern of flickering granules, pulsating cells of light, and Bergman's voice is heard offscreen: 'This time his name was Andreas Winkelmann.' On another occasion, he might have been called Jan Rosenberg or Johan Borg. As Andreas wanders in fruitless circles, like a demented patient in some infernal laboratory experiment, one thinks back to Erik Lindegren's great suite of poems from the 1940s, *the man without a way,* in which the hapless traveller stares in terror at a signpost offering him a cluster of vague and uncertain directions. In *The Passion of Anna,* Bergman still shared the anguish of those writers of his youth, still bore witness to a collapse of society's frantic attempts to maintain order in the face of war and violence.[38] As Eva asks in that film, 'What kind of poison corrodes the best in us, leaving only the shell?'

Ingmar with his long-time cinematographer, Sven Nykvist.
Courtesy of Svensk Filmindustri.

17

AT LAST, STABILITY

Dejected though he must have been at the prospect of yet another emotional separation, Bergman found once again that work proved the best therapy. In one of his early essays, he quotes Baudelaire: 'It is necessary to work, if not from inclination, at least from despair. Everything considered, work is less boring than amusing oneself.'[1] On 16 January 1969 he held a press conference at Dramaten to announce his radical staging of Georg Büchner's drama *Woyzeck*. He had originally intended to present the play when he was appointed head of Dramaten in 1963. The story of the soldier who murders his mistress in a fit of inchoate jealousy would be tackled like one of Bergman's 'chamber films'. The performance would last for an hour and a half, so Dramaten could offer two sessions each evening (much to the chagrin of Thommy Berggren, the brilliant young star of *Elvira Madigan*, who pleaded with Bergman to reduce the schedule). Tickets went on sale at a mere 5 crowns each (one US dollar at the time), and Bergman insisted on some drastic changes to the layout of the theatre. The cloakroom area became part of the auditorium, and the audience sat on benches in the stage area. *Woyzeck* was then played out in a concentrated zone between the back of the stage and the stalls – a space just 16 feet 6 inches wide and 11 feet 6 inches deep.

The mood of the rehearsals was often high-spirited. Bergman described the start of each scene to Berggren and Gunnel Lindblom (playing Marie) and outlined the particular feeling or atmosphere required. His directions were clear, concise and to the point. As Henrik Sjögren, who followed the entire rehearsal period, wrote, 'Büchner's laconic, powerful dialogue is an ideal skeleton for Ingmar's concrete vision.'[2] Although Bergman had a precise concept for each of the 28 scenes and carried around with him a copy of the play covered with sketches and notes, he allowed his performers a reasonably free rein. 'An old actor attacked me when I respectfully gave him some direction. "Mr Bergman isn't here to teach us how to perform theatre, but simply to see that we don't bash into one another on stage." I think that was rather well said!'[3]

Another radical aspect of the *Woyzeck* production was Bergman's insistence on open rehearsals. Spectators were encouraged to attend, free of charge, on various mornings prior to the opening, and the actors discussed their responses afterwards. During one of the last of these sessions, Bergman had a minor altercation in the wings with the critic Bengt Jahnsson. At one point he shoved him away, quite gently in fact, but Jahnsson lost his balance, and immediately there was a sensation. Jahnsson, drama critic for the daily *Dagens Nyheter*, took the director to court. Bergman lost the action and was fined 5,000 crowns. He paid up cheerfully, saying that he had defended the good name of his actors and would do so again in similar circumstances.

Woyzeck opened on 12 March. Three days later Per Olov Enquist, a distinguished author in his own right, noted in the evening tabloid *Expressen* that this was 'an extraordinarily neat and typical Bergman piece of work, which in its third act also possesses a certain warmth'. By then, however, Bergman had already taken the plane to Fårö, and that very same day began shooting a documentary about the island and its inhabitants.

The reaction to *Shame* may have stung Bergman into preparing his political statement. More likely, however, his years on Fårö had persuaded him that, if these people were ever to escape the leaden hand of central government, someone would have to brandish a fist in protest. So he approached Sveriges Radio and offered them the idea of a TV documentary on Fårö. They accepted. Bergman was excited by the potential of television as a political force. 'A single image on TV is a hundred times more eloquent [than theatre],' he said.[4]

'My political act', he told me, 'is to try to stop this island and its people being crushed. I live there with 700 neighbours, and there I am not confronted with the problems of Cuba because I have the problems of my neighbours. Human conscience cannot encompass sorrow for millions of people.'

Some foreign observers registered disappointment with *The Fårö Document* (*Fårö-dokument*). They could not accept that Bergman was content to make a simple, unadorned documentary on 16 mm, with grainy photography, a hand-held camera and a microphone thrust under the noses of interviewees in the tradition of *cinéma-vérité*. One of the leading figures was Valter Broman, a farmer at Dämba and Bergman's direct neighbour. A handful of colour sequences evoke the natural cycle of the island, but the rest is in monochrome. The lambing season is miraculously captured by Sven Nykvist's photography. Shorn of commentary, and with just a faint jingle of bells as the sheep give birth in the fields, this sequence serves as a counterweight to the slaughtering scenes and the skinning of the ewes (a reference to which occurs in the prologue to *Persona*). In Bergman's screenplay for *Faithless* (2000), Marianne talks of Fårö's 'pines shaped by the wind, that endless shoreline'.

The film does not obey a formal structure. There are interviews with a taxi driver, a teacher, a churchwarden, a pensioner, a farmer. Bergman records a burial service in sight of the sea as a bell tolls furiously; a homely communion service as the camera explores the room – the pictures, a clock with revolving mechanism – and a sense of time and death emerges. The people of Fårö wish to continue in the ways they have done for centuries, yet they also need better facilities. From this tension between past and future comes the gist of Bergman's interviews. Young folk want to leave the island. Their elders are suspicious of change. Ultimately, however, these people embody Bergman's own attitudes to life. As one farmer says, 'It's better to have few friends than too many.'

By early May, *The Fårö Document* was complete, and Sveriges Radio telecast it on New Year's Day 1970. More than 3 million Swedes watched the programme.

Over the previous year or two, Universal, United Artists and Warner Brothers had been flirting with Bergman in the hope that he would make a film for them. The project known as *Love Duet* proved more tempting. On 10 April 1969, Bergman's agent Paul Kohner wrote to Harry Schein with the revised agreement between Personafilm AG and Martin Poll Films for the 'loan-out of the services of Mr Ingmar Bergman'. This contract stated that the film as a whole would be directed by Fellini, Bergman and perhaps a third director. Bergman would receive $130,000 for writing the screenplay and directing the 50-minute segment. Five days later, Schein replied to Kohner saying that Bergman would shoot his segment abroad and not in Sweden as stated in the agreement.

Bergman cherished his script for this project, which he entitled *Sixty-four Minutes with Rebecka* (later referred to as *White Walls*). He even envisioned the main role being played by Katharine Ross, whose star had risen since her appearance in *The Graduate*. Rebecka Lawrence, an American and a teacher of children with hearing disabilities, is sexually frustrated even though she loves her husband. An often violent one-night stand in a club leaves her feeling guilty and disappointed. Bergman clearly wrote the script in the midst of his rupture with Liv Ullmann; he also delivers a dig to Käbi Laretei through the character of Rebecka's mother, who is a concert pianist forever on the move.

However, despite Paul Kohner's enthusiasm for the script that Bergman wrote during the summer ('a brilliant group of scenes, probing deeply into the soul and body of contemporary woman'), the agent soon realised that Martin Poll was reluctant to pay the $57,500 due on delivery of the screenplay. On 24 November, Harry Schein (by then Bergman's trusted counsellor in business matters) cabled Kohner asking for clarification of Bergman's remuneration should he alone make the film – in other words, without Fellini. A revised contract called for payment of $110,000 to Personafilm, plus participation in the profits of the picture.

By 5 December an exasperated letter from Schein to Kohner indicated that *Sixty-four Minutes with Rebecka* was unlikely to be made, especially as Bergman said that it would be sexually explicit and, therefore, all or parts of it would be unsuitable for eventual screening on TV.

Bergman's other script of the period, *The Lie*, dated from May 1969 and enjoyed more immediate success. Although he wrote this play for Eurovision, Bergman seemed quite content to let others direct it in various countries. The Swedish version (under the original title of *The Sanctuary*, or *Reservatet*) starred Gunnel Lindblom, Erland Josephson and Per Myrberg, under the direction of Jan Molander. In Britain, Alan Bridges directed the piece for the BBC, and in the United States CBS Playhouse 90 presented *The Lie* in the autumn of 1972.

In *The Lie*, Bergman again focuses on the umbilical cord that binds the married couple. Once more, the man appears the more easily undermined of the two sexes, the one who cracks first under the searching, relentless onslaught of his partner during a 24-hour time span. In Swedish, the man and the woman bear the same name as the leading characters in *The Passion of Anna*: Andreas and Anna Fromm. This, perhaps, is the story of Anna and the 'first' Andreas, the predecessor in whose tracks Max von Sydow's Andreas found himself treading. Andreas is turning forty, 'like having an unmentionable disease', comments his office superior; Anna is a few years younger. Her brother, a tormented author, languishes in hospital. 'The worst part of it is – I had hopes,' he tells her, on the verge of a breakdown. Anna has a lover who is world-weary and suffers from insomnia. The 'lie' is the very fact of the marriage. During all these eight years, Anna has never enjoyed true happiness with her husband. Their arguments rise in a crescendo until Andreas loses his temper and threatens Anna with an axe – an explosion of anger identical to the one in *The Passion of Anna*, and reminiscent of the quarrels that marred the final months of the partnership between Bergman and Liv Ullmann.

On 4 September, Liv flew to Chicago for location work on *The Emigrants*, which occupied the next five weeks in Minnesota and Wisconsin. Bergman wrote long letters to her, but during this time, she had a very brief liaison with Max von Sydow, which caused consternation back home in the von Sydow household, and which wounded Bergman sharply when he found out about it. In late 1969, they parted by mutual consent. Liv flew to Stockholm, to be greeted at the airport by Harriet Andersson, Bibi Andersson and Gunnel Lindblom. They and some other friends gathered at Bibi's house and spent most of that night lying on the floor, drinking wine and reminiscing about Bergman's behaviour in bed and elsewhere. Bergman wrote to her soon afterwards: 'Now I can see that this separation was absolutely necessary. Otherwise we would have set each other on fire.'[5] Frustrated and lonely, he contacted Käbi Laretei and asked her to come out to the island to see her 'Immi' again. But it came to naught, and the next year Bergman sent her a letter notable for its ice-cold clarity, even if he maintained his deep tenderness towards her and Daniel. He requested her to sign the divorce papers promptly, which would mean dispensing with two lawyers and long-drawn-out procedures.[6]

Bergman could never relinquish the ties with Liv. She would call him most days, and, she said, he would comfort *her*.[7] They agreed to a three-month trial separation. Linn accompanied Liv to Oslo. But although they could talk happily on the telephone, sometimes daily, they could not recover the intimacy of earlier years. Within two years of their break-up, she would be back in the Bergman team, starring in *Cries and Whispers*, and then in *Face to Face* and *The Serpent's Egg*. In 1975, he flew across the Atlantic to see her acting in Ibsen's *A Doll's House* in New York, and returned to Sweden the next day. 'He was one of two men in my life I have really loved,' she said, 'and I wanted it to last.'[8] Her role in *Saraband* was the final tribute Bergman paid to her as actress and former partner. In 1976 Liv revealed a new and unexpected talent as a writer, in her candid autobiography, *Changing*.

———

Now in middle age, Bergman could bring to *A Dream Play* a sensitivity and incipient wisdom lacking in his earlier productions of Strindberg's plays. He had directed *A Dream Play* for Swedish television in 1963, and he prepared an 'edited' version for the small auditorium (Lilla Scenen) at the rear of Dramaten. Strindberg had been fifty-two when he completed the piece, and Bergman was almost the same age when he embarked on this new production.

Resisting the temptation to evoke the spectacular production by Olof Molander in 1955, Bergman presented the play in ascetic terms, with spartan decor and the mood of a chamber work. His cuts in the text affect chiefly the third act, from which he removed many of Strindberg's digressive reflections on Eastern mysticism. 'What was left', wrote Henrik Sjögren, 'was a dream rising from the poet's imagination or, more correctly, the poet's dream, concretely materialised as a stage play precisely calculated to involve each member of the audience in its happenings.'[9]

At the heart of *A Dream Play* stands the elfin, blonde figure of Agnes. Her presence summons up memories and complexes, faded hopes and incidents, rendered either humorous or tragic by age. There is, for example, the fisherman, jolly in a bowler hat, who dreamed of catching the sun in his net when he was still youthful. The action takes place in several time planes. The Crucifixion is enacted, Chopin's Funeral March is heard, and men are crowned with laurels and thorns. Agnes was played by Malin Ek, then twenty-four and the daughter of one of Bergman's closest friends,

Anders Ek, and the choreographer Birgit Cullberg. For a brief, charmed spell, Malin Ek shared a love affair with Bergman, after they had met on *The Passion of Anna*, in which she made an uncredited appearance. More than twenty years later, Daniel Bergman would cast her as Märta in *Sunday's Children*, his father's screenplay about his childhood.

Bergman's production of *A Dream Play* abounded in nuance and invention. Groups of people stood frozen on the stage, as though rooted in time. In the funeral scene, couples dressed entirely in black gazed over black barriers. Later, everyone appeared clad in white costumes. At the end, after the cast removed their masks, in a gesture of sacrifice and self-reckoning, Agnes was left alone. She got to her feet, looked disconsolately around the low-lit stage, and then exited.

A Dream Play opened on 14 March 1970 and was the talk of the town. By November it had celebrated its hundredth performance. But in the midst of the acclaim, Bergman suffered personal grief. His father died on 26 April. Solemn, strict, a poet *manqué*, Erik Bergman had grown more and more frail since the death of his wife four years earlier. Knowing that his father was stricken with cancer of the oesophagus, Bergman visited him in his bed at Sophiahemmet just four days before the end. Erik had come to appreciate his son's accomplishments and self-discipline.

In May 1970, Bergman travelled to London to stage *Hedda Gabler*, using the same set and production notes as he had in the 1964 version at the Royal Dramatic Theatre, but featuring British actors, with Maggie Smith as Hedda. The production was staged at the Old Vic, at that point the home of the National Theatre, and friction developed between Bergman and Sir Laurence Olivier, then in charge of the NT. Each felt like a king in his domain. Bergman was accustomed to being able to switch out a light when he so desired, and Olivier was used to granting permission for such gestures. It proved an unhappy, humiliating week. Bergman comforted himself by attending concerts. 'I'd have my dinner in the hotel, and then I'd walk over to the Southbank and go to the Queen Elizabeth Hall or the Purcell Room.' He refused to write a piece for the programme booklet ('As a principle I never write or tell things about my productions or film and theatre'), and informed the National Theatre abruptly that he would give no interviews. At least he was granted a bedroom and sitting room at the prestigious Connaught Hotel.

Instead of returning directly to Stockholm, Bergman flew to Finland to supervise the presentation of *A Dream Play* at the Swedish Theatre in Helsinki. (He had declined an invitation to stage the Strindberg drama at the Comédie-Française in Paris, on the grounds that he had a poor grasp of French. But the production did go to Belgrade, where it won the Grand Prix at the Theatre Festival, and also to Venice and Vienna.)

During the brief stay in London, a significant encounter took place. On 2 May, Bergman's American agent, Paul Kohner, arranged a dinner in a private room at the Connaught Hotel. Leonard Goldenson, founder and president of ABC Corporation, was present with some of his associates. Martin Baum, head of ABC's new motion-picture division, listened as Bergman told him and his wife the outline of the next film he wanted to make, entitled *The Touch*, and which he had just started to write, with Bibi Andersson in mind for the leading role. 'We were to give our answer to Mr Kohner in a few days,' said Baum. 'But I could see from the faces that [Bergman] had sold everybody in the room. And my *wife*! With her, he scored a bullseye!'[10] Two days later, ABC Pictures Corporation confirmed its offer. Bergman would be paid a flat sum of one million dollars on delivery of a negative; ABC would also pay the salary of the English-speaking actor Bergman would choose to play the role of David in the movie ($200,000 as it happened). ABC would receive from Bergman a screenplay by 15 July 1970, and shooting would commence two months later. The eventual contract was prolix and elaborate, running to 110 pages.

Bergman had seen Elliott Gould in *Getting Straight* and felt he was ideal for the character he had in mind. He phoned him. Gould was flattered by this approach from one of the world's greatest living directors and immediately agreed to participate in the film. Bergman then embarked on the screenplay, working steadily from 9.30 a.m. to 3.30 p.m., using pads of yellow lined paper and writing in his laborious, quite large hand. If he made a mistake, he did not cross out and scratch in the new words but copied out the whole page again.[11]

On 5 September, before filming began, Bergman held a press conference at the studios in Råsunda. There was some sorrow at the thought that this marked Bergman's first real production break with Svensk Filmindustri for over fifteen years. Circumstances had changed, however. The studios were soon to be closed, and the State Theatre organisation (Riksteater) would move into Råsunda.

Much of *The Touch* was photographed in Visby, capital of Gotland, the large Baltic island of which Fårö is geographically a part. Rain pelted down continually, but Bergman maintained his sense of humour beneath a cap and plastic mac. He compared his methods with a boat lying on the Fårö shore, built according to an ancient formula. 'So I, in less than thirty years, have built up a "practical machine", a method of filmmaking. Why change something that's working so well?'[12] When Elliott Gould first came to Fårö, Bergman screened Fellini's *The White Sheik* for him, and the two men bonded immediately. Years later, Gould would still refer to himself as Ingmar's 'little brother'.[13]

Max von Sydow and Bibi Andersson were signed to play the husband and wife in *The Touch*, and Sheila Reid, who had appeared in Bergman's production of *Hedda Gabler* in London, was cast as Elliott Gould's sister. Bergman spoke of his enthusiasm for Gould: 'the impatience of a soul to find out things about reality and himself, and that is one thing that always touches me almost to tears, that impatience of the soul'.[14]

In his finest films and stage productions, Bergman had the knack of creating in his audience what the poet Samuel Taylor Coleridge termed 'the suspension of disbelief' – the appearance of Death on the shore at the outset of *The Seventh Seal* being a perfect example. That explains the failure of *The Touch* on many levels. It seems contrived; the dramatic climaxes are unconvincing, despite the excellent performance of Bibi Andersson. Although he must have believed in the film at the time, it is scarcely surprising that Bergman confessed in his workbook for 14 August 1980, '*The Touch* is still so unbearable that it makes me sick just to watch it.'

The story is as elementary and triangular as a women's picture of the 1940s. It begins and ends on a note of farewell that was excruciatingly personal to Bergman. Karin (Bibi Andersson) arrives at the hospital where her mother has just died. In the still, private room, she sits beside the dead body. A nurse gives her the wedding bands. Small things are suddenly very tangible; buses blurt past the window, and bells jostle in a nearby church. Bergman clearly recalled his mother's passing in 1966. He has said that this sequence was inspired by the death of an actor friend some fifteen years earlier, but the more immediate memory was that of his father's corpse in the clinic in 1970. 'I saw my father fifteen minutes after he died . . . His head was turned towards the window. The eyes were closed, but not completely. The illusion was that he was looking far away. I found it so extremely strange and beautiful and full of secrets.'[15]

Karin's husband Andreas (Max von Sydow) is a hospital consultant and returns home one day with David (Elliott Gould), a young archaeologist whom he has been treating for kidney trouble. For Karin, this dark handsome stranger and his abrupt declaration of love for her are auspices of deliverance from the bonds of her conventional middle-class existence. When he takes her to see a wooden sculpture of the Madonna that has been unearthed in a remote part of the island, he explains that the relic is being devoured by insects from within – insects that have lain dormant for 500 years and awoke when the statue was exposed to air and light. The parallel with Karin's social predicament is obvious. The instincts aroused in her by David are in their way as exquisite and meaningful as her own physical appeal.

An undercurrent of violence courses through the film. David's love-making is brutal and insensitive. He can slap her and, in a fit of temper, smashes furnishings in the room where they meet. Then he smarts beneath Karin's forgiving touch. Egotistical to the end, he abandons her, pregnant with his child. Bergman's mood, when writing the screenplay, echoed Graham Greene's thought from *The Heart of the Matter*: 'Human love knows nothing that might be called victory, barely a few strategic successes before the final disaster of death or indifference.' As they prepare to part, Karin tells her lover, 'No one has done me so much good as you. No one has done me so much harm as you.' They are, one suspects, lies that were addressed to Bergman by more than one lover.

Gould's characterisation resounds long after the film has ended. He mounts to a knobbly mixture of clumsiness and culture, aloofness and ardour, charm and solemnity, an exile condemned by his Jewishness to wander restlessly through the world for all time. No other Swedish actress, save perhaps Maj-Britt Nilsson, could have created such a vivid impression of Karin Vergérus as does Bibi Andersson. Bibi was expecting a child with Kjell Grede at the time and coped with the often arch English dialogue even better than Max von Sydow, whose English might have been equally assured but who was trapped in the thankless, cardboard role of Andreas.

Bergman concentrated on the editing of *The Touch* throughout the winter, and on 3 May 1971 representatives of ABC came to view the first print. They liked it, and met Bergman in the afternoon to express their delight. The following week, Dick Cavett flew to Stockholm to tape an interview with Bibi Andersson and Elliott Gould about the film. When *The Touch* opened in the United States and Britain, however, it failed to attract a wide audience. In one of the few favourable notices, *Variety* hailed it as 'both a romantic film of great poignancy and strength and an example of masterful cinema honed down to deceptively simple near perfection'.[16]

Post-production work on *The Touch* coincided with rehearsals for Bergman's production at Dramaten of *Show*, a play by Lars Forssell based on the life of the entertainer Lenny Bruce. Allan Edwall and Harriet Andersson were featured in the leading parts. Farcical and irreverent, this 'show' betrayed as much about Forssell as it did about Bruce. Few modern playwrights have been as prolific as Lars Forssell. He used poems and songs to trenchant effect and was a fierce thorn in the side of the Establishment. *Show* opened on 20 March 1971. Bergman then flew to London to prepare his cast and stage personnel for the presentation of *A Dream Play* in the World Theatre season at the Aldwych.

From late March through to early June, Bergman resumed his hermit-like existence on Fårö in order to write the screenplay for *Cries and Whispers*. He refused to interrupt his work to receive the Irving Thalberg Award in Hollywood, and Liv Ullmann accepted it on his behalf. A shadow fell over the summer, however, when his former wife Gun died in a car crash in the former Yugoslavia. Only fifty-four at the time, she had reached the pinnacle of her repute as a translator from Slavic languages, and had introduced Ivo Andrić's *The Bridge on the Drina* to Swedish readers in 1960. Andrić won the Nobel Prize for Literature the following year, and acknowledged Gun as his 'only translator' in Sweden.

By late July, the structure of *Cries and Whispers* had taken shape. Bergman considered casting Mia Farrow, Gunnel Lindblom and Birgitta Valberg, before settling on Harriet Andersson, Liv Ullmann, Ingrid Thulin and the young stage actress Kari Sylwan. At a press conference after the screening of the film at Cannes the following spring, Bergman declared, 'Some years ago I had a vision of a large red room, with three women in white whispering together. This picture came back again and again to me.' As a small boy, his image of the soul was that of a huge red monster; it had no face, and the interior of the creature appeared red and membranous. In his workbook, Bergman described the four women: 'Agnes, the dying one, Maria the most beautiful, Karin the strongest, and Anna the serving one.'[17]

The project differed in various ways from Bergman's previous work. Economically, it proceeded along rather perilous lines. Nobody wanted to invest in *Cries and Whispers* on a big scale. Bergman had to turn to the Swedish Film Institute for some aid and also to his principal colleagues – Liv Ullmann, Harriet Andersson, Ingrid Thulin and Sven Nykvist – who showed their faith in him by offering to defer their earnings from the film until it was sold.

From a thematic point of view, *Cries and Whispers* represented Bergman's most daring attempt to achieve a dream state on film. 'As I turn this project over in my mind,' he wrote to his actors and technicians, 'it never stands out as a completed whole. What it most resembles is a dark, flowing stream: faces, movements, voices, gestures, exclamations, light and shade, moods, dreams.' The title came from a music critic's review of a Mozart quartet that described it as evoking 'cries and whispers'.[18] The script was couched in the language of a story, with more stress on the milieu than the dialogue. Once more, Bergman gazed back in time, to a period at the turn of the century when religion still amounted to a significant force in Swedish life and when the social hierarchy was more pronounced. The narrative unfolded in a stately mansion set in its own ample parkland. Bergman found this manor in Taxinge-Näsby, outside Mariefred in the Mälär district west of Stockholm. The shoot lasted for 42 days, and the budget was one million crowns (just under $400,000 at the time).

Cast and crew lived in fairly spartan, but enjoyably intimate, circumstances while shooting *Cries and Whispers*. The manor offered only five rooms – one for Bergman, one for Ingrid Thulin, one for Liv Ullmann, one for Harriet Andersson and the last for Kari Sylwan. Harriet, the first to wake, would make for the single shower available and, when finished, knocked on Ingrid's door to tell her she could go next. The two of them had strong Italian coffee for breakfast and then went for a walk in the spacious park. In the evenings, the crew had dinner at their hotel in Mariefred and kept Harriet up as long as possible – so that she would look exhausted on camera. As she lay in the huge bed on camera, she would remember the agonising death of her father from cancer during the 1950s. Yet her puckish sense of humour never deserted her: when she had at last 'died' on camera, Bergman said, 'Cut!' and Harriet sat upright with a sharp jerk – and shouted, 'Booo!'

By setting *Cries and Whispers* within the fabric of a dream, Bergman could try the limits of his art, as he had done with *Persona*. The pervasive red of the film lingers on the retina like an after-image. Each sequence fades out to red. The rooms of the mansion where the three sisters live with their maid are clad in red from ceiling to floor. Bergman's vision of the interior of the soul-monster coincides with the sensation of bloodletting that the film transmits. The glistening white dresses of the women appear all the more striking, even violent, by comparison.

Like the sisters in *The Silence*, Agnes (Harriet Andersson), Karin (Ingrid Thulin) and Maria (Liv Ullmann) seem part of a single soul, and Bergman acknowledged that each evoked an aspect of his mother's personality. As Agnes sinks towards death, and Karin and Maria reveal their fundamental egoism, two other characters make a mysterious contribution to the proceedings. First the doctor (Erland Josephson), who confronts Maria with her shortcomings – coolness, indifference, indolence, impatience – just as the ballet master tormented Marie in *Summer Interlude*. Then the maid Anna (Kari Sylwan), whose warmth and sincerity bring comfort to Agnes. Anna is treated like a pariah by her employers, for her goodness disturbs and provokes them. Karin and Maria have grown up in luxury and are hopelessly impractical. Bergman gave Liv Ullmann just one comment regarding her character: 'She's the kind of woman who never closes a door behind her,' while Ingrid Thulin's Karin regards those who serve her with a hard glaze of dispassion. There is even an element of erotic subjugation in a scene where, having been struck in the face for an ill-timed remark, Anna stoops to divest Karin of her clothes.

The most taxing role was unquestionably that of Agnes. Harriet Andersson recalled that Bergman shot her death scene first because the very bright lights required had been hired for only a brief spell. Torn by spasms of pain, she eventually enters her death agony. 'Can no one help me?' she screams, and Maria turns away, horror-stricken and ashamed.

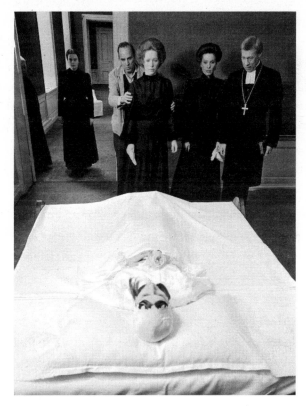

Bergman directing Liv Ullmann, Ingrid Thulin and Anders Ek, with Kari Sylwan in the background and Harriet Andersson as the dead Agnes, in *Cries and Whispers*.
Photo by Bo-Erik Gyberg.

When the priest comes to perform the traditional prayers, he speaks not of God, but 'the God'. 'Ask Him for a meaning to our lives,' he implores. At the most solemn moment of life – death – this steward of the Christian Church gives vent to his confusion and bitterness. For Bergman, the only authentic priest remains the one who admits his ignorance and impotence: Tomas Ericsson in *Winter Light* and the James Whitmore figure in *The Serpent's Egg* are men of this ilk.

Bergman, though, was never a disbeliever. For him, the distinction between the state of death and the state of life corresponded to the difference between dream and reality. Anna is haunted by the sound of her long dead baby crying in the night. She enters the large bedroom and touches both Karin and Maria; neither emerges from what seems like a trance. But when she lays her hand on Agnes, the dead woman stirs. Maria and Karin, awakened and disgusted by the idea of a corpse come to life, abandon Anna at the bedside. She takes Agnes to her bosom while the wind sighs outside the house. The image is composed with care by Bergman to convey the sense of the Pietà – the dead Christ supported by the Virgin Mary. An image so striking that the Swedish postal service would use it on a stamp in 1981.

After the funeral guests have left the manor, along with Karin and Maria, the maid lights a candle and opens Agnes's diary. The dead woman's voice speaks of an interlude of joy and tranquillity. The three sisters, dressed in white, stroll through the sunlit park. They sit beside one another in a swing-seat. 'I felt the presence of their bodies,' says Agnes wistfully. 'Come what may, this is happiness. Here for a moment, I can experience perfection.' The film concludes with a peaceful close-up of Agnes's face. It marks a release from suffering, an expectation of harmony, just like the similar close-up of Isak Borg at the end of *Wild Strawberries*.

Cries and Whispers was not screened until more than a year later, when New World Distributors purchased the American rights and rushed it into theatres in time to qualify for the Academy Awards of 1972 – a smart move, for the production received five nominations, including Best Picture. To Bergman's surprise, the film was a phenomenal success, earning $1.2 million in the US. The critics were ecstatic, and the public in New York and other major cities stood in line to see the latest Bergman masterpiece (having overlooked *Shame*, a film of equally uncompromising power, only a few years earlier). Perhaps, despite the suffering and despair of *Cries and Whispers*, its dreamlike vision proved more appealing to audiences than Bergman could have hoped – or dreamed.

———

During the spring of 1970, Ingrid von Rosen had fallen ill, and Bergman visited her in hospital. She and Ingmar had first met by chance in a shop in Stockholm in the late autumn of 1957, and in the spring of 1959 Ingrid gave birth to Maria, a daughter by Bergman. Born Ingrid Karlebo, she had been the wife of Count Jan Carl von Rosen for eighteen years and had borne three children prior to Maria, who would grow up assuming that Count von Rosen was her father. Now, twelve years later, Ingrid suggested that she and Ingmar should get married. But her parents, her sister and her closest friends took exception to the idea of her marrying Bergman.[19] The couple decided to wait for a while, although Bergman's affinity with Strindberg remained obvious. 'You probably know that as a writer I blend fiction and reality,' wrote Strindberg to his brother Axel in 1887, 'but all of my misogyny is only theoretical; I could never live without the company of a woman.'[20]

Finally, with principal photography on *Cries and Whispers* complete, Bergman and Ingrid could marry on 11 November 1971. They moved into an apartment in Karlaplan, which Bergman described as 'about as beautiful as a slab of toffee'.[21] Built on the site of Strindberg's former home, their apartment block had the advantage of being close to the Royal Dramatic Theatre, the new Swedish Film Institute headquarters and the main arteries leading out of the city. The circular park-plaza features in *Scenes from a Marriage*. Early in December, the married couple flew to Vienna and on to Sicily, where Bergman received the Pirandello Award for his achievements as a stage director.

Ingrid stood apart from Bergman's other wives and lovers. Discreet, sensitive, gracious and efficient, she became his amanuensis as well as a faithful companion for the next quarter-century. Unlike Else Fisher, Ellen Lundström, Gun Grut, Käbi Laretei or Liv Ullmann, she did not pursue a profession as such. During their years together, Bergman became less irascible and more at ease with the world. 'We had twenty-four good years together,' he said after her death. 'The most important element in our tender love was an unbroken stream of inner conversation. Ingrid always knew what I was feeling, and I always knew what she was feeling.'[22]

Despite his misgivings about his trip to London the previous year, Bergman could still write warmly to Laurence Olivier. He agreed to sign Olivier's petition to help Jews who had been secretly tried in Leningrad the previous year, and added a personal thought, saying 'how much I appreciated my personal human contact with you and your wife [Joan Plowright]. I will never forget our two lonely breakfasts when with all your generosity you told me about yourself and your relation to Shakespeare.'

18

THE CHALLENGE OF TELEVISION

By the end of 1971, Bergman was disturbed by the difficulty of financing his work in Stockholm. He had no desire to seek money from abroad, following his dissatisfaction with *The Touch*, and felt reluctant to repeat the experiment of *Cries and Whispers*, in which his colleagues had invested their salaries.

Television was the answer.

By early March 1972, Bergman had decided to shoot *Scenes from a Marriage* on 16 mm, using a tiny crew – Sven Nykvist, a focus-puller, a sound person, a production assistant and Siv Kanalv, who would double as editor and script-girl. The production was budg-eted at $240,000, and Cinematograph sold the television rights to Channel 2 of Sveriges Radio and TV for $120,000, a considerable sum by contemporary standards in Scandinavia. There would be six episodes, each to be rehearsed for five days and then filmed during the following five. Thus fifty minutes of film would be completed in ten days, and the entire series in just over two months.[1] Bergman started with the third *Scene*; then he wrote the fourth, followed by the second.

This marked a significant development in Bergman's career. He would never again embark on a film in Sweden without aiming pri-marily at the television audience. As a result, discernible changes occurred in both the style and content of his films, even if the emphasis on the pain in human relationships remained immutable.

On 9 January 1972, Ingmar's brother Dag wrote that he had reserved a suite at the best and most celebrated hotel in Athens, the Grande Bretagne, for Ingmar and Ingrid during a brief honey-moon trip in Greece. He assigned a driver named Bessie to take the

Bergmans to Delphi, and after the trip Dag reported that Bessie had said, 'What a nice chap Ingmar is and what a treasure he had found in Ingrid.'

On 17 March, Bergman's production of *The Wild Duck* opened at Dramaten. The prolixity of the dialogue was justified by Bergman's sense of the gathering wave of drama in Ibsen's play. Max von Sydow played Gregers, the characteristic Ibsen idealist who unnerves the petite bourgeoisie and is forever at the mercy of his own inferiority complex, like a huge, ungainly bird. Bergman's most imaginative device involved the construction of an area at the front of the stage that served as Hedvig's loft. In Act Five, Hedvig (Lena Nyman) could thus be seen in the foreground, gazing at her beloved bird, while Gregers and Ekdal chatted in the 'room' behind her; eventually she slumped in dejection and took her own life. This was surely the equivalent of deep focus in the cinema. Ossia Trilling in the *Financial Times* wrote that Bergman's production was 'as revolutionary as his *Hedda Gabler*. [. . .] Bergman has turned Ibsen's ailing nineteenth-century *drame à thèse* into a twentieth-century Freudian farcical tragedy.'[2]

Immediately after the premiere, Ingmar and Ingrid travelled to Fårö. 'How can it be that I have it all –' noted Bergman in his workbook, 'completeness in everyday life and reality. And I know it derives from Ingrid.'[3] Their routine on the island changed little, but their living quarters became more comfortable. Life became less spartan under the influence of Ingrid. Bergman had renovated an old barn at Dämba so that it could serve as a home cinema. Guests could sit in the fifteen 'soft moss-green armchairs' while 'two cutting-edge sea-green projectors . . . whirred softly in the darkness behind a glass panel'.[4] According to Lena Bergman, the director's eldest daughter, some films at the 3 p.m. screenings in Dämba would reappear summer after summer: *Tous les matins du monde*, *Rashomon*, *The Circus*, *Casque d'or*, *The Phantom Carriage* and Ariane Mnouchkine's film about Molière. Visitors were driven by Bergman in his red jeep at breakneck speed along the uneven roads to the cinema building. Afterwards, he would drive to the kiosk near the ferry terminal to collect the newspapers. Siri Werkelin, Bergman's housekeeper at the time, recalled his liking for fried flounder, Swedish meatballs and soup made from rose-hips. He enjoyed a cup of tea but never took coffee. He and Ingrid would walk along the seashore and beside the blue water inlets, beneath the broad skies with their scudding clouds. The landscape was dominated by scrubland and hardy grasses, with an abundance of abraded boulders and finger-pointing steles.

During the filming of *Shame* in 1967, Bergman was already contemplating his demise on Fårö: 'When I am dead, I want them to stuff me and put me in the cutting room. That's where I'll sit and nod over the desk with the help of an inserted contraption. The summer tourists will put a Swedish crown in a box to see the marvellous display. The money could go to young film producers. But until then, I just pray to be left in peace in my own home.'[5] Paradoxically, though Bergman expressed a desire to lead a hermetic existence, he also depended on being surrounded by his actors and technicians for inspiration.

The screenplay for *Scenes from a Marriage* (*Scener ur ett äktenskap*) was ready after just over four weeks in the summer of 1972. It bristled with personal references to lovers and wives who had peopled the Bergman landscape. For example, Else Fisher recognised immediately the moment when Johan tries to wriggle out of going to lunch with Marianne's parents. 'He did that during our marriage,' she recalled.

When Erland Josephson and Liv Ullmann came to the island that summer, Bergman rehearsed with them for ten days. During the shooting phase, certain exteriors were filmed in Djursholm, the Stockholm neighbourhood frequented by the characters. 'Liv and I would get up at 5 a.m. and prepare our dialogue, and Ingmar was surprised that we knew everything when we came on the set!' recalled Josephson. 'The script was very clear, and we did not in fact have lengthy discussions about each sequence, nor did we improvise stretches of conversation. We had to make jokes with each other because we simply couldn't cry all of the time!'

Scenes from a Marriage evolves around two characters. Liv Ullmann's Marianne is a woman free of Bergman's habitual personality traits. She lives and works in the Stockholm of the 1970s and suffers no religious or moral inhibitions. Erland Josephson's Johan is equally modern – as selfish and as vulnerable as the Bergman males of previous iterations, but brisk and assured in daily life. These were personalities with whom Bergman felt that a television audience could empathise. They drove a Volvo, ate in restaurants and fled like every Swede to the tranquillity and clutter of their summer cottage whenever the opportunity arose. An ardent fan of the American TV series *Dallas*, Bergman felt that by using the small-screen medium to advantage, he could communicate more intimately with his audience. He himself spoke the introduction to each of the *Scenes*, reminding viewers of what had happened in the preceding episodes.

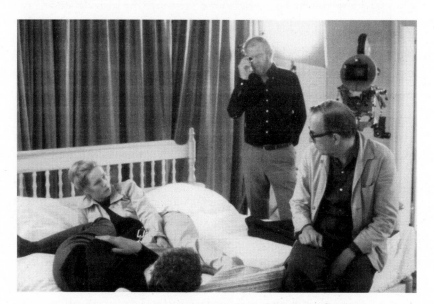

Bergman directing Liv Ullmann and Erland Josephson
for *Scenes from a Marriage*.
Copyright © AB Svensk Filmindustri 1973. Photo by Lars Karlsson.

Throughout the six episodes, Marianne and Johan are either leaving or rejoining each other. The time scale covers some years, but by the closing scene these lovers are more tightly bound in divorce than they were at the outset by marriage. For the complacent Johan ('I'm bright, youthful, successful and sexy'), wedded bliss is a renewable contract. Marianne in the early stages appears more uxorious. She cites St Paul's Letter to the Corinthians as containing the perfect definition of love. 'The trouble is, his definition squashes us flat. If love is what Paul says it is, then it's so rare that hardly anyone has known it.'

By including in his first episode a dinner sequence involving two unhappily married friends, as well as an interview with Johan and Marianne for a woman's magazine, Bergman sets the fault-lines that run through the whole series – marriage as middle-class idyll, marriage as torture chamber, abortion as a symbol of annihilation – a rejection of life, of continuity, of the very tie that binds so many couples.

The most effective sequences in *Scenes from a Marriage* are also the simplest in form. Johan and Marianne having lunch in a bistro, watched broadside by Sven Nykvist's camera. Or the painful juncture when Johan returns to their summer cottage one evening and tells his wife that he is leaving for Paris with his new mistress. (Bergman based this on the moment in 1949 when he told Ellen Lundström that he was going to Paris with Gun Grut.)

Each episode is replete with dialogue that echoes Bergman's innermost thoughts and feelings through the years. 'To me,' Johan tells Marianne, 'every domicile is always temporary.' He believes that 'loneliness is all-encompassing'. 'Must it always be', he muses, 'that two people who live together for a long time begin to tire of each other?' He, like Bergman, can give way to violent outbursts followed by tearful, shameful reconciliation. And yet Bergman's greatest accomplishment in *Scenes from a Marriage* is to apportion the viewer's sympathies between the partners. Just as Johan seems to have made a winning strike, so Marianne will emerge with a line or a monologue that restores the balance.

Bergman's limited relationship with his offspring emerges strongly in various episodes. Johan avoids seeing his children when he departs for his fling with Paula. He baulks at paying 2,000 crowns for his daughter's trip to France. In reality, the evidence suggests that Bergman's lack of interest in his sons and daughters did not go to such extremes. On the negative side, Liv Ullmann has said that Ingmar failed to attend their daughter Linn's high school and university graduation, and not even her christening. He saw little of Lill-Ingmar apart from playing trains with him on occasional Sunday visits to Gun Grut's home. He had time for Daniel only when his son had reached an age at which he could serve as projectionist for the regular screenings on Fårö. He would take Daniel out to Teatergrillen, but the meetings were stilted and intimidating for the young boy.

Against this, Bergman did contribute financially when Eva travelled to England for a course arranged in collaboration with Stockholm University, and sent her money for Christmas presents. In 1964, when the sixteen-year-old twins Mats and Anna wrote that they would be going to England to acquire the language, their father wired to say he was sending 3,000 crowns for their trip. Bergman's guilt appears in a letter dated 19 November 1961, when he told his oldest son, Jan, that 'it has been so that various circumstances have prevented the contact between us, but I often think of you and I am so glad that you are fine. Write soon again and tell about your life. As you probably understand, I am incredibly interested.'

By far the warmest relationship was with his first child, Lena. He asked her to appear in films including *The Seventh Seal*, *Wild Strawberries* and even fleetingly in *Scenes from a Marriage*. During the early 1960s, she wrote him several affectionate letters, calling him Pappa, Fader, then Ingmar, and finally 'Dearest Pappa'. On 11 October 1962 Bergman wrote to her saying that through her mother he has heard she is devoting a lot of her effort to the theatre and that 'I will not raise any threatening paternal finger if you complete school without any grades'. Three years later he composed a letter commending Lena to theatre directors and other competent authorities, saying she was intending to study theatre in Paris. Just a few months before Bergman died, he received a long letter from Lena, reminiscing about their relationship. 'Last time we spoke on the phone we talked about our tip to Dalarna. I also remember our drive in the light-blue Volvo to Våroms in late August more than fifty years ago. That's where we really made contact [. . .] You were my newly discovered, nice and venturesome father.'

Scenes from a Marriage was screened over a six-week period from 11 April to 16 May 1973 on Swedish television and subsequently on foreign stations and networks. The BBC commissioned a dubbed version, as did the American PBS, but these proved disastrous, robbing the series of its pinpoint accuracy of inflection. Subsequently, the TV version was screened in Britain with subtitles and was much more popular.

The impact on Scandinavian audiences was startling. In Denmark, police deserted point duty and left traffic congestion to fend for itself while they sat at home watching the latest confrontation between Johan and Marianne. The divorce rate jumped. ('That's got to be good!' laughed Bergman.) No less than 48 per cent of the Swedish TV audience watched *Scene 5* when it was first broadcast. While many intellectuals dismissed *Scenes* as mere soap opera, others noted that Bergman could no longer be accused of being purblind to social customs.

Economically and aesthetically, the film version was a triumph. Bergman compressed the series ruthlessly, so that the theatrical release ran for just under three hours. Almost 120 minutes of film, and certain *Scenes*, disappeared altogether: Marianne's pregnancy and abortion; the meeting in a restaurant between Johan and Marianne; a phone call from Marianne's lover in *Scene 4*; a nightwatchman's appearance in *Scene* 5, as well as large chunks of dialogue from that episode; Marianne's visit to her mother's house; and the conversation between Eva and Johan in *Scene* 6. Some omissions were regrettable, such as the chat between Katarina and Marianne in *Scene* 1, but each version worked satisfactorily.

In the summer of 1972, Bergman developed a screenplay entitled *A Spiritual Affair*, about a lonely, middle-aged woman named Victoria Egerman who suffers in a loveless marriage. Although he tinkered with it again during the 1980s, he eventually settled for directing it as a radio play, broadcast in 1990, with Jane Friedmann in the main role. Friedmann had appeared in two Bergman productions in her youth, *Hedda Gabler* and *Three Knives from Wei*.

By the early winter, however, he returned to the Royal Dramatic Theatre to prepare one of his most exciting stage productions – Strindberg's *The Ghost Sonata*. With Gunnel Lindblom as his assistant director, he gathered many of his most distinguished actors and technicians for what he told *Svenska Dagbladet* was 'a wild, terrible and beautiful piece'.[6] Toivo Pawlo played Old Man Hummel, Gertrud Fridh both the Young Lady and the Mummy, and Anders Ek the Colonel. From this fevered 'dream play', wrought during one of Strindberg's gravest troughs of melancholy, three scenes live in the mind of anyone who saw the Bergman production. There was the astonishing moment when the Milkmaid (Kari Sylwan) surged up without warning through a trap in the floor at the front of the stage, while simultaneously Bergman changed the back-projected image at the rear of the stage from an ordinary building to the stone walls of a prison, dwarfing and surrounding the Milkmaid. Towards the end of the play, the Old Man (Toivo Pawlo) forced the Colonel to his knees. The Colonel shed his wig; his uniform was torn back to reveal the quivering breast beneath. Rarely had Bergman conceived on stage such a terrifying image of humiliation. The death of the Old Man recalled the director's own mortal dread of closets. The Mummy ordered the Old Man to hang himself, and he was dragged away and thrust into the closet by his servant. Then came the noise of his neck being broken as his enemy, Bengtsson, gleefully accomplished the murder.

Meanwhile, in New York, Stephen Sondheim embarked on a Broadway musical version of *Smiles of a Summer Night*, to be entitled *A Little Night Music*. 'We decided', said Sondheim, 'that the songs should bubble and that they should be dry, unsentimental, and unsoulful.' Bergman planned to visit Manhattan to see the rehearsals and to accept the New York Film Critics' Prize for *Cries and Whispers*. But, at the last moment, he and Ingrid cancelled the trip. Instead, Bergman travelled to Copenhagen to set up a production of *The Misanthrope* at the Danish Royal Theatre. In May 1973, he was persuaded to attend the Cannes Film Festival in connection with a screening of *Cries and Whispers*. Such was the interest aroused by the visit that the press conference was held in the main auditorium of the Festival Palais, an unprecedented honour. Bergman entered like a shy monarch, almost engulfed by the photographers. When the hubbub had subsided, he spoke in careful, simple and affecting English not only of the genesis of *Cries and Whispers*, but also of his youthful fear of death, the contrast between working in the theatre and making films for the cinema, and the need for directors to learn from one another. He defended his intuitive approach to films. 'I've often been termed anti-intellectual. But art is not at all intellectual, and cannot be. Stravinsky was right when he said, "One can never understand music, only experience it."'

———

Stillborn, Bergman's film version of *The Merry Widow* proved one of the most frustrating experiences of his career. Perhaps, with the applause for his 1954 staging of Lehár's operetta in Malmö still resounding in his memory, he had felt overconfident when on 2 December 1965 he received a letter from the head of Sandrew, Göran

Lindgren, suggesting that Bergman might direct a screen version of *The Merry Widow* in the autumn of 1967, with Jarl Kulle as Danilo.

When they met subsequently, Bergman said he wanted Sven Nykvist, and Lindgren replied that Sandrew was willing to contract Nykvist but needed a firm decision from Bergman by 30 March 1966. Kenne Fant, then head of Svensk Filmindustri, suggested the same project to Bergman during an informal conversation, although this time mentioning Barbra Streisand as Hanna Glavari.[7]

The topic then slipped into limbo, while Bergman was busy with various films and the TV series *Scenes from a Marriage*. On 21 February 1973, Bergman's agent Paul Kohner wrote to Kenne Fant, 'For an Ingmar Bergman *Merry Widow* production with Barbra Streisand in co-production with Svensk Filmindustri, [Warner Bros.] are willing to subscribe a 5 million dollar budget to 80 per cent, assuming that their partner, Svensk Filmindustri, as you told me, will take 20 per cent.'

Later that summer Bergman wrote a personal letter to Streisand, whom he had met on *The Touch*, when she was visiting her husband Elliott Gould: 'It is a difficult but fascinating task to transform an old masterpiece of the stage into another medium. It is so perfect in its form and its atmosphere is so delicate. Anyway for you it's a wonderful part and I'm all the time looking forward to our working together.' They would start shooting, he said, in the middle of September 1974. He would send her the script in mid-November. 'Someone told me that you don't want to sign the contract before you have [reviewed] the script. I think that is wise. Some people involved (not me) are a little nervous because of your hesitation. Don't care. They are getting paid for their bad nerves and their ulcers.'

On a personal note, he added, 'I'm often sleepless, and then I get out of my bed into my study and sit down in my nice comfortable chair looking at the sea at dawn and listening to music. The night of July 14 there was a concert with Barbra Streisand [for] almost an hour. I felt very happy and grateful.'

The project gathered pace. On 25 July Bergman wrote to Kohner, 'I am now busy every day with *The Merry Widow* and it seems to be more and more fascinating. Today I got some wonderful photos of Al Pacino. I think [he] has a perfect face for Danilo.' But Pacino, then immersed in *The Godfather Part II*, was not available, saying that he really would like to work with Bergman in the future.

On 25 August 1973, Bergman wrote to Kohner that he felt Karl Böhm was a little bit too old for the conductor's role, and that he wanted to use Silvio Varviso, who had worked with him on *The Rake's Progress*, as well as employing the Swedish Radio Symphony Orchestra.

Dino De Laurentiis had been assigned by Warner Bros. as producer. But several weeks later Martin Erlichman, Streisand's manager, wrote at length to Bergman underlining the fact that the entry of De Laurentiis into the affair was causing his client some dismay, as it had been agreed that 'no deal will be made until [she] and Bergman meet'. By October 1973, De Laurentiis himself was growing anxious. He urged Kenne Fant to send Bergman's script to him in Rome as soon as it was ready, so that it could be translated into Italian and a budget prepared. He also asked for an English translation to be mailed to Barbra Streisand so she could give her decision, and then everyone could convene in Rome in early January 1974.

On 30 December Bergman wrote to Kohner saying that 'unfortunately due to the flu, we have to postpone the opening of [Strindberg's *To Damascus*] until Friday, February 1st. [After that date] I am ready to go to Rome or New York or anywhere else. [. . .] Please tell Dino that I will never accept Alain Delon as Danilo. [. . .] I vote for Thommy Berggren, but if somebody could find a "star" with his qualifications I will be ready to accept.'

The house of cards suddenly collapsed. On 5 February 1974, Bergman shocked Kohner by writing that 'after a very unsuccessful conversation with Barbra this Monday, I have decided to drop her. Perhaps we will work together in another project, but her lack of enthusiasm for Hanna Glavari, her lack of understanding of the script and her lack of education and professional behaviour bores me to death. [...] As soon as possible I will return to my island, where I will make up my mind what to do with the whole project.'

Six weeks later he informed Kohner that he was abandoning *The Merry Widow* because 'when I planned the picture I had the impression (false or not) of unlimited resources. [...] I was terribly stimulated and felt that I, for the first time in my life, had the chance to create a Gobelin tapestry with a crowd of artists, colours and atmosphere. [...] I have already lost too much creative time. I have always the feeling that my life as an artist is very short (even if I will go on until I'm ninety-five). I always feel that I'm in the beginning of my artistic investigations. I always feel curious to see what's going on round the corner behind the shadows in my mind, or in the workshop of my imagination. That passion is my only real treasure and I feel responsible for it in every moment.' Ironically, on that very same day, Kohner wrote to Kenne Fant at Svensk Filmindustri with the news that Warner Bros. had declined to distribute the picture, which meant that De Laurentiis 'will have to come back to the original method of financing it alone or to make a deal with another American distributor for the American motion picture and television rights. This will probably be Paramount, who have very pleasant experiences in cooperating with De Laurentiis here.' Fant assured Kohner that SF and Bergman, and even De Laurentiis, wanted to continue with the idea of an English-language *Widow*, shot as planned in 1975.

In his workbook for 13 April 1974, Bergman noted that he had 'liquidated' *The Merry Widow*, that he had said farewell to the troublesome lady with considerable relief.[8]

What would the film have been like? The screenplay is prefaced with the words 'a film by Ingmar Bergman, light-heartedly written down from Lehár's operetta'. In his Introduction, Bergman declares:

The strange magic radiating from *The Merry Widow* is a musical magic. [...] As regards the libretto, I have been rather free [...] I have left the song texts almost unchanged. [...] It is wonderful to discover how both [*The Magic Flute* and the *Widow*] are blossoming branches on the huge and inconceivably ramified tree of Viennese musical tradition. [...] I thought of beginning on the day the young Russian lieutenant Nikolai, I mean Danilo, celebrates a friend's farewell to bachelor life at the high-class brothel. And I shall finish somewhere after a hundred and forty-five minutes. Where, I shan't say. Lehár's music fits this course of events like a glove, or the other way round. And all about us there seethes, reeks, romps and roars an age unlike any other in Europe's strange history.[9]

The screenplay runs to 106 pages and pullulates with sexual innuendo and saucy imagery of the belle époque, almost as if Toulouse-Lautrec had joined forces with Bergman. Undoubtedly, the music would have carried the story forward and saved it from a rather puerile vulgarity that evokes *The Devil's Eye* or *All These Women*. With the exception of *Smiles of a Summer Night*, Bergman was never fully at ease in the frivolous society of past centuries.

At almost the same time, Bergman abandoned his plans for a film about Jesus Christ, writing in his workbook for 13 April, 'I have also said goodbye to the film about Jesus. Too long, too many togas, too many quotations.' Suggested by RAI, the Italian television network, this would have been shot in and around Fårö, with the walls of Visby standing in, as it were, for the walls around Jerusalem, and the sea beyond serving as the Sea of Galilee. But RAI preferred to entrust the project to Franco Zeffirelli. Bergman's film would have focused on Caiaphas, the high priest who was believed to have plotted the downfall of Jesus. His treatment also developed the characters of Livia, the wife of Pontius Pilate; Jesus's mother Maria; Mary Magdalene; and Rufus, son of Simon of Cyrene (who had been forced to carry Jesus's cross). 'I am not a believer,' he wrote, 'and any external salvation strikes me as blasphemous; my life is easiest expressed as being without meaning.' For Bergman, Jesus was the advocate of life and found himself confronted by a world of hatred, fear and emptiness. He dies in a human world, bereft of spiritual faith.

————

The acclaim for *Scenes from a Marriage* convinced Bergman that the future for his kind of intimate cinema lay with the small screen and, with *The Merry Widow* dead and buried, he happily accepted a commission from Sveriges Radio to make a TV film of Mozart's *The Magic Flute*. It would be broadcast on New Year's Day 1975, in celebration of SR's golden jubilee, but the search for singers began in late 1973. Eric Ericson, conductor of the Swedish Radio Symphony Orchestra, alerted opera companies throughout Scandinavia; there were major auditions at which even well-known soloists such as Håkan Hagegård were tested.

Before recording and filming began in earnest, however, Bergman devoted his energies to staging *To Damascus, Parts I and II*, at the Royal Dramatic Theatre. The production opened on 1 February 1974. There is a *Part III*, which is not often performed; the trilogy deals with Strindberg's frantic struggle with a God beneath whose aegis he had been as strictly reared as Bergman was and whose existence he came finally to accept. The play was also motivated by the turmoil of his marriage to the Austrian Frida Uhl, and by his guilt at abandoning the children of his earlier union with Siri von Essen.

Just as a sentimentalist may lurk behind every cynic, so every advocate of permissiveness conceals a puritan, and Strindberg felt trapped between these two extremes when he wrote *To Damascus* in 1898. Henrik Sjögren, an enthusiastic witness of the Bergman production, wrote, 'Swift as a dream, the play shifted virtuosically between the

moods and projections of the Stranger – i.e. of Strindberg and everyone else. It was at once defiant, absurd, grandiose, pitiable, fiercely
sarcastic and panic-stricken; torn between cruelty and tenderness,
between self-assertion on one hand and masochistic self-torment
on the other."[10] Bengt Jahnsson in *Dagens Nyheter*, though, took issue
with Bergman's considerable cuts to the text, and with his watering
down of the religious themes of the play.

Apropos of *The Magic Flute*, Bergman wrote in his memoirs,
'A production stretches its tentacle roots down through time
and dreams. I like to imagine the roots as dwelling in the special room of the soul, where they lie maturing comfortably like
mighty cheeses.'[11] Far back in the early 1940s, while helping out
at the Opera in Stockholm, Bergman heard the conductor Issay
Dobrowen say, 'In about fifteen years I hope I'll be ready to do
The Marriage of Figaro.' Bergman was puzzled by the remark, but
in 1974 he confessed that he was glad he himself had waited over
twenty years before tackling Mozart. There is a precision about the
way music is laid out and then played by an orchestra or an ensemble that appealed to Bergman. Now he was determined to involve
himself in every aspect of the production, from selecting the singers
to checking the colour release prints.

The other producers at Sveriges Radio and TV were irritated by
The Magic Flute project because it drew on the services of almost
every department and technician in the organisation. The producer,
Måns Reuterswärd, found *The Magic Flute* a thoroughly enjoyable
challenge: 'Bergman is always the first to arrive on the set in the
morning, and he's always precise in calling his coffee break at 3 p.m.
or 3.15 p.m. or whatever. You can set your watch by him more than
by any other director I've worked with. He has a great respect for all
the members of the unit; they feel this, so there is a good team spirit
as a result.'[12]

The logistical problems, however, seemed daunting. Bergman
wanted to shoot inside the celebrated Drottningholm Palace,

in the royal park outside Stockholm, but the scenery proved too delicate to accommodate all the paraphernalia of a TV crew. So Henny Noremark and his colleagues reconstructed the stage of Drottningholm in the studios of the Swedish Film Institute. Rumour has it that Schikaneder spent 6,000 florins on costumes and scenery for the original 1791 production at the Theater auf der Wieden in Vienna, and Noremark checked that each prop, curtain, wing and backdrop was painted in the same shade and tone as it would have been in Mozart's time. Bergman asserted that Mozart wrote his score with a specific stage in mind (7 metres wide, if one follows the music when Tamino goes across stage at the Temple of Wisdom).

The special effects were intricate and hard to arrange in advance. The fire at the end of the film, when Tamino and Pamina pass through apparently endless vistas of smoke and writhing bodies, was meant to be accomplished with gas. But the gas pipes in the Film Institute were too slender, and larger ducts had to be imported from all over Scandinavia. Some of the finest sections of the film, however, simply needed first-class editing to impress. The Overture is played as Bergman's editor Siv Kanalv cuts from one face to another in the theatre audience – a modern audience, including all ages and races (even Sven Nykvist himself) and, in particular, a demure young girl who serves as a tabula rasa on whose unspoilt beauty the music exercises its charm.

The devices of the cinema allow Bergman to take his audience by the throat at will. As the Queen of the Night, dagger in hand, harangues Pamina in 'Der Hölle Rache' in Act Two, her face is transformed into a mask of fury by waxen make-up and a livid green filter. Later, when Monostatos informs her of his scheme for destroying Tamino, their two faces are seen in close-up, staring slightly away from the camera, like Death and the Knight in *The Seventh Seal*; a greenish-blue light dominates the Queen's features, while a bright one illuminates the ruddy face of Monostatos.

Josef Köstlinger as Tamino and Håkan Hagegård as
Papageno in *The Magic Flute*.
Copyright © Cinematograph AB. Photo by Lars Karlsson.

Hour of the Wolf, with its numerous Mozartean and Hoffmannesque
overtones, might have led people to believe Bergman capable of
nothing but a sombre, metaphysical *Flute* in which the Queen of the
Night and Monostatos would hold sway over the spirits of Tamino
and Papageno. In fact, Bergman's judicious cuts in the libretto elim-
inated various obscure references to Masonic ritual, and the forces
of sweetness and light remain in the ascendant.

Outside the centre of Stockholm stands the huge Circus building,
and here Eric Ericson began recording the opera with the Swedish
Radio Symphony Orchestra. Bergman presided over every session.
He opted for the playback method of filming opera, whereby all
the music is pre-recorded by the artists and musicians and then
replayed in segments in the film studio until the director is satisfied with both lip synchronisation and acting performance. Tempi,
phrasing and dynamics had to be meticulously controlled for the

stereo broadcast; this was the first occasion on which the Swedes had harnessed a stereo soundtrack for a TV production. 'Bergman was as happy as a sandboy when he came out to the Circus and had a whole orchestra at his disposal,' said Reuterswärd. 'On the first day the first violin was delayed by some plane trouble, so the chair was empty. Eventually, Ingmar slipped into it, and he looked *so* happy at being in the very midst of the music-making."[13]

After the last day's shooting, Bergman joined the crew for a summer party at a restaurant outside Stockholm. He had a drink in his hand, smoked a cigar for the first time in years, and made a happy little speech thanking his collaborators. He accepted the notion of releasing *The Magic Flute* to cinemas as well as on television, outside the Nordic area. The film was blown up to 35 mm at the Filmteknik laboratory and looked superb. But it required skill and patience to convert the soundtrack to optical sound. Bergman rejected several prints before he was satisfied. For the special screening at the Cannes Festival in 1975, a magnetic stereo print was struck. All other release prints had optical sound.

19

ARRESTED ON STAGE

In 1962, Marianne Höök wrote in her book on Bergman, 'He is always primarily the man of the theatre who distrusts technical shortcuts, relying solely on the human being and on the spoken word." The observation makes sense only when Bergman is off form. By some curious process, his best films bridge the division between theatre and cinema; his worst make one aware of the exits and entrances, the tinny thunder and the false backdrop. In an interview with a Danish newspaper in 1972, he maintained that there are two kinds of reality: one that is carried within oneself and mirrored in the face, and then the outer reality. 'I work only with that little dot, the human being; that is what I try to dissect and to penetrate more and more deeply, in order to trace his secrets.'[2] While the demands of the television medium offer a mundane explanation for Bergman's increasing use of close-ups during the 1970s, the yearning to explore and lay bare the lineaments of the soul affords the more basic reason.

The screenplay of *Face to Face* (*Ansikte mot ansikte*) took almost three laborious months to write, from August to November 1974. Bergman's basic idea was that everyday events should appear unreal, while the dreams of the main character, Dr Jenny Isaksson, should have a tangible reality. In essence, Liv Ullmann was asked to play a well-established professional psychiatrist, who herself suffers a breakdown and an emotional reset. On 14 December, Bergman and his wife took the taxi-plane to Stockholm. He noted in his workbook that he was 'tired – body and soul saying STOP! Fear of people, fear of life, fear of death.'

Face to Face was shot, like *Scenes from a Marriage*, as a TV serial, but in four parts only. In early 1975, Bergman flew incognito to New

York for a series of meetings with Dino De Laurentiis, who had settled in the United States as an independent producer. The flight was rough, and the jet had to set down in Gander, Newfoundland. After two hours the tornado-like winds abated sufficiently to allow the plane to continue to Kennedy Airport. Ingmar admired Liv Ullmann's performance as Nora in *A Doll's House* at the Circle in the Square Theater.

De Laurentiis immediately agreed to finance *Face to Face*. He seemed glad to re-establish his connection with Bergman, only two years after the collapse of *The Merry Widow* project, and did not attempt to interfere with the production.

Principal photography on the film began on 28 April and ended in July with a wrap party at Stallmästaregården restaurant. Some additional material was filmed in September. During all this period, Bergman's production of *Twelfth Night* attracted huge crowds to the Royal Dramatic Theatre. They were delighted by the comfortable Tudor setting, the melodious delivery of the set speeches (Bergman regarded *Twelfth Night* as among the most musical of Shakespeare's plays) and the piquant performance of Bibi Andersson as Viola – who remained dressed as Caesario, the counterfeit man, throughout the evening.

Two studios were rented for *Face to Face* by Cinematograph at the Swedish Film Institute. One contained the sickbed of Jenny Isaksson. 'There is also her office,' wrote Liv Ullmann, 'and the corridors she runs through when she is in that borderline territory between life and death.'[3] In the other studio, the production designer Anna Hagegård had constructed Jenny's childhood home in Uppsala. Daniel, Bergman's twelve-year-old son by Käbi Laretei, rushed to the set after school and helped his father as an assiduous clapper-boy. Käbi herself played a Mozart Fantasy during a concert scene in the film.

Face to Face was an arduous production for Bergman, but at least the studio facilities enabled him to maintain a regular schedule. He would come on set in his familiar garb of sweater, trousers, house shoes and sometimes, according to Liv Ullmann, one blue and one yellow sock. At lunch he would take a hard-boiled egg, a slice of toast and jam, and a bowl of sour cream. Crackers, chocolate and bottles of Ramlösa soda water were kept in reserve on a table in the studio.

Face to Face suffers from a dearth of fire and venom, wearing instead a deadpan aspect that robs the film of the inner drama Bergman wanted so dearly to convey. Bergman is at his most persuasive when describing Jenny's return to the environment of her childhood, and least convincing when he tries to grasp the fashionable elements of 'modern' drama, such as the party scene in which Dr Tomas Jacobi (Erland Josephson) appears, and the sequence where Jenny is raped in an empty house.

The film marks Bergman's most decisive and detailed journey back to the world of his childhood since *Wild Strawberries*. The apartment in Uppsala where Jenny's grandparents live is a replica of the one Bergman visited so often during the 1920s. Gunnar Björnstrand's Grandpa suffers from the same ailment – a paralysis of the legs – that incapacitated Bergman's father. Aino Taube, playing his wife, has the dark dress, drawn-back hair and serious face of Bergman's own grandmother.

Pastor Erik Bergman had sustained a heart attack when he reached his seventies, and mother and son would sit in the hospital together day after day beside the sick man. Little by little, a reconciliation between them was brought about, a friendship regained. Something of this feeling, this craving for harmony between parent and child, is transmitted in *Face to Face*. Jenny's own failure to impart love to her daughter is echoed in her memory of disputes with her grandparents, of being locked up in a closet, or endless reproaches for being late, using lipstick, wearing the wrong clothes, not eating properly. Such experiences in youth produce what Jenny terms 'a vast army of emotional cripples', but by the close of the film she seems in an elegiac, conciliatory mood. As she watches her elderly grandparents together, the man confined to his bed, the woman watching over him, Jenny says offscreen, 'For a brief moment I realised that their love embraces everything – even death.'

Liv Ullmann's acting matches anything she has done for the cinema. She renders Jenny Isaksson in such ambivalent shades that the character cannot be dismissed as a stereotype. '[Bergman] really does have an understanding of what actors are trying to express,' she reflected. 'He always waits until you've done something and then he may say, "Why not give a little more?" or "Try not giving so much." But he never pushes.'[4] When she asked Bergman if audiences would like the film, he answered, 'Regard it like a surgeon's scalpel. Not everyone will welcome it.' Released just after Bergman's traumatic humiliation at the hands of the tax authorities, *Face to Face* failed to impress audiences either on TV or in the cinemas. The favourable reviews in the United States offered some consolation, and in *Annie Hall* Woody Allen's Alvy Singer waits for Diane Keaton outside the Beekman Cinema on Second Avenue – where *Face to Face* is showing on its first run.

On 17 September 1975, Bergman was installed as an honorary doctor of philosophy at Stockholm University. 'I just wish that my mother and father could have experienced this moment,' he said. The award inspired a burst of creative energy. In October he decided on the names of the characters in what would become *The Serpent's Egg*, and began writing the script under the title of *The Experiment*. Simultaneously, he conceived another original screenplay – *The Petrified Prince*. The idea was to create a companion piece for two other erotic fantasies to be written by Federico Fellini and Mike Nichols. Bergman devised an aphrodisiac plot involving a Prince, his Queen Mother and a young whore, set in the Napoleonic era.

Scatological in tone, the action unfolds in the Kingdom of Slavonia (presumably the same fictional land that features in Bergman's screenplay for *The Merry Widow*). The widowed Queen tries to introduce her handicapped son to the delights of sex, but when at first it fails, she puts his hand between her legs and rubs herself with it to arrive at 'a majestic climax . . . Two roars announce her deep satisfaction – a hideous sound which sets the bloodhounds in the palace yard baying.' Elise, the girl hired by the Queen to take the young Prince's virginity, is an experienced if still charming whore. There are scenes of candid sexuality, but the screenplay also smacks of the archness of *All These Women*. Exasperated by her ineffectual son, the Queen declares that she will force him back into her vagina from whence he had come as a baby – reminiscent of the Frost story in *Sawdust and Tinsel*. Then Beethoven makes an entrance, and almost immediately asks for the toilet because of his worsening diarrhoea. Finally, Napoleon, the all-conquering emperor, bursts in and, in Bergman's immortal words, 'takes the Queen offstage to fuck her'.

On 8 January 1976, the producer Kenneth Hyman wrote from Los Angeles to say that he had given much thought to this new screenplay. 'I think it is marvelous. I can't tell you how excited I am, not only with the material, but with the fact that this has finally become a reality, and that I am going to have the privilege of being associated, in whatever small way, with you and your work. [. . .] I know that we are going to have a marvelous movie.'

Bergman's agent, Paul Kohner, had also given Dino De Laurentiis the script to read, and in a telegram to Ingmar, De Laurentiis said, '[I] must say [I] am very enthusiastic about this picture. The script in my opinion is sensational and can be a fantastic movie.' Ingrid replied by cable: 'Ingmar deeply touched by your appreciation of this script and hopes that his illness will allow him to discuss casting and plans as soon as possible. I will be in constant contact with Paul about Ingmar's situation.'

The Petrified Prince project was stillborn, however. Amid the chaos of Bergman's being arrested for alleged tax fraud, his flight to Munich and his immediate plunge into *The Serpent's Egg* and then *Autumn Sonata*, the project fell into oblivion.[5]

On 19 November 1975, Bergman received what he called, with uncanny prescience, a 'first memorandum from the tax officials'. But he could hardly have foreseen the ordeal that awaited him just two months later. Having spent the autumn working on both *The Petrified Prince* and *The Serpent's Egg*, he threw himself into rehearsals for what would have been his first production of Strindberg's *The Dance of Death*. But on Friday, 30 January 1976, around noon, two plainclothes police officers called at the side entrance of Dramaten in Nybrogatan. They were told that Bergman was in rehearsal and could not be disturbed. Jan Olof Strandberg, then head of Dramaten, wrote subsequently to the newspapers refuting official police accounts of the incident, claiming that only the energetic protests of the theatre's secretary prevented the two officers from entering the stage area.

Bergman was summoned to the office of Margot Wirström, the theatre secretary, and confronted by one of the officers, while the other hastened to the stage door, stationing himself there should Bergman try to make a run for it.

Of course, he was too startled and confused to contemplate such a move. Seized by stomach cramps, he had to visit the toilet. He was then bundled into a car and driven to the local 'police tax' office, where he was questioned by Detective-Inspector Bo Stolpe about an alleged tax offence dating back to 1971. (The police later defended their precipitate action on the grounds that a statute of limitations might have placed Bergman beyond their grasp had they not moved swiftly – and Bergman's office had informed them that he would not be free for an interview until after *The Dance of Death* had opened in April.) The prosecutor had ruled that Bergman should be brought before a hearing without prior summons.

Meanwhile, the matter had been leaked to the press, and 40 minutes after Bergman had been taken away from the theatre, the first newspaper rang asking for details. Bergman was held for questioning for almost three hours before being allowed to return – under escort – to his apartment in Karlaplan. There his passport was temporarily confiscated, and other personal documents were removed by the police. Bergman's lawyer, Sven Harald Bauer, also had to surrender his passport and allow his offices to be searched for documents relating to the Bergman 'affair'.

Of what exactly was Bergman accused?

In 1967, in order to finance any productions he might undertake outside Sweden, Bergman was advised to establish a company in Switzerland. But the scheme for a film in tandem with Fellini fell through, and the Swiss company, Persona AG of Bern, went into liquidation in 1974. There was nothing illegal about this: Persona AG had been set up with the approval of the Bank of Sweden; Bauer had been scrupulous in attending to such essentials. Bergman liquidated the company only when he withdrew from a tentative arrangement with RAI, the Italian television network, to film a series of programmes on the life of Jesus Christ. About $600,000 remained in the kitty, and when Bergman transferred this to Sweden he had to pay 10 per cent capital gains tax on it immediately.

But an assiduous tax officer, Kent Karlsson, came to the conclusion – after months of investigation – that Bergman should have paid the equivalent of several hundred thousand crowns in personal income tax. In Karlsson's opinion, Bergman had used Persona AG as a front in order to avoid paying taxes in his own country, whereas Bergman maintained that he wanted to accumulate capital for film projects.

The penalty was either a massive fine or a maximum of two years in prison. Others apart from Bergman were under threat. An examination of five leading Swedish actors had been set in motion by the tax authorities, who suspected that Bergman's Swiss company had paid some of their fees directly into accounts in Liechtenstein and the Bahamas in order to evade Swedish tax. Bibi Andersson was held for more than 24 hours by the police. She protested strongly, saying that her young daughter would be anxious about her whereabouts. But she was treated with contempt, as though guilty of tax offences before even being charged. Her brassiere was confiscated, in case she should 'try to harm herself'.

Three days after his first encounter with the police, Bergman collapsed. He was not permitted to travel outside the mainland, so refuge on Fårö was out of the question. 'I am an artist,' he said somewhat disingenuously. 'I know nothing about money, and I know nothing about these charges.' He became so agitated that his wife and friends took a room for him at Karolinska Hospital. Officially, his condition was described as 'a nervous breakdown'.

By now, people in government and cultural circles were aware of the situation and very worried about its implications. The Social Democrats held a fragile coalition together in parliament, and the elections that autumn were by no means a foregone conclusion. When the world-famous author of children's stories Astrid Lindgren announced that by her calculations she was subject to 102 per cent taxation on her earnings, the government realised that the clumsy handling of the Bergman affair might have explosive consequences.

By virtue of Bergman's reputation outside Sweden, the gruesome details of his arrest and hospitalisation had already reached the front pages of the world's press. So it was not surprising that on 24 March 1976 Bergman and his lawyer were cleared of all charges and accusations. The local public prosecutor, Anders Nordenadler, announced that Bergman was exonerated as far as his own and his company's tax returns were concerned for the entire period from 1972 to 1975. Bergman had been sleeping badly, despite taking Mogadon and Valium, and one night went to his desk and scribbled down the idea for what would become *Autumn Sonata*, about a mother and daughter; Ingrid Bergman and Liv Ullmann would be ideal for the main roles.

In the public eye, the affair seemed over. But the tax authorities, smarting from their defeat, launched a new round of investigations. They concentrated on the year 1974 and claimed that Bergman was liable to double taxation, to the tune of 100,000 crowns and more, for the money that featured in the books of both his defunct Swiss company and his Swedish business concern, Cinematograph AB. According to Bergman, this claim blossomed into a massive demand for the financial year 1975. He was requested to pay tax *twice* – at rates of 85 and 45 per cent – on some 2.5 million crowns. Confident of eventual victory, the tax superintendents now made Bergman an offer they felt he could not refuse. If he agreed to pay the taxes they had claimed originally in January, they would refrain from taxing Cinematograph for 1975 as threatened.

This convinced Bergman that he had to leave Sweden. He called Katinka Faragó at Cinematograph and said he wanted her to know before the news appeared in the press. On 22 April, the readers of the largest evening paper in Stockholm, *Expressen*, were confronted by a long article headed 'Now I Am Leaving Sweden' and signed by Bergman. In the piece he attacked some of his tax tormentors by name, declaring with satisfaction that he would not submit to an underhanded deal. If found guilty of tax evasion, he would pay his dues to the last cent. But the tenor of the article left no doubt that Bergman saw exile as the only means of saving his creative sanity and taking a stand against what he termed 'a particular kind of bureaucracy, which grows like a galloping cancer'. He had, he wrote, 'espoused the ideology of grey compromise [...] My awakening was a shock, partly because of the almost unbearable humiliation, partly because I realised that anyone in this country, anytime and anyhow, can be attacked and vilified.' The article concluded with a rapier thrust at *Aftonbladet*, the paper that had branded Bergman as a tax dodger, and with a sentence of Strindberg's: 'Watch out, you bastard, we'll meet in my next play!'

There followed a characteristically precise and detailed programme of events: Bergman was shutting down his company, Cinematograph (actually, it never closed); the workers at his studios on Fårö would be laid off, and plans for enlarging the facility were shelved; all personnel were to be compensated.

Ingrid and her sister flew to Paris on 20 April, and the next day Bergman followed. Over the weekend, they took a plane to Los Angeles at the invitation of Dino De Laurentiis and Bergman's agent Paul Kohner. During a press conference at the Beverly Wilshire Hotel on 25 April, Bergman looked harassed and unnerved. When De Laurentiis suggested reviving *The Merry Widow* project, he waxed enthusiastic, comparing it to *The Magic Flute*: 'They are two branches on the same tree, and they are both very green, and the flowers are very beautiful. You have to be careful with Lehár's music – it's pure gold.' But he probably knew that such a project was offered as a mere palliative for his present woes.

Stimulated by the prospect of making *The Serpent's Egg*, produced by De Laurentiis, he and his wife moved restlessly from one temporary refuge to another – Paris, Copenhagen, Los Angeles, Oslo, Berlin and finally Munich. 'We lived at the Hilton for about six weeks, and I said to Ingrid, "Why not here? Yes, let's try to find a place." And about the same time, I attended a performance of *Hamlet* at the Residenzteater. It wasn't a very good production but, in a way, I liked it very much. I received a cable from the head of the theatre, Kurt Meisel, inviting me to go there and meet him. We had a marvellous human contact with each other, and I felt I had to be connected with that theatre.' On 16 June, Meisel offered Bergman 30,000 German Marks to direct Strindberg's *A Dream Play*, with rehearsals to begin at the end of February 1977, and to run for eight to ten weeks.

So the Bergmans remained in Munich. They found an apartment in a modern block on Titurellstrasse, with a view of the Alps in the distance. They furnished it in Scandinavian style and immersed themselves in the life of the city. Munich boasted two operas, two symphony orchestras, some thirty theatres and several museums. The weather may be mediocre, but the cultural climate in the Bavarian capital has always been lively and varied.

Swedish papers continued to comment on Bergman's exile. Bertil Bokstedt, head of the Royal Opera, thought it 'a disaster for Swedish cultural life', and he could speak with justification, for Bergman's production of *The Rake's Progress*, scheduled for TV transmission on 14 April, had been cancelled. The public commissioner (*ombudsman*) considered the Bergman case and vindicated him with few reservations. The Royal Swedish attorney gave a public rebuke to the Stockholm public attorney. Olof Palme, then prime minister, announced that he regretted Bergman's departure and hoped he would return to the country soon. In a cover story in *Time* magazine, entitled 'Sweden's Surrealistic Socialism', Bergman was quoted as saying, 'Security means a lot to us, and here we have made a great mistake. Everything must be in order. Everything must be in its own small box. There is something wrong in our way of handling these things. There is a lack of fantasy, a lack of human experience.'[6]

In the national elections that September, the Social Democrats were excluded from office for the first time since 1932. So narrow was the defeat that many believed that the scandal aroused by Bergman's persecution (and to some extent by Astrid Lindgren's attack on the tax system) persuaded moderate Swedes that the welfare state had progressed beyond desirable limits and the time had come for a change.

This sorry episode drew at last to a close on 28 November 1979, when Bergman's lawyer announced that the dispute with the government was over. The Supreme Administrative Court upheld a lower court ruling that Cinematograph need pay only 150,000 crowns in back taxes, or some 7 per cent of the original demand. The Swedish government was obliged to cover the vast legal costs the case had entailed, amounting to almost 2 million crowns, or half a million dollars. Long before that date, Bergman had returned to Sweden in all but name, spending summers on Fårö and meeting friends and associates in Stockholm. But the wounds inflicted on him by his arrest that winter morning in 1976 remained painfully visible in the films that followed.

Disharmony reigns in all Bergman's films, but in *The Serpent's Egg* the pessimism is almost cosmic, no longer restricted to one couple, one family. 'Man is an abyss,' wrote Georg Büchner, 'and I turn giddy when I look down into it.' Bergman sets this quotation at the head of his screenplay for *The Serpent's Egg* (*Ormens ägg*).

The narrative unfolds like a murder mystery thriller during a single week, 3–11 November 1923, during which the value of the German Mark dwindled virtually to nought, the Bavarian government seemed about to use armed force to eradicate communist elements in the south of the country, other provincial governments were preparing to resist possible fascist coups, and everywhere the Jews were being branded as both Marxists and the manipulators of international finance. Adolf Hitler, at the head of a tiny but vociferous National Socialist German Workers' Party, was laying plans for a putsch. 'Herr Hitler and his gang underrated the strength of German democracy,' says Inspector Bauer in the final line of the film, unaware of the chaos to come.

The city of Berlin always fascinated Bergman. 'Berlin exerted an almost demonic suggestiveness over me, due to an early collection of short stories by Siegfried Siwertz. So Berlin wasn't the real Berlin at all, but a city of black destruction.'[7] During the 1950s, he had been inspired by the awesome anonymity of the place to draft a screenplay about a pair of acrobats who had lost their third partner and were trapped in a German city during the final phase of the war. 'As the end approaches, their relationship gradually falls to pieces.' But in a process of sea change, that script developed into *The Silence*.

The strain on Bergman must have been immense. In the aftermath of his departure from Sweden, he had to cope with the logistical issues attached to an international production, budgeted by Dino De Laurentiis and Rialto Film of West Berlin at $3,266,000. It was the first time he had shot a film outside his native country. Max von Sydow had been mentioned as a probable star for the role of Abel, but Bergman had to look elsewhere. Dustin Hoffman, Al Pacino and George Segal were all reputedly considered, before Bergman decided on Richard Harris. But Harris fell sick, and the part went finally to David Carradine, whose work on *Bound for Glory* Bergman had admired. There were some 3,000 extras to be supervised, a gigantic set by Rolf Zehetbauer, recreating an entire block from the Berlin of the 1920s, and a shooting schedule of fifteen weeks over the autumn of 1976. Apart from Sven Nykvist as cinematographer and Liv Ullmann as Manuela, Bergman had to rely on a new team of actors and technicians. And all the while he was keeping in touch with his associates in Stockholm, giving advice to Gunnel Lindblom, whose *Paradise Place* was being produced under the Cinematograph banner.

Liv Ullmann visited various tatty nightclubs in West Berlin to give her the mood of the cabaret sequences. She and the other actors watched documentaries from the 1920s, as well as films such as Phil Jutzi's *Mutter Krausens Fahrt ins Glück* (1929). Bergman pays homage to Fritz Lang both covertly and overtly. At one point Inspector Bauer calls up a colleague named Lohmann – the name of the police officer in *The Testament of Dr Mabuse* – and says he is involved in a similarly insane case. (Bauer himself bears the same name as Bergman's lawyer in Stockholm.)

Each stage of *The Serpent's Egg* traces the impact on Abel Rosenberg of the all-pervasive despair that seems to rise from the very pavements and streets of the city. In the opening sequence, Abel returns slightly drunk to his shabby boarding house, blunders by mistake into a lavatory, where a stout woman screams with indignation, and glimpses in another room a group of well-dressed men singing lustily around a table. He plods up to his quarters, opens the door and is confronted by the corpse of his brother, Max. Bergman uses a medium shot – almost a long shot – to register the shock of the dead man's shattered face; most directors would have chosen a gruesome close-up. Offscreen, there is just the vague sound of the men singing downstairs. Bergman's technique was similarly dispassionate in *Winter Light*, when he viewed the fisherman's corpse from a distance. 'It's good sometimes to jump back with the camera,' he told Vilgot Sjöman, 'and just stand far away and register.'[8]

Tracking down Manuela, Max's estranged wife, in the cabaret where she performs, Abel discusses the curious letter that the dead man has left at his bedside: 'There's poisoning going on here.' Strolling back through the dark streets, he witnesses the humiliation of an innocent man at the hands of Neues Vaterland thugs. After a sleepless night in Manuela's apartment, he sees through the window a line of people in the snow, waiting for a bakery to open at dawn. 'It's like waking up and finding that the reality is worse than the nightmare,' he mutters. The remark springs from Bergman's heart. The reality of his interrogation by the tax authorities in 1976 exceeded his nightmares.

Perhaps *The Serpent's Egg* could have been a great film had it been made prior to Bergman's departure from Sweden. Its crushing despair might have been couched in less garish and hysterical terms. To audiences without knowledge of Bergman's state of mind at that juncture, the film seemed overheated, melodramatic and occasionally turgid. The confrontation between Abel and the mad scientist Dr Vergérus (played by Heinz Bennent) has none of the subtlety of the meeting between Vogler and that other Dr Vergérus in *The Magician*. Liv Ullmann commented later, and with justification, that Bergman might have been carried away by having so much money at his disposal.[9]

Although it attracted a respectable number of people in West Germany, *The Serpent's Egg* was a resounding failure in the United States, France, Britain and even Sweden. It soon became clear that the best the producers could hope for was an art-house success, which could never recoup the high budget of the film. Nevertheless, Bergman wrote in his workbook some months later, '*The Serpent's Egg* is one of my best films, that I know and I'm not mistaken.'[10]

Fortunately, before *The Serpent's Egg* opened simultaneously in Stockholm, Paris and New York, on 28 October 1977, Bergman had already shot his next feature, *Autumn Sonata*, which was financed for the most part by an advance sale of rights to Lord Lew Grade and his American production partner, Martin Starger. So the familiar caveat 'You're only as good as your last film' did not apply to Bergman as it would after *From the Life of the Marionettes*.

During the particularly harmonious July of 1977, he enjoyed making a short, private film about his father-in-law, Carl Selim Karlebo, a distinguished engineer and businessman. Bibi Andersson came to Fårö to visit Ingmar and Ingrid, as did Harry Schein, who had remained a good friend across the years. The screenplay for *Autumn Sonata* (*Höstsonaten*) took shape during the summer, and was virtually complete almost a year before shooting. Bergman confessed later that he had written it as 'a back-up' should *The Serpent's Egg* prove a failure. The force of *Autumn Sonata* lies in its reflection of Bergman's relationship with his children. Charlotte, the concert pianist played by Ingrid Bergman, might at first seem more akin to Käbi Laretei, but she embodies many of Bergman's own traits and flaws. Her fame has taken her away from domestic life to the point where she no longer understands her two daughters and assumes that the occasional royal visit, along with gifts, can compensate for her absence and emotional incapacity. Ingrid Bergman must have been reminded of her own difficulties in seeing her daughter Pia after she had left Petter Lindström for Roberto Rossellini.

On Tuesday, 20 September 1977, at 10 a.m. precisely, Bergman began shooting *Autumn Sonata* in the studios of Norsk Film in Oslo. He had formed his own company in Munich, Personafilm, and *Autumn Sonata* was pre-sold throughout the world before a metre of film was in the can. The shoot occupied only 40 days (including some exteriors around Molde), but prior to that Bergman had been rehearsing for two weeks at the Swedish Film Institute – without too much publicity, as this was the first time during his exile that he had returned openly to mainland Sweden. The first script, according to Ingrid Bergman, would have run for four and a half hours had Ingmar not removed significant chunks of dialogue during the rehearsal period.

The two Bergmans, *monstres sacrés* of the Swedish cinema, were working in tandem for the first and only time. At Cannes in 1973, when Ingrid was president of the jury, and Ingmar a rare guest on account of *Cries and Whispers*, she reminded him of his promise to write a story to feature her on screen. Two years later he called her and suggested the idea of *Autumn Sonata*, with Ingrid playing the mother of Liv Ullmann. 'I heard he was a beast,' she said, 'very temperamental, always yelling and screaming, but he never raised his voice once to me. He was a lamb.'[11] She did not relish the long takes but accepted when Bergman explained their necessity. However, the mood on set was often very tense.

Bergman relished the opportunity to film again in Swedish (even if the tax problems had led him to use the studios in Oslo). Only fifteen people were involved in the day-to-day production, in complete contrast to the huge crew Bergman had orchestrated for *The Serpent's Egg* at Bavaria Studios. Two-thirds of them were women; Bergman told Ingrid that he found them much more efficient and less hysterical than men – and, he might have added, more in awe of his reputation.

On a technical level, Ingrid Bergman was surprised by the number of close-ups he demanded. 'I'd been so long in the theatre where you have to play out to people up in the third balcony that I'd always been very big in my gestures and my voice.'[12] *Autumn Sonata* is held in a miraculous balance by the revelation of these close-ups and by the stream of incisive, searching dialogue. No action whatever occurs, in the accepted sense of the word. Bergman is audacious in his use of theatrical devices: for instance, he allows both Viktor (Liv Ullmann's husband, played by Halvar Björk) and Charlotte to address the camera with no other character within earshot, as though they were talking to a close friend or even an interviewer.

It's a film fraught with pain. Eva's son, Erik, has drowned at the age of four. Her younger sister, Helena, suffers from cerebral palsy. Charlotte's partner of thirteen years has just died. Eva had undergone an abortion at the age of eighteen. The mental and psychological anguish provoked in both Eva and Charlotte by these losses wells up in a prolonged nocturnal argument, with the two women torturing each other like figures in a Strindberg play. Each, in the end, pleads for help and forgiveness.

The crowning sequence in *Autumn Sonata* entails Eva's being urged by her mother to play Chopin's A minor Prelude. Charlotte listens to her daughter as she essays the piece with worthy, conventional technique but also a kind of stunted emotional intensity, and she shrinks back with alarm and suspicion. She recognises perhaps that had she spent time with Eva as a child she might have ironed out the flaws in her playing and allowed that emotion to flower in a more rewarding and fulfilling interpretation of life. By contrast, when Eva watches Charlotte embark on the prelude, she is aghast at her mother's capacity for feeling and realises that she has poured

Liv Ullmann and Ingrid Bergman in *Autumn Sonata*.
Copyright © AB Svensk Filmindustri 1978. Photo by Arne Carlsson.

that feeling exclusively into her career and her music. *That* is where she was during Eva's lonely youth.

Charlotte's declaration about the meaning of the prelude, just before she plays it, houses words of great perspicacity and understanding, but Ingrid Bergman speaks with just the right hint of condescension. She addresses Eva as a pupil rather than as a relative. This becomes one of the great anthology pieces of Bergman's cinema, showing with aching accuracy the gulf between art and life. Charlotte comprehends the music to the last note, yet she fails to read her daughter.

Käbi Laretei supervised the playing of the two actresses during the scene at the piano. She herself played the prelude twice, first as it would be performed 'by a naive amateur with a stereotyped conception of Chopin', and then as a professional pianist would do it. 'Behind the camera stood Sven Nykvist. To the left of it sat Ingmar giving the odd word of direction, almost inaudibly, to Liv. I crouched on the other side of the camera, telling Ingrid just as quietly when, for instance, both hands were to be still during a pause, when the left hand was to play, or when her eyes were to follow the movements of her hands on the keyboard.'[13]

At the Residenzteater in Munich, Bergman could relax and produce work of which he might be proud, even if the critics were sometimes hostile to it. Kurt Meisel in the early months proved the perfect foil and administrative boss for Bergman; an excellent actor himself, he radiated a calmness and sanity that touched everyone in the theatre.

There were difficulties concerning the language, for Bergman found himself unable to communicate the nuances of his thought in German. 'Suddenly you're in the rehearsal room in front of an actor from Austria or Germany, and although you may understand *A Dream Play* emotionally – you can't understand it any other way – you want to translate thoughts you have, and you realise you don't have the words at your command. You speak German fluently, but you cannot explain to these people what the meaning of *your idea* about the play actually is."[14]

He insisted on a room temperature of 12°C for stage rehearsals (for which he was always half an hour early). Johannes Kaetzler, his assistant at the Residenzteater, said that Bergman had the chance to undergo primal-scream therapy, but was warned that it might affect his creativity, and so he stepped back.[15] The work of Arthur Janov had impressed Bergman, notably his idea that childhood trauma could cause neuroses throughout adult life.

A Dream Play, Bergman's first production in Munich, opened on 19 May 1977. It was the third time he had staged the Strindberg play but, according to his custom, he ignored his notes on previous approaches to it and started from scratch. 'That's the most fascinating way to deal with a play,' he said. The local press seemed baffled and profoundly disappointed by Bergman's approach to Strindberg, whose plays had been brought to Germany so unforgettably by Max Reinhardt before the war. Georg Hensel in the *Frankfurter Allgemeine Zeitung* complained that Strindberg's grandiose hallucinations were never shown. '[Bergman] has staged Strindberg's weaknesses: the escapist thoughts of an insomniac, not the visionary flow of a dreamer.'[16] Indeed, Bergman never slept well, and had been complaining since leaving Stockholm of insomnia and the tinnitus that had plagued him since his early twenties.[17]

20

ILL AT EASE IN MUNICH

In the final months of 1977, while still working on *Autumn Sonata*, Bergman requested that the cameraman Arne Carlsson (a Fårö resident) and a sound engineer commence filming material for a sequel to *The Fårö Document*. This continued for almost two years. Everything of any significance was recorded: 'Work, salmon fishing, funerals, weddings, auctions, christenings, home-guard manoeuvres, shooting competitions, autumn sowing, flounder fishing, the tourist invasion, the eternal caravan of cars . . . What we have filmed', said Bergman, 'lasts for 28 hours but will finally become a film of 1 hour 58 minutes.'[1]

The island yields a certain type of human being; the inhabitants of Fårö dwell in a remarkable, inexplicable symbiosis with the environment. The rhythm of life there appealed to Bergman. 'When one has had all the success, all the money, everything one has ever wanted, ever striven for – power – the lot – then one discovers that it's nothingness,' he confessed to me in Munich in 1980. His second tribute to Fårö is both less ascetic and more optimistic than its predecessor. Some of the 673 people who lived and worked on the island have left since 1969, but the young no longer deny their birthplace. Bergman traces a calendar year as it elapses on Fårö: the lambing, the shearing, the thatching, the slaughter of sheep and pigs, a funeral and, eternally, the fishing smacks plying their trade in the waters of the Baltic. A fatalism imbues these frugal people, a quality exemplified to haunting effect in Walter, the solitary, self-sufficient farmer observed cooking a meal for himself with all the solemn ritual of a priest preparing Communion.

In March 1978, Bergman completed a screenplay entitled *Love without Lovers*, and Ingrid took the lengthy manuscript to Stockholm for clean typing. Nobody wanted to invest in this project, but little by little it morphed into *From the Life of the Marionettes*, which received the backing of Austrian television, the second West German channel and Lord Grade's ITC Entertainment. *Love without Lovers* featured an ageing producer and his film editor trying to make a film out of a vast amount of footage shot by the director, who is, according to Bergman's introduction to the screenplay, 'crazy, intoxicated with power, desperate, alcoholic, and homosexual'. This individual would become Tim in *Marionettes*, and drew on Bergman's memories of Lenn Hjortzberg, his long-time assistant during the 1960s. The two main characters emerged in the later film as variations on Peter and Katarina from *Scenes from a Marriage*.

In June, Bergman's production of Chekhov's *Three Sisters* opened at the Residenzteater, but reviewers reacted with suspicion in the face of Bergman's ascetic interpretation of the play, compared as it was by the director to a Mozart symphony, with the musical score being followed rigorously and free of directorial interpretation.[2] One journalist told Bergman, 'You're ruining the theatre by working with such bad actors!' Bergman himself railed against the 'politically infected' atmosphere at the Residenzteater, even as he noted the attendance levels were reaching 95 per cent of capacity.[3] Bergman had been complaining of violent stomach cramps and diarrhoea, blood-pressure issues and loss of balance.[4]

Ingrid, however, remained steadfast. She 'has never failed me', noted Bergman. 'She's never been cruel or nasty or small-minded.'[5] She restored her husband's spirits the following month by bringing all his children out to the island to celebrate Bergman's sixtieth birthday. Some did not know each other well, and this marked the first time that Lill-Ingmar had met Daniel. In a family photo Bergman sits smiling on the steps with a floral wreath around his head.

In August Bergman tried to resume rehearsals for *The Dance of Death*, which had been interrupted by the tax officials back in 1976, but Anders Ek was terminally ill, and so the production fell by the wayside once more. The next month, the first thoughts about *Fanny and Alexander* surface in Bergman's workbook (although the setting, in his grandmother's apartment in Uppsala, had already been described in an essay published by Bergman in Gothenburg in October 1947).[6]

Back in Munich the following month, *From the Life of the Marionettes* came into focus, with Bergman writing the sequence in which Peter Egermann visits his psychiatrist, and noting that Peter would murder the prostitute, Ka, as a surrogate for his wife. 'Why does a short-circuit action occur in a person who is in every way well adjusted and well established?' asked Bergman in his introduction to the screenplay. By late October, the structure of the film seemed complete, but would be set aside for most of the following year, during which time Bergman devoted his attention to developing the story of *Fanny and Alexander*.

After Bergman returned from a private visit to New York in early 1979, he received an effusive letter from Woody Allen: 'I am still glowing from the evening we spent together, and I hope we have the chance to meet and talk again. [...] I hope you are formulating a new work and I hope you are pleased with the wonderful reception *Autumn Sonata* has had here in America. It is well deserved.' Bergman replied on 13 February, thanking Allen and saying that he 'would be deeply grateful if there is any chance to meet with you again to discuss common problems or just to be together as friends'.

More alarming to Bergman was a letter from his brother dated 26 January. Dag announced that their common friend Sigvard Hammar would come out to Hong Kong (where Dag had been appointed Swedish Consul General) to interview him for Swedish television. 'The first part of my memoirs, "In the Shadow of Ingmar Bergman", is now ready,' he added. 'I have treated you with brotherly love, reverence, and a little bit of neglect.' The second part of his memoir would be entitled 'From the Depths of My Wheelchair' (Dag having been unable to walk since the 1960s as a consequence of polio). The manuscript undoubtedly reached Bergman, and in his autobiography he claimed to have had the material typed out – running to some 800 pages. But the manuscript then vanished, possibly because Dag's memories conflicted with Bergman's own carefully orchestrated recollection of their childhood. The TV interview did not appear in Sweden, probably because Bergman disapproved of Dag's comments. Dag said that Ingmar knew how to ingratiate himself with his father by asking him questions about angels and heaven. He felt that he was dealing out to Ingmar the kind of calculated punishments that he himself had received from Pastor Erik Bergman. Ingmar, he claimed, had succeeded 'almost effortlessly' at school, and when his career took flight, his father was jealous because his films had bigger audiences than he did for his sermons in church.

The first months of 1979 saw the premiere of two Bergman stage productions at the Residenzteater: Molière's *Tartuffe* and Ibsen's *Hedda Gabler*. The production of *Tartuffe*, he told some American visitors, was consciously designed to emphasise the 'ironic charm' of the play rather than its 'blackness'. He felt concerned 'not with the religious imposter who hoodwinks those around him, but rather with the nature of the absurd society – epitomised by Orgon's upside-down household – which allows such a creature as Tartuffe to flourish'.[7]

Bergman would weather the fairly savage reviews that *Tartuffe* provoked, and revived his production of *Hedda Gabler*, this time with the Austrian actress Christine Buchegger in the title role. Mago's marvellous blood-red set again dominated the evening, and if the character of Hedda herself had changed at all, it was towards a greater composure and detachment from her fate. In August, Bergman's charming version of *Twelfth Night* was revived at Dramaten, with Bibi Andersson once more the boyish Viola. The crowds were huge and fervent. Bergman was, he could sense, welcome in his own country again.

From the Life of the Marionettes was shot at the Bavaria Studios on the outskirts of Munich. Like *The Serpent's Egg*, the film hinges on a violent, squalid incident. A Munich businessman, Peter Egermann (Robert Atzorn), murders and then rapes a prostitute. The victim is known simply as Ka (Rita Russek), short for Katarina – which also happens to be the name of Egermann's wife (Christine Buchegger). In his dreams, Egermann has imagined himself killing his wife, and now, in a brief, horrible moment, the savagery of the dream invades his conscious state.

The opening sequence, describing the murder, assaults the audience with garish colours and flashing, pulsating lights in the prostitute's boudoir. Then, as the scene ends, Bergman reverts to black-and-white cinematography – to the austerity in which his characters have so often been immured and against which they struggle to assert their true desires. Only in the conclusion does the colour return, showing Peter in an asylum cell, playing with a chess computer and then, with a listless gesture reminiscent of Abel in *The Serpent's Egg*, reaching his hand up to the barred window. The Bergman alter ego finds himself thus totally emasculated, deprived of resistance. As another character has commented earlier, Peter Egermann is dying emotionally as some people die of hunger and thirst.

The psychiatrist seeks to peel away the various layers of fear and dissimulation that mask the motives for Peter's crime. Like a perverse net of Chinese boxes, however, the crime refuses to divulge its secret heart. The atmosphere recalls that of Fritz Lang's *Dr Mabuse* dramas of the early 1920s. Humiliation permeates the film, touching each character in turn. No doubt *Marionettes* approximated an act of revenge against the tormentors who provoked Bergman's exile from Sweden. The most sympathetic figure is Tim (Walter Schmidinger), a Jewish homosexual whose inferiority complex, allied to a refined intelligence and articulacy, produces one of the finest soliloquies in Bergman's work. Entertaining Katarina in his fastidious apartment, he gazes into the mirror and traces the lines of incipient age in his face, kneading and squeezing the flesh as though it were a mask that might be removed.

He soon confesses to the investigator that he introduced Egermann to the prostitute as a means of detaching him from his wife: 'I saw the awful lovelessness of his marriage and was obsessed by the thought that he would turn to me, that at last he would discover me, that he would realise I loved him deeply.' This refers to Bergman's assistant Lenn Hjortzberg, who had craved to be more than a mere servant to Bergman. Strindberg, too, had dealt with gay relationships in *The Confession of a Fool*, and Bergman also admired Rainer Werner Fassbinder for using the cinema to flirt with his own sexual ambivalence.

If *Marionettes*, for all its intensity of feeling (and it cost Bergman 'blood, sweat and tears'[8]), failed to touch the imagination of a wide audience, the character of Peter Egermann may be to blame. Robert Atzorn, an excellent stage actor, appears too wooden, too limited in

Robert Atzorn and Christine Buchegger in *From the Life of the Marionettes*. Copyright © *AB Svensk Filmindustri 1980. Photo by Arne Carlsson.*

his expressiveness. Christine Buchegger as Katarina is much more akin to Bergman's strong female personalities.

Meanwhile, Bergman's relations at the Residenzteater became strained. Some of the actors, including Walter Schmidinger and Gaby Dohm, wrote an open letter pleading for Bergman and Kurt Meisel to settle their differences in the interest of the entire company. Bergman disliked Meisel's tendency to criticise his actors as disloyal and ungrateful. On 5 November, he asked Meisel 'to forgive my insulting and brutal behaviour. I am working and living under exceptional stress, it is no excuse, just an explanation. [...] I feel very unhappy with your relation to your actors. [...] When we signed the contract, we all made a gentlemen's agreement that if one of us deeply disagreed with the opinion of the other, we had the right to cancel the contract. Dear Kurt, perhaps you find this letter like a threat. It is not. I write to you in a feeling of close friendship . . .'

The following day, Bergman received an invitation from Robert Favre Le Bret, director of the Cannes Film Festival, to be president of the jury in 1980. On 26 November, Bergman replied by telegram, 'Happy and proud having accepted your invitation and looking forward to seeing many wonderful pictures in Cannes.' He believed that 'after the disaster of last year, when Françoise Sagan was president [and had subsequently complained about venal pressures on the jury], and the scandal after the awards, I had the feeling that with some small changes in the regulations, and with a very tough president, the honour and absolute integrity of the Cannes Jury could be restored'.[9] Accommodations were reserved for Ingmar and Ingrid at the luxurious Hôtel du Cap-Eden-Roc in Antibes, but in April he resigned. The festival had doubtless refused to amend the rules as he had suggested. Kirk Douglas assumed the presidency.

In March 1980, Bergman began rehearsals at the Residenzteater for *Yvonne, Princess of Burgundy*, by the Polish author Witold Gombrowicz. Instead of judging films on the French Riviera, Bergman stayed in Munich for the premiere on 10 May, with a critical reaction more favourable than for his earlier productions at the Residenzteater.

From the Life of the Marionettes did not reap the box-office rewards that Lord Grade had anticipated. Even in Paris, respectable opening figures could not conceal the failure. In the United States, the picture met with somewhat dismissive notices and flopped. In Sweden, the average attendance at each cinema on the film's first run was a mere 64 people. In Malmö, only twelve tickets were sold at one performance.[10] Bergman had agreed to lead a delegation of Scandinavian film personalities to the US in the autumn of 1980, coinciding with a special week at the Museum of Modern Art and further tributes (to contemporary Nordic cinema as much as to Bergman himself) at the Chicago Festival and in Los Angeles.

At the very last moment, Bergman cabled his regrets at being unable to attend the various functions. Word had reached him that *Marionettes* would open a few days after his scheduled arrival and that the distributors had chosen such a release pattern in order to capitalise on the interviews and publicity accruing from Bergman's appearance. 'I was not informed', he declared, 'of this tie-in of my film and my presence in the United States. It has long been my policy not to participate, directly or indirectly, in the promotion of my films.'[11]

Even before his contract with the Residenzteater expired in 1982, Bergman had begun spending more and more time in Sweden, less and less in Munich. Fårö had become once again a solid base for him and his wife. On the stage, the 1980–1 season was marked by just one startling achievement, the staging of a triptych: Ibsen's *A Doll's House*, Strindberg's *Miss Julie* and a theatrical version of Bergman's own *Scenes from a Marriage*. The Ibsen and Strindberg works followed each other with barely a half-hour's interval in the Residenzteater, while *Scenes from a Marriage* was performed in the little annexe, Theatre am Marstall. Spectators in this small auditorium were surprised to find that the interviewer who addresses

Johann and Marianne at the beginning of *Scenes* did so from among the audience itself. Much abbreviated from its original length, Bergman's vision of the sex war had a lightness lacking in its Swedish original, thanks in part to the effervescent performance of Gaby Dohm, an actress with whom Bergman felt a particular kinship. Åke Janzon in *Svenska Dagbladet* spoke of the almost spectral opening of *A Doll's House*, with Nora seated on a gigantic neo-rococo sofa, 'an image of comfortable yet unconscious imprisonment'. Robert Atzorn, thought Janzon, was the most natural Helmer he had seen; Rita Russek, the prostitute in *From the Life of the Marionettes*, played Nora. Bergman treated the play's famous coda with astonishing audacity: 'Nora rises up like a phoenix from the marital bed. Torvald awakens and sees to his amazement his wife dressed for travel.'[12] *Miss Julie*, featuring a classical Swedish set by Gunilla Palmstierna-Weiss, was the most realistically staged of the three plays; Janzon saw Michael Degen's Jean, the groom, as a marionette at the mercy of women and of life in general. The extraordinary triple bill, known informally in Munich as 'The Bergman Project', opened on 30 April.

The festering issues between Bergman and Kurt Meisel came to a head in June 1981. Meisel wrote a final, lengthy letter to Bergman, by then back on Fårö, attesting that the theatre had lost considerable sums of money on his 'Bergman Project'. Further, he told Bergman that his leading actress, Christine Buchegger, had tried to commit suicide and was, at that juncture, confined to the Max Planck Institute. Bergman was fired. 'My productions were taken out of the repertoire,' he wrote in *The Magic Lantern*, 'and I was banned from the theatre.'[13] He was reinstated in December, however, after Meisel himself had been ousted and the Residenzteater was under new management.

21

AT HOME WITH *FANNY AND ALEXANDER*

An entry in Bergman's workbook for 27 September 1978 indicates he had already begun thinking about *Fanny and Alexander*. In his book *Images*, he said that he wrote the screenplay during the spring of 1979, 'and by that time, many things had eased up. *Autumn Sonata* had a successful premiere, and the whole tax business had dissolved into thin air. I found myself liberated suddenly.' He cited E. T. A. Hoffmann as one of the 'godfathers' to *Fanny and Alexander*.

The project proved more difficult to finance than any previous film by Bergman, who was insisting on a TV version of some five hours and a theatrical version running to 2 hours 45 minutes. Lew Grade and his financiers withdrew their initial interest, but Jörn Donner, at that time managing director of the Swedish Film Institute, read the screenplay, liked it, and told Bergman that if he proceeded with his plans to make the film in Sweden in Swedish, then the cash would somehow be raised.

And it was. The bulk of the $6 million budget was covered by the Swedish Film Institute, Gaumont in Paris and West German television (ZDF in Mainz). The cast included some 60 speaking parts and around 1,200 extras.

At a press conference in Stockholm in November 1980, Bergman said:

It has been suggested that *Fanny and Alexander* is autobiographical, that it portrays my childhood, and that twelve-year-old Alexander is my alter ego. But this is not quite true. *Fanny and Alexander* is a story, the chronicle of a middle-class, perhaps upper middle-class

Jarl Kulle feeding oysters to Pernilla August in *Fanny and Alexander*.
Copyright AB Svensk Filmindustri 1982. Photo by Arne Carlsson.

family, sticking closely together and set in a medium-sized Swedish
town in 1910. The materfamilias is the paternal grandmother
with three married sons who in their turn have children. The
film shows a little over a year of their lives. It is, as I see it, a huge
tapestry filled with masses of colour and people, houses and forests,
mysterious haunts of caves and grottoes, secrets and night skies.

Fanny and Alexander mingles elements of comedy, tragedy, farce
and horror. 'It's not so much a chronicle', reflected Bergman towards
the close of the shoot, 'as a Gobelin tapestry, from which you can
pick the images and the incidents and the characters that fascinate
you.' The film encompasses both business and the arts. Oscar Ekdahl
was sufficiently wealthy at the end of the nineteenth century to pur-
chase the theatre in the university town (clearly Uppsala) where he
lived with his actress wife, Helena Mandelbaum (Gunn Wållgren).
But on his death Helena confided the management of the theatre to

her eldest son, Oscar (Allan Edwall), and his wife Emilie – she too an actress (Ewa Fröling). Oscar suffers a stroke during a rehearsal of *Hamlet*, in which he has been playing, grudgingly and appropriately, the Ghost. Emilie falls victim in her widowhood to the charms of the local Bishop (Jan Malmsjö). The life of the family undergoes a dramatic change; the Bishop's ways are harsh, and his house damp and inhospitable. Eventually, with the help of a merchant friend, Isak Jacobi (Erland Josephson), Emilie's children – Fanny (Pernilla Allwin) and Alexander (Bertil Guve) – are delivered from this virtual prison, while the Bishop is given an overdose of sleeping pills by Emilie and is then consumed in a fire initiated by paranormal energy stemming from the young Alexander.

God and the Devil confront each other throughout *Fanny and Alexander*. The Bishop, says Carl Gustav (Jarl Kulle), is 'the Devil himself', while Emilie believes in a higher power, even if she does not espouse orthodox Lutheranism. 'My God wears a thousand masks,' she says. In a wider context, the film involves a struggle between three domains: the haute bourgeoisie, with its creature comforts and vacuous chatter; the Church, with its austerity and latent violence; and the imagination, exemplified by the theatre and the magic invocations of Isak Jacobi and his androgynous nephew Ismael.

'There's a lot of me in the Bishop, rather than in Alexander,' Bergman conceded cheerfully. 'He's haunted by his own devils.' One thinks of Bergman, indeed, when the Bishop tells Alexander that 'imagination is something splendid, a mighty force, a gift from God. It is held in trust for us by the great artists, writers, and musicians.' The ritual punishment meted out to Alexander by the Bishop may evoke Pastor Erik Bergman's conduct towards his own son, but in almost a caricatural way; the Bishop remains light years away from the father who enjoys a pastoral adventure with young Ingmar in *Sunday's Children*. Fanny, on the other hand, may have been modelled on Bergman's younger sister, Margareta, who shared his incipient love of puppet theatre and silent movies.

If Bergman was obsessed by God in some form, he also never abandoned his fascination with the Devil and his demons, and even in his late seventies he signed his approval of Criterion's DVDs and Blu-rays of his films with his name and the trident-wielding devil that had accompanied him since the early 1950s. 'I believe that a person is his own god and his own devil,' he told an interviewer on Fårö.[2] Tim makes an intriguing comment in *From the Life of the Marionettes* about the sacred and the profane, two incompatibles: 'the dream of closeness, tenderness, community . . .' and on the other hand 'violence, disgrace, terror, and the threat of death'.

Bergman's diabolical characters remain more beguiling than their pseudo-heroic antagonists, which is why he made Mephistopheles so charismatic a presence in his version of Goethe's *Urfaust* at Malmö in 1958. Bishop Vergérus in *Fanny and Alexander* may be the representative of God on earth, but he is in fact the embodiment of the Devil. Among all Bergman's diabolical characters, the Bishop appears the most subtle and the most deadly. More so than those played with sinister aplomb by Stig Olin in early films such as *Crisis*, *Prison* and *Summer Interlude*. More so than the Frans of *Sawdust and Tinsel*. More so than the seminarist Raval in *The Seventh Seal*. And more so than those other male members of the Vergérus clan – in *The Magician*, *The Passion of Anna* or *The Serpent's Egg*. His only rival in the Bergman canon may be Caligula, the sadistic schoolteacher in *Frenzy*. And one should not forget the engaging personality of Satan in *The Devil's Eye*, who is weary and bent on retirement – 'and then Heaven will have to do without Hell!' Ahead, in 2003, lay *Saraband*, with the character of Johan, of whom Erland Josephson (who played the role) said, 'The malice is oozing out of him, out of every bloody pore.'[3]

Although fatigued at the end of six months' shooting, Bergman relished *Fanny and Alexander*. He could once again direct in his native tongue, and he was ogled and applauded like royalty whenever he appeared on location in Uppsala, where several major sequences were shot. Bertil Guve, his choice to play Alexander, was just eleven years of age, but proved a resilient and natural performer. The film's vast list of credits includes various Bergmans: Anna, Ingmar's daughter, as the ingénue Hanna Schwartz; Mats, his son, as Aron; Käbi Laretei, his fourth wife, as Aunt Anna; Daniel, their son, as grip; and his final wife, Ingrid, as an invaluable solvent of production problems. There were parts, too, for some of Bergman's oldest friends: an ailing Gunnar Björnstrand, struggling to recite 'When that I was and a little tiny boy' from *Twelfth Night* with a candle balanced on his head; and Erland Josephson as Isak Jacobi, who not only saves the children but verbalises thoughts that come from Bergman's heart and mind – 'Every man bears within him hopes, fears, longings. Every man cries his despair aloud. Some pray to a particular god, others utter their shouts into the void.'

There was but one frustration: in January 1982, Bergman caught influenza, and for several days languished in bed. Peter Schildt, the assistant director, had to film a massive funeral cortège through Uppsala – and by all accounts acquitted himself with agility and resourcefulness. For Bergman, the interruption was exasperating, because he liked to attend to the tiniest detail of production. Sven Nykvist remarked that in Hollywood such scenes as a procession of flagellants (one of the fantasies imagined by Alexander as he listens to old Isak Jacobi) would require up to fifteen takes. 'With Ingmar, two or three, and it's in the can.'

Katinka Faragó, production manager on the film, recalled that she and her husband went to Spain to seek a good location for what Bergman termed 'The Desert Walk' in the script. They found the ideal stretch of desert, and Bergman said, 'That's perfect – exactly what I want.' But Faragó knew the budget would not allow them to return to Spain with a thousand extras and the required crew. When she confessed this to Bergman, he said, 'Don't worry, I'll fix it.' He devised a scheme whereby both studios, large and small, were used, a grip brandished an old vacuum cleaner that blew out dust, and 400 extras (not 1,000) trudged slowly towards the camera and quickly out one door, before doubling round to come back again. 'He was smart. He could cheat with film,' said Faragó.

Not since *Smiles of a Summer Night* had Bergman shown himself in such an expansive mood. *Fanny and Alexander* becomes a pageant, which – consciously, one feels – recalls Dickens with its extremes of fun and cruelty. The range of moods is startling. When Alexander's father dies and his mother marries the Bishop, the children are torn from their home and flung into a bare, barred room, policed by ruthless maids. The halcyon days have vanished, and so the sly, watchful Alexander embarks on a battle of wills with his stepfather. In some of the film's most compelling sequences, Bergman conveys the hatred that religious bigotry can cause: for example, the flagrant injustice of the Bishop's attitude when, after Alexander has sworn on the Bible, he is accused of lying and forced to undergo a severe beating. For a boy weak in body and argument, the only refuge lies in fantasy – a fantasy peopled with angels and demons; childhood may be a place of slavery but it is also a sort of paradise. Only Alexander has the vision to 'see' his father's white-suited ghost walking among the rooms of his granny's home (cream or white always being associated with death in Bergman). Only he has the capacity to imagine the terrifying procession of flagellants, with Death whirling his scythe, in the story recounted by Isak Jacobi. Only he, finally, possesses the extrasensory perception required to 'will' the immolation of his arch-enemy, the Bishop.

More than 25 hours of film had been shot for *Fanny and Alexander*. The TV series was closer to Bergman's heart than the theatrical version, which unfortunately had wider distribution abroad than the five-part TV series. Despite this, *Fanny and Alexander* met with a triumphant reception around the world. The film's warmth and generosity of spirit prevailed. Jan Malmsjö's smug, ice-cold Bishop (a part initially conceived for Max von Sydow) could be a target for the hisses of the audience, but so many of the other characters radiate a profound and, by Bergman's standards, unusually human glow. Allan

Edwall's Oscar Ekdahl, in his speech after the Christmas stage show, enunciates much of Bergman's philosophy: the theatre as 'a little room of order, clarity, care, and love'. As he speaks, Oscar removes his false beard, as though to reveal the vulnerable human creature beneath. Uncle Carl (Börje Ahlstedt) shocks and delights the children with a display of controlled flatulence, but once closeted alone with his crass, inhibited German wife, he succumbs to bitterness and self-pity. 'How is it that one becomes second-rate?' he exclaims in frustration. His brother Gustav Adolf (Jarl Kulle) rejoices in life's lusty vices and yet has difficulty completing the sexual act unless the woman takes the initiative.

The concluding dinner scene in *Fanny and Alexander*.
Copyright © AB Svensk Filmindustri 1982. Photo by Arne Carlsson.

At the close of the film, addressing the assembled Ekdahls on the occasion of a double christening, he seizes on an issue dear to Bergman's heart. 'We shall go on living in the little world. We shall stay there and cultivate it, and make the best of it. Suddenly Death strikes, Hell yawns open, the storm howls and disaster overwhelms us – all that we *know*. But we will not dwell on such unpleasant things.'

So many of these personalities brimmed up from Bergman's childhood (Maj, for example, who is lame, plump and red-haired, just like Marit in the Bergman household, or Emma, a corpulent aunt), and he would render them in even more vivid terms in his later screenplays. (Uncle Carl and Lalla the cook are well described in *Sunday's Children*.)

Bergman had declared to the press on several occasions that *Fanny and Alexander* would be his last film. 'I want to stop,' he told me in March 1982. 'I want to stay on Fårö and read the books I haven't read, find out things I haven't yet found out. I want to write things I haven't written. To listen to music, and talk to my neighbours. To live together with my wife a very calm, very secure, very lazy existence, for the rest of my life.' He cited the sheer fatigue brought about by the logistical challenge of dealing with a large crew and coping with the vagaries of shooting on location. But, as the ensuing twenty years would demonstrate, his career was by no means over. He would never again direct a theatrical feature, but he continued to work in television and for the stage.

In September, with *Fanny and Alexander* in the final throes of post-production, Bergman agreed to come to London to talk about his mentor, Alf Sjöberg, who had died in a bicycle accident in Stockholm two years earlier. He and Ingrid stayed at the Savoy Hotel, and the National Film Theatre was packed to the rafters when he clambered shyly on stage.

After about twenty minutes, the conversation shifted to Bergman's own early films, and then to general issues. Relaxed and smiling amid the adulation, he used this author's back as an impromptu desk for signing autographs. At the restaurant afterwards, he had two beers with his meal. Ingrid whispered happily, 'Ingmar *never* has more than one beer. This is really something!' A few weeks later, he wrote to me: 'The visit to London was in fact really nice, the first

Ingmar and his fifth wife Ingrid meeting John Boorman, with
Peter Cowie, at the National Film Theatre, London, in 1982.
Courtesy of the BFI National Archive. Photo by Sten Rosenlund.

and, until now, only comfortable experience I have had in that city
[. . .] It's difficult to say something subtle and substantial in a foreign language, and that evening just happened to be more "foreign"
than usual!'

On 17 December, the five-part TV version of *Fanny and
Alexander* opened in Sweden, and proved the joyous highlight of
the Christmas season. Most mainstream newspapers and magazines welcomed Bergman's magnum opus without reserve. Some
influential critics such as Jan Aghed and Stig Larsson treated the
film with condescension, underlining Bergman's lack of social conscience vis-à-vis the entrenched sexism and patriarchal attitudes.
Chris Mosey, in the London Sunday *Observer*, sneered at Bergman
as he traversed 'the same psychological landscape again and again,
unable to change course'.[4]

As *Fanny and Alexander* made its triumphant way around various countries on screens big and small, Bergman returned for the third time to Molière's play *Don Juan ou Le Festin de pierre*, which he directed for the Salzburg Festival in July 1983. Calling on his troupe of actors from Munich, and the eternal skill of Gunilla Palmstierna-Weiss as production designer, he presented Don Juan as a libidinous lover stricken with any number of anxieties. While in Salzburg, Bergman encountered Herbert von Karajan. The maestro urged him to direct Puccini's opera *Turandot* for television, with Karajan conducting the Vienna Philharmonic. Soon it became apparent that this production would be scheduled for a distant 1989, and based on a recording of the opera Karajan would make in 1987. Not surprisingly, the project failed to materialise.

Even in what Bergman might have considered a fallow year, his output in 1983 was impressive: making *After the Rehearsal*, as well as a short tribute to his mother entitled *Karin's Face*; shooting a TV production of Sjöberg's *School for Wives*; and attending the Venice Film Festival in September with the complete version of *Fanny and Alexander*.

Stig Olin had been a comrade-in-arms for Bergman during the 1940s, starring as the director's alter ego in films such as *Crisis*, *Prison* and *To Joy*. Now his daughter Lena became a muse in *After the Rehearsal*. She had appeared briefly in *Face to Face* and *Fanny and Alexander*, but in the role of Anna Egerman she flexed her talent as a screen actress. It was only a TV movie and ran for just 70 minutes, but it enabled Bergman to meditate on his craft and his vocation. His films were often reflections of what actually happened in his life at such and such a time. As a young theatre-school student in the spring of 1975 Lena Olin had met him, and she worshipped his work. 'Dearest, dearest Ingmar' were often her opening words, well into the 1990s, while 'All my love and a thousand hugs' typically ended her handwritten letters to Bergman. A few months after completing *After the Rehearsal*, Bergman would cast her as Cordelia in his production of *King Lear* at the Royal Dramatic Theatre, and two years later as Agnes in *A Dream Play*.

During these later years, Erland Josephson (also a friend since the 1940s) felt like a soulmate to Bergman, and would play a thinly disguised version of the director not just in *After the Rehearsal* but also in *Faithless*, the screenplay Bergman wrote for Liv Ullmann. His character in *After the Rehearsal*, Henrik Vogler, had emerged in Bergman's imagination already in the summer of 1980, alongside Olin's Anna Egerman, whose 'beauty, erotic sparkle, guileless vision, natural curiosity and secret disdain' he refers to in his workbook.[5]

After the Rehearsal marked a return to the 'chamber cinema' so beloved of Bergman during the 1960s. Ascetic in the extreme, it is a conversation piece involving just three characters – Vogler, Anna and Rakel, the playwright's former mistress. The action never strays beyond the confines of a theatre stage. There is no music. No special effects. The only concessions to fantasy are a brief image of Henrik as a young boy (played by Bertil Guve, Bergman's 'Alexander') and the subtle concept of Anna's metamorphosing from herself as an adult into the figure of Henrik's illegitimate daughter (by Rakel).

The thematic material of *After the Rehearsal* appears to be closely interwoven with that of Strindberg's *A Dream Play*. Anna herself is playing Indra's Daughter in the play – and would do so in reality for Bergman two years later. Strindberg wrote his drama during the months of his most passionate and exasperating involvement with his third wife, Norwegian actress Harriet Bosse. Harriet was almost thirty years younger than Strindberg (just as Anna is the same age as Henrik's elder daughter).

The extreme intimacy of the film, and especially the cunning camerawork of Sven Nykvist, closing in on faces and gestures, suggests the confessional. Bergman repeatedly expresses his doubts and anxieties through the mouth of Henrik. 'At my age,' he concedes, 'one bows to old age and faces another kind of reality.' To Rakel, he declares, 'My rehearsal is like an operation. Self-discipline, cleanliness and stillness prevail. Then we approach the infinite, the enigmas, the darkness. Then we solve the riddles and learn the mechanism of repetition.' Together, he and Anna take pleasure in imagining an affair that progresses during rehearsals for the play.

When Anna accuses him of professional cruelty, Henrik/ Bergman responds with an encomium: 'I adore actors. I love them as a phenomenon. I love their profession. Love their courage or hatred of death or whatever you care to call it. I understand their escapism. Also their dark, brutal honesty. I adore them when they try to manipulate me. And I envy them their credulity – and their sharp-sightedness. I adore actors, I can never hurt them.'

Bergman the director concludes *After the Rehearsal* with the screen changing suddenly to total blackness, almost as though a light had been switched off – the light, perhaps, that Henrik presses on and off in the very first moments of the film, symbolising the division between dream and reality, death and life. As Strindberg wrote to the painter Carl Larsson while he was developing *A Dream Play*, 'Life becomes more and more dreamlike and inexplicable to me. Perhaps death really is the awakening.'

So the long coda of introspection began. During the last twenty-odd years of his life, Bergman would write his autobiography, publish a detailed analysis of many of his films and produce screenplays that sought to resuscitate the loves and struggles of his forebears. He grew inclined to look back at his reckless youth, notably in *Faithless*. In 1983, he also composed a tiny, elegiac tribute to his mother, *Karin's Face*, remembering her life through old family photos – some of which show the young Ingmar himself – with the aid of a poignant piano accompaniment by his ex-wife Käbi Laretei. 'The Åkerblom family adored photographs,' he said. 'After the death of my father and mother, I inherited a considerable quantity of albums, the earliest tracing back to the mid-nineteenth century, the most recent covering the early 1960s. There is so much magic in these images, especially if you look at them through a large magnifying glass.'[6]

Jarl Kulle in Bergman's production of *King Lear* at the Royal
Dramatic Theatre, Stockholm, in 1984.
Courtesy of Bengt Wanselius.

Bergman returned to Dramaten on 9 March 1984 with a compelling production of *King Lear*, starring Jarl Kulle. Fifteen minutes
before the performance was due to commence, the stage was peopled
with knights and courtiers, paying homage to the king. Not a single
piece of furniture was to be seen. Nor did anyone *leave* the stage
during the evening. Instead, players retreated into the sombre shadows of the screened stage and 'froze' until their next incursion into
the drama. For chairs, or even a throne, an actor's bent back was put
to use. Add to this a scintillating visual concept – costumes of pastel
pink, magenta, sea green and vermilion, against a scarlet backdrop;
knights clad in black leather and heavy visors, as though imported
from *Star Wars* – and the evening was as rich in theatrical magic
as any in Bergman's career. Much of the credit for the look of this
production must go to Gunilla Palmstierna-Weiss, who designed
the sets and costumes.

Jarl Kulle's Lear dominated the proceedings, at once nimble and labouring, petulant and compassionate. Bergman related Shakespeare's themes to the superpower struggles of the twentieth century (for example, the tempest suggested by the roar of B-52s thundering overhead). The Fool embraced Lear like a father, or perhaps a lover. The final duel was interrupted by a *coup de théâtre* apocalyptic in significance and extraordinary in its impact on an audience about to leave the auditorium: during Lear's funeral procession, the main elements of the central set suddenly collapsed backwards, leaving Gloucester's son and the Duke of Albany facing each other with swords drawn.

One month later, on 9 April 1984, *Fanny and Alexander* won four Academy Awards in Hollywood, including Best Foreign Language Film, accepted on stage on behalf of Bergman by Ingrid and the producer, Jörn Donner. *After the Rehearsal* premiered on Swedish television the same evening.

Bergman's brother Dag and his wife somehow made the long journey from the Far East to see Ingmar and Ingrid on Fårö during that summer. The brothers spent hours reminiscing about their childhood. 'He remembered much more than I did,' wrote Ingmar. 'He spoke of his hatred of Father and his strong ties to Mother.' Some months after his return to Greece, Dag died of asphyxiation in hospital. 'He was conscious all the time,' according to Ingmar, 'but unable to speak as they had made a hole in his windpipe. As he could not communicate, he died raging and struck dumb.'[7]

In June 1985, Bergman staged Ibsen's *John Gabriel Borkman* in Munich – his final production at the Residenzteater. Armin Eichholz in *Münchner Merkur* called it 'a noble farewell', but some reviewers criticised Bergman's introduction of comic moments and Gunilla Palmstierna-Weiss's stage design as being too formalistic. Three of his stalwart actors of the period graced the play: Christine Buchegger, Heinz Bennent and Rita Russek.

As Ingrid had to go to Stockholm, Bergman spent midsummer alone on Farö – 'Alone but not sad,' he wrote in his workbook.[8]

Far more successful than *John Gabriel Borkman* was Bergman's new production of *Miss Julie*, starring Marie Göranzon and Peter Stormare (who bore in his youth a startling resemblance to Bergman himself). Bergman admitted to being influenced by Alf Sjöberg's legendary stage production of the Strindberg masterpiece in 1949. He now brought the character of Kristin the cook into sharper focus and smoothed out the vulgar, even violent traits of Jean, the valet. A subtle, narcissistic moment occurred when Julie prepared to slit her throat, and Jean gave her a mirror, thus endorsing the act. Few Bergman stage triumphs have travelled so much as *Miss Julie* – the original cast appeared in no fewer than eight cities, culminating in New York at the Brooklyn Academy of Music in June of 1991 (with Lena Olin as Julie). Clive Barnes in the *New York Times* hailed it as 'a great classic perfectly fulfilled'.

Bergman's return to filmmaking failed to excite the same enthusiasm, however. *The Blessed Ones* (*De två saliga* in Swedish) had been written by Ulla Isaksson, who had scripted both *So Close to Life* and *The Virgin Spring* for Bergman. This dour autopsy of a marriage between two middle-aged social misfits, filmed in the late summer of 1985, failed to ignite on television. Harriet Andersson and Per Myrberg performed with admirable commitment, but Isaksson's dialogue lacks the bittersweet irony of Bergman's conversations and from a visual point of view the film appeared undistinguished. Bergman seems not to have been in the best of moods. Tarkovsky was filming *The Sacrifice* in the Swedish Film Institute studios at the same time. Bergman had muttered, 'Tarkovsky's finished. He shouldn't do that film,' and when the two auteurs passed each other in the corridor, they did not acknowledge each other in any way.[9] Bergman regretted the fact that he could not use Sven Nykvist on *The Blessed Ones* and was irritated that his greatest collaborator was on a neighbouring stage shooting *The Sacrifice*.

22

RESURRECTING THE FAMILY PAST

On 28 February 1986, the Swedish prime minister, Olof Palme, was assassinated as he walked through the streets of central Stockholm after watching a new Swedish film comedy, *The Mozart Brothers*. At that juncture, Bergman was absorbed by two projects: staging Strindberg's *A Dream Play* for the fourth time, and writing an autobiography, which he called *The Magic Lantern* (having at first conceived the tongue-in-cheek title 'In the Hands of His Stomach').

Perhaps depressed in the wake of Palme's murder, he fell ill with flu during the first run-through of *A Dream Play*. Nonetheless, he completed rehearsals on 9 April, and sixteen days later the production opened on the Lilla Scenen of the Royal Dramatic Theatre and brought to the limelight a future star of stage and cinema, Stellan Skarsgård, as the Officer. The reviews were lukewarm at best. The 'most controversial feature was the scene in Fingal's Cave,' noted Birgitta Steene, 'which [Bergman] turned into a stage rehearsal with the Poet and Indra's Daughter memorising, in a deliberately amateurish way, Strindberg's lines to the sounds of an old-fashioned record-player and in front of a parodic projection of Böcklin's painting *Töteninsel*.'[1]

By September, the manuscript of *The Magic Lantern* was ready to go to Norstedts, Bergman's faithful publisher since the early days of his career. The rights to his memoirs yielded advances of $500,000 from the United States, £90,000 from the UK and DM 400,000 from West Germany. Hardback sales in Scandinavia reached 60,000 copies in Sweden, 48,000 in Norway and 15,000 in Denmark.[2] Few filmmakers have written such an engaging autobiography as Bergman did with *The Magic Lantern*. It ranks with the memoirs of Rousseau, Cellini, Renoir, Chaplin, Buñuel and Kazan in its intensity of feeling, its candour and its description of both private and professional life. Although film buffs would have to wait some years more to read Bergman's detailed analysis of his greatest films in *Images* (1991), *The Magic Lantern* remains the primary background source for any study of Bergman's theatrical work. He had no hesitation in criticising figures who rivalled him in the artistic firmament – Herbert von Karajan, Laurence Olivier and even his early idol, Olof Molander. He all but ignored Bibi Andersson, and aroused the ire of his second wife, Ellen Lundström, for not confirming that their first child, Eva, was wanted and planned.[3]

At the end of October, Bergman and Ingrid flew to Greece for a rare holiday abroad, taking Linn with them. They were impressed by Delphi, with its oracle and open-air theatre. With Bergman suffering from pain in his leg, they continued to Epidaurus and then to other sites in the Peloponnese. The experience must have restored his energies, for on 20 December his first production of *Hamlet* opened at Dramaten, with Peter Stormare as the Prince, Gunilla Lindblom as Gertrude and Pernilla Östergren as Ophelia. Bergman's aged mentor and collaborator, Herbert Grevenius, was billed as dramaturge alongside Erland Josephson's partner, Ulla Åberg. Bergman's audacious changes to the text distressed several reviewers in Sweden ('To be or not to be' inserted arbitrarily into the scene with the players, for example). The production made the rounds of major theatres outside Sweden, including London's National, and not all critics treated it with reverence. John Peter, in the *Sunday Times*, wrote, 'This is not Shakespeare's *Hamlet* but an expressionist fantasy on the same theme, called, presumably, Ingmar the Black Prince [...] I've never seen a performance of this role so harshly and wilfully deprived of a sense of intelligence, nor of any quality that could be called noble, or even likeable.'[4] Blake Morrison, in the *Observer*, however, described how 'a play long interpreted as Shakespeare's most linguistically complex and cerebral is restored to us – clearly and movingly – as a drama of great visual force'.[5]

The pace of life gradually slackened. Bergman directed no new stage productions in 1987, although his *Hamlet* and *Miss Julie* continued to grace theatres in Europe and beyond. Bergman felt depressed and conscious that he was overweight during the spring of that year. Indeed, on 20 January he wrote in his workbook that he was 'on the brink of suicide this morning'. He disliked his medication, Tenormin (Atenolol), a beta-blocker that affects the heart and blood circulation. In June, he reflected, 'My creativity has caged me my entire life and shoved me over every obstacle and steered me clear of every precipice. Now, when that creativity has abandoned me and left me in confusion and anxiety, it's vital to remain sensible, and not surrender to panic.' The reception for *The Magic Lantern* in September, however, spurred him to embark on further literary adventures.

If, to paraphrase Dr Johnson, nostalgia is the last refuge of those in fear of the future, then Bergman contrived to make it a virtue, resurrecting his parents and forebears in three 'novels' that would be directed for the screen by his son Daniel, by Bille August and Liv Ullmann. He began work on *The Best Intentions* in May 1988. 'The story unfolded during six months on Fårö. I contemplated my parents' faces and cautiously fingered their destinies and felt I learned quite a bit about myself.' His lengthy screenplay dealt with the life of his mother and father from roughly 1905 to 1918 (the year of his own birth). Bergman confided the direction to Bille August, whose epic about life in early-twentieth-century Denmark, *Pelle the Conqueror*, had impressed him.

A poignant bass line runs through the entire story, with its moments of genuine companionship, passion and strife. This was a marriage subject to violent extremes, akin to the climate in northern Sweden, with its brief, idyllic summer interlude and the harsh, bitter cold of winter. No doubt Anna and Henrik love each other, but they must struggle not just against their own 'best intentions' but also against the very fabric of early-twentieth-century society.

Class divisions in Sweden remained acute until the Social Democrat Party won a landslide election victory in 1932. The Åkerbloms typified the strait-laced attitude of the haute bourgeoisie before the Great War. Anna's bigoted if graceful mother Karin (Ghita Nørby) opposes her daughter's relationship with the impoverished young priest, even going so far as to intercept and burn a letter from Anna to Henrik. The father, played with sensitivity by Max von Sydow, is more accommodating; having built the Southern Dalarna Railroad in the late nineteenth century, he could spend his final years watching, literally, the trains go by.

The social gulf between Anna (Pernilla August) and Henrik (Samuel Fröler) exacerbates the tensions of their early years together. Henrik is shy, laconic and prone to sudden outbursts of violence that come and go like a summer storm. By his own admission, he's 'a spoiler of games'. Anna can be meek but also uncompromising. Together they fling themselves into the rigorous routine of running a parsonage, helping local folk and their children, and rearing their own first-born, Ingmar's brother Dag. Anna's is the decisive voice in the marriage, just as her mother's was in hers. Henrik would have liked a simple wedding; instead Anna prevails, and the ceremony in Uppsala Cathedral becomes a huge social event. When, after years of service in the north, Henrik is invited by the Swedish Queen Victoria to become her personal Chaplain for Sophiahemmet, where Anna herself had studied nursing, the story takes an unexpected turn. Bergman relates the anguish that divides the couple and leads to Anna's returning to her mother's embrace in Uppsala.

In his screenplay, running to more than 450 pages, Bergman reflects with affection and understanding on the troubled relationship between his mother and father. This is not a documentary reconstruction of their early life. Bergman has taken dramatic licence with names, places and facts. What counts is the veracity of the emotions and the relationships. While the arguments and misunderstandings in the relationship between Anna and Henrik sustain the underlying tension (reminiscent of *Scenes from a Marriage*), there are dramatic incidents to match the best such scenes in Bergman's own œuvre: when the mysterious, waif-like foster child Petrus tries to kill the infant Dag Bergman, or when Henrik defies the boss of the local ironworks, who tries to remove his children from confirmation class. One wonders if Petrus really existed in the life of the young Bergman couple. In the screenplay he lurks like a guilty conscience, a figure akin to the androgynous boy who preys on Max von Sydow in *Hour of the Wolf.*

A co-production of various TV channels in Europe, *The Best Intentions* was broadcast first as a four-part series on 25 December 1991. So faithfully does August embrace his master's classical style of filmmaking that *The Best Intentions* feels like an extension of Bergman's life, and not just the appendix it could so easily have been. An abridged version running three hours brought August his second Palme d'Or at the Cannes Film Festival, and Bergman gave the film his seal of approval.

In April 1988, Bergman's production of Eugene O'Neill's *Long Day's Journey into Night* opened at Dramaten, with Jarl Kulle as the father; Bibi Andersson as Mary, the mother; Thommy Berggren as the elder son, Jamie; and Peter Stormare as his younger brother. In 1956, Bengt Ekerot not only played Death in *The Seventh Seal* but also directed a majestic production of *Long Day's Journey into Night*, the rights to which had been willed to the Royal Dramatic Theatre by O'Neill's widow. Bergman told Berggren that he had never actually liked the play, and that Dramaten had urged him to direct it as a favour to the ailing Jarl Kulle.[6] But 'Dramaten is a strong and addictive poison,' he had noted in his workbook.[7] Rehearsals frequently degenerated into arguments between Bergman and Berggren, who claimed that Jamie's role had been arbitrarily trimmed. Certainly, Bergman reduced the running time of the play from more than four and a half hours to just over three. Reviewers discussed the production in ecstatic terms, however, and the acclaim continued when the cast and crew presented the play in Bergen, Rome, Paris, Hamburg, Barcelona and New York.

On 31 May 1988, Bergman confided to his workbook that he was keen to develop a kind of 'dialogue drama' about the silent-film director, Georg af Klercker. This would become *The Last Gasp* some seven years later. The publication some weeks afterwards of a special issue of *Chaplin* magazine, to celebrate Bergman's seventieth birthday, must have encouraged him to pursue both writing and directing. Some great names saluted him, including Kurosawa, Fellini and Woody Allen. Andrzej Wajda wrote, 'Throughout my life as a film director, I have admired Ingmar Bergman and been envious of the serenity that has made it possible for him to choose man and woman as his subject, not lancer and girl.' For the birthday itself, Ingmar invited to Fårö some of the women who had meant so much to him, including Bibi Andersson and Käbi Laretei.

Ingmar and Ingrid's life on Fårö and in Stockholm (when stage work dictated) was perhaps the happiest period of their relationship. Bergman had written in his workbook, 'Between me and death stands Ingrid. Only Ingrid, and nothing else.'[8] During the summer of 1990, one of his most productive spells, he regretted that his father had never visited him on the island. 'But it was difficult at the time with transportation, and we didn't have the resources for such a visit.'[9] Erik Bergman dominated his thoughts that summer, for he was engrossed in the writing of *Sunday's Children*. 'I can't love him. I can forgive him, understand him, explain him, whatever. But I can't love him and my heart is shut tight.'[10]

Sunday's Children, like *The Best Intentions*, was not just another screenplay turned out to order like his scripts of the 1940s and 1950s. Bergman now had the power and the eminence that enabled him to control every scene, even if it were directed by someone else. *Sunday's Children* started as an idea for a short film put forward by his son Daniel, but Bergman said that instead he wanted, while he was still alive, to write a feature film that Daniel would direct. It would be set in the summer of 1926. Bergman called the script 'God's Love', but Ingrid did not like it.[11] He used his own childhood nickname, 'Pu', for the main character, but in the first draft of the screenplay he was called 'Alexander'.[12]

Daniel Bergman had caught the attention of some observers in 1987 with his quirky short film, *The Egg*, presented at the Berlin Festival. He worked in television before agreeing to bring his father's script to the screen. *Sunday's Children* dwelt on an incident when the young Ingmar, aged eight, accompanied his father when he went to preach in a nearby church in Dalarna. Daniel injected a full-blooded emotional charge, rich in nostalgia and understanding, into the story. He shot mostly on location, around Borlänge, with an excursion to Styggforsen (where Ingmar had filmed *The Virgin Spring* more than thirty years earlier). The inspired acting of Thommy Berggren as the father and Henrik Linnros as the young Ingmar radiates compassion and sensitivity. The film throbs with the pleasure of holidays in the countryside, picnics, cycle rides and so on, while always in the background, like storm clouds, lurk the repressed grievances of the adult world. The grey and futile attempts at reconciliation between a Bergman now in his fifties and his widowed father were also treated honestly by Daniel in a chilling encounter in Pastor Erik's office. When Ingmar saw the scene as it had been shot, he instructed his son to cut it out of the film. Daniel refused, arguing that it gave balance to the relationship between father and son. A row ensued, but Daniel succeeded in retaining the sequence.[13] Until his death, Ingmar referred to the film as a masterpiece.[14]

Rita Russek, the German actress with whom Bergman had worked on several occasions in Munich, had played Marianne over a hundred times in the stage version of *Scenes from a Marriage*. When the Chichester Festival in England invited the production, Russek became the director, with Alan Howard and Penny Downie as Johan and Marianne. The show opened on 4 September 1990.

Bergman enjoyed working with a sextet of actresses for *Madame de Sade*, an adaptation in Swedish of Yukio Mishima's play, which consists of a discussion of the much-vilified Marquis. Stina Ekblad had appeared in *Fanny and Alexander*, Anita Björk was a stalwart of Nordic theatre across more than three decades, and Agneta Ekmanner would incarnate Death in *In the Presence of a Clown* in 1997. *Madame de Sade* opened in the Royal Dramatic Theatre's Lilla Scenen in April 1989. The visual scheme included costumes and wigs from the French Revolutionary period and the hieratic gestures so integral to Noh theatre. When, the following winter, the production appeared in Tokyo, the Japanese critics praised Bergman's intimate familiarity with Noh.

An even greater *succès d'estime* awaited Bergman's production of *A Doll's House* in November 1989, with Pernilla Östergren as Nora and Erland Josephson as Dr Rank. Leif Zern in *Expressen* wrote an ecstatic notice: 'What Bergman has done with *A Doll's House* is a performance so beautiful, so moving, so incomparably rich that I have to go back to 1969 to find anything similar in his and Dramaten's modern history.'[15] When the production played at the Brooklyn Academy of Music in New York more than eighteen months later, Michael Feingold ended his rave review in the *Village Voice*, 'It would be hard to imagine art more complete or transfiguring.'[16]

In November 1991, after a long period of gestation, Bergman staged an opera based on Euripides' *The Bacchae* written by the composer Daniel Börtz. Working closely with Börtz, he decided to give the various women individual voices rather than the traditional sense of a collective chorus. The soprano Sylvia Lindenstrand sang the part of the god Dionysus as he exacts a gory revenge on the ruling family of Thebes, who have caused the death of his human mother, Semele. 'It was Bergman's total concentration on the Aristotelian ideal,' wrote James Helme Sutcliffe in the *New York Times*, 'getting the story across directly and clearly without decorative detours, which makes *The Bacchae* such a shattering evening of musical drama.'[17]

Maria von Rosen, who had learned only at the age of twenty-two that she was Bergman's illegitimate daughter, wrote an ecstatic letter to her father after seeing the opera. She addressed him as 'Dearest Ingmar-Father', and her handwritten letters, in red ink, are warm, affectionate and concerned.

Bergman's production of Ibsen's *Peer Gynt* at the Royal
Dramatic Theatre, Stockholm, in 1991.
Courtesy of Bengt Wanselius.

During what was probably the busiest of his remaining years, Bergman had also mounted his second production of Ibsen's *Peer Gynt*, on the smallest of the three stages at the Royal Dramatic Theatre, based on his own translation from the Norwegian. Bibi Andersson played Mother Åse, with Börje Ahlstedt as Peer and Lena Endre as Solveig. Lars Ring in *Sydsvenska Dagbladet* exclaimed, 'In Bergman's *Peer Gynt* there isn't a dead moment, it feels like a big popular feast.' Despite the cuts made by Bergman, the evening's entertainment still ran to some 4 hours, with the vast ensemble interacting with their spectators in the tiny theatre along a walkway that reached into the audience area.

Drawn increasingly to writing, now that the physical strain of directing and staging weighed on him, Bergman completed his trilogy of novels about his parents and family in 1992. The third volume, entitled *Private Confessions*, filled six exercise books, and confirmed Bergman's resolve to pay tribute to his mother's tenacious hold on life, even when suffering guilt during her extramarital affair with a student called 'Thomas' in the book. *Private Confessions* also demonstrated Bergman's skill as a writer of quasi-fiction, as Jan Holmberg shows in his magisterial study, *Författaren Ingmar Bergman*.[18]

His schedule on Fårö seemed inviolable: breakfast at 7 a.m., a brisk walk along the shore or in the surrounding woods, then work at his desk, writing in long-hand that really only Ingrid could decipher. Lunch was served at 1 p.m. on the dot, and then Bergman would work some more, before, on most days, driving ten minutes to the converted barn in Dämba to screen a film at 3 p.m. He enjoyed a rather late siesta, from 4 p.m. to 5 p.m. In the evening he indulged his taste for TV series such as *Dallas*, *The Muppet Show* and *Sex and the City*.

On 29 February 1992, Bergman wrote a heartfelt letter to Gilles Jacob, director of the Cannes Film Festival, declining an invitation to attend the 45th anniversary of the event. 'I have indeed withdrawn from filmmaking, and almost also from theatre,' he said. 'I hate travelling. I love silence, quiet days and good nights. I love to live on my island. Although I am very flattered by your invitation, a visit in Cannes would strike me with horror and will probably be stopped in the last minute due to some inexplicable illness.' He could hardly have known that illness would indeed strike Ingrid so abruptly in the late spring of 1994. In the interim, however, he rushed from one new creative venture to another: *Room and Time*, the German play by Botho Strauss much haunted by death, with Lena Endre and Erland Josephson in the lead roles and Bergman's son Mats in a smaller one; George Tabori's *The Goldberg Variations*, a morality piece starring Erland Josephson and Johan Rabaeus; and

Shakespeare's *The Winter's Tale*, with Börje Ahlstedt as King Leontes and Pernilla August as Queen Hermione, on the main stage at the Royal Dramatic Theatre.

He also wrote two mini-dramas that would subsequently become TV movies: *The Last Gasp* and *In the Presence of a Clown*. But in mid-May 1994 he noted in his diary that Ingrid often suffered from abdominal pains. On 4 October she had an X-ray and a gastric ulcer was revealed. One week later she was told that she had a cancerous tumour in her stomach. That same day, at the Ersta Hospital in Södermalm, she learned that an operation was essential.

Ten years later, Bergman would publish with his daughter Maria a poignant, unflinching account of the progression of Ingrid's cancer.[19] Bergman had tried to maintain a regular daily schedule: he attended concerts in Hedvig Eleonora Church, survived on a diet of fishballs and ice cream and struggled with the translation, rehearsals and preparations for his production of *The Misanthrope*. Ingrid would still drive him, more often than not, to the theatre. The operation on 31 October was drastic, reported Dr Farago, 'stomach, spleen, lymph glands, and some suspect rough tissue in the diaphragm'.[20] Three days later, after visiting his wife, Bergman went to his office in Dramaten, lit a candle and wept. On 11 November, their twenty-third wedding anniversary, Ingrid wrote him a heartfelt letter of love and devotion – 'Beloved Gubbis!'

By mid-November 1994, Ingrid had recovered sufficiently to return home to the apartment in Karlaplan for a few hours each day. Bergman somehow contrived to check the final edit of *The Last Gasp* with Sylvia Ingemarsson and polish the dialogue for *In the Presence of a Clown*. On 6 December, Ingrid commenced a course of radiation treatment. On Christmas Eve, Bergman attended the service in Hedvig Eleonora 'as usual. But it was fruitless. What was I expecting?' Over the next few days, he brought Ingrid her breakfast in bed, and they would take a short walk around Karlaplan. On 6

January *The Last Gasp* was broadcast on Swedish television and met with a favourable reception.

Four days later, Ingrid began the second phase of her radiation treatment, while Bergman tried to concentrate on rehearsing *The Misanthrope*. When the play opened, with Torsten Flinck in the role of Alceste, which Max von Sydow had inhabited so memorably in 1957, the reviews were kind. John Lahr in *The New Yorker* went so far as to write that 'taken together with [Bergman's] previous two productions, Shakespeare's *The Winter's Tale* and Yukio Mishima's *Madame de Sade* – these are the finest displays of stagecraft I have ever seen'.[21] Bergman had shown his dark side by humiliating Flinck in front of other actors on stage during the rehearsals, and then cancelling performances of the play in New York. He may have been envious of the successes Flinck had enjoyed, or just strained to breaking point by Ingrid's illness.

A third phase of chemotherapy treatment caused Ingrid to vomit frequently, but she continued to drive Ingmar to the theatre and to work on the accounts for Cinematograph. On 1 March Bergman insisted she return to Sophiahemmet, and one week later Ingrid underwent a second operation. Dr Sundblad called Bergman to say that a large tumour could not be completely excised, and that the situation was hopeless – 'a matter of months'. Resolute but badly stricken by the news, Bergman continued to work on the translation of *The Bacchae* with the dramaturge Ulla Åberg.

Ingrid's health declined swiftly. By 14 April her weight had fallen to 47 kilos. She had lost 20 kilos in just five months. Bergman noted in his diary, 'I'm trying to master a profound confusion and perplexity. No consolation.' *Madame de Sade* was due to be presented again in New York, and Bergman insisted on attending rehearsals.

On 26 April Ingrid told Ingmar that she would prefer not to see him, and Maria von Rosen, writing some years afterwards, believed that she saw her own death reflected in his face when they did meet. On 1 May Bergman entered Hedvig Eleonora, lit a candle, and suddenly the organist started playing Bach, and the sunlight formed a striking pattern on one of the pulpit ornaments. Bergman would recreate this experience in his final film, *Saraband*.

Ingrid Bergman, née Karlebo, died in the very early hours of 20 May 1995. She was only sixty-five years of age and had been in love with Ingmar for almost half her life. Their daughter Maria – the ninth of his children – was finally written into Bergman's will on 4 October 1996.

23

A FINAL FLOURISH

Bereaved, Bergman reached for the two lifebelts that had sustained him throughout his career – work and his own particular brand of faith.

On the island, he pursued his hermit-like existence, with two local women, Cecilia and Maja, helping to manage his daily routine. Linn Ullmann recalls that 'after Ingrid died, [Cecilia] handled everything to do with the houses, in addition to being the appointed projectionist'.[1] Bergman continued to write each day between 9 a.m. and noon, stopping after 3 hours, even if he was in the middle of a sentence, a habit he shared with Ernest Hemingway, Somerset Maugham and other authors. Days could go by without his talking to anyone. He grew more introspective, and imagined that he might in some dimension be reunited with Ingrid. He wept more than ever, and the tears flowed, especially from his right eye. He rejected almost all invitations to travel, declining, for example, to join an honorary committee to mark the fiftieth anniversary of the Cannes Festival.

The Last Gasp had seen the light of day first as a one-act play, performed on 5 February 1993 in the larger of the Swedish Film Institute's two auditoria. Bergman then adapted it into a TV movie, which was broadcast on 6 January 1995, during the final months of Ingrid's life. It recalled Strindberg's play *The Stronger*, in which one woman talks almost continuously, but ends by failing to dominate the other. In *The Last Gasp* the film director Georg af Klercker (1877–1951) cajoles and harangues his boss, Charles Magnusson, the legendary producer at Svensk Filmindustri. Magnusson, calm and ruthless despite being on the cusp of senility, dismisses his pleas for the chance to make one final film. Björn Granath, who had played Oskar Åkerblom in *The Best Intentions*, delivered his virtual monologue with fiendish application. Bergman admired Klercker enormously and worked to restore his reputation as the third great filmmaker of Swedish silent cinema, worthy to stand alongside Sjöström and Stiller. *The Last Gasp* begins, in fact, with an 8-minute survey of that period, emphasising the rivalry between Svensk Filmindustri in Stockholm and the Hasselblad Studios in Gothenburg, where Klercker directed his remarkably atmospheric films.

Six months after his wife's death, Bergman staged Witold Gombrowicz's *Yvonne, Princess of Burgundy* at the Royal Dramatic Theatre, with Nadja Weiss as Yvonne and Erland Josephson and Kristina Adolphson as the King and Queen. Birgitta Steene noted that it 'was presented by Bergman as a morality play, a farce and a tragedy at the same time'.[2] Many reviewers lamented the news that Bergman would retire from Dramaten at the end of the season, and, on 15 March 1996, his stage version of *The Bacchae* closed that phase of his career with a flourish. Leif Zern in *Dagens Nyheter* wrote, 'Nothing I have seen by this almost seventy-eight-year-old director has moved me so right down to my bare bones. He stages *The Bacchae* with a self-evident authority that makes the cruel play speak directly to our own time.'[3] Malin Ek sent Bergman a postcard featuring a wise owl, thanking him for the production and saying it was wonderful. Bergman always kept such items, as he did the long letters from Peter Stormare, in whom he could see much of his younger self, and from Rune Waldekranz, who had produced *Sawdust and Tinsel* and who received the Ingmar Bergman Prize at the annual film gala in February 1996.

On Christmas Day 1996, *Private Confessions* premiered on Swedish television, in two parts. Bergman's screenplay was directed by Liv Ullmann. Once again Bergman's own family web intermingled with the fictional one. The story begins in 1925, with Anna (based on Bergman's mother Karin) involved in an extramarital affair with a man 'ten, well, eleven years younger' than she is. Her husband Henrik is, she admits, 'good to the children. Maybe too strict, especially with the boys, but he's loving and tender-hearted with them.' She confesses this situation to her Uncle Jacob, played by Max von Sydow: 'How shall I describe the poisoning that imperceptibly fills the home like a nerve gas, corroding everyone's mind for lengthy periods, perhaps a lifetime?'

Clearly drawn from the diaries that Karin Bergman had kept in secret for decades, *Private Confessions* confirms the origin of various Bergman characters – Miss Agda the housekeeper in *Wild Strawberries*, or Pastor Tomas Ericsson in *Winter Light*, for example, who 'is always ill. A priest who can't preach? What will it be like when he's there in the pulpit and it's crowded with people and everyone's face is turned towards him? And then he has nothing to say?'

Liv Ullmann brings her own talent to bear on the film. The close-ups of Pernilla August as Anna recall those of Ullmann herself in films of the 1960s. She renders Anna's undressing into an act of beauty and grace. She relies on close-ups for the long monologue in which Anna tells her mother about Henrik's sickness. She creates a final shot with Anna smiling shyly into the camera as if telling the spectator, as well as herself, that she has come to terms with life.

Private Confessions never quite escapes its dark, even lugubrious theme, and the extracts from Bach, Shostakovich and Albinoni's Adagio in G minor only underline this impression.

After Ingrid's death, Bergman grew more introspective, with the fear of Death once again dominating his thoughts and becoming a more palpable concept than any God. He confided to his workbook that 'I have always been afraid. I think I was born afraid.'[4] Birds frightened him, as did all kinds of animals except for dogs. Sleep grew more difficult. To banish the demons, he would drink mineral water, listen to music on the radio in the small hours, go to the toilet even when he did not need to, and sometimes take a Valium tablet.[5] Although Bergman's existence on Fårö appeared spartan, he leavened it with regular Sunday phone calls to friends and, on Saturday morning, to some of his former wives and lovers. According to Linn, he liked 'putting on his chalk-white sneakers and taking walks on the beach or bicycling through the forest', with often an omelette to follow for lunch.[6] He had lost almost all his remaining hair in the wake of Ingrid's death and acquired a monkish look. He grew a moustache and an incipient beard. Happy to relinquish the last vestiges of formality, he wore checked flannel shirts and sleeveless sweaters, often with brown corduroy trousers. For his brisk walks he wore a warm jacket, but always took a stick with him. His eyesight continued to decline. A grandfather clock would tick away in the main room of his house, reminding him of his childhood. Memories of his happy days with Gun Grut surfaced often: 'I think of her with joy and I see her mostly naked in the light from the small lamp on the coffee table, or dancing alone in her yellow nightgown.'[7]

On 17 March 1997, Gilles Jacob told Bergman in confidence that he had been elected to receive 'The Palm of Palms' by 'an overwhelming majority' of his peers, and in the presence of the French president, Jacques Chirac. Needless to say, Bergman responded graciously, but did not make the journey to Cannes. Liv Ullmann presented the award on stage to their daughter Linn.

For the first time since Ingrid's death, Bergman returned behind the camera, directing a TV play entitled *In the Presence of a Clown* (the English title for *Larmar och gör sig till*, which refers to the line 'sound and fury, signifying nothing' from Shakespeare's *Macbeth*). Börje Ahlstedt, who had become one of Bergman's favoured actors, plays the eccentric engineer, Carl Åkerblom (based on Bergman's uncle, who appeared in *Fanny and Alexander*). Åkerblom loves the music of Schubert and, with his friends Osvald and Emma (Erland Josephson and Gunnel Fred), contrives to make a film, or rather a play, about the composer's relationship with the showgirl Mizzi Vieth.

Set in Uppsala in 1925, the film indulges many of Bergman's fetishes: his affection for silent cinema, for classical music and for smutty humour. As he aged, so he became more vulgar, deliberately intending to shock like a naughty schoolboy. Cherished players including Inga Landgré, Birgitta Pettersson, Anita Björk and Lena Endre flit in and out of the proceedings. Death looms over the film, suggested by the projectionist who is discreetly coughing up blood, and metaphorically by Agneta Ekmanner's clown, whose presence is a riff on that of Bengt Ekerot's Death in *The Seventh Seal*.

Despite his having resigned from the Royal Dramatic Theatre in 1996, Bergman returned for a final flurry of productions before his definitive retirement. By late May 1997, he had completed an original screenplay entitled *Faithless*, inspired by his escapade with Gun Grut in Paris in 1949. He asked Liv Ullmann to direct it, but the film was completed only in early 2000 and premiered at the Cannes Festival that spring. The story of an extramarital fling is told from the woman's standpoint, as she confides in a thinly disguised Ingmar Bergman (played by Erland Josephson) in his study on Fårö. Lena Endre bears the name Marianne, like all the characters Bergman shaped in the memory of Gun Grut. Ullmann's direction makes the older Bergman a tangible personality, not just a presence in the background, as Bergman's screenplay indicated.

Faithless attempted to exorcise issues that had plagued Bergman throughout his earlier life – his debts, his violent jealousy of rival lovers, his neglect of his children's birthdays, and the effect of divorce on a child. Immaculately shot by cinematographer Jörgen Persson, and with imaginative production design by Göran Wassberg, the film remains too good-looking for its theme of squalid self-pity. Liv Ullmann does, however, steep the story in remorse and regret, and evokes a sense of time and place with sequences set in the Thielska Gallery in Stockholm, in a Paris hotel room and in Bergman's home on the island.

Having paid tribute to Georg af Klercker in *The Last Gasp*, Bergman leapt at the opportunity to return to the personality of Victor Sjöström. When he read Per Olov Enquist's play *The Image Makers*, he felt that this was a piece he had to direct, dealing as it did with the relationship between the writer Selma Lagerlöf and a Sjöström at the height of his powers after shooting *The Phantom Carriage* in 1920. Anita Björk's performance as Selma on the small stage at Dramaten delighted the critics. Bergman allowed Enquist's incisive and allusive dialogue to command the evening, with just a spare set and occasional snippets of film projected on a screen. His television version, broadcast on 14 November 2000, heightened the drama, with the relationship between Selma and Sjöström's young lover, the actress Tora Teje, exacerbating the mood of desperation and sexual jealousy. The costumes were designed by Bergman's old friend and colleague Mago, while Schubert's quartet 'Death and the Maiden' gave the film an austere, controlled atmosphere.

'For me,' said Bergman in his final years, 'the Royal Dramatic Theatre is the beginning and the end, and almost everything in between.'[8] So he returned to Dramaten and his austere office high in the great building on Nybroplan, producing Strindberg's *The Ghost Sonata*, Schiller's *Maria Stuart* in 2000 and Ibsen's *Ghosts* in 2002. Generations of actors had come and gone, but some of Bergman's loyal colleagues continued at his side at Dramaten – Erland Josephson, Gunnel Lindblom and Per Myrberg among them. Appropriately for Bergman's final stage production, the critics discerned the parallels between the play and its characters and Bergman's own life. Amelie Björck in *Göteborgs-Posten* wrote that Bergman had approached Ibsen 'as if he were Strindberg [...] or why not Bergman himself, all his marriages, all his agony of death'.[9] It certainly marked a radical, often irreverent approach to Ibsen. Mrs Alving was played by Pernilla August and Pastor Manders by Jan Malmsjö, who, though burnt to a cinder in *Fanny and Alexander*, himself provokes a huge conflagration at the climax of Bergman's *Ghosts*.

In the summer of 2001, Bergman said, 'Just like Sarah in the Bible, I was, much to my amazement, pregnant (with a film project!) at an advanced age. At the beginning, it made me feel quite ill, but then it was both funny and astonishing to sense the desire coming back.[10] *Saraband*, which he declared as his farewell to the world of moving pictures, was released on 1 December 2003. He wanted to shoot it with the new Sony digital camera, CineAlta DV24, but in the end used the Thomson 6000. The noise of the three cameras exasperated Bergman, even though he loved the idea of HDTV.

Unlike *Scenes from a Marriage*, to which it is intimately related, *Saraband* runs a mere 105 minutes, involving 10 scenes and an epilogue. Erland Josephson and Liv Ullmann again play the characters of Johan and Marianne, thirty years after their last encounter in *Scenes*. Marianne arrives at Johan's country place for a reunion, only to find her former husband embroiled in an emotional conflict with Henrik, his son from an earlier marriage.

Saraband is not quite a sequel to *Scenes from a Marriage*. Both films have the same pattern, but the colours and textures are different. Johan is eighty-six years of age, and Marianne sixty-three, whereas in the first film there were only seven years between them. Johan has inherited a handsome sum of money from an aunt, and Marianne serves as narrator, looking out of the screen in collusion with her audience. The emphasis shifts in *Saraband* from the relationship of Johan and Marianne to those between Johan and Henrik, and Henrik and his daughter Karin (who, Bergman noted, 'in all probability have a sexual relationship').[11] Like the slow and stately saraband dance, the film demands that two people are always meeting each other.

Excellent though Ullmann and Josephson are, they are upstaged by an extraordinarily intense performance by Börje Ahlstedt as Henrik. He may be miscast in a technical sense, for he looks almost as old as his screen father, but he oscillates between selfish fury and filial vulnerability with uncanny skill.

Ever aware of fresh talent, Bergman chose Julia Dufvenius to make her screen debut as Johan's granddaughter Karin, the cellist. He discovered her while rehearsing Schiller's *Maria Stuart* for the

The last film: Bergman with Liv Ullmann and Erland Josephson,
discussing a scene for *Saraband* in the autumn of 2002.
Photo by Bengt Wanselius.

stage. She played a lady-in-waiting, but 'Julia was special. She had
her own unique light. Even though she was doing exactly the same
as the other three [ladies-in-waiting].'¹² Karin's almost incestuous
passion for her father becomes a metaphor for the love that's been
so conspicuously missing in the relationships around her.

The film resounds with echoes from Bergman's earlier work and
his own life. The handicapped daughter of Johan and Marianne
recalls Helena in *Autumn Sonata*; Johan's housekeeper may not be
seen on camera, but she's called 'Agda', just like Isak Borg's housekeeper in *Wild Strawberries*. Indeed, Johan at one point quotes a
psalm to Marianne, reminding us of the scene in *Wild Strawberries*
where Isak recites the Swedish psalm at the lunch table. Henrik and
Johan merge to form a portrait of Bergman himself in some degree.
'Life itself has become a ritual,' says Henrik, referring to his status
as widower (and Bergman dedicated *Saraband* to his late wife, even

noting in his workbook, 'Thank you, dearest Ingrid, for without you there would be no *Saraband*!').[13] Henrik is preparing a book about Bach's *St John's Passion*, something that Bergman himself contemplated during the early 1960s. Music looms large in the existence of both Johan and Henrik, whether it be Bach or Brahms, or Bruckner, whose majestic Ninth Symphony adds dramatic impulse to one particular sequence. There are mentions of everything from the toy soldiers Bergman had as a child, to the hostility between father and son, to his inadequacy as a father, and even the phone calls he made to close friends and parents on Sunday mornings.

Although predominantly a chamber play, *Saraband* has one or two shocks up its sleeve, notably a moment when Erland Josephson is seen fully nude, and another when Karin plays the cello in a white space and then shrinks at 'light speed' into infinity, like an illusion dwindling to nothing. Using digital equipment, and various cameramen, Bergman even deploys a Steadicam during Karin's frantic run through the forest after being attacked by her father. The film is bracketed with a prologue and epilogue in which Marianne addresses us, the audience, in a tone of complicity that dissolves the formal barrier created by the screen.

The dialogue, which could so easily become arch and theatrical at times, reveals the characters as brilliantly as it did in *Scenes from a Marriage*. Johan refers to his 'anxiety' as a kind of mental diarrhoea, and on learning of Henrik's suicide attempt, sneers that his son always fails at everything – even suicide. Yet his contempt for himself and for others is balanced by an acerbic wit and a recognition that he loves to control those around him. Bergman has rarely made such a candid, unflinching analysis of family relationships. Liv Ullmann recalls that when shooting was complete, Bergman said goodbye, flew to Fårö and never returned to either the theatre or the film studios in Stockholm. He would remain on the island for the rest of his life.

24

AFTERMATH AND LEGACY

In 2002 Bergman presented to the Swedish Film Institute his huge collection of personal papers, letters, screenplays and other archival items. As a result of this benefaction, SFI and Svensk Filmindustri established the Bergman Foundation, which is devoted to furnishing information about Bergman's career to a worldwide constituency.

Less than two years later, in January 2004, he decided to remain permanently on Fårö. This meant leaving the apartment he had shared with Ingrid in Stockholm, and also vacating the room he had occupied for so many decades at the Royal Dramatic Theatre. 'The people I know [on Fårö], my neighbours, have accepted me even though I'm not a local,' he told an interviewer on the island, 'and I have never felt that they keep their distance or that they make a fuss of me. There has always been mutual respect and contact between us.'[1]

In his senior years, Bergman used to count his cramps, recalled his son Daniel. 'If there were no more than seven, he got out of bed. If there were more than seven, he got up anyway.'[2] Reading remained a pleasure, although he needed about six weeks to finish a novel of three hundred pages, 'assuming I immerse myself for an hour each day'.[3] He may, by his own admission, have lacked an ear or a memory for melody, but his love of music sustained him to the end of his life. Dag Kronlund, chief archivist at Dramaten, acquired numerous books on music for Bergman, and would often talk to him about Schubert.

Bergman's memory remained in excellent shape until his death. In perhaps the most intimate interview he ever gave, to the TV journalist Marie Nyreröd, Bergman in 2004 recalled his emotional relationships with candour and little remorse. ('A guilty conscience is pure vanity,' he reflected.) 'I have been married to, or have lived with, a number of women. Not that many, but wonderful, gifted people. I'm proud of them and they've taught me a great deal.'[4] He conceded that he had not 'put an ounce of effort' into his families.

Marie Nyreröd came like a new light into Bergman's final years. She was bright and good-humoured, and above all, she listened. The result was a stream of videos, short and long, in which Bergman revealed much about his innermost anxieties and beliefs. He trusted Marie implicitly, and she did not betray his confidence. He even gave her his beloved teddy bear, 'Baloo', which he had cherished for eighty years. The relationship was so secure that it survived one unusually embarrassing incident. A final version of *Saraband* arrived in the postbox at Hammars one day, and Bergman asked her to watch it with him. 'I always like to see my own films for the very first time without anybody in the room,' he told her. 'But for you I'll make an exception.' Marie had slept badly the previous night, however, and soon fell asleep, only to be awakened by Bergman jabbing his elbow into her ribs. She nodded off a second time, and when the lights came up, Bergman said, 'Marie, it's a sign of how much I like you that I'm not really angry!'

Marie persuaded Bergman to introduce each of his major films on video, and these informal yet very revealing shorts, photographed at the cinema in Dämba, have been used in accompaniment with the DVD and Blu-ray releases of many of Bergman's works. Marie was a last gleam of joy in his life. The relationship remained platonic, but the feelings between them were deep and sincere.

During his last years, Bergman ate very little, according to his daughter Linn: 'A slice of toast and a cup of tea for breakfast, yogurt for lunch, and a piece of meat or fish (no spices, no vegetables) in the evening.'[5] Loyal local women would prepare his supper and wash and iron his clothes. 'I rather like being old,' he had told Anna Larsson, a schoolteacher on the island, many years before. 'It's a bit like climbing a mountain. You climb from one plateau to the next. The higher you get, the more tired and breathless you become, but the view gets better and better.'[6] He retained his insatiable curiosity about what each new day would bring. Old friends and lovers continued to come to the island to see him – Liv Ullmann, Harry Schein, Erland Josephson and Käbi Laretei, who played Brahms waltzes for him upstairs in the barn at Dämba. During Bergman Week, which was inaugurated in 2004, distinguished visitors such as Ang Lee would pay court to Bergman when he put in an appearance.

He had long ceased driving due to cataracts and, in the wake of a hip operation and other ailments, had been confined to a wheelchair for some time. Liv Ullmann flew to Fårö on the spur of the moment to see him towards the end. She found him in bed, unable to speak. 'I quoted lines from *Saraband* to him – "Why did you come here today?" . . . "Because you called for me."'[7] The following morning, at 'the hour of the wolf', on Monday, 30 July 2007, Bergman passed away in his sleep. As Linn Ullmann wrote, 'He had made arrangements for dying. *I will lie in my own bed, in my own house, looking across the stony shore, the gnawed pines, the sea, and the ever-shifting light.*'[8]

He had chosen his own spot near the church wall in the cemetery of Fårö Parish Church. He left instructions for the burial – no flowers, no wreaths, no speeches at the graveside. The funeral took place on 18 August, and was arranged primarily by Lill-Ingmar and his wife. The local pastor, Agneta Söderdahl, conducted the service. 'She was certainly very much liked and respected by my father,' said Ingmar Bergman Jr, 'and I know that they used to meet frequently to have philosophical discussions around life and death.' A cellist performed the *Sarabande* from Bach's Cello Suite No. 5 in C minor. The six pallbearers included Arne Carlsson, the stills photographer on Bergman's later films, who himself was a long-time resident of Fårö and had shot Marie Nyeröd's documentary about Bergman some three years earlier. The coffin had been made of plain white pine to Bergman's specifications and kept in the barn in advance of his death.

The grave of Ingrid and Ingmar Bergman in a sheltered
corner of the churchyard on the island of Fårö.
Courtesy of the author.

Harriet Andersson, who was among the seventy or so invited
guests, felt that the funeral was 'a grand affair – with fine wines and
food'. There she finally met Lill-Ingmar, Ingmar Bergman Jr, who
had been one year old when his father had begun his affair with
Harriet, fifty-five years earlier. But Veronica Ralston, Bergman's
niece, remembers the occasion as 'very dour, with no speeches and
everybody sitting quietly, and not eating much of the buffet which
had been set out in a tent'. Understandably, Bergman's nine children
had not wished for a frivolous gathering, with actors and actresses
prancing around in their finery. Bergman's funeral occurred in stark
contrast to that of Strindberg, whose funeral cortège brought some
60,000 people into the streets of Stockholm.

The *New York Times* devoted a long obituary to him, quoting
the French director Bertrand Tavernier as saying, 'But the best

of Bergman is the way he speaks of women, of the relationship between men and women. He's like a miner digging in search of purity."[9] In the *Guardian*, British filmmaker Michael Winterbottom said, 'Ingmar Bergman was one of the great directors of cinema. He was a man of great integrity, honesty and energy [. . .] It's impossible to imagine anyone contributing more to the history of cinema."[10] On National Public Radio, Melissa Block referred to him as 'the director of some of the greatest films ever made'.[11] In France, his career was also extolled, for example in *Libération*: 'He created a body of work of great emotional richness, in which he brought to light the tragedy of the human condition.' Other, earlier paeans of praise were revived, such as Woody Allen's declaration: 'Ingmar Bergman, who is probably the greatest film artist, all things considered, since the invention of the motion-picture camera."[12]

This outpouring of appreciation for Bergman startled many Swedes, who had thought of him as an icon of stage and screen but not on such a lofty pedestal as the world seemed to think on 30 July 2007. Only in the aftermath of his passing did the Swedish authorities acknowledge that Bergman had been a cultural giant as important as Strindberg before him. He would feature some years later on the 200-crown banknote (ironically, just before cash virtually disappeared in Sweden), and in 2008 a small square and a street between Birger Jarlsgatan and Nybrogatan in Stockholm were named after him – a few steps from the Royal Dramatic Theatre, and on the corner where he used to wait for his taxi. The following year the Swedish government gave one million euros for the organising of a Bergman Festival at Dramaten, and a further million for the restoration of his films and the digitisation of his archives.

Bergman had left instructions that his possessions were to be sold at auction. In September 2009, Bukowskis of Stockholm succeeded in selling 1,837 articles in 337 lots, and nothing was left without a buyer. The sum of 18 million crowns ($2.56 million at the time) was realised, and the majority of the lots were bought by one individual.

These included the chess pieces used in *The Seventh Seal* (1,200,000 crowns), Bergman's writing desk (192,000 crowns) and his magic lantern (600,000 crowns). The identity of the anonymous main bidder emerged the following month – Hans Gude Gudesen, a Norwegian inventor and businessman who had heeded his friend Liv Ullmann's fervent wish that Bergman's house should become a retreat for artists, writers and filmmakers rather than be exploited for financial gain.

In 2010, the film scholar and distinguished university teacher Jan Holmberg became head of the Bergman Foundation and set in train a series of initiatives that bore fruit at the time of the centenary of Bergman's birth in 2018. Careful planning led to his films being screened at 550 cinematheques, festivals and regular cinemas during the year. Criterion in New York released a massive box set of 39 Bergman films in restored versions on Blu-ray and DVD. Seventy-four stage productions of Bergman's plays and films took place.

Filmmakers in Europe and the United States were inspired to pay tribute to Bergman in various ways. In 2021 Mia Hansen-Løve directed *Bergman Island*, with Tim Roth and Vicky Krieps, focusing on a couple who visit Fårö in the hope of writing a script worthy of the Master. In the US, Hagai Levi directed a remake of *Scenes from a Marriage*, in five episodes for HBO, adhering closely to the original, but with a twist – the wife breaking away from her husband rather than vice versa as in the original. Various documentaries explored Bergman's life and work, among them Margarethe von Trotta's *Searching for Ingmar Bergman* and Jane Magnusson's four-part *Bergman – A Life in Four Acts*.

Although Bergman's influence may be felt most vividly in filmmakers who came of age in the 1960s (Woody Allen, Philip Kaufman, David Lynch), the intensity of his approach, the need to question life at every turn, emerges in the work of more recent auteurs such as Pedro Almodóvar, David Fincher, Lukas Moodysson, Todd Haynes, Ang Lee, Olivier Assayas and Noah Baumbach. David Mamet paid specific tribute to Bergman's *Persona* in his film *House of Games* (1987): Lindsay Crouse's haircut is like Bibi Andersson's, and she combs her hair abstractedly in a mirror just as Bibi does in *Persona*. As an aside, one notes that as of July 2023, there are almost 10 million references to Bergman in the search engine Google.

———

From his earliest days as a director, Bergman grasped the essentials of film technology. He felt as much at home in the laboratory as he did on the set. He loved the editing process, and nothing more than the moment when, in creating a dissolve between shots, *both* pictures lie double *in each other* for thirty frames.[13] And in 1969 he told me, 'Film is above all concerned with rhythm. The primary factor is the image; the secondary factor the dialogue; and the tension between these two creates the third dimension.'

On the set, Bergman invariably tried to shoot his scenes in chronological order. 'I always re-shoot the first day's work,' he said.[14] In the broadest sense of the term, improvisation played a major role in his strategy. Actors were not allowed to ramble on, Cassavetes-fashion, until the camera ran out of film, but nothing was specified too rigidly in advance. A study of Bergman's published screenplays shows that incidents and movements within a scene are subject to change as frequently as lines of dialogue. Some scripts (for example, *The Touch* and *Cries and Whispers*) are more evocative than precise. Close-ups are never indicated, even though they constitute one of the director's favourite means of expression. Bergman prepared each scene well in advance. Often he made a sketch of it, asking himself where the camera should be placed. 'He allows technical rehearsals,' said Liv Ullmann, 'but then he likes to take on the first emotional reading, because sometimes that is the best take.'[15] The secret of Bergman's mesmeric hold over the audience lies in his control of 'pitch', in the way that Bach controls the pitch in his greatest partitas.

'He is courageous enough to follow his own intuition,' according to Käbi Laretei, 'and nothing can change his mind. He's one of those rare people who really *believes* in his intuition.'[16] Bergman himself told an interviewer, 'My impulse has nothing to do with intellect or symbolism; it has only to do with dreams and longing, with hope and desire, with passion.'[17]

While he may have shaped some of cinema's most exalted moments, at the other extreme Bergman remained throughout his life fascinated by the scatological aspects of the human condition. Ester in *The Silence* refers to herself smelling like a rotten fish after intercourse, and Rakel in *After the Rehearsal* complains that she is 'rotting, bit by bit . . . some fluid is oozing from my skin that smells like carrion . . .' Carl Åkerblom declares in *In the Presence of a Clown*, 'I've fouled myself and vomited and the smell is abominable.' Judge Abrahamson in *The Ritual* apologises for the odour of his sweat, and *Cries and Whispers* reeks of death and decay. Bergman accepts that while the spirit may fly as free as a bird, the body is doomed to putrefaction and dissolution.

Bergman has his detractors. His rigid, some would say inflexible, view of the world led to a certain repetition of themes, doubts and aspirations. The unremitting obsession with death and betrayal, belief and disillusionment, produced in the 1950s and 1960s a style ripe for parody, as the American directors Davis and Coe achieved so beautifully in their short film *The Dove* (showing Death playing badminton and an old man speculating on life while emerging from an outdoor privy). Woody Allen paid affectionate tribute to the scene on the beach in *The Seventh Seal* in his film *Rifkin's Festival* (2020), with Christoph Waltz playing Death.

Bergman cannot be accused of religious sentimentality, but many of his characters suffer from a self-pity that becomes tiresome and overweening. The men in his films are rarely lit by any kind of enduring virtue. Sterile more often than not, they appear damned by the director from the outset. Abortion in Bergman's world still carries a sense of sin, turpitude even. The contradiction, as Denis Marion has pointed out, is that if human beings are led inexorably towards unhappiness in this life, and if no hereafter exists, why give birth to future unfortunate creatures?[18]

Humour, in spite of the epigrammatic dialogue in films such as *A Lesson in Love* and *Smiles of a Summer Night*, did not burst easily through the brooding pessimism of Bergman's cinema. At certain moments, the spectator may be forgiven for sighing with intolerance at the dismal, stolid attitudes of many characters in the Bergman canon. When Bergman did try to present a scene free of psychological tensions, the result could be disastrous – for instance, the meeting on the ferry between Jan, Eva and the Major and his wife at the beginning of *Shame*. Smiles, lines and gestures – all theatrical and unconvincing.

It is undeniable that Bergman was rarely engaged by the political issues of his time. If the society he evoked is maladjusted, it is maladjusted in a spiritual rather than any socio-economic sense. Yet *Shame* may outlast many a strident war movie, and *Scenes from a Marriage* may have influenced more couples than any number of pious TV documentaries on divorce. The particular truth, in Bergman's work, becomes by some magic formula the universal truth.

Bergman has been accused of a certain detachment. His films radiate compassion, however, because they pity human beings. Man has the instincts and the body of an animal, yet he still cherishes the unconquerable hope. He is embittered by the gift of reason that fate has somehow forced on him. Bergman's characters seek always to extent their range of experience, as if eager to cram as much into life as possible. In the absence of the Christian God, they are confronted with a loss of identity. For Bergman, the lapsed Christian who cannot quite dispense with the Christian idiom, the difficulty lies in finding some compensation for the apparent lack of purpose in life. Against the encroaching darkness, love forms a fragile shield. Art no longer serves as either protection or justification. In the 1950s,

Bergman described the artist as a martyr to the cause of lost faith. Subsequently, his 'artists' were discredited, even cowardly figures, reluctant to assume responsibility for the affairs of the world.

The concern with the human soul, the Puritanism and sense of sin that colours even Bergman's most elegant work, belong to the Nordic temperament. Given the historical and religious background from which Bergman sprang, one can scarcely blame him for dwelling on matters of guilt and expiation, any more than one could take Fellini to task for his Latin insistence on the lewd and grotesque, or reproach Renoir for the casual, even frivolous Gallic grace of his films. Like Shakespeare, Bergman analysed all the stages of life, from childbirth through adolescence, first love, the tumult of life's prime, marriage, divorce, middle age and advancing years, even senility. He certainly 'lived' almost all the great scenes that he wrote. He preferred to ignore the rigours of a professional working routine and the challenge of raising children, but his range is still extraordinary. In 2003, when asked what still drove him to continue working, he responded, 'You play. It's a game of life and death. I started with a doll's theatre when I was eight years old. I have the same feeling now, when I come into the studio, as I had when I started to assemble my doll's theatre. I have a need to create a reality I can control and manoeuvre.' On the other hand, his conscience may have been at work when David, the writer, declared in *Through a Glass Darkly*, 'It makes me sick to think of the life I sacrificed to my so-called art.' In the early 1960s, he admitted, 'My great weakness (also as a private person, it usually goes together) is, I suppose, my "bossiness". The fact that I have an awful need to order people about and tell them what to do – of course it's a sense of power or a need for power.'[19]

Bergman's most abiding virtue remains the personal quality of his filmmaking. It is this that strikes a chord of identification in audiences the world over. People recognise in Bergman's straitened characters some replica of themselves. No film director, with the exception of Rainer Werner Fassbinder, has been at once so prolific and so spurred by the need to bare his sores on screen. As Eva chastises her mother in *Autumn Sonata*: 'Have you ever given a damn about any living soul except yourself? You're emotionally crippled.' Yet self-esteem was alien to Bergman, even in the face of the international acclaim that through his films he acquired during the late 1950s. The notion of being an anonymous artist, like the builder of Chartres Cathedral, came to him while he was working in Malmö, as a kind of reaction to the pressure of fame.

Bergman has never pretended to hold an answer to the problems of human existence. He neither denies nor affirms the Christian tradition in which he was so sternly educated. Instead, he probes, he interrogates. In one of his most revealing interviews, he admitted, 'Now I believe that all the qualities I used to associate with God – love, tenderness, grace, all those beautiful things – are created by human beings themselves, they come from inside us. That, for me, is the big miracle.'[20]

Bergman was driven by a compulsive need to create, above all in his chosen fields of film and theatre. Like Hokusai, who drew or painted every day of his life from the age of six to when he was ninety, he was always seeking to refreshen his art or, as he would say, *métier*. Like Johann Sebastian Bach, who composed 1,128 pieces of music in a life that lasted just sixty-five years, Bergman committed his waking hours to work for the cinema or the stage. When once I asked him how he could find the time to watch a TV series like *Dallas*, he reflected that 'Only the truly efficient can be truly lazy.'

In part, this unrelenting work ethic originated in his youth, as he grew up in the shadow of his parents' churchgoing routine and observed his father's constant need to preach or perform religious ceremonies. Work for Bergman offered an escape from emotional entanglements and, on a mundane level, from financial and paternal responsibilities. Deep down, there festered a need to experiment, as Swedish writers such as C. J. Almqvist, Strindberg and Hjalmar Bergman had before him. He drew infinite scenes from private life, with dialogue torn bluntly and unembellished from quarrels with his female companion of the hour. That did not disconcert him. 'You must be obsessed by the feeling that you want to touch people with your emotions,' he said, when I interviewed him at London's National Film Theatre in 1982. 'A director is somebody who is obsessed with the need to get in touch with other human beings.'

He could be a martinet, and a stickler as far as punctuality was concerned. When I had my first formal interview with him in 1969, his assistant warned me to be absolutely on the dot. This precision applied to everything he did, for he sought to wring as much as possible from each passing minute. He inherited this punctiliousness from his father; but while in Pastor Erik it seemed merely pompous, in Bergman it often descended into anger at colleagues who failed to arrive on time for a meeting.

———

With few exceptions, 'tele-recordings' of his stage productions cannot capture the magic that Bergman conjured up every time he stepped into the theatre. He returned often to the work of a handful of playwrights – Strindberg, Ibsen, Molière, Shakespeare. On each occasion he found new means of illuminating the text. He was as much at home on the huge stages of Malmö City Theatre as he was in the Lilla Scenen at the Royal Dramatic Theatre in Stockholm. He could work with the most elaborate of stage settings, and with literally no furniture at all (e.g. *King Lear* in 1984). He knew how to inspire the loyalty of a troupe of actors from season to season, year to year. Some proved stronger on film than they did on stage, and vice versa.

Forever obsessed with God and his demons, reckless in love, and relentless in his commitment to film and theatre. Such was the long and rewarding life of Ernst Ingmar Bergman.

FILMOGRAPHY

SCREENPLAYS BY INGMAR BERGMAN

1944   *Frenzy/Torment* (*Hets*), dir. Alf Sjöberg

1947   *Woman without a Face* (*Kvinna utan ansikte*), dir. Gustaf Molander

1948   *Eva*, dir. and co-scripted Gustaf Molander

1950   *While the City Sleeps* (*Medan staden sover*), dir. Lars-Eric Kjellgren. Bergman wrote only the synopsis; the screenplay is by Kjellgren and Per Anders Fogelström

1956   *Last Couple Out* (*Sista paret ut*), dir. Alf Sjöberg

1961   *The Pleasure Garden* (*Lustgården*), dir. Alf Kjellin. Bergman co-wrote the screenplay with Erland Josephson, under the pseudonym 'Buntel Eriksson'

1970   *The Lie* (*Reservatet*), dir. Jan Molander

1992   *The Best Intentions* (*Den goda viljan*), dir. Bille August

        Sunday's Children (*Söndagsbarn*), dir. Daniel Bergman

1996   *Private Confessions* (*Enskilda samtal*), dir. Liv Ullmann

2000   *Faithless* (*Trolösa*), dir. Liv Ullmann

FILMS SCRIPTED AND DIRECTED BY INGMAR BERGMAN

1946   *Crisis* (*Kris*)

        It Rains on Our Love/The Man with an Umbrella (*Det regnar på vår kärlek*)

1947   *A Ship Bound for India/The Land of Desire* (*Skepp till Indialand*)

1948   *Music in Darkness/Night Is My Future* (*Musik i mörker*)

        Port of Call (*Hamnstadt*)

1949   *Prison/The Devil's Wanton* (*Fängelse*)

        Thirst/Three Strange Loves (*Törst*)

1950   *To Joy* (*Till glädje*)

        This Can't Happen Here/High Tension (*Sånt händer inte här*)

1951   *Summer Interlude* (*Sommarlek*)

1952   *Waiting Women/Secrets of Women* (*Kvinnors väntan*)

1953	Summer with Monika (*Sommaren med Monika*)
	Sawdust and Tinsel/The Naked Night (*Gycklarnas afton*)
1954	A Lesson in Love (*En lektion i kärlek*)
1955	Journey into Autumn/Dreams (*Kvinnodröm*)
	Smiles of a Summer Night (*Sommarnattens leende*)
1957	The Seventh Seal (*Det sjunde inseglet*)
	Wild Strawberries (*Smultronstället*)
1958	So Close to Life/Brink of Life (*Nära livet*)
	The Magician/The Face (*Ansiktet*)
1960	The Virgin Spring (*Jungfrukällan*)
	The Devil's Eye (*Djävulens öga*)
1961	Through a Glass Darkly (*Såsom i en spegel*)
1963	Winter Light (*Nattsvardsgästerna*)
	The Silence (*Tystnaden*)
1964	All These Women (*För att inte tala om alla dessa kvinnor*)
1966	Persona
1967	Daniel (episode of *Stimulantia*)
1968	Hour of the Wolf (*Vargtimmen*)
	Shame (*Skammen*)
1969	The Ritual/The Rite (*Riten*), TV movie
	The Passion of Anna (*En passion*)
	The Fårö Document (*Fårö-dokument*), TV documentary
1971	The Touch (*Beröringen*)
1973	Cries and Whispers (*Viskningar och rop*)
	Scenes from a Marriage (*Scener ur ett äktenskap*), TV series in six episodes
1975	The Magic Flute (*Trollflöjten*), TV movie
1976	Face to Face (*Ansikte mot ansikte*), TV series in four episodes
1977	The Serpent's Egg (*Das Schlangenei/Örmens ägg*)
1978	Autumn Sonata (*Höstsonat*)
1979	Fårö 1979 (*Fårö-dokument 1979*), TV documentary
1980	From the Life of the Marionettes (*Aus dem Leben der Marionetten*)
1982	Fanny and Alexander (*Fanny och Alexander*), TV series in four episodes
1984	After the Rehearsal (*Efter repetitionen*), TV movie
1986	The Blessed Ones (*De två saliga*), TV movie
	Karin's Face (*Karins ansikte*), short
1992	Madame de Sade, TV movie
1993	The Bacchae (*Backanterna*), TV movie
1995	The Last Gasp (*Sista skriket*), TV movie

1996	*Harald & Harald,* TV short
1997	*In the Presence of a Clown* (*Larmar och gör sig till*), TV movie
2000	*The Image Makers* (*Bildmakarna*), TV movie written by Per Olov Enquist
2003	*Saraband,* TV movie

STAGE PRODUCTIONS

1938   *Outward Bound* (Sutton Vane), Mäster-Olofsgården, Stockholm

1939   *Guldkarossen/The Golden Chariot* (Axel Bentzonich), Nicolai
Elementary School, Stockholm
Galgmannen/The Hangman (Runar Schildt), Nicolai Public School,
Stockholm
Lycko-Pers resa/Lucky-Per's Travels (August Strindberg), Mäster-
Olofsgården, Stockholm
Kvällskabaret/Evening Cabaret (Bergman himself and his team)
Mäster-Olofsgården, Stockholm
Romanesques (Edmond Rostand), Mäster-Olofsgården, Stockholm
Höstrapsodi/Autumn Rhapsody (Doris Rönnkvist), Mäster-
Olofsgården, Stockholm
Han som fick leva om sit liv/He Who Lived Twice (Pär Lagerkvist),
Mäster-Olofsgården, Stockholm
Jul/Christmas (August Strindberg), Mäster-Olofsgården, Stockholm

1940   *I Bethlehem – ett julspel /In Bethlehem, A Christmas Play* (unknown
author), Mäster-Olofsgården and Hedvig Eleonora Church,
Stockholm
Svarta handsken/The Black Glove (August Strindberg), Mäster-
Olofsgården, Stockholm
Macbeth (Shakespeare), Assembly Hall at girls' school in Sveaplan,
Stockholm
The Pot of Broth (W. B. Yeats), Mäster-Olofsgården, Stockholm
The Hour Glass (W. B. Yeats), Mäster-Olofsgården, Stockholm
Tillbaka/Return (Gregor Ges), Mäster-Olofsgården, Stockholm
Melodin som kom bort/The Tune that Disappeared (Kjeld Abell),
Mäster-Olofsgården and State Mission Assembly Hall, Stockholm
Svanevit/Swanwhite (August Strindberg), Sveaplan Girls High
School
Pelikanen/The Pelican (August Strindberg), Stockholm Student
Union

1941   *Fadren/The Father* (August Strindberg), Stockholm Student Theatre
Elddonet. Saga I atta bilder/The Tinder Box, Fairy Tale in Eight

Tableaux (Hans Christian Andersen), Sagoteatern, Stockholm
The Merchant of Venice (Shakespeare), Norra Latin High School
Spöksonaten/ The Ghost Sonata (August Strindberg),
Medborgarhusteatern, Civic Centre, Stockholm
A Midsummer Night's Dream (Shakespeare), Sagoteatern, Stockholm
Fågel blå/ Bluebird (Zacharias Topelius), Medborgarhusteatern, Civic
Centre, Stockholm

1942   *Sniggel-Snuggel, sagospel i 9 bilder/ Sniggel-Snuggel, Fairy Play
in 9 Scenes* (Hugo Valentin and Torunn Munthe), Sagoteatern,
Stockholm
*De tre dumheterna. Skämtsaga I 6 bilder/ The Three Stupidities.
Humorous Fairy Tale in 6 Scenes* (Torun Munthe), Sagoteatern,
Stockholm
Kaspers död/ The Death of Punch (Ingmar Bergman), Stockholm
Student Theatre
Rödluvan/ Little Red Riding Hood (Brothers Grimm/Robert
Bürkner), Sagoteatern, Stockholm
*Clownen Beppo eller den bortrövade Camomilla/ Beppo the Clown or the
Abducted Camomilla* (Else Fisher, Ingmar Bergman), Sagoteatern,
Stockholm
A Midsummer Night's Dream (Shakespeare), Norra Latin School,
Stockholm

1943   *Vem är jag? Eller när fan ger ett anbud/ Who Am I? or When the Devil
Makes an Offer* (Carl-Erik Soya), Stockholm Student Theatre
Strax innan man vaknar/ Just Before Awakening (Bengt Olof Vos),
Stockholm Student Theatre
Tivolit/ The Tivoli (Ingmar Bergman), Stockholm Student Theatre
U 39/ U-boat 39 (Rudolf Värnlund), Dramatikerstudion,
Stockholm
Geografi och kärlek / Geography and Love (Bjørnstierne Bjørnson),
Folkparksteatern, Frösunda
Niels Ebbesen (Kaj Munk), Dramatikerstudion, Stockholm

1944   *Hjalmar Bergman afton/ Hjalmar Bergman Evening* (Hjalmar
Bergman), Dramatikerstudion, Stockholm
Hotellrummet/ The Hotel Room (Pierre Rocher), The Boulevard
Theatre/Scala Theatre, Stockholm
Aschebergskan på Wittskövle/ The Ascheberg Widow at Wittskövle (Brita
von Horn), Helsingborg City Theatre
Fan ger ett anbud/ The Devil Makes an Offer (Carl-Erik Soya),
Helsingborg City Theatre

Macbeth (Shakespeare), Helsingborg City Theatre

Elddonet/The Tinder Box (Hans Christian Andersen), Helsingborg
City Theatre

1945   *Kriss-krass-Filibom/Scapin, Pimpel & Kasper (Punch)* (Sture Ericson,
Rune Moberg, Ingmar Bergman), Helsingborg City Theatre

Sagan/The Legend (Hjalmar Bergman), Helsingborg City Theatre

Reducera moralen/Down with Morality (Sune Bergström),
Helsingborg City Theatre

Katedralen/The Cathedral (Jules Baillod), Helsingborg City Theatre

Jacobowsky och Översten/Jacobowsky and the Colonel (Franz Werfel),
Helsingborg City Theatre

Rabies: scener ur livet/Rabies: Scenes from Life (Olle Hedberg),
Helsingborg City Theatre

Pelikanen/The Pelican (August Strindberg), Malmö City Theatre

Utan en tråd/Without a Shred (Rune Moberg), Helsingborg City
Theatre

1946   *Rekviem/Requiem* (Björn-Erik Höijer), Helsingborg City Theatre

Rakel och biografvaktmästaren/Rachel and the Cinema Doorman
(Ingmar Bergman), Malmö Intiman Theatre

Caligula (Albert Camus), Gothenburg City Theatre

1947   *Dagen slutar tidigt/Early Ends the Day* (Ingmar Bergman),
Gothenburg City Theatre

Magi/Magic (G. K. Chesterton), Gothenburg City Theatre

Mig till skräck/Unto My Fear (Ingmar Bergman), Gothenburg City
Theatre

1948   *Dans på bryggen/Dancing on Deck* (Björn-Erik Höijer), Gothenburg
City Theatre

Macbeth (Shakespeare), Gothenburg City Theatre

Tjuvarnas bal/Thieves' Carnival (Jean Anouilh), Gothenburg City
Theatre

Kamma noll/Come Up Empty/Draw Zero (Ingmar Bergman),
Gothenburg City Theatre

1949   *En vildfågel/The Wild Bird* (Jean Anouilh), Gothenburg City
Theatre

A Streetcar Named Desire (Tennessee Williams), Gothenburg City
Theatre

Rakel och biografvaktmästaren/Rachel and the Cinema Doorman
(Ingmar Bergman), Boulevard Theatre, Stockholm

1950   *Guds ord på landet/Divine Words* (Don Ramon del Valle-Inclan),
Gothenburg City Theatre

Die Dreigroschenoper/ The Threepenny Opera (Bertolt Brecht), Intima Teatern, Stockholm

Medea (Jean Anouilh), Intima Teatern, Stockholm

En skugga/ A Shadow (Hjalmar Bergman), Intima Teatern, Stockholm

1951   *Det lyser I kåken/ Lights in the Shack* (Björn-Erik Höijer), Royal Dramatic Theatre, Stockholm

Mannen du gav mig/ The Country Girl (Clifford Odets), Folksparksteatern, Eskilstuna

The Rose Tattoo (Tennessee Williams), Norrköping-Linköping City Theatre

1952   *Mordet I Barjärna – Ett passionsspell Murder in Barjärna – A Passion Play* (Ingmar Bergman), Malmö City Theatre

Kronbruden/ The Crown Bride (August Strindberg), Malmö City Theatre

1953   *Jack hos skådespelarna/ Jack among the Actors* (Ingmar Bergman), Lilla Teatren, Lund

Six Characters in Search of an Author (Luigi Pirandello), Malmö City Theatre

Slottet/ The Castle (Max Brod, based on the novel by Franz Kafka), Malmö City Theatre

1954   *Spöksonaten/ The Ghost Sonata* (August Strindberg), Malmö City Theatre

Glada änkan/ The Merry Widow (Franz Lehár, libretto by Viktor Léon and Leo Stein), Malmö City Theatre

Skymningslekar/ Twilight Games (Carl Gustaf Kruuse and Ingmar Bergman), Malmö City Theatre

1955   *Don Juan* (Molière), Malmö City Theatre

Teahouse of the August Moon (John Patrick), Malmö City Theatre

Trämålning/ Wood Painting/ Painting on Wood (Ingmar Bergman), Malmö City Theatre

Lea och Rakel/ Leah and Rachel (Vilhelm Moberg), Malmö City Theatre

1956   *Bruden utan hemgift/ The Dowerless Bride* (Alexander Ostrovsky), Malmö City Theatre

Cat on a Hot Tin Roof (Tennessee Williams), Malmö City Theatre

Erik XIV (August Strindberg), Malmö City Theatre

1957   *Peer Gynt* (Henrik Ibsen), Malmö City Theatre

Misantropen/ The Misanthrope (Molière), Malmö City Theatre

1958   *Sagan/ The Legend* (Hjalmar Bergman), Malmö City Theatre

Urfaust (Goethe), Malmö City Theatre

Värmlänningarna (F. A. Dahlgren), Malmö City Theatre

1961 *Måsen/ The Seagull* (Anton Chekhov), Royal Dramatic Theatre, Stockholm

Rucklarens väg/ The Rake's Progress (Stravinsky), Royal Swedish Opera, Stockholm

1963 *Who's Afraid of Virginia Woolf?* (Edward Albee), Royal Dramatic Theatre, Stockholm

Sagan/ The Legend (Hjalmar Bergman), Royal Dramatic Theatre, Stockholm

1964 *Tre knivar från Wei/ Three Knives from Wei* (Harry Martinson), Royal Dramatic Theatre, Stockholm

Hedda Gabler (Henrik Ibsen), Royal Dramatic Theatre, Stockholm

1965 *Don Juan eller stengästen/ Don Juan or The Stone Guest* (Molière), Royal Dramatic Theatre, Stockholm

För Alice/ Tiny Alice (Edward Albee), Royal Dramatic Theatre, Stockholm

1966 *Die Ermittlung/ The Investigation* (Peter Weiss), Royal Dramatic Theatre, Stockholm

School for Wives and *Critique of School for Wives* (Molière), Royal Dramatic Theatre

1967 *Six Characters in Search of an Author* (Luigi Pirandello), National Theatre, Oslo

1969 *Woyzeck* (Georg Büchner), Royal Dramatic Theatre, Stockholm

1970 *Ett drömspel/ A Dream Play* (August Strindberg), Royal Dramatic Theatre, Stockholm

Hedda Gabler (Henrik Ibsen), National Theatre, London

1971 *Show* (Lars Forssell), Royal Dramatic Theatre, Stockholm

1972 *Vildanden/ The Wild Duck* (Henrik Ibsen), Royal Dramatic Theatre, Stockholm

1973 *Spöksonaten/ The Ghost Sonata* (August Strindberg), Royal Dramatic Theatre, Stockholm

Misantropen/ The Misanthrope (Molière), Royal Dramatic Theatre, Copenhagen

1974 *Till Damaskus/ To Damascus* (August Strindberg), Royal Dramatic Theatre, Stockholm

1975 *Twelfth Night* (Shakespeare), Royal Dramatic Theatre, Stockholm

1977 *Ein Traumspiel/ A Dream Play* (August Strindberg), Residenztheater, Munich

1978 *Drei Schwestern/ Three Sisters* (Anton Chekhov), Residenztheater, Munich

1979	*Tartuffe* (Molière), Residenztheater, Munich
	Hedda Gabler (Henrik Ibsen), Residenztheater, Munich
1980	*Yvonne: Prinzess von Bourgogne* (Witold Gombrowicz), Residenztheater, Munich
1981	*Nora und Julie; Szenen einer Ehe; The Bergman Project* (Henrik Ibsen, August Strindberg, Ingmar Bergman), Residenztheater, Munich and Theater am Marstall
1983	*Dom Juan* (Molière), Cuvilliés-Theater, Munich/Salzburg Festival
1984	*Vom Leben der Regenschlangen/From the Life of the Rain Worms* (Per Olov Enquist), Residenztheater, Munich
1985	*John Gabriel Borkman* (Henrik Ibsen), Residenztheater, Munich
1984	*Kung Lear/King Lear* (Shakespeare), Royal Dramatic Theatre, Stockholm
1985	*Fröken Julie/Miss Julie* (August Strindberg), Royal Dramatic Theatre, Stockholm
1986	*Ett drömspel/A Dream Play* (August Strindberg), Royal Dramatic Theatre, Stockholm
	Hamlet (Shakespeare), Royal Dramatic Theatre, Stockholm
1988	*Lång dags färd mot natt/Long Day's Journey into Night* (Eugene O'Neill), Royal Dramatic Theatre, Stockholm
1989	*Markisinnan de Sade/Madame de Sade* (Yukio Mishima), Royal Dramatic Theatre, Stockholm
	A Doll's House (Henrik Ibsen), Royal Dramatic Theatre, Stockholm
1991	*Peer Gynt* (Henrik Ibsen), Royal Dramatic Theatre, Stockholm
1993	*Sista skriket – en lätt tintad moralitet/The Last Cry – a slightly tinted morality play* (Ingmar Bergman), Royal Dramatic Theatre, Stockholm; also in Gothenburg and Malmö
	Rummet och tiden/Room and Time (Botho Strauss), Royal Dramatic Theatre, Stockholm
1994	*Goldbergvariationerna/The Goldberg Variations* (George Tabori), Royal Dramatic Theatre, Stockholm
	Vintersagan/The Winter's Tale (Shakespeare), Royal Dramatic Theatre, Stockholm
1995	*Misantropen/The Misanthrope* (Molière), Royal Dramatic Theatre, Stockholm
	Yvonne, prinsessa av Burgund/Yvonne, Princess of Burgundy (Witold Gombrowicz), Royal Dramatic Theatre, Stockholm
1996	*Backanterna/The Bacchae* (Euripides), Royal Dramatic Theatre, Stockholm

1998   *Bildmakarna/The Image Makers* (Ingmar Bergman), Royal Dramatic
       Theatre, Stockholm
2000   *Spöksonaten/The Ghost Sonata* (August Strindberg), Royal Dramatic
       Theatre, Stockholm
       Maria Stuart (Friedrich Schiller), Royal Dramatic Theatre,
       Stockholm
2002   *Gengångare/Ghosts* (Henrik Ibsen), Royal Dramatic Theatre,
       Stockholm

For fuller details of each production, and also the various guest performances
outside Sweden, see Birgitta Steene's admirably comprehensive *Ingmar
Bergman, A Reference Guide* (Amsterdam University Press, Amsterdam, 2005).

ACKNOWLEDGEMENTS

All sources are noted in the text, apart from comments taken from conversations or correspondence between the author and one of the following individuals, who kindly gave their time to this project, first in the 1970s and 1980s, and more recently in the period 2018–21. Quotations from letters to and from Bergman come from the collection in the Bergman Foundation in Stockholm.

I am grateful for conversations with, and advice from, Kjell Albin Abrahamson, Jan Aghed, Bibi Andersson, Harriet Andersson, Ornólfur Árnason, Paul Britten Austin, Aina Bellis, Yngve Bengtsson, Daniel Bergman, Ingmar Bergman, Ingmar Bergman Jr, Gunnar Björnstrand, Jacob Boëthius, Gudrun Brost, Peter Darvill, Jörn Donner, Allan Ekelund, Arne Ericsson, Kenne Fant, Katinka Faragó, Gunnar Fischer, Else Fisher-Bergman, Bengt Forslund, Christer Frunck, Herbert Grevenius, Erik Hedling, Ann-Marie Hedwall, Jan Holmberg, Kerstin Högvall, Claes Hooglund, Gun Hyltén-Cavallius, Christer Jönsson, Erland Josephson, Stefan Klockby, Hauke Lange-Fuchs, Käbi Laretei, Lars-Olof Löthwall, Torborg Lundell, Mago, Aito Mäkinen, Birger Malmsten, Maj-Britt Nilsson, Erik Nordgren, Marie Nyreröd, Stig Olin, Lennart Olsson, Birgitta Pettersson, Veronica Ralston, Måns Reuterswärd, Olle Rosberg, Ulla Ryghe, Maud Sandvall, Alf Sjöberg, Henrik Sjögren, Vilgot Sjöman, Nils Petter Sundgren, Ove Svensson, Henrik von Sydow, Max von Sydow, Sven Tollin, Hartvig Torngren, Liv Ullmann, Rune Waldekranz, Gertrud Wincrantz, Dieter Winter and Bertil Wredlund. All too many of these friends and acquaintances have passed away, but their contribution to my work will not be forgotten.

I am most grateful for a generous grant from the Lauritzen Foundation in Stockholm, and also to the following individuals, who proved so invaluable to my research: Hélène Dahl (*prima inter pares*), Charlotta Bjuvman, Krister Collin, Claes Du Rietz, Derek Elley, Leif Engberg, Jan Göransson, Bo-Erik Gyberg, Lars Hedenstedt, Jan Holmberg, Dag Kronlund, Pia Lundberg, Lena Mauler, Torgny Nilsson and Kasia Syty.

I salute my editor at Faber and Faber, Walter Donohue, who has encouraged my work for more than thirty years; and my tireless, ever-optimistic agent, Laura Morris. Joanna Harwood, Jill Burrows and Ian Bahrami have shepherded the book to its final form with grace and vigilance. Finally, my wife Françoise has served as a constant inspiration to me, as well as proffering astute observations on Bergman's individual films.

NOTES

See References Cited in the Text (p. 389) for full details of abbreviated titles.

1 CHILDHOOD SHOWS THE MAN

1 Ingmar Bergman, *Sunday's Children* (Vintage Classics, London, 2018).
2 Ingmar Bergman, *The Best Intentions* (Vintage Classics, London, 2018), p. 229.
3 Interview with Dag Bergman recorded by Sveriges Television in September 1981.
4 Margareta Bergman, *Karin vid havet* (Stockholm, Raben & Sjögren, 1980); unpublished English translation by Paul Britten Austin.
5 Quoted in Veronica Ralston, *The Love Child* (unpublished manuscript).
6 Ingmar Bergman, *Private Confessions* (Vintage Classics, London, 2018), p. 76.
7 Interview with author, Munich, October 1980.
8 *L136, Diary*, p. 34.
9 *Bergman on Bergman*, p. 132.
10 Introduction to *Four Screenplays*.
11 Jörn Donner, *Three Scenes with Ingmar Bergman* (documentary film, 1975).
12 Ingmar Bergman, 'Self-analysis of a Filmmaker', in *Films and Filming* (London), September 1956.
13 Donner, *Three Scenes*.
14 *Lantern*, p. 57.
15 *Bergman on Bergman*, p. 7.
16 Ibid., p. 8.
17 Gösta Werner, *Victor Sjöström, A Portrait* (documentary film, 1981).

2 FIRST FORAYS INTO THEATRE

1 *Lantern*, p. 78.
2 Barbro Hiort af Ornäs maintained sporadic contact with Bergman across the years, always concluding by thanking him for what he had

done for her. 'Sometimes I think of that summer when you wore a machine-gun pipe on your shoulder and celebrated your twentieth birthday by dropping your watch. Too bad I was still an uneducated and inexperienced child at the time, otherwise we might have had more fun moments together.'

3 *Lantern*, p. 123.
4 Ibid, p. 129.
5 Jörn Donner, *Three Scenes with Ingmar Bergman* (documentary film, 1975).
6 Birgitta Steene, 'Words and Whisperings: An Interview with Ingmar Bergman', in *Focus on The Seventh Seal* (Prentice-Hall, Englewood Cliffs, New Jersey, 1972).
7 *Ofilmat*, p. 55.
8 *The Fifth Act.*
9 *Bergman på teatern.*
10 *Lantern*, p. 138.
11 'Monologue', *The Fifth Act.*
12 Anders Thunberg, *Karin Lannby – Ingmar Bergman's Mata Hari* (Natur & Kultur, Stockholm, 2009), p. 244.
13 Ibid., p. 262.

3 FIRST MARRIAGE, FIRST SCREENPLAYS

1 Quoted in *Nutid* (Stockholm), no. 16 (1955).
2 Author's interview with Gunnar Fischer, Bromma, November 1979.
3 *Arbetsboken 1975–2001*, p. 418.
4 *Lantern*, p. 142.
5 Ibid.
6 *Artiklar*, p. 170.
7 In 1942, Bergman had written *Om en mördare*, describing two men, one an out-of-work musician, the other a sadist much akin to Caligula in *Frenzy* (*Ofilmat*, pp. 55 *et seq.*).
8 *Images*, p. 119.
9 Letter to author, 25 February 1983.
10 *Lantern*, p. 146.
11 Ibid.
12 Henrik Sjögren, *Stage and Society in Sweden* (Swedish Institute, Stockholm, 1979).
13 *Artiklar*, p. 94.
14 Letter to author, 5 December 1979.
15 Unpublished memoirs (Bergman Foundation, Stockholm).

16 Anna Bergman, *Inte Pappas Flicka* (Bra Böcker, Höganäs, 1988).

4 WORKING AT TERRAFILM

1 *Artiklar*, p. 269.
2 Unpublished memoir by Gunnar Fischer (Bergman Foundation, Stockholm).
3 Unpublished memoir by Ellen Lundström (Bergman Foundation, Stockholm).
4 Ibid.
5 *Lantern*, p. 155.
6 Interview in *Playboy* (Chicago), June 1964.
7 *Bergman on Bergman*, p. 34.
8 *Ny Tid* (Stockholm), no. 14, 30 November 1946.
9 *Artiklar*, p. 211.
10 *Filmnyheter* (Svensk Filmindustri, Stockholm), no. 11 (1947).
11 Charles Thomas Samuels, *Encountering Directors* (Putnam's, New York, 1972), p. 192.
12 Bengt Forslund, 'Prästsonen Ingmar Bergman', *Ord & Bild* (Stockholm, 1957).
13 Samuels, *Encountering Directors*.
14 *Ny Tid*, no. 16 (1955).
15 *Lantern*, p. 168.
16 *Bergman on Bergman*, p. 33.

5 FROM *PRISON* TO EMOTIONAL LIBERTY

1 *Images*, p. 144.
2 Interviewed in *Vänd* (Stockholm), 1960.
3 The character of Grandé may be found in an unperformed play by Bergman, *The Puzzle Makes Eros* (dated 9 October 1946), as well as in *Woman without a Face*.
4 *Lantern*, p. 152.
5 *Reference*, p. 545.
6 François Truffaut, *The Films in My Life* (Simon & Schuster, New York, 1978).
7 *Lantern*, p. 159.
8 Ibid.
9 Interview with Cynthia Grenier, *Oui* (Paris), no. 3 (1974).
10 Amita Malik, *Sunday Statesman* (New Delhi), 12 December 1965.

11 Interview with author, Munich, 9 February 1980.
12 Ellen Lundström, *År med Ingmar*, manuscript (Bergman Foundation, Stockholm).
13 *Bergman on Bergman*, p. 78.
14 Lorens Marmstedt, 'Ruda eller Gamba?', *Obs* (Stockholm), 13 September 1950.
15 *Theater* (New Haven, Connecticut), vol. 11, no. 1 (fall 1979).

6 SUMMER LOVE

1 *Bergman on Bergman*, p. 51.
2 *Artiklar*, p. 42.
3 Interview with Edwin Newman, in the WNBC-TV *Open Mind* series, printed in *Film Comment* (New York), vol. 4, nos. 2, 3 (fall–winter 1967).
4 *Lantern*, p. 60.
5 *Bergman on Bergman*, p. 50.
6 See *Chaplin* (Stockholm), special issue for Bergman's seventieth birthday, 1988.
7 'Lill-Ingmar', named after the character in Selma Lagerlöf's *Jerusalem*, filmed by Victor Sjöström in 1919. Lill-Ingmar Bergman would not see his father much during his childhood, except for the occasional Sunday, when Ingmar Sr would visit the apartment and play with an electric train set that was the delight of Lill-Ingmar and his two half-brothers.
8 *Bergman on Bergman*, p. 67.
9 Ibid., p. 75.
10 *Images*, p. 295.
11 Interview with the author for the Criterion Blu-ray release of *Summer with Monika* (2012).
12 Ibid.
13 Ibid.
14 *Arbetsboken 1955–1974*, p. 424.

7 TRIUMPH AND DISASTER

1 *Images*, p. 184.
2 *Bergman på teatern*.
3 Interview in *Expressen* (Stockholm), 15 March 1980.
4 *Bergman on Bergman*, p. 96.
5 Author's interview with Harriet Andersson, 2021.
6 Maaret Koskinen, in *Ofilmat*, p. 320.

7 Charles Thomas Samuels, *Encountering Directors* (Putnam's, New York, 1972), p. 205.
8 Author's interview with Rune Waldekranz, 1979.
9 *Bergman på teatern*, p. 140.
10 Ibid.
11 Henrik Sjögren, *Stage and Society in Sweden* (Swedish Institute, Stockholm, 1979).
12 Introduction to the film for the Criterion DVD (2018).
13 *Bergman on Bergman*, p. 57.
14 Author's interview with Katinka Faragó, Stockholm, 18 March 2019.

8 THE GOLDEN YEARS BEGIN

1 *Bergman på teatern*, p. 151.
2 Carl Anders Dymling, Preface to *Four Screenplays*.
3 Tillie Björnstrand, *Inte båra applader* (Tidens Förlag, Stockholm, 1975), p. 145.
4 Richard Meryman, 'I Live at the Edge of a Very Strange Country', in *Life* magazine (New York), 15 October 1971.
5 In *Chaplin* (Stockholm), special issue to celebrate Bergman's seventieth birthday, 1988.
6 *Lantern*, p. 179.
7 *Bergman on Bergman*, p. 102.
8 *L136, Diary*, p. 233.
9 In the wake of the shoot of *Smiles*, Bergman published a script entitled *Falskspelet* (*Foul Play*), which was, by his own admission, 'awful'. (See *Ofilmat*, p. 215.)
10 *Arbetsboken 1955–1974*, p. 32.
11 Ibid.
12 Ibid., p. 57.
13 Bibi Andersson, *Ett ögonblick* (Saga Egmont, Stockholm, 1996).
14 Ibid.
15 Henrik Sjögren, *Stage and Society in Sweden* (Swedish Institute, Stockholm, 1979).
16 Roland Huntford, *The New Totalitarians* (Allen Lane, Penguin Press, London, 1971), p. 24.
17 *Images*, p. 234.
18 Lars-Olof Löthwall, 'Ingmar Bergman och Diger döden', *Stockholms-Tidningen*, 5 July 1956.
19 *Bergman on Bergman*, p. 113.

20 Charles Thomas Samuels, *Encountering Directors* (Putnam's, New York, 1972), p. 204.
21 Ibid.
22 *Variety* (New York), 21 May 1957.
23 Daniel Bergman, *Hjärtat* (Bokförlaget Polaris, Stockholm, 2021), p. 399.
24 *Bergman on Bergman*, p. 227.
25 Interview with Marie Nyreröd for DVD of *Smiles of a Summer Night* (Criterion).

9 BEHIND THE MASK

1 Jean Béranger, *Ingmar Bergman et ses films* (Le Terrain Vague, Paris, 1960), p. 87.
2 *Bergman på teatern*, p. 172.
3 Michael Meyer, *Ibsen, A Biography* (Doubleday, Garden City, New Jersey, 1971), p. 252.
4 Henrik Sjögren, *Stage and Society in Sweden* (Swedish Institute, Stockholm, 1979), p. 54.
5 *Bergman on Bergman*, p. 132.
6 *Arbetsboken 1955–1974*, p. 62.
7 *Images*, p. 20.
8 Ibid., pp. 16–20.
9 *Arbetsboken 1955–1974*, 2 May 1957.
10 *Images*, p. 22.
11 August Strindberg, *Three Plays*, trans. Peter Watts (Penguin Classics, London, 1958), p. 110.
12 Ibid.
13 *Arbetsboken 1955–1974*.
14 *Bergman on Bergman*, p. 136.
15 'Bergman on Victor Sjöström', in *Sight and Sound* (London), spring 1960.
16 Denis Marion, *Ingmar Bergman* (Gallimard, Paris, 1979).
17 Interview in *Året runt* (Stockholm), no. 17 (1964).
18 Martin Lamm, *August Strindberg*, translated and edited by Harry G. Carlson (B. Blom, New York, 1971), p. 208.
19 Peter Cowie, 'Janus and the Art House Legacy', *Essential Art House* (Criterion Collection, New York, 2006), p. 17.
20 Ibid.

10 THEATRE AS WIFE, FILM AS MISTRESS

1 On 29 August 2006, she wrote him a final letter, saying she had just turned eighty-five and that 'it is sixty-eight years since we met for the first time'. Only he and her mother had called her 'Babs'.
2 Henrik Sjögren, *Stage and Society in Sweden* (Swedish Institute, Stockholm, 1979), p. 59.
3 Ibid.
4 *Filmnytt* (Stockholm), no. 6 (1950).
5 Vernon Young, *Cinema Borealis* (David Lewis, New York, 1971), p. 184.
6 *Arbetsboken 1955–1974*, p. 74.
7 Ibid.
8 *Images*, p. 164.
9 Ibid., p. 172.
10 *L136, Diary*, pp. 63–4.
11 *Bergman on Bergman*, p. 187.
12 Gunnar Oldin, 'Ingmar Bergman', *American–Scandinavian Review* (Philadelphia), fall 1959.
13 Sjögren, *Stage and Society in Sweden*, p. 62.
14 Ibid., p. 63.

11 NEW DIRECTIONS

1 *L136, Diary*, p. 128.
2 Käbi Laretei, *Vart tog all denna kärlek vägen?* (Norstedts, Stockholm, 2009).
3 Jean Béranger, *Ingmar Bergman et ses films* (Le Terrain Vague, Paris, 1960), p. 101.
4 Note on Dramaten notepaper, dated 2 September 1973.
5 Béranger, p. 103.
6 Erik Ulrichsen, 'Ingmar Bergman and the Devil', *Sight and Sound* (London), summer 1958.
7 From booklet on *The Virgin Spring* issued by Svensk Filmindustri in 1960.
8 *Bergman on Bergman*, p. 128.
9 Edith Sorel, 'Ingmar Bergman: I Confect Dreams and Anguish', *New York Times*, 22 January 1978.

12 THE DISCOVERY OF FÅRÖ

1 *Arbetsboken 1955–1974*, p. 99.

2 *L136, Diary*, p. 173.

3 Arne Sellermark, 'Den okände Ingmar Bergman', *Hemmets Journal* (Stockholm), 1959.

4 *L136, Diary*, p. 5.

5 *Lantern*, p. 208.

6 Carl Anders Dymling, Preface to *Four Screenplays*.

7 Minus is referred to as fifteen years of age in Bergman's early notes for the screenplay.

8 *Images*, p. 254.

9 *Bergman on Bergman*, p. 164.

10 *Arbetsboken 1955–1974*, p. 102.

11 *Lantern*, p. 226.

12 Ernst Riffe was the name of a hairdresser in Paris frequented by Gun Grut during her escapade with Bergman in 1949.

13 *Chaplin* (Stockholm), no. 14, 1960.

13 A NEW LANGUAGE

1 Amita Malik, *Sunday Statesman* (New Delhi), 12 December 1965.

2 *Bergman on Bergman*, p. 173.

3 *Arbetsboken 1955–1974*, p. 112.

4 Ibid., 12 June 1961.

5 Ellen Lundström, *År med Ingmar*, manuscript (Bergman Foundation, Stockholm).

6 Sven Nykvist, 'Photographing the Films of Ingmar Bergman', *American Cinematographer* (Los Angeles), vol. 43, no. 10 (October 1962).

7 *L136, Diary*, p. 184.

8 Ibid., p. 89.

9 Ibid., p. 73.

10 She does not blink throughout her monologue. 'I thought it was the only way to hold the audience's attention during such a long close-up.' (*L136, Diary*, p. 228.)

11 *L136, Diary*, p. 170.

12 *Bergman on Bergman*, p. 175.

13 *Arbetsboken 1955–1974*, 30 December 1962.

14 *L136, Diary*, p. 163.

15 Ibid., p. 162.

16 *Bergman on Bergman*, p. 181.

17 *Arbetsboken 1955–1974*, 28 March 1962.

18 *The Times* (London), 11 February 1961.

19 Mårten Blomkvist, *Höggradigt jävla excentrisk* (Norstedts, Stockholm, 2011), p. 89.

20 *L136, Diary*, p. 194.

21 See *The Undefeated Woman*, film by Marie Nyreröd, made for Sveriges Television (2018).

22 Tommy Berggren, *Tommy* (Albert Bonniers Förlag, Stockholm, 2017), p. 167.

23 *L136, Diary*, p. 185.

24 Nykvist, 'Photographing the Films of Ingmar Bergman'.

25 Author's interview with Katinka Faragó, Stockholm, 18 March 2019.

26 *Arbetsboken 1955–1974*, 17 August 1962.

27 See *Searching for Ingmar Bergman*, documentary film (2018).

28 Linn Ullmann, *Unquiet* (W. W. Norton, New York, 2019), p. 126.

14 ADMINISTRATOR, INNOVATOR

1 See https://www.media.volvocars.com/global/en-gb/media/press; accessed May 2023.

2 Käbi Laretei, *Vart tog all denna kärlek vägen?* (Norstedts, Stockholm, 2009).

3 Interview with Matts Rying, *Röster I radio TV* (Stockholm), 3–9 February 1963.

4 *L136, Diary*, p. 136.

5 *Bergman on Bergman*, p. 21.

6 Mårten Blomkvist, *Höggradigt jävla excentrisk* (Norstedts, Stockholm, 2011), p. 90.

7 *Chaplin* (Stockholm), no. 42, December 1963.

8 Author's interview with Nils Petter Sundgren in Stockholm, December 1979.

9 John Simon, *Ingmar Bergman Directs* (Harcourt, Brace, Jovanovich, New York, 1972).

10 *Lantern*, p. 191.

11 Derek Prouse, 'Ingmar Bergman: A Problem Genius', *Washington Post*, 5 April 1964.

15 *PERSONA* AND LIV ULLMANN

1 *Arbetsboken 1955–1974*, 30 June 1964 and 22 July 1964.

2 Randolph Goodman, *From Script to Stage: Eight Modern Plays* (Brooklyn College, City University of New York, Rinehart Press, 1971).

3 John Simon, *Ingmar Bergman Directs* (Harcourt, Brace, Jovanovich, New York, 1972), p. 30.
4 Käbi Laretei, *Vart tog all denna kärlek vägen?* (Norstedts, Stockholm, 2009).
5 Daniel Bergman, *Hjärtat* (Bokförlaget Polaris, Stockholm, 2021), p. 48.
6 *Arbetsboken 1955–1974*, 19 May 1965.
7 *Bergman on Bergman*, p. 199.
8 Martin Lamm, *August Strindberg*, translated and edited by Harry G. Carlsson (B. Blom, New York, 1971), p. 226.
9 Simon, *Ingmar Bergman Directs*, p. 215.
10 *Ingmar Bergman*, documentary film by Stig Björkman (1971).
11 Liv Ullmann, quoted in *Newsweek* (New York), 17 March 1975.
12 Bergman, *Hjärtat*, p. 29.
13 Liv Ullmann, *Changing* (Knopf, New York, 1977), p. 113.
14 Liv Ullmann, quoted in *Time* magazine (New York), 4 December 1972.
15 Oscar Hedlund, 'Ingmar Bergman: The Listener', *Saturday Review* (New York), 29 February 1964.
16 *Bergman on Bergman*, p. 208.

16 AT WORK ON THE ISLAND

1 *Arbetsboken 1975–2001*, p. 368.
2 Charles Thomas Samuels, *Encountering Directors* (Putnam's, New York, 1972), p. 190.
3 *Nya Svensk Damtidning* (Stockholm), 1972.
4 *Bergman on Bergman*, p. 249.
5 *Liv & Ingmar*, documentary film by Dheeraj Akolkar (2012).
6 Richard Meryman, 'I Live at the Edge of a Very Strange Country', in *Life* magazine (New York), 15 October 1971.
7 *Images*, p. 42.
8 Liv Ullmann, *Changing* (Knopf, New York, 1977), p. 116.
9 Interview with Gordon Gow, *Films and Filming* (London), 30 January 1975.
10 Linn Ullmann, *Unquiet* (W. W. Norton, New York, 2019), p. 137.
11 Edith Sorel, 'Ingmar Bergman: I Confect Dreams and Anguish', *New York Times*, 22 January 1978.
12 Interview with Cynthia Grenier, *Oui* (Paris), no. 3 (1974).
13 Interview with Nils Petter Sundgren on Swedish TV, 21 February 1968.
14 Ibid.
15 Daniel Bergman, *Hjärtat* (Bokförlaget Polaris, Stockholm, 2021), p. 24.
16 *Arbetsboken 1955–1974*, 24 April 1971.

17 Quoted in Richard Kaplan, *A Look at Liv*, a documentary screened on BBC Television, 3 October 1979.
18 Quoted in *Film in Sweden* (Stockholm), no. 3, 1966–7.
19 *Bergman on Bergman*, p. 231.
20 *Arbetsboken 1955–1974*, 25 February 1967.
21 In *Chaplin* (Stockholm), special issue to celebrate Bergman's seventieth birthday, 1988.
22 *Fårö and Ingmar Bergman* (Fårö Local Heritage Association Publishers, 2015).
23 *Liv & Ingmar*.
24 *Bergman on Bergman*, p. 229.
25 Ibid., p. 228.
26 https://margot-quotes.livejournal.com/135645.html; accessed May 2023.
27 *Liv & Ingmar*.
28 *Images*, p. 299.
29 Ullmann, *Changing*, p. 128.
30 *Chaplin* (Stockholm), special issue to celebrate Bergman's seventieth birthday, 1988.
31 *Chaplin*, no. 80 (March 1968).
32 *Bergman on Bergman*, p. 162.
33 Maria Bergom-Larsson, *Ingmar Bergman and Society* (Norstedts, Stockholm, 1978), p. 100.
34 Ibid.
35 Author's interview with Nils Petter Sundgren in Stockholm, December 1979.
36 *Arbetsboken 1955–1974*, pp. 244 and 254.
37 *Images*, p. 306.
38 Alrik Gustafson, *A History of Swedish Literature* (University of Minnesota Press, Minneapolis, 1961), pp. 438 *et seq.*

17 AT LAST, STABILITY

1 *Artiklar*, p. 269.
2 Henrik Sjögren, *Regi: Ingmar Bergman* (Aldus Books, Stockholm, 1970), p. 98.
3 Ibid.
4 *Bergman på teatern*, p. 291.
5 *Liv & Ingmar*, documentary film by Dheeraj Akolkar (2012).
6 Daniel Bergman, *Hjärtat* (Bokförlaget Polaris, Stockholm, 2021), p. 231.
7 *Liv & Ingmar*.

8 *Newsweek* (New York), 17 March 1975.
9 Henrik Sjögren, *Stage and Society in Sweden* (Swedish Institute, Stockholm, 1979), p. 148.
10 Richard Meryman, 'I Live at the Edge of a Very Strange Country', in *Life* magazine (New York), 15 October 1971.
11 Ibid.
12 *Ingmar Bergman*, documentary film by Stig Björkman (1971).
13 Postcard sent to Bergman, dated 15 April 1988.
14 Meryman, 'I Live at the Edge of a Very Strange Country'.
15 Ibid.
16 *Variety* (New York), 7 July 1971.
17 *Arbetsboken 1975–2001*, p. 306.
18 *Images*, p. 86.
19 *Tre dagböcker, sammanställda av Maria von Rosen och Ingmar Bergman* (Norstedts, Stockholm, 2004), p. 5.
20 Martin Lamm, *August Strindberg*, translated and edited by Harry G. Carlsson (B. Blom, New York, 1971), p. 196.
21 *Lantern*, p. 229.
22 *Tre dagböcker*.

18 THE CHALLENGE OF TELEVISION

1 *Images*, p. 212.
2 *Financial Times* (London), 6 May 1972.
3 *Arbetsboken 1955–1974*, 28 March 1972.
4 Linn Ullmann, *Unquiet* (W. W. Norton, New York, 2019), p. 26.
5 From an interview Bergman gave to *Vecko-revyn* in 1967, during the shooting of *Shame*.
6 *Svenska Dagbladet* (Stockholm), 12 December 1972.
7 Kenne Fant, *Nära bilder* (Norstedts, Stockholm, 1997), p. 5.
8 In his interview with me in Munich, on 9 February 1980, Bergman explained the cancellation of the project in more mundane terms: 'The oil crisis came and everything became more expensive, and then we had to start it all over, we had to see what we had to take away here and take away there, and then I said, "I'm bored, I don't want to do it."'
9 Introduction to screenplay, 31 October 1973 (Bergman Foundation, Stockholm).
10 Henrik Sjögren, *Stage and Society in Sweden* (Swedish Institute, Stockholm, 1979), p. 149.
11 *Lantern*, p. 227.

12 Author's interview with Måns Reuterswärd in Stockholm, November 1979.
13 Ibid.

19 ARRESTED ON STAGE

1 Marianne Höök, *Ingmar Bergman* (Wahlström & Widstrand, Stockholm, 1962).
2 *Theater* (New Haven, Conn.), vol. ii, no. 1 (fall 1979).
3 Liv Ullmann, *Changing* (Knopf, New York, 1977), p. 212.
4 Guy Flatley, 'Liv and Ingmar Bergman Remain . . . Such Good Friends', *New York Times*, 9 April 1972.
5 On 21 March 1978, a settlement was signed between Bergman, Cinematograph AB, Kenneth Hyman, Inter-Hemisphere Productions Ltd and Warner Bros. At length, an elaborate contract was drawn up in 1990 reciting all the previous claims and counter-claims.
6 *Time* magazine (New York), 7 June 1976.
7 *Bergman on Bergman*, p. 181.
8 *L136, Diary*, p. 164.
9 In the documentary *Far from Home* on the DVD of *The Serpent's Egg*.
10 *Arbetsboken 1975–2001*, 31 January 1978.
11 Emma Andrews, 'The Bergman Principle', in *Films Illustrated* (London), February 1978.
12 Ingrid Bergman with Alan Burgess, *My Story* (Delacorte Press, New York, 1980), p. 444.
13 Sleeve notes to *Närbilder: Käbi Laretei spelar musiken till Ingmar Bergmans filmer*, PROP 7809 (Proprius Förlag, Stockholm, 1980).
14 Interview with author, Munich, 9 February 1980.
15 *Searching for Ingmar Bergman*, documentary film by Margarethe von Trotta (2018).
16 *Frankfurter Allgemeine Zeitung*, 21 May 1977.
17 *Arbetsboken 1975–2001*, 19 November 1976.

20 ILL AT EASE IN MUNICH

1 *News* (Swedish Film Institute, Stockholm), vol. 1, no. 19 (1979).
2 *Reference*, p. 654.
3 *Artiklar*, pp. 101–3.
4 *Arbetsboken 1975–2001*, 8 June 1977.
5 Ibid.

6 Programme leaflet for Bergman's play *Mig till skräck*, 26 October 1947, Gothenburg City Theatre.

7 *Theater* (New Haven, Conn.), vol. 11, no. 1 (fall 1979).

8 In a letter to the author, November 1980.

9 Interview with author, Munich, 9 February 1980.

10 Reprinted in *Film og Kino* (Oslo), no. 1, 1981.

11 Quoted in *Variety* (New York), 29 October 1980.

12 Åke Janzon, 'Tre utsökta uppvisningar av tvåsamhetens diabolik', *Svenska Dagbladet* (Stockholm), early May 1981.

13 *Lantern*, p. 250.

21 AT HOME WITH *FANNY AND ALEXANDER*

1 *Images*, p. 362.

2 *Nya Svensk Damtidning* (Stockholm), 1972.

3 Erland Josephson, *Rollen* (Brombergs, Stockholm, 1989).

4 *Reference*, p. 333.

5 *Arbetsboken 1975–2001*, 8 June 1980.

6 Gilles Jacob (ed.), *Les Visiteurs de Cannes* (Hatier, Paris, 1992), p. 274.

7 *Lantern*, pp. 57–8.

8 *Arbetsboken 1975–2001*, p. 228.

9 Author's interview with Katinka Faragó, Stockholm, 18 March 2019.

22 RESURRECTING THE FAMILY PAST

1 *Reference*, p. 686.

2 *Veckans Affärer* (Stockholm), no. 41 (8 October 1987).

3 Ellen Lundström, *År med Ingmar*, manuscript (Bergman Foundation, Stockholm). As noted on pp. 47–8, however, Bergman was not the natural father.

4 *Sunday Times* (London), 14 June 1987.

5 *Observer* (London), 14 June 1987.

6 Tommy Berggren, *Tommy* (Albert Bonniers Förlag, Stockholm, 2017), p. 444.

7 *Arbetsboken 1975–2001*, Week 8, 1987.

8 Ibid., Week 3, 1988.

9 Ibid., 27 July 1990.

10 Ibid., 1 August 1990.

11 Daniel Bergman, *Hjärtat* (Bokförlaget Polaris, Stockholm, 2021), pp. 169 and 171.

12 *Arbetsboken 1975–2001*, p. 294.
13 Daniel Bergman, *Hjärtat*, pp. 185 *et seq.*
14 *Searching for Ingmar Bergman*, documentary film by Margarethe von Trotta (2018).
15 *Expressen* (Stockholm), 18 November 1989.
16 *Village Voice* (New York), 2 July 1991.
17 *New York Times*, 6 November 1991.
18 Jan Holmberg, *Författaren Ingmar Bergman* (Norstedts, Stockholm, 2018).
19 *Tre dagböcker, sammanställda av Maria von Rosen och Ingmar Bergman* (Norstedts, Stockholm, 2004).
20 Ibid., p. 35.
21 *The New Yorker*, 8 May 1995.

23 A FINAL FLOURISH

1 Linn Ullmann, *Unquiet* (W. W. Norton, New York, 2019), p. 45.
2 *Reference*, p. 741.
3 *Dagens Nyheter* (Stockholm), 16 March 1996.
4 *Arbetsboken 1975–2001*, 5 May 1997.
5 Ibid., p. 417.
6 Linn Ullmann, *Unquiet*, p. 338.
7 *Arbetsboken 1975–2001*, p. 424.
8 *Bergman Island*, documentary film by Marie Nyreröd (2006).
9 *Göteborgs Posten* (Göteborg), 10 February 2002.
10 Stig Björkman, *Sight and Sound* (London), summer 2001.
11 *Arbetsboken 1975–2001*, p. 431.
12 Björkman, *Sight and Sound.*
13 *Arbetsboken 1975–2001*, 19 July 2001.

24 AFTERMATH AND LEGACY

1 *Fårö and Ingmar Bergman* (Fårö Local Heritage Association Publishers, 2015).
2 Daniel Bergman, *Hjärtat* (Bokförlaget Polaris, Stockholm, 2021), p. 256.
3 *The Fifth Act*, p. 3.
4 *Bergman Island*, documentary broadcast by SVT in 2004.
5 Linn Ullmann, *Unquiet* (W. W. Norton, New York, 2019), p. 335.
6 Interview in *Fårö and Ingmar Bergman, A Mutual Bond* (Fårö Local Heritage Association Publishers, Fårö, 2015), p. 237.

7 *Liv & Ingmar*, documentary film by Dheeraj Akolkar (2012).

8 Linn Ullmann, *Unquiet*, p. 261.

9 *New York Times*, 30 July 2007.

10 *Guardian* (London), 30 July 2007.

11 National Public Radio (Washington, D.C.), 30 July 2007.

12 *Chaplin* (Stockholm), special issue for Bergman's seventieth birthday, 1988.

13 *L136, Diary*, p. 212.

14 Charles Thomas Samuels, *Encountering Directors* (Putnam's, New York, 1972), p. 189.

15 Interview with the author in Stockholm, January 1975.

16 Interview with the author in Stockholm, November 1979.

17 Samuels, *Encountering Directors*, p. 183.

18 Denis Marion, *Ingmar Bergman* (Gallimard, Paris, 1979), p. 84.

19 *L136, Diary*, p. 188.

20 A. Alvarez, 'A Visit with Ingmar Bergman', *New York Times*, 7 December 1975.

REFERENCES CITED IN THE TEXT

WRITINGS BY INGMAR BERGMAN

Arbetsboken 1955–1974	*Arbetsboken 1955–1974* (Norstedts, Stockholm, 2018)
Arbetsboken 1975–2001	*Arbetsboken 1975–2001* (Norstedts, Stockholm, 2018)
Artiklar	*Artiklar, Essäer, Föredrag* (Norstedts, Stockholm, 2018)
Fifth Act	*The Fifth Act* (The New Press, New York, 2001)
Four Screenplays	*Four Screenplays of Ingmar Bergman*, trans. Lars Malmström and David Kushner (Simon & Schuster, New York, 1960)
Images	*Images* (Faber and Faber, London, 1994)
Lantern	*The Magic Lantern*, trans. Joan Tate (Hamish Hamilton, London, 1988)
Ofilmat	*Ofilmat, ospelat, outgivet* (Norstedts, Stockholm, 2018)

WRITINGS ON INGMAR BERGMAN

Bergman on Bergman	Stig Björkman, Torsten Manns and Jonas Sima (eds), *Bergman on Bergman*, trans. Paul Britten Austin (Simon & Schuster, New York, 1973)
Bergman på teatern	Henrik Sjögren, *Ingmar Bergman på teatern* (Almqvist & Wiksell, Stockholm, 1968).
L136, Diary	Vilgot Sjöman, *L136, Diary with Ingmar Bergman* (Karoma, Ann Arbor, Michigan, 1978)
Reference	Birgitta Steene, *Ingmar Bergman, A Reference Guide* (Amsterdam University Press, Amsterdam, 2005)

INDEX

Page numbers in *italics* denote images; IB denotes Ingmar Bergman.

and *Dracula*, 226; IB on, 225; plot, 20, 141, 225–6, 227–8, 229, 234, 235, 330; reception, 238; as remake of *The Magician*, 227

Hovs Hallar, Skåne, 124–5, 225

Howard, Alan, 332

Huntford, Roland: *The New Totalitarians*, 121

Hyman, Kenneth, 287

Ibsen, Henrik: *Brand*, 121; see also *A Doll's House*; *Ghosts*; *Hedda Gabler*; *John Gabriel Borkman*; *Peer Gynt*; *Wild Duck*

Idestam-Almquist, Bengt, 104

The Image Makers (TV movie), 343–4

In the Presence of a Clown (TV movie), 333, 336, 342, 355

Ingemarsson, Sylvia, 336

Ingmar Bergman Prize, 340

The Investigation (Weiss), 29, 220, 221

Isaksson, Ulla: *The Blessed Ones*, 325; and *So Close to Life*, 144–5; *The Virgin Spring*, 156, 158

Isedal, Tor, 159

It Rains on Our Love (1946 film), 29, 51–2, 57, 59

ITC Entertainment, 303

Jack Among the Actors, 36

'Jacob' (raven), 161

Jacob, Gilles, 335, 342

Jacobsson, Ulla, 113, 115, 116, 119

Jahnsson, Bengt, 247, 279

Jannings, Emil, 102

Janov, Arthur, 301

Janus Films, 142–3, 149, 164, 168, 169, 178, 180, 196

Janzon, Åke, 310

Japanese cinema, 163

Järrel, Stig, 38

Jaubert, Maurice, 63

Jesus film project (RAI), 277–8, 289

Joakim Naked, 73

John Gabriel Borkman (Ibsen), 324

Jönsson, Nine-Christine, 63; 121

Jordeberga Castle, 114

Josephson, Erland: head of Royal Dramatic Theatre, 231; on IB, 33, 45; IB friendship, 28, 344, 350; portrayal of IB in films, 321; in *After the Rehearsal*, 321–2; and *All These Women*, 197–8; in *Cries and Whispers*, 70;

in *A Doll's House*, 333; in *Face to Face*, 285; 268; in *Faithless*, 83, 321, 343; in *Fanny and Alexander*, 313, 315; in *Hour of the Wolf*, 226; in *The Passion of Anna*, 243; and *The Pleasure Garden*, 182; in *In the Presence of a Clown*, 342; in *Room and Time*, 335; in *The Sanctuary*, 250; in *Saraband*, 345, 346, 347; in *Scenes from a Marriage*, 267–8; in *The Silence*, 260; in *So Close to Life*, 145; in *Yvonne, Princess of Burgundy*, 340

Jung, Carl, 215

Jutzi, Phil: *Mutter Krausens Fahrt ins Glück*, 295

Kael, Pauline, 241

Kaetzler, Johannes, 301

Kafka, Franz: *The Castle*, 96, 105

Kanalv, Siv, 265, 280

Karajan, Herbert von, 206, 320

Karin Månsdotter (Sjöberg), 99

Karin's Face, 320, 322

Karlebo, Carl Selim, 297

Karlebo, Ingrid, *see* von Rosen, Ingrid

Karlsson, Anne, 61

Karlsson, Kent, 289

Karlstad, Sweden, 104

Kauffmann, Stanley, 164

Kaufman, Philip, 353

Kavli, Karin, 61, 62, 94, 95, 200, 204

Kindal, Jullan, 26

King Lear (Shakespeare), 321, 323–4, 323, 359

Kjellgren, Lars-Eric, 37, 76

Kjellin, Alf, 20, 43, 56, 57, 182

Klercker, Georg af, 339, 340

Koch, Erland von, 58, 63

Kohner, Paul, 249, 254, 274, 275, 287, 292

Koskinen, Maaret, 84–5, 101

Köstlinger, Josef, 281

Krieps, Vicky, 353

Kronlund, Dag, 348

Kubrick, Stanley, 168

Kulle, Jarl: in *All These Women*, 198; in *The Devil's Eye*, 165; in *Fanny and Alexander*, 312, 313, 317; in *King Lear*, 323, 324; in *Long Day's Journey into Night*, 330; in *The Merry Widow*, 274; in *Smiles of a Summer Night*, 116, 117; in *Waiting Women*, 86

Kurosawa, Akira, 237, 331; *Rashomon*, 163

Kvällsposten, 147